WORKERS GO SHOPPING IN ARGENTINA

WORKERS GO SHOPPING IN *Argentina*

The Rise of Popular Consumer Culture

NATALIA MILANESIO

UNIVERSITY OF NEW MEXICO ALBUQUERQUE

© 2013 by the University of New Mexico Press
All rights reserved. Published 2013
Printed in the United States of America
First paperbound printing, 2015
Paperbound ISBN: 978-0-8263-5242-2

20   19   18   17   16   15   1   2   3   4   5   6

Library of Congress Cataloging-in-Publication Data

Milanesio, Natalia, 1974–
  Workers go shopping in Argentina : The rise of popular consumer culture /
    Natalia Milanesio.
    p. cm.
  Includes bibliographical references and index.
  ISBN 978-0-8263-5241-5 (cloth : alk. paper) —
    ISBN 978-0-8263-5243-9 (electronic)
1. Consumption (Economics)—Argentina.
2. Consumers—Argentina—History—20th century.
3. Working class—Argentina—History.
4. Argentina—Economic conditions—20th century.
I. Title.
  HC180.C6M55 2013
  306.30982—dc23

2012032707

Cover design and type composition by Lila Sanchez
Composed in New Caledonia LT Std 10.25/13
Display type is New Caledonia LT Std

COVER: A shoe store in Buenos Aires and a grocery store run by the
        Eva Perón Foundation. Photos courtesy of Archivo General de la Nación.

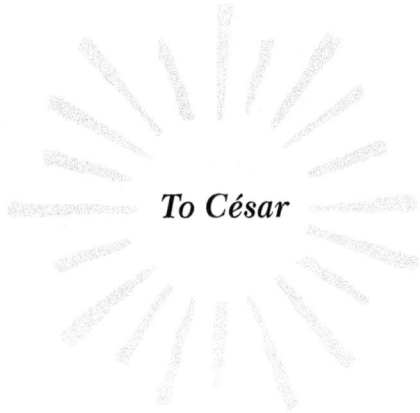

To César

CONTENTS

ACKNOWLEDGMENTS

During my time as a graduate student at Indiana University, I benefited from the expertise of a group of talented historians of Latin America. Arlene Díaz, Jeff Gould, Peter Guardino, and Danny James made graduate school unceremonious and intellectually stimulating. I want to thank Danny especially for supporting my choices throughout my studies and Peter for his frank advice in all things academic. Konstantin Dierks was truly generous with his counsel and encouragement throughout graduate school. I would like to thank him for being an avid and thoughtful reader from the start. Mike Grossberg offered his invaluable advice at a key moment during the final stage of graduate school.

I am also grateful to Matt Karush, Eduardo Elena, Rebekah Pite, Katharine French-Fuller, and Oscar Chamosa for sharing their enthusiasm and knowledge of Argentine history in conferences and conversations, and to Julio Moreno, Jeffrey Pilcher, Ricardo Salvatore, and Donna Guy for their comments on my work at different stages of this project. Thanks also go to William Ratliff at the Hoover Institution Library and Archives at Stanford University; to Rosario Bernatene, Karina Ramacciotti, Fernando Remedi, and Pablo Gerchunoff for answering my queries; and to Cecilia Wingerter for her help with research in Rosario. I greatly appreciate the constructive comments Monica Perales and Sandra McGee Deutsch made after reading chapter 6. I owe thanks to Wendy Gosselin for proofreading my writing and to Beatriz "Tati" Muñoz at the Communist Party Archives in Buenos Aires for her kindness and aid over the years. I am truly grateful to Giovanna Urdangarain and Craig Wayson for their endless generosity, friendship, and unfailing support both in Bloomington and beyond.

I want to express my profound gratitude to all the men and women who spent days sharing their memories and stories with me. Their generosity, thoughtfulness, and insights made me think of the past in a different way and contributed to my understanding of methodology, ethical research, and the subjectivity of knowledge in ways I could not have imagined before meeting them.

I also want to convey my appreciation to the several institutions that have provided generous financial assistance throughout many phases of my research: the Andrew W. Mellon Foundation, the American Council of Learned Societies, the John W. Hartman Center at Duke University, the Social Science Research Council, the American Historical Association, the Indiana University Department of History and Graduate School, the Indiana University Graduate and Professional Student Organization, and the Center for Latin American and Caribbean Studies also at Indiana University. At the University of Houston, I want to thank the Department of History, the College of Arts and Sciences, the Provost Office, and the Division of Research.

Many colleagues at the University of Houston have read proposals or chapters and offered me valuable advice and guidance about several aspects of this project and academic life in general. Thanks go to Susan Kellogg, Thomas O'Brien, John Hart, Kathleen Brosnan, Martin Melosi, Catherine Patterson, Monica Perales, James Schafer, Landon Storrs, Nancy Young, Xiaoping Cong, Todd Romero, Guadalupe San Miguel, Philip Howard, and Eric Walther. I am also very grateful to Lorena López at the Department of History for her valuable assistance.

Special thanks go to W. Clark Whitehorn, editor in chief of the University of New Mexico Press, for his engagement with this project from the very beginning, his sound guidance, and his enormous patience. I also extend thanks to Liam Utz Wiegner for the editing and to Elise McHugh, Felicia Cedillos, and Elizabeth Hadas for their assistance at the Press. I would also like to thank the two outside readers for their constructive suggestions and kind assessment of my work.

My friends in Argentina—Vanina Broda, Julieta Viglioni, Mariela Rodriguez, Julieta López, María José Ceruti, Milena Paglini, and Gabriela Terrazino—helped me reconnect with "real life" after too many hours in the archives and provided unconditional reassurance, optimism, and a lot of fun. Finally, I could not have completed this book without the love and encouragement of César Seveso. I owe him many things, from incisive readings of my work and domestic multitasking to the laughter he always managed to bring to my desk, with the help of our dog Fredo, when writing became frustrating. César is a true example of honesty and dedication. His passion for life and his integrity have encouraged me to never stop searching for what I believe is important and right.

Introduction

In 2005, Juan Carlos Legas was seventy-three years old. He grew up in a small town in the province of Santa Fe where he lived until he moved to Rosario, the second largest city in Argentina, at the age of seventeen. It was 1949. That year, wages reached a record high in the country, workers' rights were included in the national constitution for the first time, and Juan Domingo Perón successfully completed his third year as president. Upon his arrival to Rosario, Juan Carlos was employed in several workshops and soon got a job he cherished deeply in the largest textile factory in the city. Life as a well-paid industrial worker, Juan Carlos remembered more than fifty years later, was full of possibilities. In the next five years, Juan Carlos got married, bought a small plot of land where he built a home he then diligently equipped, and went on vacation for the first time in his life. His tale of uprooting, hard work, and fulfillment was not exceptional. In 1947, 17 percent of Argentines had migrated from the provinces where they were born in search of a better life in the big cities of the *pampeana* region where most industries were located. In fact, Juan Carlos was following others who had set the example a few years earlier, going on a journey that many remember as one of discovery and prosperity. With nostalgia, Juan Carlos recounted that

> life was much better for everyone back then. People ate well, dressed well, went out to eat, and went to the movies. As workers, we had money in our pockets for the first time, and this was evident. I will never forget the first boy who left my town for Buenos Aires. His name was Gregorio Valdéz, and we all admired him because he came back three months later in a suit and tie . . . His salary was so high that none of us could believe it. Many more followed.[1]

The stories of young workers like Juan Carlos and Gregorio are snapshots of a historical period marked by industrialization, high purchasing power, internal migration, and consumption. This book is a study of the exceptional experience that lay at the center of it all: the emergence of the working-class consumer as a powerful force that transformed modern Argentina. This book explores the mid-twentieth-century conditions that triggered the transformation of the national market culture, but the aim of the analysis is to reveal what changed when vast sectors of the population became consumers of industrial goods and participants in spaces and practices of consumption they had rarely or never enjoyed before. *Workers Go Shopping in Argentina: The Rise of Popular Consumer Culture* points to the historical novelty of the worker-consumer based on the idea that mass consumption developed incrementally by increasingly incorporating different sectors of the society over time. While the Argentine middle classes opened the doors of the marketplace in the 1920s, I maintain that the lower-income sectors of the population had to wait until the middle decades of the twentieth century to gain full access to the world of consumption.[2] *Workers Go Shopping in Argentina* demonstrates that, when the time came, these sectors made a grand entrance, stretching the limits of inclusion to impressive new levels. My argument does not dispute that the working classes had participated in the consumer market in the past but suggests that this participation did not become a massive phenomenon until the mid-twentieth century and, most importantly, that this was the first time that the worker-consumer became a definitive historical agent of enormous cultural and social visibility and unprecedented political and economic influence.

Thus the consumer society that arose from this incorporation was novel in nature as well as extent.

Although they surface throughout the book, the qualitative or quantitative aspects of working-class consumption are not the focus of my study; instead, I seek to understand its social and, above all, cultural consequences. In other words, this is a history of consumption that places the working class at the core of an interpretation of postwar Argentine consumer culture rather than a labor history linking consumption, work, and labor politics. The central premise is that working-class consumers were a new modernizing social actor who shaped a different commercial ethos, transformed social relations and collective identities, and redefined the role of the state as a mediator between business and consumers. From the new language and aesthetics of advertisement to the new form and content of consumer goods, from the rise of middle- and upper-class anxieties to the changes in gender expectations, from the redefinition of working-class standards of living to the creation of new government institutions, I show that the transformations fueled by the worker-consumer were remarkable and far-reaching.

The story this book tells unfolds at the juncture of a unique process of economic development, social modernization, and nationalistic populist politics that peaked during Juan Domingo Perón's government between 1946 and 1955. Peronism changed the course of twentieth-century Argentina so profoundly that this period became a critical turning point in national history whose legacy still shapes the country today. Following its entry into the international market as a free nation after gaining its independence from Spain in the early nineteenth century, Argentina experienced a long period of economic expansion based on the exportation of agricultural products. This growth was made possible by fertile lands, British capital, and manual labor provided by European immigrants attracted by the prospects of abundance. Until 1916, however, the landed oligarchy whose wealth was amassed on the export market not only exercised full political control over the country but also refused to concede a fair share of the economic pie to the masses. The upper social sector not only kept the working population socially and economically marginalized but also excluded them from the political system by means of electoral fraud and coercion. In 1916, the Radical Party gained power after a law opened political participation by establishing secret ballots and mandatory universal suffrage for all males over eighteen years of age. Although the state took on a more active and interventionist role in social issues than it had in the recent past, political and economic power remained concentrated among the agro-exporters and their foreign allies and, increasingly, among a small group of industrialists who had close personal and commercial ties with the landed elites.

The First World War and the Great Depression exposed the vulnerability of Argentina's export-based economy and contributed to consolidating the industrial sector. At the same time, the growing urban working class and communist and anarchist leaders began to challenge the reigning social order, actively demanding better working and living conditions. Still, the fight for their rights was unsuccessful. Activists were frequently persecuted, and the labor movement was constantly subjected to government harassment. In 1930, economic difficulties and a climate of increasing political and social unrest prompted a military coup backed by the most traditional sectors of the landed elites. The coup inaugurated a period known as the "Infamous Decade" characterized by fraudulent elections, widespread government corruption, and repression of any form of protest. In 1943, a group of military officers allied with new industrialist sectors whose interests and power had grown during the Second World War led a military coup in an effort to redefine national politics and economic development. Colonel Juan Domingo Perón was one of the members of the new government. From the Ministry of War, the vice-presidency, and especially the Secretariat of Labor, Perón was able to rally a vast political movement, winning the presidential elections in 1946 and again in 1951. The epitome of Latin American populism, Peronism was founded on a multiclass alliance that included industrialists, some sectors of the military, and, most significantly, labor organizations. The working class provided Peronism with its main base of support as wage earners became rapidly attracted by Perón's strong nationalistic and antioligarchic discourse and his promises for a better life.[3]

Most of these promises depended on an economic plan aimed at developing the national industry and consolidating the internal market and on unparalleled policies of income redistribution. Although business and economic historians have studied these processes, we know little about their implications for consumer culture. To expand our knowledge, *Workers Go Shopping in Argentina* is focused on consumption, a multifaceted phenomenon that involves a vast range of practices like shopping, buying, using, displaying, and desiring, all of which entail complex relations among subjects and between subjects and goods. As a particular historical form of consumption, mass consumer culture represents the unprecedented interpenetration of economic and cultural forces: the intersection of growing markets—resulting from increasing manufacturing and the democratization of goods—with new cultural logics of commercial advertising, mass marketing, and new forms of merchandising.[4] Here consumption is defined as more than an economic act intended to satisfy needs and wants through the acquisition and use of commodities. It is, in fact, both a subjective and a sociocultural practice that individuals and groups use to validate existing identities or create new ones, express a sense of selfhood and otherness, and manifest membership and social standing. In other words, consumer culture is a system of signification. This argument, put forward by theorist Jean Baudrillard, became highly influential in cultural anthropology and the sociological study of consumption, a body of scholarship that has deeply shaped my understanding of consumption. This book is then a historical examination of the meanings that consumers, producers, businessmen, advertising agents, and state officials assigned to and conveyed through experiences of consumption and consumer goods.[5]

As the analysis delves into processes of self-definition and personal and collective fulfillment, the creation of stereotypes, and the construction of social distinction and political legitimacy, it also dissects what sociologist Robert G. Dunn has termed the "economic and signifying apparatuses of consumer culture," most notably, production, advertising, and marketing.[6] The mid-twentieth-century market culture was indeed not only marked by the emergence of new social actors, or of old actors in new roles, but also by new structural conditions that included growing national industrialization, expansive commercial infrastructure, state regulation of the economy, and innovative forms of publicity. My analysis positions the worker-consumer at the center of this transformation, both as a cause and as an outcome. Interdisciplinary in nature, this book combines theories of the anthropology of consumption, cultural studies, and gender studies with the methodologies of cultural, social, and oral histories. The result is a complex object of study: the worker-consumer emerges as many sided. First, the working-class consumer is a social subject who worked, shopped, and desired, a historical actor consciously seeking to satisfy material needs and wants but whose actions were, at the same time, largely contingent upon independent economic, social, and political forces. Still, in this book, the worker-consumer is, in particular, a historical cultural category that was studied, imagined, invented, and debated in the mid-twentieth century by industrialists, ad-makers, the press, the state, and the middle and upper classes for a broad range of purposes. Thus, in this cultural history, the worker-consumer takes on multiple forms, materializing differently in diverse settings: a concept resulting from market research, the icon of a political movement, the personification of progressive social policies, the leading character of advertisements, a social type disseminated in the media, and a stereotype born out of class resentment. Finally, the worker-consumer is also embodied by the individuals who, in the last chapter, remember their past as young working-class men and women who longed for and purchased consumer goods in the mid-twentieth century. In their recollections, a new form of worker-consumer arises, this time as the product of personal and collective memories.

The Historiography of Consumption

A history of consumption, *Workers Go Shopping in Argentina* belongs to a body of historical scholarship that is novel, exhilarating, and extremely diverse. The research topics, the methodologies, the theoretical frameworks, the historical arguments, and even the conceptualization—ranging from consumerism and consumption to consumer society and consumerist behavior—are wide ranging, and thus the discipline has both suffered and benefited from its fluid contour. Yet, in contrast to this multiplicity, the initial focus on the United States and Western Europe conferred upon the history of consumption great geographical uniformity as well as two traditional lines of inquiry. One of these examined the origins of consumer society, tracing its birth in Europe (and some more broadly in the Atlantic world) in the seventeenth and eighteenth centuries and arguing that consumption even predated the Industrial Revolution. The periodization of consumer society has been central among historians of early modern and modern Europe, although it has remained largely unresolved.[7] If the beginnings of consumer culture have sparked much debate, it has been even more challenging to establish a proper chronology for its later evolution, both in regional and national contexts, and to determine which factors have prompted the transition between phases.

In spite of differences in time, place, arguments, and scope, this scholarship drove me to examine the development of consumer culture in Argentina while trying to thoroughly comprehend what was really novel about mid-twentieth-century consumption in terms of social and cultural actors, politics, and structural economic conditions. Although my study is not a genealogy, I understand consumption in terms of "stages" and, as a result, question how "massive" "mass consumption" was before the mid-twentieth century. This premise led me to constantly go back in time to assert the originality of this period in a compelling way. To this end, and because of the few studies on consumption in Argentina—a subject I address below—I conducted extensive research on the early twentieth century and wove the patterns of historical change within each chapter. This strategy has allowed me to offer a broader narrative of historical change while keeping the analysis focused on the 1940s and 1950s.

The second traditional approach to consumption has prioritized the nineteenth and twentieth centuries while looking at the mechanisms, institutions, and practices that made it a true mass phenomenon. With an interest in the combination of ever-expanding goods and desires rather than the origins of consumption, these historians have looked at the many manifestations of consumer culture, particularly department stores, advertising, and leisure.[8] Most of these scholars have firmly grounded their arguments on social history and gender studies, except for historians of advertising who have been more inclined to cultural analysis and to the study of representations.[9] Scholars within this group questioned the feminization of consumption and considered the impact of commercial culture on notions of femininity and masculinity. They also explored the tensions between retailers and consumers, reconsidered racial issues, and reassessed the "power of the purse" interrogating the oppressive and liberating aspects of consumer practices.[10] Rich and original, this body of work reached illuminating conclusions. In many cases, however, rather than prompting historical and geographical comparative analysis and remaining open to critical questioning, some of these conclusions became ossified truisms and standardized and axiomatic analytical lenses. This occurred, for example, with the equation between consumption and consumerism (the modern principle that consumption is an end in itself and that material possessions bring happiness and personal fulfillment) and between consumption and abundance. It also occurred with the focus on conspicuous or "spectacular" forms of consumption to the detriment of necessities like food. Similarly, the favoring of commercial settings over less strident spaces of consumption like the household became commonplace while attention to politics and social solidarities born out of consumer practices was rare.

The explosion of studies on the politics of consumption moved history away from the shop counter and began to address this last omission. Historians began to examine the political organization of consumers and the definition of consumer rights and then turned to the role of the state in creating different "consumption regimes" with their distinct marketplaces, forms of representation, and interpretation of needs and wants.[11] Yet this scholarship pushed the boundaries of the political further by asking broader questions about the creation of a civic culture organized around consumption. Issues of civic identity, the meanings of nationalism and democracy, and the conflation of spending with voting became central topics of inquiry, and the citizen-consumer came out as the sovereign historical character in the field.[12] These questions produced a protean and provocative scholarship in spite of the fact that, in many cases, consumption was not so much a primary object of study in its own right but more of a means to explore the foundations of political culture, especially in terms of the connection between liberal democracy and capitalism.

While gender, race, ethnicity, and increasingly age have figured prominently in histories of consumption, class has played a far more obscure role in the analysis.[13] Insofar as consumption was about class, it particularly referred to the bourgeoisie in modern Europe and the American middle class, both of which became "paradigmatic consumer classes" and strengthened an archetypical notion of consumption based on plenty, conspicuousness, and emulation.[14] While many labor historians criticized historians of consumption for their emphasis on a consumer society where wage earners were invisible and others regretted the emphasis on consumption over production, most labor historians evaded the study of consumption, at least explicitly. Paradoxically, subsistence, moral economy, cooperativism, and standard of living have been a traditional part of their research agendas since the 1960s.[15] Ultimately, the interest in consumption that has grown in other fields also reached labor history. For the most part, labor historians stayed within the boundaries of social history and avoided the arguments and methodologies of cultural studies. Consequently, they approached consumption through the discipline's traditional focus on work and distributionist policies and, from this angle, conducted outstanding studies about the gendered spending patterns of the working-class household and the historical significance of the living wage in consolidating consumer society. Furthermore, labor historians drew attention to the impact of consumption practices in working-class community life and sociability as well as to the transformation of leisure when workers had to choose between higher income and more free time. In contrast to those who had dismissed consumption as a threat to working-class agency, labor histories of consumption avoided sterile dichotomies between producer and consumer, explaining how consumption facilitated unionism and showing the vast political and social effects of the consumer power of labor.[16] Due to its methodological focus and conceptual interests, the labor history of consumption has largely overlooked issues of identity and cultural meanings—which anthropologists and sociologists have thoroughly exam-ined—and has rarely gone beyond the union hall and the working-class neighborhood. For this reason, class relations and the role of consump-tion in social stratification have remained largely unnoticed in this scholar-ship which, by and large, has not provided an interpretation of the broader social and cultural impact of working-class consumption.

In all its variants, the history of consumption collectively contributed to the creation of influential arguments about modernity, capitalism, democ-racy, the marketplace, and collective identities. Many of these arguments took the form of definitive historical conclusions and paradigmatic inter-pretations applicable to different geographical locales worldwide while others have been employed as proof of the historical exceptionality of par-ticular case studies. However, both historical generalizations and claims of the distinctiveness of Western European and American historiographies have been frequently postulated without real comparative or transnational analyses to substantiate or enrich them. Although the history of consump-tion in the "non-Western world" is proportionally smaller than in Western European and American historiographies, the main problem has been what historian Craig Clunas illustrated by arguing that in the history of con-sumption, "China must be just about China; what is about England must be about the world."[17] Historians of consumption in Africa, Asia, Canada, and Eastern Europe have responded by setting original research agendas and studying forms and functions of consumption and types of consumers that can hardly be explained by using American or European "models." Although they have actively engaged with the history of consumption in European countries and the United States, these scholars have also defined consumption on their own terms, in relation to scarcity, nonmonetary exchanges, and socialism, thus challenging old-standing characterizations. Recently, others have shaken arguments about American consumption from within by looking at the borderlands as a site for a distinct consumer culture while rethinking the reified distinctions between Mexico and the United States. Furthermore, through a transnational perspective, new historical research has contested the supposed secondary position of colonies or "the periphery" in the world of goods, opposing a simplistic interpretation of con-sumption in these regions as mere reception or resistance. Works of this kind have showed that, in many cases, local consumers not only developed tastes and practices independent from colonial powers or foreign companies, but also had a dramatic impact on the production and consumption that took place in the metropolises or, more generally, in the Western world.[18]

Workers Go Shopping in Argentina joins this scholarship by studying consumption in an overlooked and thus unexpected historical setting: a traditional export economy in search of a future as an industrial power and a populist government that, profoundly pervaded by the idea of social justice, employed income redistribution as a political weapon and proposed an original strategy of development conceived as an alternative to capitalism and communism. Most importantly, this book shows that the making of a consumer culture is not only about the volume of goods produced, the numbers of consumers, and the size of the stores, but also about the cultural manifestations and social perceptions of these changes.

Consumption in Latin American and Argentine History

In the last few years, historians of Europe and the United States have disapproved of the "inflation" of consumption that is making its definition inconsequential—if everything is consumption, what makes it distinct?—and others have asked for some "breathing space" arguing that consumption has threatened to engulf other subjects.[19] However, while the history of consumption has flourished across geographical fields, historians of Latin America have lagged far behind. As a result, consumption in Latin American historiography is incipient, small, fresh, and full of challenges and opportunities; it is a nonconformist newcomer rather than an overpowering "colonizing force." It is difficult to understand why historians of Latin America have taken so long to ask questions about consumption, particularly in a field traditionally interested in modernity and economic development, one that has been characterized by a strong tradition of social history and the study of popular culture, and which has been receptive to the theoretical influences of cultural studies, especially issues of identity construction. The paucity of archival materials, the constraints of the publishing market, and the prevalence of other research agendas might explain why historians of Latin America have shelved the study of consumption. Still, I think that the main problem has been the persistent mistake of equating consumption with rich countries and expensive goods, the incorrect assumption that poor people and peasants are not consumers, and, more generally, the even more problematical supposition that Latin America is, unequivocally, a region of poor people and peasants. Interestingly, as scholars have analyzed the transition between modes of production and Latin American participation in the world economy and interrogated the limits and effects of industrialization, the proletarianization of former campesinos, and the economic outcomes of land reforms, the many complex consequences of these processes for consumers both in cities and the countryside have remained largely unexplored. Two notable exceptions are Arnold J. Bauer's *Goods, Power, History*, a rich social history of material culture in the region from precolonial times to the present day, and Julio Moreno's *Yankee Don't Go Home!*, an illuminating examination of the intersection among U.S. business, consumption, and nationalism in Mexico in the first half of the twentieth century.[20]

Historians of Latin America have generally privileged the examination of the region as a producer of goods—from cocoa beans and bananas to cocaine—for consumers in other parts of the world.[21] When they have studied Latin American consumers, the focus has been either on food consumption—an incipient subfield that holds many promises and thus should be developed much further—or the elites. In this case, scholars have been particularly interested in how the upper classes have prioritized imports as markers of modernity and distinction. In other instances, historians of the middle classes have explored their consumer practices in order to offer a broader understanding of social identity.[22] In this scholarship, consumption is thus instrumentalized; it is not the principal question that historians examine but a necessary facet of a broader subject, from business culture, pawning, tourism, and fashion writing to the construction of racial and national categories and the masculine self-fashioning of political leaders.[23] Consequently, historical knowledge about consumption in Latin America is restricted and incomplete. In contrast, *Workers Go Shopping in Argentina* positions the consolidation of mass consumption at the center of the story, as the key to understanding the formation of a new commercial culture, class and gender identities, and a new relationship between society and the state in Argentina.

In so doing, this book combines the history of consumption and of the working class in a unique way. While labor historians who specialize in different parts of the world incorporated the study of consumption in their research agendas, their colleagues studying Latin America have disregarded it. Conscientious about gender, ethnic, and racial dynamics both in industrial and nonindustrial settings, the new labor history of Latin America born in the late 1990s moved from the factory and the union hall to the household and community but disregarded consumer issues. Although these scholars contested long-established historical arguments about the working class in Latin America by examining sexuality, civic culture, the state, and communal solidarities, they persisted in the conventional analytical division between producers and consumers.[24] The omission is particularly notable in Argentine historiography, which has been fundamentally shaped by social and institutional history, and thus reluctant to look beyond the labor unions and labor parties, both before and after Peronism. Even proponents of a new labor history that includes cultural sensibilities and that is more concerned with everyday life have overlooked the forms and functions of consumption among workers.[25] Although *Workers Go Shopping in Argentina* has not been conceived as a study of this sort, it is my hope that by examining the major influence of working-class consumption in market culture, the state, and the political and social imagination, it will shed light onto workers' history while encouraging others to follow the many research and theoretical paths I did not pursue.

Finally, the study of advertising, which has carved out a niche for itself in other historiographies, remains embryonic in Latin American history. In fact, there is still no book-length study on the topic, and with the exception of Moreno's analysis of advertisements produced by the J. Walter Thompson Company in Mexico, historians of Latin America have been primarily interested in the institutional history of major advertising agencies and the success and failure of foreign admen and their clients in the region. The content of ads, advertising as a cultural artifact, and its complex relationship with consumers, all aspects I explore extensively in the first part of this book, have been generally overlooked.[26]

In comparison with the general pattern in Latin American historiography, the historical study of consumption in Argentina is even more limited and fragmented.[27] The lack of attention to consumption in Argentine historiography is especially surprising among historians of the Peronist years, when workers enjoyed the highest rise in their standard of living in the history of the country. Only recently a small number of historians in Argentina have started examining the Peronist "democratization of wellbeing"—that is, the improvement of living conditions based on new forms of government planning for housing, education, tourism, and health.[28] Notably, these scholars have generally overlooked the consumerist edge of many of these subjects, privileging a political and institutional approach over research on cultural and social aspects. The few analyses that have explicitly engaged the topic of consumption have addressed it as inevitably dependent on Peronism, as part of the efforts of the government to control the economy, build the state, and appeal to its constituency.[29]

In contrast, my book moves from the state to culture and from political clients and citizens to consumers. *Workers Go Shopping in Argentina* offers a cultural and social analysis that privileges the perspective of buyers, admen, and business. This study cannot (and should not) elude Peronism, one of the most historically resilient and analytically captivating phenomena in Latin American history and thus under thorough and innovative reexamination.[30] Yet, rather than making consumption secondary to Peronism, I have employed Peronism as one of many means to understand consumption in the mid-twentieth century. My research approaches the state as a moderator among consumers, advertising agencies, industrialists, and merchants and shows that, by playing this role, the Peronist administration undertook a new historical task: it offered consumers protection by supervising the quality and marketing of consumer goods and by launching educational campaigns that urged consumers to be discerning and informed. Furthermore, by using the oral testimonies of workers, I examine the place of Peronism in historical memory, question common historical assumptions about working-class agency, and address how low-income consumers have understood their relationship with the Peronist government.

This Book

The first three chapters explore the economic, social, and political transformations that led to increased purchasing power among the working population, define the working-class consumers, and examine the changes these new consumers triggered in commercial culture. Chapter 1 analyzes the historical conditions that created a larger and more socially inclusive market: nationalistic economic policies, import substitution industrialization, the new politics of income redistribution, and the role of consumption in the Peronist ideal of social justice. However, the aim of the chapter is to show that beyond these aspects, one of the most important factors in advancing consumption among the working class was the new state regulation of consumer goods and practices. Based on high standards of quality and the recognition of consumer rights, the government launched a far-reaching institutional and legal crusade aimed at defending consumers and, most particularly, buyers from the low-income sectors.

Chapter 2 looks at how admen characterized the new consumers along class, gender, and geographical lines. The analysis shows that in order to reach working-class consumers, advertising companies and their clients embarked on a process of discovery and study that made the low-income population the object of market surveys and the targets of consumer education for the first time. Here I argue that advertising agents envisioned a market that was not only more socially inclusive, but also more comprehensive in geographical terms. This chapter demonstrates how industrial and economic development as well as the expansion of their field encouraged admen to reach an array of towns and cities in the interior of the country that they had traditionally overlooked. Moreover, the analysis reveals the centrality of gender in the demarcation of the new market. Consumer campaigns innovatively singled out working-class women as the recipients of potent messages that stressed the social and economic relevance of defending purchasing power, being knowledgeable shoppers, and standing up against manipulative business practices. Chapter 3 focuses on the transformation of mid-twentieth-century advertising. To this end, I delve into the creation of new advertising discourses and images based on the use of working-class characters, female visual clichés, colloquial language, straightforward messages, and humor. I argue that, in contrast to the recent past, mid-twentieth-century advertising became nationalistic, accessible, festive, and unpretentious. Beyond visual and discursive contents, the chapter examines a significant change in advertising mediums. A shortage of paper reduced advertising space in the printed press in the early 1950s and provoked a new dynamism in outdoor advertisement. With vast appeal among the working sectors, outdoor displays became the embodiment of truly democratic advertising and the means for a broader incorporation of the worker-consumer into commercial culture.

The last three chapters center on how working-class consumers changed gender and class imaginaries and how these transformations had an impact on social identity. In chapter 4, I argue that the new participation of the working class in a flourishing urban mass consumer culture fueled acute anxieties among the middle and upper classes. I also reveal how practices of consumption, like going to the movies, dining out, and shopping, and the spaces where they took place were both the trigger and the stage for the surfacing of growing concerns among the affluent sectors. These groups felt distressed because of the perceived threat of "social mingling" with people of lower status and by an alleged loss of monopolist access to diverse realms of the consumer market, from stores to movie theaters and restaurants. Consequently, these middle- and upper-class consumers feared that they would be unable to assert class belonging, a process I consider in detail.

Chapter 5 contends that consumption generated mounting tensions in gender relations. I show that money management, patterns of spending, and individual outlooks toward consumption and savings became fundamental when choosing a partner, when planning a wedding, and, later, in achieving a happy marriage. Images of comfortable singlehood circulated alongside the idea that materialism dominated the lives of young working-class consumers who were more interested in material goods than in family life. As consumer expectations rose for working-class men and women who remained single, they also heightened for those who opted to marry. In this regard, I argue that consumer culture was a crucial force in redefining gender roles and stereotypes like the male provider and the frugal stay-at-home wife as well as a decisive factor in transforming gender expectations, including the financial dependence of married women and women's subordination of personal gratification to marriage, home, and romantic love. Finally, through the analysis of working-class testimonies, chapter 6 explores the role of consumption as an arena of subjective self-creation and representation. Here I show how interviewees used memories of consumption to reaffirm their working-class identity. I argue that, in so doing, they contested public discourses that have traditionally downplayed the agency of workers in attaining a better standard of living and have interpreted higher consumer power as a means of social emulation. Furthermore, recollections reveal the crucial role of consumer goods both in shaping personal narratives of the past and in configuring collective memory.

In the epilogue, I outline the almost six decades after Perón was overthrown and discuss the consumer culture that surfaced following the 1990s neoliberal reforms and the 2001 crisis. In these last pages, I briefly go back to some of the characteristics of the mid-twentieth century in the light of current consumer practices in Argentina.

CHAPTER 1

Industry, Wages, and the State

The Rise of Popular Consumer Culture

In the early 1940s, the Corporación para la Promoción del Intercambio (Corporation for the Promotion of Trade), an agency whose executive board consisted of the directors of the most powerful industrial firms in Argentina, hired the U.S.-based Armour Research Foundation to conduct a study on the state of Argentina's national industry and the prospects for further development. A private agency specializing on business and economic consulting, the Armour Research Foundation did an in-depth assessment of agricultural and industrial activities, demographics, commerce, banking, transportation, and communication systems, but what really caught the researchers' attention was the low wages of the working class. Between 1937 and 1939, an Argentine worker earned half the income of an English laborer and one-third of the salary paid to his American counterpart. Although food was generally less expensive in Argentina, the report asserted, low wages prevented the working class from reaching the same consumption levels as workers in England and the United States, even in terms of the amounts of bread, potatoes, and sugar they could afford.

Most importantly, meager earnings barred Argentine workers from spending on durable consumer goods. For example, they could buy only one-third to one-fourth of the same clothing purchased by their peers in the United States. Similarly, for workers in Argentina a sewing machine was three times more expensive and a radio cost seven times more than for an American worker. In fact, the research team had been warned about the limited participation of the low-income sectors in the consumer market. Upon their arrival, a local businessman told them, "You must never forget that the Argentine market has three and a half million people—not thirteen million." In the final report, the researchers explained the pessimistic view of their informant by arguing that to keep labor costs low, industrialists refused to pay higher wages, but, as a result, sales of their products were poor and industrial development was hindered. The addition of new technology on shop floors, the consolidation of mass production, and the advancement of the secondary sector as a whole was dependent on mass consumption, but the size of the internal market was too small.[1]

Less than a decade later, headlines conveyed an entirely different view. In 1947, the newspaper *Democracia* proclaimed that "Argentina is the country where living is cheapest and the worker earns more." Four years later, the celebration of good times continued as the weekly *Mundo Argentino* announced that "the standard of living of Argentine workers is the highest in the world."[2] As an expression of the late 1940s spirit, the press depicted a triumphant age that has remained in the popular memory as the "golden years of Peronism." For many Argentines, this was a time of bonanza and achievement with the working masses partaking in the social feast. María Roldán, a meatpacking worker in those years, adhered to this view when she recalled many decades later: "With Perón we discovered many things. A pair of nylons, a nice dress. Life changed. We could buy things like refrigerators. I bought mine in 1947."[3] In her memories of increasingly affordable consumer goods that transformed everyday life and broadened horizons, Roldán synthesized an original historical process that peaked in the years following the visit of the Armour researchers, a process in which workers turned into consumers.

This chapter explores the structural conditions and the political decisions that contributed to the emergence of the worker-consumer. As the exceptional circumstances of international trade caused by the Second

World War were soon to come to an end, several local interest groups—from powerful long-standing industrial firms and the agro-export sector to small factory owners and the military—planned different paths to industrialization to overcome the obstacles identified by the Armour report. The chapter examines these conflicting views of national development and focuses on the triumphant one: a vision of growth rooted in industrialization for the domestic market and high purchasing power for the working population. As an icon of widespread well-being, the worker-consumer was the essential articulator of Juan Domingo Perón's project of national industry and full employment, an inward-looking economic model based on the expansion of internal demand and aimed at economic independence. The unprecedented participation of low-income sectors on the consumer market became the banner of the Peronist cause for social justice that championed the rise of the working-class standard of living through a combination of minimum wages, unionization, work regulations, and assistance programs. Purchasing power, the chapter shows, turned into the epitome of national progress and social equality while the working-class consumer became a central component of government propaganda but, most notably, a major focus of state policy.

Indeed, the expansion of the consumer market extensively altered the role of the state, which began to actively intervene in areas of economic life that had traditionally remained outside government control. From generous credits for the industrial sector to monitoring commercial activities, from mandating annual bonuses for workers to standardizing packages, from regulating advertising to controlling product quality, the Peronist government ventured into unknown territory while reinforcing and transforming state agencies, laws, and the overall process of policy making. The analysis demonstrates that promoting working-class consumption involved more than increasing wages and fixing prices; it entailed a new conceptualization of the consumer right to access both reliable products as well as accurate information about these products. As the state acknowledged this right, which became critical to making the consumer market truly massive, it combined a battery of legal and institutional measures to safeguard it against the abuses committed by certain industrial, commercial, and advertising sectors.

Industrial Argentina

Industrialization started in the late nineteenth century in Argentina but was subordinated to the country's role as the world's breadbasket. By the turn of the twentieth century, Argentina was one of the top world exporters of wheat, beef, wool, and leather, and a leading economic power in Latin America. Economic prosperity attracted massive numbers of European immigrants who fueled population and urban growth and stimulated a demand for consumer goods that was largely met through imports and, increasingly, through locally produced goods. Industrial enterprises grew from 22,804 in 1895 to 48,799 in 1914. The birth of the national industry, strongly dependent on imported supplies, encountered a favorable open economy that guaranteed easy access to foreign raw materials and machinery. Furthermore, real wages remained low due to immigration, and the labor market was unregulated, two factors of great appeal for foreign capitalists searching to maximize profits. But the favorable conditions that had made Argentina one of the most prosperous countries in the world deteriorated when the First World War and later the Great Depression caused a sharp decline in the sale of agricultural products on the international market while preventing the arrival of imports. In some sectors, the lack of imported supplies strangled industrial activity; in others, it contributed to a process of industrialization by import substitution, especially when factories used domestic raw materials like in the case of leather and wool activities. Yet throughout the early twentieth century, industry lingered behind the agricultural sector and remained frequently troubled by shortages of imports, fuel, and capital, and in spite of increasing tariff rates aimed at protecting local manufacturers, Argentine administrations lacked long-term industrial planning.[4]

Therefore, by 1930, Argentine manufacture remained relatively underdeveloped, concentrated, and dominated by a few big companies whereas most nondurable consumer goods were produced in small and labor-intensive shops. Agro-industries like food processing of beef, flour, and dairy pushed the rate of industrial growth, but metallurgy and consumer goods like soap remained embryonic. Several factors contributed to this situation. Dependent on agro-exports cycles, manufacturers only secured investments when agro-exports went up, suffered from banks' restrictive lending practices, and were hindered by inefficient industrial legislation. Furthermore, labor productivity was generally low, imported machinery generated high production costs, and local companies frequently faced difficulties when it came time to incorporate new technology. By the mid-1930s, however, government control of foreign exchange and tariff increases strengthened import substitution. The rate of substitution—defined as the fraction of consumer goods produced domestically—went from 50 percent between 1925 and 1929 to 63 percent between 1930 and 1939. Oil by-products, rubber products, and cement expanded greatly in this period, but cotton textiles, especially the production of fabrics and yarns, led the growth. As evidence of this trend, between 1930 and 1937, the number of cotton spinning mills more than tripled.[5]

The Second World War and the consequent crisis on the international market contributed to intensifying the process of import substitution industrialization. Many new small and medium-sized national firms appeared in traditional sectors such as textiles and food processing as well as in newer sectors like electric appliances. The number of factories grew from 38,456 in 1935 to 86,440 in 1946. Industrial production doubled and the number of workers grew accordingly due to the arrival of internal migrants from the interior. The war also provided the unique opportunity to increase industrial exports to countries that had formerly imported consumer goods from the belligerent nations. In fact, from the years 1937–1939 to the years 1943–1945, the percentages of exports to the Americas more than doubled.[6] As import substitution increased, both the export and manufacturing sectors came to the conclusion that industrial development should be reinforced after the war and that the state, in contrast to the past, should play a key role in protecting and consolidating the secondary sector. The postwar years, all economic sectors agreed, would bring a period of uncertainty and critical decisions as the end of the conflict would reestablish nations' traditional roles in the world economy. In 1942, the Unión Industrial Argentina (UIA), which grouped the most powerful industrial interests, expressed concerns about the future when it asked:

> What will happen once the war has ended? What will be our situation
> in the near future when the war has finished and the countries of the
> Old World as well as the largest country of North America have not
> only restored their economies but also begun to place their industrial
> surplus on world markets—particularly our own?[7]

Arguments regarding future industrial development were polarized into two different fields. The 1940 *Plan de Reactivación Económica* put forth by Federico Pinedo, the head of the Treasury Department during the presidency of Ramón Castillo, represented the ideas of the traditional export sector and the most powerful industrial interests organized within the UIA. The *Plan* encouraged "natural" industries that, like the food industry, used domestic raw materials and thus competitively produced for the foreign market. Pinedo promoted the balance between the industrial and agricultural sectors because the latter provided the foreign currency required by manufacturers, and endorsed a close association with the United States. The military coup that overthrew President Castillo in 1943 prevented Pinedo's proposal from being implemented, but several other problems contributed to making it an unviable strategy. Due to Argentina's neutrality during the war, the U.S. government not only prohibited the European countries from using the funds obtained through the Marshall Plan to buy Argentine agricultural products, but also flooded the continent with subsidized grains. Similarly, American imports rapidly began to replace Argentine industrial goods in neighboring countries where Argentina exported extensively during the war. Pinedo's strategy also had a high social cost because by privileging internationally competitive industries, less efficient sectors that had grown during the war would be eliminated and countless workers would be laid off.[8]

In contrast, the military men congregated in the Grupo de Oficiales Unidos (GOU), a lodge of army colonels and lower-ranking officers that took power in the 1943 June Revolution, endorsed an alternative view of industrialization firmly rooted in a nationalist tradition aimed at economic autarchy. The armed forces proposed going well beyond "natural" industries by increasing industrialization through import substitution and expanding it to the production of basic inputs like steel and oil. In fact, this group even questioned the very distinction between natural and artificial industries by claiming that in a country as rich in minerals as Argentina, mining was just as "natural" as agriculture. Furthermore, these sectors, which yearned for a model of technocratic government, envisioned a far more active intervention of the state in the economy both as a regulating agent and a manufacturer. Supporters of this alternative conceived of industrialization as the motor of national development and, most importantly, as the answer to the postwar threat of unemployment, social unrest, and political upheaval. In contrast to Pinedo's emphasis on industrial exports, military proponents of this alternative saw industrial production for the internal market as the foundation for change. This view brought them closer to new industrial sectors that had flourished during the war and which, dependent on internal demand, challenged the model that conferred primacy to national "natural" industries.[9]

A member of the GOU, Perón had shared these arguments since his early days as the head of the Secretariat of Labor and of the National Postwar Council, a federal planning board in charge of industrial policy established by the military government. Still, during the three years that led to his meteoric rise to the presidency in 1946—a period marked by Perón's alliance with the labor unions, the rejection of certain factions of the military, and the unification of conservatives, the Left, and some of the most powerful economic interests that opposed him—the emphasis placed on different industrial sectors shifted. During Perón's first few years in power, the internal market and the development of industries based on national raw materials, including metals, gained preponderance over the GOU's traditional goal of national autarchy based on the expansion of heavy industry. For Perón, industry was the only path to economic independence as well as the road to collective well-being. Therefore, workers were more than an instrument for industrial development—they also had to benefit from such development. Perón's nationalist vision of the future categorically opposed the past oligarchic order, but most importantly, the exploitation of the workforce that had characterized the export economy mostly subordinated to foreign interests. Perón maintained that in creating a "New Argentina," socially just, economically free, and politically sovereign,

> we will either win our right to compete industrially with the rest of the countries of the world—if only to satisfy our needs—or we will eternally remain a dependent nation. And by being a dependent nation, every industrialist, every one of us, every Argentine will pay the cost of this dependence, because dependency is never free.[10]

The 1946 Five-Year Plan, Perón's first body of economic policies as president, promoted industrial sectors that had expanded during the war and required protection from imports, such as some textiles and metallurgy, supported new import substitution sectors that needed basic inputs, and assisted some sectors with export potential like vegetable oils. Most of the production in these industries took place in labor-intensive small- and medium-sized establishments of no more than five hundred workers. The prominence of these industrial sectors in the government became evident with the designation of Perón's first economic team. For the first three years of the government, the president of the Central Bank and of the powerful Instituto Argentino para la Promoción del Intercambio (IAPI) was Miguel Miranda, a manufacturer of tinplate containers, seconded by Raúl Lagomarsino, the minister of industry and commerce, a textile industrialist. Both represented a sector that historians James P. Brennan and Marcelo Rougier have called "the Peronist industrial bourgeoisie," a diverse group that included producers of refrigerators, auto parts, stoves, wool textiles, and cotton clothing among other goods. Many of these industrialists belonged to the Confederación General Económica (CGE), a business association that, unlike the UIA, fully represented the interests of manufacturers from the provinces. These were the *bolicheros*, a term used by the Buenos Aires industrial and commercial elites to belittle these self-made men whose enterprises had grown remarkably over the previous decade.[11] For their part, large industries, foreign capital, and export-market producers such as meatpackers and flour-millers generally opposed the Peronist government. Largely represented by the UIA, these sectors openly objected to government policies that jeopardized their interests, like the liberal importation of equipment that hurt the local manufacturers of capital goods or the restrictions on imported silk that endangered the production of big textile industries dependent on foreign fibers.[12]

Divisions between supporters and opponents of the regime notwithstanding, manufacturing activities and the gross domestic product expanded rapidly thanks to government protection and support. Industrial plants went from 86,440 in 1946 to 181,000 in 1954. In the textile sector, for example, the number of factories grew 43 percent, the number of workers increased by 35 percent, and installed power experienced a sweeping 78 percent growth from 1946 to 1950. The progress of the electric appliances sector was an even more impressive example of increased industrialization by import substitution. Between 1946 and 1953, the number of workers in the electric appliances sector increased by 151 percent and the amount of installed power rose 384 percent. As a result, electric refrigerators manufactured in the country went from 12,000 units in 1947 to 152,000 in 1955, a year when imports drastically dropped to only 500 units.[13] The expansion in the production and commercialization of refrigerators is remarkable when compared with the extremely insignificant number of refrigerators of any kind existing in the previous decade. While even the poorest family had some kind of rudimentary cooking artifact, in 1947 only 20.4 percent of households in the country had iceboxes and just 3.4 percent had electric refrigerators. Moreover, half of all artifacts for food conservation were in Buenos Aires.[14] The mid-twentieth-century boom of refrigerators is even more striking due to the constraints in the supply of electrical energy that affected the period. Postwar industrial growth generated an unprecedented demand for electricity that providers could not satisfy, and therefore, the government established strict limitations on the supply of electricity to domestic users in order to privilege industry. Even in this context, the sale

TERMINACION Y PRUEBA DE HELADERAS FAMILIARES

FIGURE 1: Workers finish assembling refrigerators at SIAM. Photo courtesy of Archivo General de la Nación.

of electric refrigerators boomed, and so half of all electric appliances manufactured in the sector were refrigerators, which came to be aptly considered the "stars of the industry."[15]

As a firm that went from a small manufacturer of bread-kneading machines to the largest metalworking company in the country, SIAM (Sociedad Industrial Americana de Maquinarias) offers an excellent example of the dynamics of industrial expansion in the postwar era. Founded by Italian immigrant Torcuato Di Tella and two partners in the 1910s, SIAM started as a small workshop that manufactured bakery equipment and that expanded production to gasoline pumps and water softeners in the 1920s. An imaginative planner who was eager to diversify his business, Di Tella started producing commercial refrigerators in the early 1930s. This was a small market of high-priced, custom-made artifacts that required minimal advertising and only a small number of salesmen and servicemen. At this time, SIAM technicians started experimenting with household refrigerators. However, the unsuccessful results and high costs, especially with compressors, the most difficult element of the assembly, led Di Tella to sign a license with the American Kelvinator company in 1937. SIAM purchased all refrigerator parts from Kelvinator and either marketed 20 percent of its products under the Kelvinator brand or linked both trade names on all refrigerators. Although production grew, the market remained small since refrigerators were too expensive for the majority of the population.

In 1940, Kelvinator adopted a standardized and single-model line that prompted SIAM, whose production was based on variety and flexibility, to terminate the agreement and to sign a contract with Westinghouse for materials and technical advice. However, when the United States entered the Second World War at the end of 1941, the American government included most metals and machineries on a list of restricted export materials, severing the supplies that SIAM received from Westinghouse. While the numbers of refrigerators dropped, SIAM continued production by manufacturing parts and buying them from local producers. At the end of the war, the company maintained its contract with Westinghouse but diversified its products through new agreements with the Swedish company Electrolux for the production of kerosene-absorption refrigerators marketed for residents in the countryside, and with Hoover for the manufacture of washing machines. Still, SIAM continued a process of vertical integration that led to self-sufficiency. By the early 1950s, SIAM manufactured practically all parts of several appliances, an achievement that had required the complete physical reorganization of the factory, the introduction of the assembly line, and higher levels of technical expertise. In 1955, SIAM was not only producing its own compressors for refrigerators, the main technological obstacle in previous decades, but also selling them to competitors. Between 1950 and 1955, SIAM's production of electric refrigerators tripled and the company supplied between 60 and 80 percent of all electric refrigerators sold in the country.[16]

The remarkable industrial development in the postwar years was contingent upon several critical conditions. Through generous long-term loans at low interest rates, the Central Bank and the Industrial Bank, founded by the military government in 1944, became decisive in supporting and promoting industrialization during Perón's government. Despite the official rhetoric, which emphasized assistance to industries throughout the country, close to half of all credits went to companies operating in the capital city and the province of Buenos Aires. Until 1950, the textile and metallurgic sectors were the two primary beneficiaries of official credits. From that year on, and as a result of the increased credit for agricultural producers triggered by the difficulties in the balance of payments, most industrial loans went to the food sector. Generally, manufacturers invested only a small portion of loans in infrastructure and technology. Most borrowers used credit to pay wages and purchase supplies, a practice that in many cases had a negative effect on industrial productivity.[17]

To further promote industrial development, the government combined generous loans with tariff protection to prevent foreign competition. Moreover, foreign currency acquired at preferential rates allowed manufacturers to advantageously purchase machinery and inputs. In addition to the abundant foreign currency reserves accumulated during the Second World War, the IAPI, controlled by Minister Miranda, had monopolized foreign trade. It thus became a crucial instrument in generating the foreign currency needed to import technology and capital goods for the secondary sector. As a mediator between local farmers and buyers abroad, the IAPI paid agricultural producers half of the current foreign exchange rate and sold agro-exports at international prices. Then, the government transferred the profits to the industrial sector and channeled them into social programs and federal spending. The IAPI delivered a serious blow to the agricultural sector, which also suffered from rising labor costs, the decline in cultivated land, and lack of inputs.[18]

The initial industrial success of the "Peronist golden years" could not mask the weak foundations of the government's plan for industrialization. A sign of the changing times was evident when Minister Miranda and his staff were replaced by a team of professional economists headed by Alfredo Gómez Morales in 1949. By that year, the accumulated reserves had been exhausted, the international prices of grains and meat were returning to normal, and the markets were shrinking. While Argentine exports reached a total of 1.6 billion dollars in 1948, a year later, total revenue dropped to 933 million. Lower prices and smaller markets for Argentine agricultural products—aggravated by the competition of abundant American grains— threatened the flow of imports needed by the industrial sector. The industry was both a victim and the culprit of its own situation since the negative trade balance and the shortage of foreign currency were largely due to the sector's needs for imported inputs and its reduced exporting capacity.

If the Argentine industry had exported its products, it could have obtained the currency it needed to match its import requirements. However, this change would have demanded the reduction of wages and domestic consumption, both nonnegotiable components of the Peronist industrialist strategy and the source of the government's popular support. At the same time, inflation was becoming a distressing factor in the national economy. Increasing bank credits, which were greater than the growth of savings, and escalating government expenses that upped the state's fiscal deficit brought about an expansion of the monetary supply and its resulting inflationary tendencies. In 1949, annual inflation reached 31 percent, a record high since the late nineteenth century. To remedy this situation, the government decreased the amount of money in circulation, rationalized the public sector, and most significantly, tightened restrictions on credit, reduced the amounts of loans, and raised interest rates.[19]

These measures, however, were unable to prevent serious difficulties a few years later. In 1952, two successive droughts aggravated the negative trade balance and prompted the application of an austerity plan to resolve the lack of foreign currency and the rise in prices. The plan, implemented the first year of Perón's second presidency, precluded the Second Five-Year Plan, which was launched by the government one year later. In its "return to the countryside," aimed at reversing the negative trade balance, the government encouraged agricultural producers with competitive prices and gave priority to the importation of agricultural machinery in order to increase production. To rationalize spending and control inflation, industrial credit and the use of foreign exchange were further restricted. At the same time, the Second Five-Year Plan gave new support to heavy industry, evident in the revitalized SOMISA (Sociedad Mixta Siderúrgica Argentina) project to build a national steel mill and the creation of the Industrias Aeronaúticas y Mecánicas del Estado (IAME), a state conglomerate of automobile and aircraft factories. The goal was to move industrialization beyond sectors such as food processing and textiles, which had reached a limit in terms of growth and fully supplied the domestic market.[20]

In addition, and in contrast to the recent past, the Peronist state courted foreign capital as the foundation for further industrial development. The courtship proved successful with the arrival of American car manufacturer Kaiser and the Standard Oil Company in the mid 1950s. Regarding sectors such as domestic appliances, rubber, and petrochemicals, whose inefficient productive practices prevented them from satisfying the increasing internal consumer demand, the state focused on boosting productivity and fervently exhorted workers to "produce, produce, produce," the new ubiquitous motto. Thus, in 1955, the government convoked business and labor to the Congress on Productivity in which it made recommendations to discourage absenteeism, proposed modern managerial practices, and encouraged the reduction of the power that trade unions had on the shop floor. Official discourse pivoted on appeals to personal commitment and effort to fulfill the new national industrialization goals and, most concretely, on demands of discipline at the plant, longer working hours, and more proficient collective and individual performance.[21]

The 1950s economic policies became a subject of great interest for the group that overthrew Perón in 1955. During the brief administration of General Eduardo Lonardi, one of the leaders of the *Revolución Libertadora*, Raúl Prebisch, the director of the United Nations Economic Commission for Latin America and the Caribbean, was hired by the new government to draft a report on the national economic situation. The Prebisch Report, as it became widely known, offered an extremely disapproving view of the Peronist economic plans and presented a highly unfavorable characterization of the current state of the economy. This evaluation fueled an explanation of the coup against Perón as a necessary remedy to prevent economic debacle, a version of the events that economists and economic historians have successfully contested. In fact, trade balances were highly positive for 1953 and 1954, government spending had been cut 35 percent by 1955, inflation was kept in the single digits, and in the last year in which Perón was in power, the economy grew 7 percent.

In spite of the shortcomings of the postwar industrialization plan in Argentina, historians Pablo Gerchunoff and Lucas Llach have shown that the rate of industrial substitution in the country remained one of the highest in the semi-industrialized world. Equally significant, although the national industry was dependent on imported machinery throughout the Peronist government, national production of capital goods grew by 102 percent in this period. In contrast to what anti-Peronists have suggested, the Perón administration was highly successful at adapting its economic policy to challenging new conditions while sustaining employment levels, maintaining the supply of consumer goods, and avoiding a devaluation that, by carrying out substantial income redistribution, would have seriously afflicted the newly acquired consumer power of the working class.[22]

High Wages and the "Chain Effect of Prosperity"

The rise of popular purchasing power was the driving force of the industrialization plan adopted in the postwar years. In contrast to Pinedo's proposal in which industrialization was oriented to the export market, Perón's plan for industrial growth and full employment depended on turning Argentine workers into consumers. In 1944, Perón declared:

> When exportation is no longer feasible, if we only consume 50 percent of what we are manufacturing, what will be the state of our industry, of our production? The remaining 50 percent will be paralyzed and we will have one million unemployed Argentines with nothing to live on. The only solution is to increase consumption. And we can only increase consumption by increasing salaries so that every Argentine can consume more than he or she currently consumes, thus allowing every manufacturer and every merchant to produce the same amount that he produces today without the need to bring machinery to a standstill and fire workers.[23]

While Perón originally placed consumer spending at the center of his industrial policy and political project, popular consumption, or better yet, its paucity, had long been an object of public debate and of reformist attention, albeit futile. At least since the early twentieth century, when doctor and lawyer Juan Bialet Massé denounced, in a now classic study, the severe deprivation of workers in the provincial interior, physicians, social reformers, and leftist thinkers had been warning state officials against the unmet materials needs of the country's working population. The vulnerability of the low-income sectors was evident in the testimony of Pedro Escudero, a pioneer of food research in Argentina who, in his visit to the western province of San Juan in the 1930s, witnessed in dismay how the poor sectors lived on a daily diet of grapes, the regional staple, and a stew made of dog meat.[24]

Although low standards of living were especially alarming in the poorer northern and rural regions of Argentina, many social commentators expressed serious concern about the *subconsumo* (underconsumption) of the low-income sectors throughout the country. In contrast to the common trope of national plenty based on abundant grains and meat, the reality showed that most working-class families lived on the border of subsistence in even the most prosperous cities of the rich pampeana and littoral provinces.[25] Critics like Communist leader Paulino González Alberdi explained that low wages and high prices condemned workers in Buenos Aires to a constant struggle to pay the rent and buy milk and bread for their children, a fight so difficult that in many cases these working-class families were set on a dangerous path of undernourishment and illness.[26]

Communists pointed to employers as the culprits and portrayed them as greedy, parasitic, and exploitative characters like the one that a trade journal of textile workers ridiculed for complaining about the demands of his workforce in these terms: "How can I think about workers who dare to demand a raise when I just lost 50,000 pesos playing roulette!"[27]

Industrialists, indeed, had been traditionally reticent to address their share of responsibility in the wage earners' low standard of living. In the early 1940s, Luis Colombo, president of the UIA, delivered grandiloquent claims about the association's commitment to defend workers "from the cradle to the grave," but the UIA lobbied against congressional proposals for a minimum wage. The very few voices that advocated an improvement of working-class living conditions approached it in an individual, paternalistic fashion with the goal of reducing class tensions and disciplining the workforce. Concerned about the potential postwar scenario of unemployment and consequent turmoil, Torcuato Di Tella, the owner of metalworking company SIAM, advised his fellow businessmen to help laborers earn enough to rise above the subsistence level and to provide some social security. According to Di Tella, these were investments in "social pacification." A curious, well-read, and well-travelled admirer of Fordism and the New Deal, Di Tella offered wage subsidies for workers with children, implemented company-administered welfare programs, and gave laborers bonuses when they got married or had a baby. However, he was largely unsuccessful at rallying industrialists in support of these kinds of measures. In fact, Di Tella frequently resented UIA members, the most powerful referents of the industrial sector, for having a vision of labor problems and a conception of their role in improving the life of workers that resembled those of the "simple-minded, greedy owners of small shops."[28]

In the 1930s and early 1940s, the National Department of Labor conducted a series of surveys that documented working-class living conditions in Buenos Aires, confirming what researchers and manufacturers had known for decades. A 1937 survey showed that the "average working-class family," consisting of a male wage earner, his wife, and three children under the age of 14, spent more than 60 percent of their budget on food and fuel for cooking and heating, assigned around 20 percent of their funds to pay for inadequate housing, and employed around 10 percent of their money to purchase inexpensive consumer goods, mainly clothing. The rest of the budget was spent on a miscellaneous category that included entertainment, transportation, and medical expenses. The picture of quotidian working-class consumption was extremely ascetic and constricted at best. The survey, which offered no information on the wages earned by women and children, further revealed that while the male head of the household earned 127 pesos per month, household expenditures totaled 164 pesos per month. The resulting monthly deficit of 37 pesos, which represented nearly 30 percent of the average worker's income, reinforced traditional views of working-class subconsumo. Furthermore, it substantiated the central conclusion of all surveys conducted by the National Department of Labor in this period: working-class families did not earn enough to satisfy their basic needs.[29]

As had happened in the past, state authorities filed the surveys away and the troubling conclusion of the research did not translate into any official attempts of rectification. Shortly after taking power, the officials of the 1943 June Revolution reduced the rent and enforced price controls on consumables, but between 1943 and 1945, real wages barely increased. This changed when Perón was appointed to the National Department of Labor—soon to become the Secretariat of Labor—and José Figuerola, the head of the statistics team who had directed the surveys, became his closest policy advisor. With Perón in this position, the problem of meager wages took center stage. If industrial growth and full employment depended on internal consumption, good wages were the motor of the "chain effect of prosperity": high income fueled aggregate demand and thus triggered production, which in turn boosted salaries.[30] In 1951, reflecting on his postwar policy of income redistribution, Perón explained this virtuous cycle in simple terms:

> We use a system that is different from all of those used in the rest of the world during times of crisis and need. When they said they needed to economize, they reduced the wages of the workers. We said, "Are they [the workers] poor? Pay them five times more than what they used to be paid." This way, the economy was revived and everything turned out just fine.[31]

The Secretariat of Labor sided with the labor unions, and through collective bargaining, a process of negotiation between employers and labor leaders to regulate working conditions and remuneration, minimum wages began to increase considerably. This was the long overdue achievement of a major goal of the workforce. Between 1937 and 1943, salary demands were behind more than half of all strikes. In 1944 alone, close to one thousand collective agreements were negotiated with the support of the secretariat, and in that year and the following, a higher proportion of strikes were settled in the workers' favor than in any other previous year.[32] Not surprisingly, on the first anniversary of the secretariat, the leader of the sugar workers union celebrated it as "our hope," linking the bright prospects of the labor movement and a higher standard of living for working-class families to the future of the agency and its continuing defense of the workforce:

> Never before have workers had so much state support for union activity, which allows them to defend their economic and social interests. [. . .] The more powerful unions become, the more workers will enjoy better living conditions, higher salaries, and more comfortable homes. All of this will be possible because we will have government institutions that protect us against capitalist greed.[33]

Perón's wage policy as president significantly surpassed this initial progress, reinforcing his image as the architect of historical reparation, an aspect chapter 6 examines in detail. Urban, industrial, and unionized workers particularly benefited from higher compensation. Yet as the numbers of unions grew exponentially and membership expanded remarkably—from 434,814 affiliates in 1946 to close to 2.5 million in 1951—better wages rapidly became enjoyed by most. Between 1946 and 1949, real wages increased by 62 percent prompting an unprecedented rise in consumer spending that grew faster than savings and investments. In other words, the chain effect of prosperity had begun.[34]

Even traditionally vulnerable occupations experienced a significant boost in their salaries. At a meeting with Perón, the leader of the gastronomic labor union that grouped restaurant workers claimed that tips challenged the dignity of waiters since they "have to accept as alms what is in fact due to them as compensation for their work day."[35] Echoing this view, the government abolished "humiliating" tips and mandated a *laudo gastronómico* by decree. The laudo was a percentage of the monthly earnings of restaurants and cafés—between 8 to 18 percent according to the type of establishment—that was added to the staff's wages. Employers resented the access of labor union officials to their ledgers while insisting that the percentage owed to waiters would make many businesses go bankrupt. Some commentators reinforced this view by sarcastically arguing that since the laudo had been imposed, architects, doctors, and lawyers were seriously contemplating the possibility of becoming servers.[36] Still, in contrast to the apocalyptic prediction of restaurant owners, in 1951, there were four times more restaurants in Buenos Aires than in 1945. More than 30 percent of the

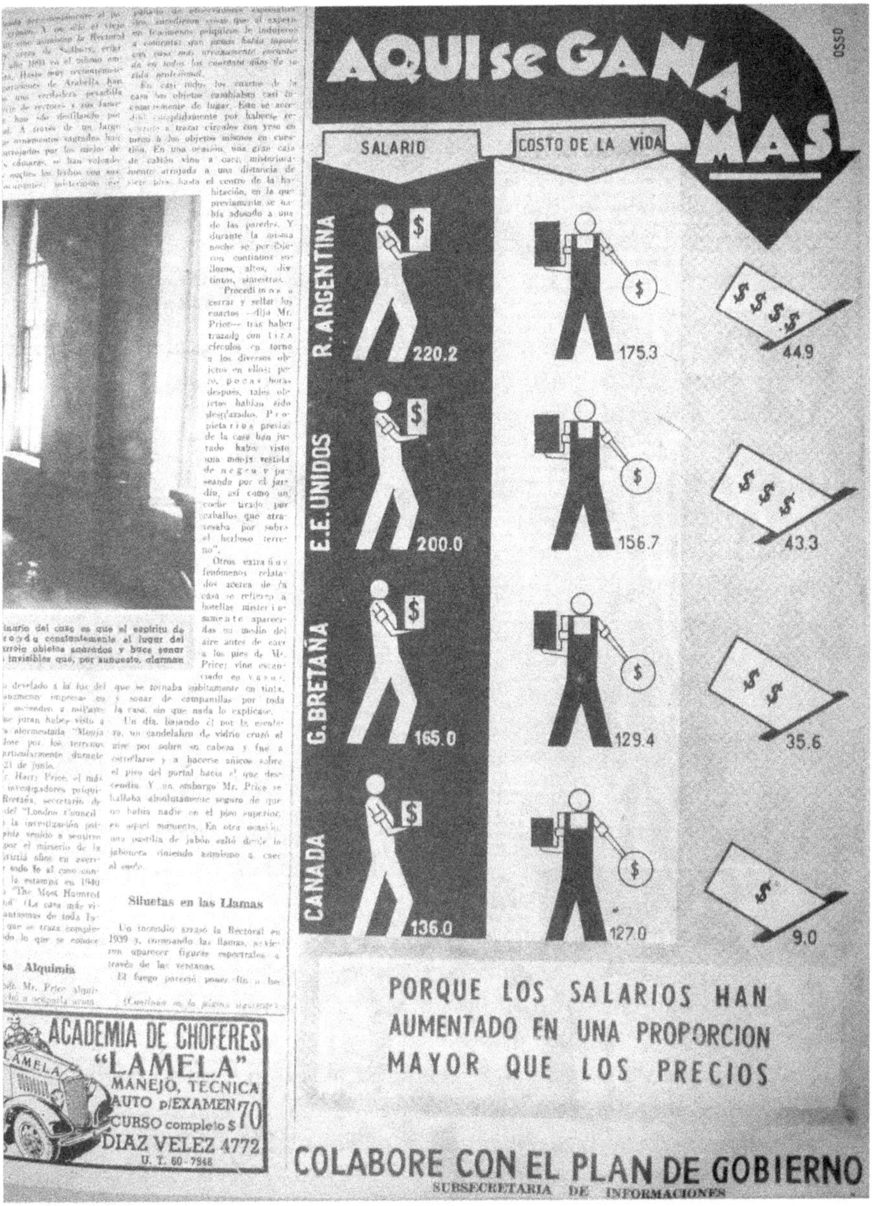

FIGURE 2: "Here we earn more." Government propaganda celebrated the remuneration of Argentine workers in a comparison with wages in other parts of the world. *Ahora*, August 3, 1947, 7.

Industry, Wages, and the State

urban grounds were occupied by restaurants, and on streets like Leandro Alem Avenue, the level of concentration was so high that there were more than twenty-five restaurants on just two city blocks.[37]

All in all, in 1954, wages represented 58 percent of the national income, the highest level ever reached in the history of the country. Income redistribution favorable to the workforce was fundamental for the Peronist conception of the economic system in which "capital serves the economy and the economy serves mankind."[38] Between 1948 and 1955, however, profit margins in industry also rose. Cheap credit to manufacturers largely allowed them to compensate for increasing wages since most bank loans were employed to pay salaries. These essentially subsidized wage increases did not make income redistribution a less thorny issue. Perón's platform based on a minimum wage, social insurance, unionization, and work regulations served him well in structuring the lasting alliance with the unionized workforce that would put him in power but also permanently severed the relationship with some industrial sectors, especially big businesses.[39]

Early on, displeased by what they viewed as the politicization of labor matters and the imposition of detrimental policies without consultation, the UIA rallied the business community against the minimum wage and especially the *aguinaldo*, the yearly bonus that Perón successfully promoted while in the Secretariat of Labor and that would become a banner of his government. Two months before the electoral victory that made Perón president, the UIA, the Sociedad Rural Argentina (SRA)—the powerful organization of large landowners—and other business organizations undertook a three-day lockout to protest executive decree 33,302, which, among other things, raised wages and established the aguinaldo.[40] The bonus, equivalent to a month of wages and paid in December, had a significant impact on the working-class budget. Official statistics reported that the purchasing power of an unskilled worker had increased 25 percent between 1939 and 1945 and that the aguinaldo boosted it to 35 percent. This did not go unnoticed by the business community. Paradoxically, at the same time that manufacturers and commerce had participated in the lockout and resisted the annual bonus, many firms centered their holiday advertisements on the aguinaldo and urged workers to spend it on the advertised goods, a marketing strategy that became widespread throughout this period.[41]

Besides higher wages and yearly bonuses, ten- to fifteen-day paid vacations, sick leave, social programs covering health care, public housing projects, and frozen rents greatly contributed to increasing the disposable income of the working population. Rent freezes, for example, had a huge impact on working-class budgets, as the share of what workers devoted to housing went from an estimated 18 percent in 1943 to 2.6 percent in 1957.[42] As workers' wallets got thicker, the expansion of modern commercial practices, particularly consumer credit, advanced their purchasing power. No interest rates and no down payments, widespread in department, clothing, and appliances stores, further allowed worker-consumers to have access to pricey durables that would otherwise have been out of their reach. Between 1950 and 1955, for example, the use of installment plans to buy domestic appliances almost doubled in the city of Buenos Aires. As evidence of this trend, in 1954, SIAM sold 63 percent of its refrigerators through installment plans.[43]

A source of political support and the motor to industrialize the country, working-class consumer power was also central to the definition of *justicialismo*. Justicialismo was based on strong egalitarian impulses that proposed a fairer distribution of wealth and the end of privileges. "We want to produce, consume, enjoy or suffer—but equally, with no preferential treatment for anyone in particular," announced Perón.[44] Social equality, harmonious class relations, and the condemnation of capitalism and communism for their exploitation of the working population, all aspects that were fundamental to Peronism, were equally central to the *Quadragesimo Anno*, the influential 1931 encyclical written by Pope Pius XI. Thus, although subjects like education, divorce, the separation between church and state, and even consumption would lately severely damage the relation between the Catholic Church and Peronism, justicialismo held a wide appeal in a "Catholic nation" like Argentina. Furthermore, for the Church, the Peronist policies of income redistribution and the regulation of working conditions initially represented a welcomed antidote to the expansion of communism, reinforced the traditional male role of the breadwinner therefore protecting women and children, and contributed to the social uplift of the low-income sectors.[45]

The Peronist definition of social justice required the expansion of citizenship beyond formal political rights to guarantee the social and economic inclusion of the masses. In 1946, Perón responded to accusations of fascism by arguing that although the opposition portrayed the upcoming presidential election as a contest between freedom and tyranny, the real challenge for workers would be to rightfully choose a high standard of living over the perpetuation of social inequality.[46] A cartoon titled *Lo que va de ayer a hoy* (From Yesterday to Today), published in the newspaper *La Época* in 1947, illustrates this vision. It shows an overweight capitalist with a cigar and elegant pocket watch, handing bills that read "Free Press" and "Constitution" to a disheartened and emaciated worker who asks:

"This is all good but . . . What do I eat?" Below, the current times are represented through Juan Pueblo (John People), an exultant and good-looking worker firmly holding bills including "Aguinaldo," "Raises," and "Paid Vacations" while thankfully shaking hands with Perón as the president advises him to defend his newly acquired privileges. In this view, social justice represented access to genuine economic citizenship, the foundation of what Perón considered to be a "true democracy."[47]

Most communist activists dismissed this vision as the ploy of a rabble-rouser and tempered their classist labor militancy to join the elites in an anti-Peronist alliance, a move that inexorably alienated broad sectors of the rank and file. Still, many union leaders—some out of true ideological conviction, others out of political opportunism—eagerly adopted the Peronist language of social justice and its emphasis on remedying long-standing economic grievances. As early as July 1945, for example, a spokesman for the Unión Ferroviaria, the railroad workers union, announced, "We want democracy, liberty, institutional normality but we also want above everything else a minimum of social justice that assures the working classes a dignified and humane standard of living to which they legitimately have a right to aspire."[48]

In line with this aspiration, Peronist authorities disputed accusations of demagogy and anti-intellectualism—which the opposition based on Peronist chants like "Alpargatas yes, books no!" that exalted the preference for material items like the inexpensive canvas shoe, over education—with a notion of a resourceful state attentive to the essential needs of the working people. Although the government stressed the innovation and originality of its policies, Peronism relied heavily on the past, launching projects—especially formulated by the Socialist Party—that had never come to fruition, revitalizing crucial but historically undeveloped and overlooked institutions, and resolutely applying labor laws, like those that limited working hours and ordered no work on Sundays, that had never been enforced for many occupations.[49] If the conception was not entirely new, it was the implementation of changes that truly substantiated claims of the historical uniqueness of the regime. Prompt accomplishment was critical to Perón's self-presentation as a hands-on leader who "delivers" (*cumple*) and to his appeal among union leaders and the rank and file frustrated with governments that had ranged from coldly indifferent to outright hostile toward the labor movement.

The famous 1947 Declaration of Workers' Rights perfectly combined the concept of material comfort central to social justice with the Peronist motto "Doing is better than promising." Later incorporated into the 1949 Constitution, workers' rights included fair wages, the right to well-being—defined as the access to housing, adequate clothing, and nutrition—and the right to a better economic situation. The declaration stated that "a worker should be able to satisfy his and his family's necessities, work with satisfaction without excessive toil, rest free of worry, and enjoy spiritual and material freedom. The right of well-being imposes the social necessity of raising the standard of living as far as our level of economic development allows."[50] Based on an all-encompassing idea of needs, the *justicialista* concept of remuneration surpassed mere survival to guarantee a virtuous and comfortable life.

According to the Peronist ideology and in spite of their profound differences, the capitalist and communist systems equally infringed on the right to well-being. Both lowered wages to either capitalize the state or private business, thus limiting popular consumption. Peronism, for its part, offered an option. The "third position" was a society where *el capital humanizado* (humane capital) served the interests of the community and an interventionist state ensured the entitlement of workers. At the same time that the state regulated working hours and conditions, protecting the right of laborers to a comfortable livelihood went from being a prerogative to one of the state's central duties. In spite of state officials' incendiary discourses and the characterization of the regime as revolutionary, the Peronist third position was a reformist ideology that advanced the conciliation between classes and the consequent end of class struggle, and endorsed a conception of the state as an impartial mediator that prevented social exploitation. Paradise, the magazine *Mundo Peronista* claimed, was neither to the right nor to the left, but "just in the middle, in the harmonic balance of productive forces which is the guarantee of freedom and justice for the people."[51]

In the third position, the well-being of workers depended on fair prices as much as on adequate wages. The rise in loans to sustain industrial growth, the increase of money in circulation, the higher wages, rising consumer demand, the government deficit, and later, the deteriorating balance of payments, all contributed to an inflationary process that progressively pushed up the cost of living. In spite of the complex variables that triggered the problem, until 1949, the government misjudged inflation as a temporary complication that essentially resulted from a lack of consumer goods—mainly due to the scarcity of raw materials and capital goods—in a context of higher purchasing power.[52] In addition to policies aimed at boosting industrial production to satisfy the expanding demand, the government established maximum prices on key products, including food and clothing. By the late 1940s, a wide array of goods and services, from a haircut to a movie ticket, had fixed prices, and merchandise such as clothing items had to have price tags. To monitor observance, the police was in charge of inspections of retail shops and industries. At the beginning, and due to the highest concentration of consumers, inspections were restricted to the capital and its metropolitan region, but progressively, local governments or the increasing presence of federal officials extended surveillance in the provinces. In 1948, the government created the Dirección Nacional de Vigilancia de Precios (National Office of Price Surveillance) to respond to consumer complaints and reports against noncompliant shops and to coordinate inspections and price enforcement among different state agencies.[53]

Although official propaganda singled out wholesalers and manufacturers as defiant of state regulation and, as a consequence, under stricter government control, the campaign particularly targeted small shopkeepers. In "the war on speculation," as the Peronist administration termed the arsenal of measures to control prices, noncompliance was punished with fines, the confiscation of merchandise, and jail terms. Since the impact of the war on speculation varied greatly throughout the country, both the success of government enforcement and the level of compliance are difficult to assess. Yet despite business complaints against the damaging effects of state controls over commerce, the number of commercial establishments in the country increased 70 percent between 1946 and 1954. Furthermore, the rise of alternative commercial venues, particularly in big cities and especially in Buenos Aires, offered working-class consumers an attractive option. Municipal markets, consumer cooperatives, and *proveedurías*—grocery stores managed by unions or by the Eva Perón Foundation—sold a variety of consumer goods at fixed prices.[54]

By 1952, as the balance of payments deteriorated, domestic manufacturing declined, and consumers suffered shortages of foods, fuel, and other staples, the issue of the rising cost of living became serious. With real wages that were 13 percent less than in 1943, the Peronist ideal of working-class well-being was at risk. In response, the government launched a massive campaign of austere consumption. Consumer frugality was critical to ease the pressures on prices and to contribute to greater surpluses for export. Therefore, the government portrayed thriftiness as the patriotic responsibility of citizen-consumers, an interpretation of civic duty that is common during economic crises and in contexts of war.[55] To fight inflation and improve the balance of payments, the government asked consumers to reduce superfluous purchases and cut down on waste while emphasizing that wise spending was meant to defend purchasing power rather than to sacrifice the "necessities of life." Perón affirmed that as a "natural" response after decades of extreme privation, the working classes had embraced their new role of consumers too wholeheartedly, and sometimes even negligently. However, after this initial period of lavish expenditures when wage earners had filled their closets and dined out every night, it was time to rationalize consumer spending and restore a simple life-style.[56] In achieving these goals, the government enlisted the cooperation of labor unions and rank-and-file workers to freeze wages for two years. By 1954, efforts to moderate consumption had succeeded and, as a result, inflation dropped to 3 percent and the government increased wages between 15 and 20 percent.[57]

Defending the Worker-Consumer, Protecting Purchasing Power

High wages and fixed prices were critical in awakening the chain effect of prosperity, but the government knew that safeguarding high purchasing power involved more than checking price tags: it required an exhaustive control of the quality of consumer goods. The principle was particularly relevant for food products. The food industry was the biggest manufacturer in the country as well as the largest industrial employer. A very disparate sector, it combined new and old companies—modern, large, and efficient factories that sold their products throughout the country along with small and makeshift workshops that served local communities. By the mid-twentieth century, Argentine food manufacturing not only firmly controlled the domestic market, but also experienced remarkable expansion. In 1946, for example, fish canneries produced close to 5.5 million kilos of canned products. Six years later, production had tripled and the industry had completely substituted imports. Similarly, the manufacturing of canned peaches went from 5 million cans in 1939 to almost 20 million in 1953, and wine production more than doubled in the same period.[58]

Higher production responded to the higher demand caused by a rising population but, most importantly, by the increasing spending power. Working-class consumers, who traditionally spent around 50 percent of their income on food, could now choose to diversify their diets and spend on better products. Similarly, internal migrants who moved to major cities began to abandon local fresh foods in exchange for canned and packaged groceries. New levels of consumption among low-income sectors, for instance, triggered the demand for products like beer, chocolates, and cookies. By investing a larger share of their budgets in food while paying higher prices for lower-quality items, working-class consumers had traditionally been at a disadvantage with regard to the quality-price ratio of food products. Indeed, class difference in food distribution went beyond quantity since historically low-income sectors not only ate less, but also consumed unhealthy food. Thus, the mid-twentieth-century Peronist banner of nutritious and reliable food for workers had a strong democratizing effect and became yet another way in which the government conveyed its powerful message of social justice.[59] Beyond health reasons, good food for working-class consumers was a key aspect of the war on speculation since it ensured that low-income sectors got what they paid for, preserved their overall purchasing power, and consequently, increased their disposable income. In support of this argument, Congressman Eloy Camus argued that

> it is not only urgent but absolutely essential to actively keep the working-class consumer from being defrauded. Otherwise laws against usury are simply ineffective since commerce takes away the quality or quantity of the merchandise sold, eliminating the advantage of reasonable prices that the legislator wished to position within the public's reach.[60]

Ironically, a country known as the world's breadbasket, Argentina was also one in which food adulteration was as widespread as the wheat fields that made it famous. Consumer fraud commonly involved adulteration with both harmless and noxious substances, like watering down and adding sugar to milk and wine, coloring old meat, diluting beverages with contaminating liquids, and using toxic additives for preservation. But consumer fraud had still many other manifestations. Producers and sellers made false claims about the weight, ingredients, and nutritional value of products, and especially the quality of the ingredients used in the elaboration of canned food, the percentages of different types of cooking oil combined in a bottle, and the vitamin and mineral contents. Also, consumers were victims of foods that had been spoiled due to unsanitary and inappropriate production, transportation, storage, and commercialization.[61] Experts argued that rising consumer demand led to the emergence of unqualified manufacturers only interested in fast and easy profits at the expense of consumers.

A 1942 report by the U.S. Office of Foreign Agricultural Relations affirmed that if sanitary laws were passed and enforced, smaller food-processing plants would be forced either to make drastic changes or to go out of business.[62] Yet, new producers were just part of the problem. Experts did not spare older and well-established manufacturers from criticism, as such producers lowered the quality of their goods in pursuit of higher profits, thus damaging the creditability of the food sector as a whole.[63]

The state, for its part, had traditionally failed to hold manufacturers accountable for the products they put on the market. In the early 1940s, food researcher Jorge Mullor discovered that 80 percent of the national population consumed food products that had not been inspected or approved by the state. Government attempts to control food production and commerce were limited to the exclusive jurisdiction of local authorities, especially municipalities that struggled with the application of local laws and decrees that were generally ineffective or unenforceable. Local agencies lacked clear roles, were poorly staffed, and suffered from insufficient financial and technological resources. For these reasons, government control mainly focused on milk, fresh meat, and bread. They not only were the most common components of the popular diet but also required minimal industrialization, thus allowing for easy detection of adulteration and decay.[64] In addition, local authorities concentrated on stopping clandestine activities, particularly illegal abattoirs, but attempts to stop them were only minimally effective and government corruption often made regulation even more ineffectual.[65]

In this context, the Peronist government launched major reform initiatives that sought to protect public health, set the foundations for a vigorous population, and safeguard household economies. For the first time ever, the federal state articulated a far-reaching web of institutions and regulations to inspect and guarantee the quality and price of hundreds of products, from factory to local market. State authorities realized that even if food prices were stable, lower-quality products would continue to hurt the budgets of the low-income sectors. The major overhaul of institutions resulted in the creation of the Dirección Nacional de Alimentación (National Food Department) in 1949. Organized by Minister of Health Ramón Carrillo, it was an agency that experts in the fields of public health and nutrition had been enthusiastically, though unsuccessfully, promoting for decades.[66] The National Food Department had six divisions that carried out distinct tasks: researching nutritional conditions across the country; organizing educational activities and informational campaigns; offering technical and organizational support for the food industry; conducting periodic inspections and monitoring food factories directly through the newly created Policía Alimentaria (Food Police) or by coordinating and assisting local agents; gathering statistics; and creating and regularly updating a national registry of food companies. The National Food Department also supervised the National Institute of Nutrition, the National School of Dieticians, and the Institute of Bromatology, which was in charge of lab research and collaborated closely with the Food Police.[67] In a typical celebratory statement, the pro-Peronist newspaper *La Época* affirmed that the department detected ninety-nine out of one hundred adulterated products, a degree of accuracy that made it "a true shield that protects the people [from unscrupulous merchants and manufacturers]."[68]

Although the lack of surviving internal records and the partiality of the press work against a detailed assessment of the Food Department, the level of intervention of the federal administration in the food industry was unprecedented. Also, at the lead of the federal government, local agencies became increasingly more active in food quality control. In 1949, a national decree mandated that all food products marketed in the city of Buenos Aires and the *territorios nacionales* had to be inspected by the Ministry of Health.[69] That same year, the Chemistry Department of Buenos Aires found 15,310 cases of sanitary infringement, confiscated 90,300 kilos of products, and inspected more than 8 million cans of food and more than 4 million beverage bottles.[70]

The most publicized case of the period was the "Mu-Mu scandal," a perfect example of the changing role of the state, the implementation of control mechanisms in the quest for healthy and quality food, and the public expectations of hygiene and commercial honesty that were transforming the consumer market. Mu-Mu, a candy and chocolate factory located in Buenos Aires that commercialized several popular brand names on the national market, was paradigmatic of the rising numbers of food factories and the increasing volumes of processed food in mid-twentieth-century Argentina. It all started when the national Ministry of Health coordinated an inspection of the Mu-Mu factory that revealed the appalling and unhygienic conditions of production and storage. The lab results showed that candy elaborated in the factory had larvae, harmful bacteria, fragments of insects, and mice hair. Working together and assisted by the police, national and municipal officials confiscated and incinerated more than sixty thousand kilos of candy and chocolate in the capital city alone in just a few days and ordered the confiscation of products in the rest of the country.

Mu-Mu was shut down from 1949 to 1953 while the government further inspected all candy and chocolate factories closing down another company due to insalubrious conditions and spoiled products.[71]

The case of Mu-Mu underlined the need to create a detailed and vast legal apparatus to assist federal and local food agencies. With the exception of Buenos Aires, which approved a food code in the late 1920s, the rest of the country lagged far behind. Córdoba sanctioned a provincial code in 1937, and Santa Fe in 1941.[72] In 1951, to systematize food regulation, the Ministry of Health appointed a commission of eight government authorities and four representatives of the food industry to study municipal and provincial food laws and to draw up the first National Food Code.[73] Approved by decree two years later, the exhaustive National Food Code comprised more than 950 articles, established standards for food elaboration, storage, wrapping, labeling, and commercialization, and regulated methods for pasteurization, sterilization, and preservation. Detention, fines, the seizure of products, the closing of production facilities, and the cancellation of production permits were common punishments for infringement.[74] In spite of the expectations of food experts, the 1953 code was initially enforced only in the city of Buenos Aires and the federal territories rather than throughout the country. Still, most provinces adhered by organizing new control and research agencies, providing certifications, and implementing the recent national legislation.[75]

The quality-price ratio was not only about how food products were elaborated, what their ingredients were, or how they were stored and transported—it was also about what consumers actually knew about the products they bought, the accuracy of the information they received from the manufacturers, and how and where they were packaged. Watered down wine and jellies with more sugar and colorants than actual fruit were not necessarily a cause of illness, but they certainly constituted commercial fraud when, based on the information supplied by the producer, consumers purchased these products believing they were paying for top-quality goods. Chances that the information was erroneous were high since labels, containers, and advertisements were unregulated in Argentina. The only legislation on the subject was law 11,275 that, passed in 1925, mandated the use of the "Argentine Industry" stamp on all national products and determined that goods elaborated in Argentina with foreign materials or ingredients were considered of national origin. The law was a reaction against manufacturers who, eager to attract upper- and middle-class consumers with a marked preference for imports, had adopted the practice of giving

Argentine products foreign names, writing labels in foreign languages, and even stating that they were elaborated in other countries in order to conceal their true provenance.[76]

By the mid-1940s, the expansive food industry, the growing consumer market, and the consequent rising levels of business competition required stricter regulations on product information disclosure. Congress discussions on law 11,275 focused on the right of consumers to know exactly what they paid for, thus making the education of the worker-consumer another aspect of the all-encompassing Peronist state. When buying cooking oils, for example, shoppers were frequently defrauded since labels commonly stated that a bottle contained 100 percent pure olive oil when in reality the contents were a mix of lower-quality oils. Similarly, labels were illustrated with olives, easily misleading consumers to believe they were purchasing olive oil when they were actually buying peanut or sunflower oil.[77]

In 1949, law 11,275 underwent two critical changes to correct these problems. The first article now prohibited both labels and advertisements containing inexact, exaggerated, or concealed information about the quality, quantity, origins, properties, and contents of the product that could confuse or deceive consumers. To make this regulation effective, the law gave the executive branch enormous new power to control, prohibit, and punish in all matters related to labeling, advertising, quality control, and product registration.[78] At the same time that old decrees began to be widely implemented, new rules were passed with directives so detailed that they even specified the size of the font to be employed on labels.[79] Therefore, the archaic Commercial Loyalty Department (Dirección de Lealtad Comercial), the federal agency that had been in charge of investigating infringements on law 11,275, acquired new and unprecedented significance. As the agency went from almost exclusively controlling the use of the "Argentine Industry" stamp on products to monitoring label information in detail, the number of infractions went from twenty-nine in 1943 to five hundred in 1949.[80]

Control over the contents of labels was only one part of the process to guarantee that consumers would be well informed since, before they found the products in the store, shoppers learned about them through advertisements. The impressive increase in the quantity and sophistication of food advertisement in the print media, on the radio, and through billboards was part of a larger trend in advertising as a whole. Between 1943 and 1948, and as a direct response to the increasing consumer market, the numbers of column ads in newspapers and magazines more than doubled.[81]

In the same period, food companies represented close to 40 percent of the biggest clients of ten major advertising agencies in the country and, as a result, the variety of advertised food products greatly expanded. This was a noteworthy change since food advertisement in newspapers had been very limited in the two previous decades. Food ads had been more common in magazines, but the number of products and companies was small, and instead of an articulated campaign sustained over time, the same ad appeared inconsistently.[82]

Until the mid-1940s, misleading ads were a common concern among consumers. Neighborhood organizations and labor unions, in particular, complained about the lack of control evident in cases like beer companies that advertised malt extracts as invigorating beverages for new mothers when the actual product was just regular beer sold at twice the price. Such companies successfully swindled consumers because the government did not certify the contents.[83] Since the mid-1930s, several decrees had attempted to monitor advertising, mainly by establishing that information on ads should be in accordance with that on labels. Provincial and municipal authorities also legislated on these matters but lacked the necessary institutional structure to apply those regulations consistently.[84] Like the control of labeling, the previously weak and unsystematic monitoring of advertisements substantially changed in the late 1940s when law 11,275 prohibited the use of false statements in advertising and imposed high fines on lawbreakers. Submission of ads for federal inspection was voluntary, but trade organizations urged producers to present their advertisements for evaluation and approval since the government could immediately prohibit the circulation of ads contravening the law.[85]

Most importantly, some product claims required state approval before publication. In 1949, decree 7,358 mandated that statements about the nutritional and therapeutic properties of food products, quality, and characteristics that appeared in all types of advertisements needed the previous approval of the Ministry of Health. In the case of the capital city, the municipal government ordered advertisers to submit all food and beverage ads to the Institute of Bromatology for approval before their media release. In Santa Fe, this task fell to the provincial Health Department, an agency that admen considered to be stricter than the national ministry and thus dreaded in the profession.[86] In fact, after decades of working without much interference, manufacturers and their advertising agents gave the new rules an unenthusiastic welcome. One of the heads of the advertising company J. Walter Thompson in Argentina complained that in Rosario ad copies could never suggest a product was "the best" or "the only one" for certain purposes because state officials wanted these facts carefully documented before approving the publication of ads.[87] Admen strongly believed that control over advertising should come from within their own ranks since the intervention of government authorities made the already complicated creation of ads even more problematic.[88]

While the quality, origin, and properties of a food product could be misrepresented on labels and ads, quantity could be distorted in the very vessels that carried the product. Experts and consumers complained that quantities, net weight, and measures stated on labels did not coincide with the real contents of the package or were not properly disclosed. The regulation on labels that prohibited false and inexact information was aimed at correcting these inaccuracies. This, however, offered only a partial solution, since the crux of the problem remained in the packages themselves. The lack of uniform and consistent shapes, capacity, materials, and size of packages for the same types of products created confusion among consumers and dishonest commercial competition among producers. The most problematic aspect was the relation between the size and shape of the package and the weight of its contents. Free to establish this ratio as they chose, some manufacturers used boxes, cans, and bottles much bigger than the contents they enclosed, misleading consumers to believe they were purchasing a larger amount of the product than they actually were.[89] These irregularities contravened the very purpose of packaged foods, that is, the economy of buying small quantities. For low-income consumers, packaged foods allowed them to buy exactly what they needed, making the most of available money, and avoiding loss through spoiling. The purchase of small rations also benefited working-class consumers who lived in small residences and had no sufficient or adequate storage space.[90]

Some sectors of the food industry actively sought out state involvement in regulating packaging, another example of how the Peronist government and the private sector found it equally rewarding to keep the chain effect of prosperity in motion. Coffee producers, for example, believed that the regimentation of packaging was essential to achieve fair competition and echoed economic and legal scholars who agreed on the need to standardize containers in order to expand the consumer market and defend popular purchasing power.[91] By the mid-1930s, the continual and extended use of tin containers had informally, though incompletely, helped to homogenize packaging. However, the Second World War restricted the importation of tin and laminated zinc to a minimum and forced food producers to seek out viable alternatives. In the case of products such as edible oils and coffee, glass became a convenient substitute that combined economy, accessibility, and the adequate preservation of perishable contents. After the war, many manufactures continued using glass while others returned to tin packages, further expanding the already varied universe of unregulated food containers.[92]

Beyond the restrictions on materials, incipient changes in commercialization contributed to the transformation of food packaging. In the early 1950s, the first self-service grocery stores appeared in Argentine big cities. Advertising agents and food manufacturers knew that the new stores required well-designed, descriptive, appealing, and standard packages not only to successfully attract the consumer, but also to neatly group items on the shelves. Also, a renewed interest in food packaging reflected the current concerns over the sanitary conditions of production and commercialization of food items. In addition to offering arguments about economy, practicality, and rich flavor, food ads insistently promised shoppers that bottles, boxes, sealed paper wraps, and cans delivered products fresh, hygienic, and free from "dirty hands."[93]

FIGURE 3: President Juan Domingo Perón is informed about the benefits of self-service grocery stores that sold government-inspected foods in sanitary packaging. Photo courtesy of Archivo General de la Nación.

In this context, the old demands of certain food industry sectors to standardize packaging successfully overlapped with the government's goal of cutting pricey imports and effectively monitoring whether consumers got their money's worth. The enactment of several presidential decrees and resolutions of the Ministry of Industry and Commerce led to two major changes. The government prohibited the use of certain materials in product packaging and ordered the exact measures, sizes, design, and capacity of packages for several food products. To make the new regulation effective, authorities enforced the inscription of manufacturers of containers in a state registry. After registration, the Commercial Control Department gave manufacturers a certification number that they were required to print or stamp on their containers to attest that they had been officially approved. The decree further standardized containers by specifying the exact height, width, length, and diameter of the packages while stating that only a difference of up to two millimeters in measurements would be allowed. Infringement would result in fines, closedowns, incarceration, confiscation of products, and prohibition of commercialization. With these changes, the state strengthened the control over industry and further consolidated its role as a mediator between producers and consumers.[94]

The emergence of the worker-consumer in Argentina inaugurated a new chapter in the collective search to become a modern nation. The positive effects of import substitution industrialization during the 1930s and early 1940s produced two alternative views and contrasting economic policies. Those who rallied behind the Plan Pinedo and favored a delicate balance between agriculture and industry were displaced when a group of nationalist military officers took power in June 1943. Their belief in channeling industrial production to supply the internal market and in an ever-increasing government intervention into a wide array of social, political, and economic spheres unleashed one of the greatest transformations the country had seen since its independence from Spain. The Peronist project, which developed within the military, appealed to sectors beyond the labor unions, mobilizing apparently disparate interests groups, from manufacturers to social reformists, who were eager to contribute to a "New Argentina" founded on strong nationalistic and egalitarian premises. When inflation and droughts forced a "return to the countryside" and a new emphasis on heavy industry during the early 1950s, the Perón government showed that it still could effectively manage the volatile assemblage it had established barely a decade earlier.

Since its very beginning, the Peronist decade was marked by the self-reinforcing effect of rising income on demand, production, and employment. A minimum wage, aguinaldos, sick leave, fixed prices, and frozen rents quickly eliminated the scourge of underconsumption while consolidating a production- and consumption-driven economy. The rise of the purchasing power among the working class came to define the very essence of justicialismo and the "third position" as well as the power of the state to shape the marketplace according to vested interests and particular ideologies. Even in times of crisis, such as during the war on speculation and the campaign for austere consumption, Peronism was intrinsically rooted in the expansion, consolidation, and defense of popular consumer power. Indeed, the enjoyment of full citizenship was inextricably tied to policies that favored social inclusion and expansive economic rights, and was ultimately guaranteed by a vast network of far-reaching institutions and laws.

The right of workers to a comfortable standard of living demanded an interventionist state that regulated wages, prices, and consumer goods. In particular, in a context in which working-class consumers spent around 50 percent of their income on food, the Perón administration embarked on an ambitious plan to control food quality and to counter widespread consumer fraud. The creation of the National Food Department, the inspections carried out by the Ministry of Health, and the enactment of the National Food Code are examples of a little known aspect of Peronism, yet one that set the foundations for a modern consumer market in Argentina. The regulation of labels, food packaging, and advertising educated the worker-consumer and made everyday commercial transactions fairer. Yet none of this would have been possible without the collaboration of the private sector, even if this collaboration was frequently brought about through enforcement. For their part, different firms and production sectors sought out state intervention to advance their own position on the market and to receive generous government loans.

The new economically enfranchised sectors not only changed the face of the consumer, but also created a true mass market. With the inclusion of a well-remunerated working class, the mid-twentieth-century consumer culture acquired its firmest and broadest social base to that date. As a mass of consumers, workers made the market large, fluid, dynamic, and inclusive, a stepping stone in the long and harrowing historical construction of a more egalitarian society. This mass of working-class consumers was the unquestionable protagonist of many crucial transformations that defined the times, thus imprinting its identity on scenarios that exceeded the market. Working-class consumers were the "horde" that sparked both fascination and hatred among the critics of Peronism who resented the emergence of a mass society and mass politics under the auspices of what they viewed as a local version of fascism. They were the multitudes that filled the factories, nourishing the industrialization of the country and consolidating the labor movement. And they were the crowd of recent internal migrants to the city that unleashed an electrifying process of urbanization and cultural modernization. As a market, political constituency, and labor force, workers monopolized the attention of politicians, academics, the media, the state, and manufacturers. As an audience of potential consumers, they fully captured the imagination of advertising agents.

CHAPTER 2

Surveys and Campaigns

Discovering and Reaching the Worker-Consumer

In 1949, the pro-Peronist magazine *Argentina* published an article about an ordinary day in the life of an Argentine worker. The piece, profusely illustrated with photographs detailing every activity from the moment the worker woke up in the morning, showed the man leaving the factory after work to meet his wife and child and the family stopping together for snacks at a fancy café, window-shopping, and buying shoes for his wife on Florida Street. The article emphasized that the famous and elegant Florida Street, once an elitist commercial venue, "is no longer the thoroughfare of bigwigs who have made their fortunes by exploiting workers."[1] This argument reproduced a common notion of the official discourse in which shopping and spending were emblems of historical rectification after the deprivation that workers had suffered at the hands of the greedy and unprincipled national oligarchy. As the piece in *Argentina* suggests, the government liberally employed working-class consumption to high-light the radical transformation brought about by Peronism. The worker-consumer was a central character in ubiquitous stories about working-class prosperity and even overindulgence, the triumph of the third position over capitalism and communism, and the achievement of a new condition of collective happiness.[2]

Beyond the propagandistic efforts of the government, the figure of the working-class consumer, which came to occupy a remarkable place in the mid-twentieth-century social imaginary, was a palpable social reality. In 1948, the participation of workers in the national income had reached an impressive 53 percent for the first time in the history of the country. That same year, domestic consumption was 50 percent higher than it had been just three years earlier. This increment was evident in the prolifer-ation of retailers across the country. Between 1946 and 1954, the quan-tity of retailers almost doubled in order to meet the rising demand.[3] The transformation was so noteworthy that it caught the attention of American observers who looked to Argentina as a growing market. Reflecting on the 1950s economic conditions, a marketing professor at the University of Miami and a specialist in Latin America enthusiastically affirmed that

cash is getting into the pockets of peasants and laborers who never before had a *peso* in their *pantalones*. Until now they have gone through life unaware of Tide, or Colgate, or Frigidaire. They listened to no radio, read no newspaper, saw no television. For the seller of goods they did not exist. They were the "inactives." Today they are passing over to the "active" side at the rate of millions per year. Workers who never purchased a cake of soap six years ago bought radio sets this year.[4]

In the new scenario, previous interpretations about who consumers were, what they wanted, and how they spent their money did not explain the latest trends in consumption. For admen, finding the answers to those ques-tions was crucial to successfully design advertising strategies that would appeal to a new audience that had played a minimal or marginal market role in the recent past. How could advertising agencies help clients sell their products if they were not familiar with the buyers? This was more than a conceptual question; it was a strategic issue, one intrinsically linked to the transformation of advertising in Argentina. In fact, in order to take advan-tage of the expanding consumer demand, admen redefined the profession, its goals, and its scope. By 1947, more than half of the twenty-four most renowned national advertising companies in the country—and members of the national society of advertising agencies—had been in business for only a decade or less. Echoing this rapid growth, by 1948, the volume of print advertisements in the country had reached a record high. One example is *Clarín*, a popular daily founded in 1945, which grew by leaps and bounds. In its third year of circulation, the paper's advertisements had grown by 140 percent. This substantial increase in the volume of advertisements was closely related to the steady expansion of advertising agencies. In 1948, these agencies employed around 1,200 people—mostly men—while hundreds more worked for the advertising departments of large companies and stores. Omnipresent in daily life, mid-twentieth-century advertising became a prominent social and economic activity regularly covered in the news and highly praised by businessmen, journalists, and state officials. In 1955, the newspaper *La Razón* asserted that "the spiritual development, material capacity and the level of progress of our country can be seen in the quality and importance of its commercial advertising." Advertisement was a sign of mercantile development and a major contributor to industrial growth, and as such, it was a motor of national advancement.[5]

On December 2, 1948, at the annual gala where the government honored admen as part of the celebration of national advertising, Minister of Industry and Commerce José Constantino Barro reflected on the new role of advertisement as a mass medium for the democratic distribution of information to all sectors of society. Minister Barro argued that advertising agents made a significant contribution to the Peronist mission of creating an egalitarian society when he affirmed:

> You are agents of the project of social justice to which we aspire, working to help spread the riches and the goods that modern civilization has offered mankind. You spark the hope of the working people and acknowledge their dignity. [. . .] Managers of an impersonal and anonymous clientele, you are less interested in the full pockets of a few than in the more democratic pockets of the majority.[6]

This celebratory rhetoric of social democratization offers but a glimpse into the process that turned admen into agents of market inclusiveness. The aim of this chapter is to reconstruct this process by arguing that working-class consumers, who were the social outcome of the structural conditions and policy making analyzed in chapter 1, were also a social and cultural category created by advertising experts. Instrumental in the reconceptualization of market culture, this category both defined the new consumers and prescribed ideal consumer behavior. This chapter explores how in crafting this new social type, admen made low-income consumers into objects of study, targets of education, and new icons of commercial culture while creating a new geographical, gendered, and class characterization of the national market. The flourishing economic conditions of the postwar years prompted advertising experts to look beyond the ideal upper- and middle-class consumer of expensive goods from Buenos Aires, the city they had largely focused on in the past. In a more socially inclusive market, admen discovered the consumer potential of working-class sectors from prosperous regions that had been traditionally overlooked in earlier decades and positioned women from these sectors at the center of their strategy to understand, instruct, and reach these new consumers.

The New Worker-Consumer

Historically, consumer research in Argentina—though limited—focused on the affluent sectors, following a worldwide trend in market surveys. Studies of upper-income consumers started with the local branches of foreign advertising companies like the pioneering American J. Walter Thompson, which opened its Buenos Aires office in 1929 after obtaining General Motors' advertising account in Argentina. Like their colleagues in São Paulo, Cape Town, and Bombay, Buenos Aires admen concentrated on the consumer patterns of the A group, a term they used to refer to the highest category of consumers based on income level. The A group comprised industrialists, owners of major commercial businesses, and large landowners. These were the upper classes that could pay for technology-intense goods like automobiles and cameras, most of which were manufactured in the United States and were out of reach for the majority of the population. In the late 1930s, for example, a Ford or a Chevrolet cost twice the annual salary of a white-collar worker. In addition to the wealthy, the second most important consumer segment was the middle class. This was the B group, made up of less prosperous merchants and farmers, professionals, and upper-level civil servants who could afford radios, small appliances, and cosmetics.[7]

Market research on consumption patterns among affluent consumers provided agencies with cachet in the marketplace, giving the profession a scientific air. However, research was less instrumental in the design of advertising campaigns than general, commonsensible assumptions about those consumers, whom admen considered a uniform and unvarying group. Advertising agents viewed potential upper-class shoppers as modern and sophisticated, that is, brand-conscious, obsessed with imitating foreign and especially European fashions and life-style, and eager to display imports and expensive novelties as markers of class status. Given the consensus on these assumptions, studies were less focused on consumers than on consumer goods, especially consumer durables.

One of the first advocates of "scientific advertising," J. Walter Thompson conducted simple market investigations based on demographic and economic statistics and questionnaires. This research predominantly focused on the sale and consumption of specific brands or types of products, mostly General Motors automobiles. In these surveys, foreign advertising agents primarily sought to strike a balance between a universalistic view of consumer desires—in which people were considered fundamentally alike the world over and could be reached exactly in the same way—and the need to identify the local characteristics of affluent Argentine consumers. In spite of the information they gathered on these consumers, advertising agents favored a universalistic approach to promote foreign technology. This trend was evident in the use of "pattern" ads that, generated by the New York–based international department, underwent only slight modifications for publication in other countries. Although they were very popular among admen, marketing experts frequently singled out pattern ads as "horrible examples" of advertisements that revealed that their creators had little knowledge of the country, its history, and its customs. In these ads, for example, copywriters frequently misused Spanish and Argentine idioms, among other shortcomings.[8]

As admen focused on selling prestige goods to a consumer market that was mainly urban, numerically small—the income groups A and B constituted around 24 percent of the population—and socially homogenous, the low-income sectors were of no interest to the advertising profession. In fact, the working class was hardly perceived as consumers. In 1936, an editorial in the Communist newspaper *Orientación* lamented the living conditions of a working-class family by humorously arguing that family members took a shower every four years because of the price of charcoal necessary to heat the water, ate bananas with the peel to satiate their hunger, and were considering nudism due to the high cost of clothing. The piece ended on a more serious note, asserting that the working-class standard of living was so low that it was not only ridiculous, but also tragic.[9] The situation was particularly evident for foreigners who contrasted the growing spending power of workers in their home countries with the economic hardship experienced by the local population. Ruth and Leonard Greenup, two American journalists living in Buenos Aires, contended that in Argentina, "a humble-born youth could seldom hope to earn enough in his lifetime to own an automobile, a house or the gadgets that people in the United States look on as ordinary tools of comforts; this was true, no matter how smart he was, how hard he worked, or how assiduously he cultivated his economic betters."[10]

In this context, as chapter 1 shows, only the state, social reformists—mostly physicians and economists—and socialists and communists researched popular living conditions and elaborated more or less comprehensive studies of working-class spending habits in the early twentieth century. Social reformers, who were interested in categorizing the population and designing public policies, focused their research on "underconsumption," and particularly highlighted the physical and moral consequences of meager purchasing power. Leftist and labor union leaders, for their part, documented working-class living conditions to denounce the capitalist exploitation that condemned workers to poverty while business owners grew richer.[11]

The lack of purchasing power only partially explains why admen concentrated on the affluent sectors and disregarded working-class consumers. In the period when foreigners dominated advertising in Argentina, cultural, class, and racial prejudice strongly permeated ad-makers' views of the low-income sectors, who were considered primitive and backward. Beyond their limited understanding of local popular traditions and ways of life, some admen believed that the Argentine working sectors were intrinsically at odds with the advancement of consumerism in the country. Considering Argentina "probably the most unionized country in the world" in 1929, Henry Flower, the founder of J. Walter Thompson's Buenos Aires office, saw workers as a force opposite to the well-off shoppers targeted by his advertising campaigns. Top executives like Flower accused workers of obstructing the market with strikes that paralyzed production and left wealthy consumers discontent and empty-handed, as in the case of the six-month walkout of General Motors workers who stopped the assembly line and radicalized their protest by throwing acid on General Motors cars.[12]

Prejudice and indifference toward low-income sectors began to fade in the early 1940s when many advertising experts acknowledged that better living conditions for the working classes were crucial for industrial growth and commercial development, and thus for more successful, profitable, and productive advertising. In following with this view, Manuel Mórtola, the assistant manager at J. Walter Thompson Argentina, argued that beyond slow demographic growth, the second factor that represented an obstacle to progress in advertising was the low living conditions of the working population. Mórtola affirmed that "it is impossible to dream of a country with commercial strength if our workers and employees [. . .] are earning just $105 per month."[13] Admen like Mórtola shared the view of some businessmen, sectors of the military, and policy-makers who wanted to strengthen national industrialization, which had soared during the Second World War, by expanding the internal market.

When in the mid-1940s this project of development triumphed over the strategy that favored the external market, the participation of workers in the national income reached a record high in the country and low-income sectors went from irrelevant to fundamental for admen and their clients. Government statistics showed that working-class families were better fed and had plenty of disposable income to spend on clothing, home appliances, and entertainment. Therefore, products that had previously been bought by a relatively small number of consumers—from food and clothing to household appliances—now had a potentially larger market. In the early 1950s, for example, a bus driver or a metallurgical worker was able to buy an electric refrigerator by making monthly installments that required between 10 to 17 percent of their wages. Therefore, while in 1946, one out of twenty-eight families had a refrigerator in Argentina, by 1955, the ratio had risen to one out of six.[14]

In 1949, the advertising journal *Ímpetu* acknowledged the impressive expansion of the consumer market in an editorial that stated:

> The buying power of Argentina's consumer masses has increased exponentially in certain segments. [. . .] The consumer population categories which are referred to as A, B, C and D have undergone a fundamental change. People in the two lowest categories are now potential consumers of many products that were previously out of their reach. These are, indeed, the *new consumers* in spite of the fact that the country's population has remained steady.[15]

The consumers in the C group included skilled factory workers, train and tram conductors, clerks, small farmers, and federal employees while the D group consisted of unskilled laborers, household servants, and farm workers, among other occupations. Only a decade earlier, the families of any of these workers had struggled to satisfy their basic needs. Now, in contrast, advertising specialists urged admen to do in-depth analyses of this new prosperous market, warning them that "whoever does not embrace the sign of the times will risk getting left behind."[16] And indeed, most admen did embrace the sign of the times, and their renewed interest in the standard of living of low-income sectors produced new studies on family, housing, indexes of comfort—frequently defined by the number and type of household appliances—types of expenditures, exposure to the media, and recreational activities. Similarly, variations in real wages and the cost of living were central aspects covered in every issue of advertising journals, in a striking contrast with the recent past.[17]

In 1947, the International Advertising Association (IAA) published a study on the Buenos Aires market sponsored by the American Export Advertising Association. Research centered on a sample of 2,030 families carefully distributed among all the city districts. The focus on the family as a unit of consumption coincided with a new national and international trend in statistics that became most evident in the Fourth National Census of 1947. Both in the census and in the IAA survey, the household overtook the individual as the crucial subject of investigation. The IAA study—the first of its kind ever conducted in a South American city, according to its authors—was not intended to reveal the purchase or use of specific brands by consumers but to offer an analysis of family composition, spendable income, dwelling, possessions, spending habits, and contact with advertising. For a profession that had been exclusively interested in the preferences of the upper and middle classes, the most original aspect of this research was the fact that over half of the families were comprised of skilled and semiskilled workers while around 13 percent were unskilled workers. Household heads held a great variety of occupations, from janitors, electricians, and assembly men to stenographers, telephone operators, and sale clerks. These working-class families represented the lowest two categories on a list of five different income groups. Researchers maintained that more than 40 percent of these families belonged to low-income sectors and 27 percent to very low-income groups. However, the study concluded, these groups were spending more—both in terms of quantity and quality—on essential expenditures like food and clothing than they had in the recent past. Most important, they had a marginal income reserved for discretionary spending that could be devoted to entertainment, nonessential items, and consumer durable goods aimed at higher levels of comfort.[18]

The need to replace speculation with specific and systematic knowledge of the new potential consumers brought business closer to academic experts in an alliance that would have been unlikely only a few years earlier. In 1954, the Asociación de Dirigentes de Ventas (Sales Managers Association), a trade organization for merchants, sponsored a series of lectures for members by pioneering sociologist Gino Germani. Entitled "The Consumer," the talks aptly combined notions of social psychology and theories of consumption with comprehensive national statistics. Germani warned businessmen and tradesmen not to misinterpret how workers would spend their money in a context of higher income and to recognize their specific role as consumers. In Germani's view, middle-class spending patterns could only be imitated selectively. Workers had habits, tastes, and values that could change independently of parameters set by middle-class living standards––or not change at all. For example, Germani argued that both the middle classes and workers tended to spend their surplus income on recreation and entertainment. However, workers invested more in household technology and food, buying in greater quantities and with an eye for novel products and better quality, while the middle sectors saved for a house or spent extra income on home improvements and, predominantly, furniture. According to Germani, both classes also reacted differently in times of hardship. Workers, the sociologist claimed, cut back on additional spending on clothing during economic crises. In contrast, the middle classes were too concerned with their image and prestige to forgo this expense even in difficult times.[19]

Germani's message to entrepreneurs was categorical: selling to an expanding market required knowledge of the new consumer. For admen, this meant a different approach than that adopted in the past. Reflecting on his years in Buenos Aires as the director of J. Walter Thompson Argentina in the early 1930s, Russell Pierce remembered how he used to leave his office to walk down Florida Street and mingle with the consumers he and his colleagues envisioned when planning their campaigns. These consumers "were the upper- and middle-class Argentines who we hoped read our advertisements and bought our client's products."[20] Experts like Germani rightly believed that admen who had focused on upper-class consumers of high-priced goods had traditionally learned about potential consumers through first-hand contact with friends and acquaintances. Because most admen belonged to the social sectors their campaigns targeted, their entry into the spaces of socialization, commerce, and recreation patronized by prospective buyers supplied them with both formal knowledge and casual insights for their ads. To supplement these observations, admen had also relied on upper- and middle-class members of the agencies' staff as sources for useful information.

The exclusive social makeup of the advertising profession was particularly evident in the early twentieth century when American admen dominated the trade. Adventurous entrepreneurs in foreign lands, these men were incontestable members of both foreign and local elites. Henry Flower, for instance, the founder of J. Walter Thompson Argentina, was the son of a prosperous banker. Flower had attended Harvard and run a family business before coming to Buenos Aires. Pierce, for his part, had served as assistant to the president of the University of Chicago and worked under Nelson Rockefeller at the Office of Inter-American Affairs after leaving J. Walter Thompson in the mid-1940s. At this time, when local admen began to outnumber foreigners, the figure of the self-made man became more prevalent. Argentine admen were generally university graduates with impressive résumés who boasted the highest positions in first-rate companies and the print media. Although local admen came from comparatively less wealthy backgrounds than their foreign counterparts, the profession continued to be synonymous with privilege. In the mid-1940s, the salary of an account executive in an advertising agency or the advertising manager of a large department store was comparable to that of the manager of a large factory or a leading hotel. The salaries of copywriters and advertising artists, on their part, equaled those of assistant bank managers or chemists working for a cosmetics company.[21]

The growing social diversity of markets challenged these ad-makers to move past the recognizable social milieus. Market researchers recommended that advertising agents go beyond surveys and questionnaires and relate to low-income consumers in a more informal and open manner. According to this perspective, the adman had to become a sort of flaneur who left his office to stroll along city streets and study the crowd. Observing and socializing with workers in stores, public spaces, commercial venues, and public transportation was crucial to gaining firsthand knowledge of prospective buyers and to developing the empathy required to effectively establish a long-lasting commercial relationship. By visiting cafés in working-class neighborhoods and observing how customers behaved, for instance, admen became familiar with the popular custom of ordering drinks through gestures and used these gestures to design a successful marketing campaign for an alcoholic beverage. In a show of support for these practices and echoing sociologist Gino Germani's recommendation, an editorial in *Ímpetu* asserted that, in order to sell, it was essential "to know the people, *to feel and think* the way they do in order to stay one step ahead of their needs, desires and tastes and then offer products and services that satisfy them."[22] Admen further agreed that they needed to be familiar with the types of inexpensive merchandise purchased by low-income consumers in order to successfully market such merchandise. This was a tricky task, because as members of the middle and upper classes, advertising agents were not the usual consumers of some of the products marketed for working-class shoppers. To face this challenge, every male member of the J. Walter Thompson staff in Buenos Aires wore low-priced Mérito shoes for a month before designing the advertising campaign.[23]

More methodically, all major advertising agencies conducted some sort of research before designing campaigns in the mid-1940s. Specialists agreed that "a market study that is done correctly at the right time is a precautionary measure and a guarantee of success."[24] Market surveys became a dominant and high-regarded pursuit that professionals in the field considered indispensable for understanding consumers and successfully convincing them to make a purchase. Furthermore, while market research had been reserved for prestige goods in the past, a larger and stronger consumer market for nondurable goods led investigators to focus on inexpensive products and their buyers. Admen chatted with clients in bars and restaurants to learn what they liked to mix with their vermouth; they conducted surveys to determine the role of advertising in the purchase of inexpensive toothpaste and interviewed working-class housewives to learn what they were looking for in laundry detergent. Findings were commonly the key to success. Research allowed admen working for a canned fish company to discover that consumers had accidentally purchased the competitor's product because they had mixed up the brands. In fact, the names were highly similar and the logo of both cans showed a woman. This information prompted admen to create a new slogan and update the logo to unequivocally distinguish their client's brand from its most important competitor on the market. To contribute to this type of research, marketing experts further urged manufacturers and large retailers to collect and systematize information about consumers, products, and sales to assist admen when creating campaigns.[25]

While market investigation had grown broader and more substantial by the mid-twentieth century and the study of consumption had become a disciplinary field led by specialists, research methods from the previous two decades had suffered only minor modifications. Personal interviews with consumers, retailers, and store managers; mail-in questionnaires; the preparation and collection of statistics; and participant observation were still the predominant research tools. These methods, which may seem rudimentary by today's standards, were the norm for the period and reinforced the reputation of advertising as a technically sophisticated field. Furthermore, the job of survey-takers became less complicated in the mid-twentieth century. Unlike the previous decades, when many upper-class consumers had refused to take surveys and considered questionnaires and interviews an intrusion, the rising visibility of advertising and frequent coverage in the media facilitated the task of admen, who now encountered agreeable and cooperative consumers who were more willing to share their insights and habits. The professionals who interviewed these more courteous consumers were also more qualified than they had been in the past. In 1942, the Asociación de Agentes de Publicidad (Association of Advertising Agents), the oldest advertising organization in the country, opened the first advertising school to educate new agents in the methodological tools required in this increasingly specialized discipline. Graduates found employment in advertising agencies, but also in big industrial and commercial companies that had opened or expanded their own departments for market surveys.[26]

Furthermore, both advertisers and admen could benefit from the services of consulting firms specializing in market research for the first time. "Watch where you step" was the phrase with which one of these firms warned clients to advertise carefully, with an illustration of a confident businessman about to walk into a pothole. The extraordinary increase in the number of publications devoted to advertising, commerce, and consumption that appeared between the mid-1940s and the mid-1950s is further evidence of the growing interest in the new market conditions. While these publications targeted a specialized audience of advertisers, economists, and admen, many others—from popular magazines to trade journals—increasingly addressed the topic of consumer research, emphasizing its importance and popularizing its precepts among a broader audience.[27] Notably, while articles on the consumer market in Buenos Aires captivated readers with its tales of sold-out movie theaters and crowded shops, statistics showed that the increasing numbers of new consumers who entered into department stores, restaurants, and entertainment venues in Buenos Aires were representative of a social transformation that went beyond the capital city. When the opportunity arose, admen began to envision a larger pool of consumers and the subsequent need for companies to extend their ads to entire regions that had been traditionally overlooked in their campaigns.

Buenos Aires and Beyond

The economic preponderance of Buenos Aires over the rest of the nation had a long history. Traditionally, Buenos Aires had had the highest concentration of manufacturers as well as the largest population in the republic. In addition, it was the center of the federal government and home to the country's leading port. The city had been the epicenter of the transportation and communication systems, and its residents traditionally enjoyed the highest wages, the broadest selection of jobs, and the greatest purchasing power. Consequently, Buenos Aires had the largest and strongest pool of consumers, especially for domestic supplies.[28]

In the late 1930s, economist Alejandro Bunge revealed this distinctive aspect of the capital city when he described Argentina as a "fan-shaped country." Bunge argued that Argentina consisted of three different regions defined by three concentric arches that converged in Buenos Aires. Bunge used the arches to show the severe imbalances between the first region and the remaining two. The first arch, with a radius of 360 miles, included the provinces of Buenos Aires, most of Santa Fe, half of Córdoba, part of northern La Pampa, Entre Ríos, and southern Corrientes. This arch encompassed 20 percent of the national territory, almost 70 percent of the national population, and about 80 percent of the invested industrial capital. Bunge concluded that the further away an inhabitant was from the epicenter of Buenos Aires and the further into the two largest but poorest arches he lived, the lower his economic power and standard of living. Categorically stated, Bunge's argument was not new. Since the early twentieth century, researchers and social thinkers had warned authorities about the appalling living conditions in the northern and southern regions, the high levels of unemployment and malnutrition, and the widespread underconsumption that characterized those areas. In the 1930s, advertising experts argued that this accurate diagnosis had led manufacturers, merchants, and admen to overlook deprived and distant regions with disappointing commercial prospects.[29]

In the mid-twentieth century, the economic disparity between Buenos Aires and the rest of the country continued. The concentration of the new working-class consumers in both the city and the province of Buenos Aires was persuasive evidence of such disparity. In 1946, 39 percent of all industrial workers lived in the city of Buenos Aires, which housed 30 percent of all industrial factories in Argentina. The gap between the regions was a challenging issue for the Peronist government, which was publicly committed to the development of the whole country, especially the most disadvantaged provinces. Regardless of state efforts to reduce inequality, in the mid-1950s, 30 percent of the total national population continued to reside in the capital city and Greater Buenos Aires while enjoying 40 percent of the total income. The northeast, in contrast, had only 7 percent of the national income and 14 percent of the national population. For these reasons, in the 1940s and 1950s, the interest of advertisers in Bunge's second and third arches remained slight. Businessmen were well aware that advertisements could not sell what people could not afford.[30]

In contrast, in those same years, advertising agents began to promote the unprecedented marketing potential of the first arch, the vast and economically thriving central region beyond Buenos Aires. Traditionally, advertising agencies had refrained from launching campaigns directly in these provinces. Experts explained that advertising agents from Buenos Aires were as culturally imperceptive and disengaged when addressing consumers in the provinces as their foreign colleagues had been toward Argentine consumers in the early twentieth century. Without any knowledge or interest in the regional press, admen published their ads in national rather than local publications. This miscalculation was the result of the unfounded and excessive confidence that both advertisers and advertising agents had in the reach and influence of magazines and newspapers edited in Buenos Aires.[31]

A decade later, when the Fourth National Census disclosed the market potential of Argentina's interior, advertising agents began to change their views. The census revealed that the interior had 13 million inhabitants who represented four-fifths of the total population of the country. With close to 4.5 million inhabitants, Santa Fe, Córdoba, and Mendoza alone grew 14 percent between 1947 and 1953. Due to postwar prosperity, advertising experts began focusing on these central provinces, where industrial expansion and better wages for workers replicated the conditions of Buenos Aires on a smaller scale. Santa Fe was home to 12 percent of industrial factories in the country and close to 10 percent of industrial workers while Córdoba had approximately 10 and 5 percent respectively. These two provinces took second and third place respectively behind Buenos Aires in terms of the number of businesses in their territories; Entre Ríos occupied fourth place.[32] In 1949, one adman acknowledged these favorable conditions when he declared that "the inland has its own life. Argentina's interior has likes and dislikes, spends money and has fun. Today, the interior enjoys comfort and progress that reflect the advances of modern life and coincide with those of our beautiful, attractive and powerful metropolis [Buenos Aires]."[33]

Though the commercial significance of the central region was not new, the attention of the most important advertising specialists from Buenos Aires was. Within this territory, admen focused on the capital cities of the provinces and other large and prosperous industrial centers like Rosario in Santa Fe. With close to half a million inhabitants, Rosario was the second largest city after Buenos Aires and boasted a large port for exporting grain and other agricultural products. Also, in contrast to the recent past, admen's awareness of consumer potential extended to small towns and medium-sized cities. Newspaper editors from the interior greatly contributed to this discovery by constantly reminding admen that the local media was the best venue to reach more consumers. The editor of the newspaper *La Acción* from Rosario exemplified this argument by affirming that "the city of Córdoba is not all there is to the province of Córdoba: there are an infinite number of towns and cities that stand on their own thanks to their large populations and industrial activities, such as Río Cuarto, San Francisco and Villa María, among others."[34] Advertising experts even discovered the market possibilities of otherwise overlooked towns and cities in the province of Buenos Aires as well as the thriving communities of Greater Buenos Aires that had traditionally been eclipsed by the capital city.[35]

The great mobility of inhabitants of the interior during this period gave advertising agents additional incentive to persuade clients to reach potential consumers outside big cities. Better economic conditions and reduced trans-portation costs allowed residents of small towns to pay more frequent visits to large cities near their towns for both shopping and entertainment. Ads in local papers gave visitors valuable information on sales, new products, and new shops before their trip and even encouraged consumers to head to the city for store clearances and deals publicized in local newspapers. More systematically, the massive migration from the interior to the cities in the pampeana region—and most especially to Buenos Aires—meant that vast numbers of prospective consumers were moving each year. Between 1936 and 1947, around seventy thousand people arrived to Buenos Aires annually, mostly from central provinces like Entre Ríos, Santa Fe, and Córdoba and, to a lesser extent, from Santiago del Estero, Corrientes, and La Pampa.[36]

For admen from Buenos Aires who had the chance of securing campaigns for the most important manufacturers of the country, the provinces opened up splendid possibilities. In the 1940s, advertising agencies from the interior were generally no competition since they mostly worked for local industries. Taking advantage of this opportunity, important agencies operating in Buenos Aires opened branches in large cities, particularly Rosario. In other cases, they formed alliances with local admen who did local campaigns for national clients or served as liaisons between provincial clients and the agency in Buenos Aires. Advertising agencies planning a campaign in the interior could also offer their services to national clients cost-effectively since the local press in the provinces had more affordable rates than the Buenos Aires media. Furthermore, campaigns for some cities in the interior were generally less demanding in creative terms because artistic standards in local advertising were usually low and local campaigns were likely to be rudimentary.[37]

For their part, businesses from Buenos Aires preferred advertising companies from the capital city to manage their national campaigns. Yet, business changed its view of the role of advertising in the interior. In previous decades, even important manufacturers had believed that sales agents and personal contacts in the provinces were their main allies in promoting their products and increasing retail sales. Consequently, they made only minimal investments in advertisement to reach the provinces. In the mid-twentieth century, industrial development and a rising demand for industrial goods made many manufacturers fully aware of the importance of advertising outside Buenos Aires. The growing number of companies in several industrial sectors exacerbated market competition, and thus advertising campaigns became an excellent tool to win consumers away from rival firms. In addition, new market statistics played a fundamental role in changing the views of manufacturers. Comparative studies indicated that for some goods, the markets of the interior were even stronger than that of Buenos Aires. In 1953, a survey revealed that more sewing machines were purchased in Olavarría (Buenos Aires Province), Mendoza, and Cañada de Gómez (Santa Fe) than in the city of Buenos Aires—and that there were more potential buyers in these cities as well. Increasingly, this type of evidence persuaded manufacturers that advertising was the best way to reach consumers from the interior who had money to spend but lacked the information or the motivation to buy.[38]

Besides the auspicious industrial development of the 1940s, the professionalization of ad-makers, and the new importance of advertising for business, improvements in shipping also strengthened the role of advertising in the interior. In 1935, a report by the U.S. Bureau of Foreign and Domestic Commerce noted that advertising was inefficient due to the lack of coordination between advertising campaigns and the systematic supplies of products. Ads were pointless when distribution was insufficient and stores lacked stock, adequate merchandise, and sales information. Traditionally, supplying goods to the provinces had been a challenging task due to serious shortcomings in infrastructure, particularly the fact that there were only a few stretches of paved highways in Argentina outside of the city of Buenos Aires. Although big companies had started to modernize delivery fleets in the 1930s to replace freight trains, maintenance and operating costs—gas, drivers, and license plates—were very expensive and inadequate roads made ground transportation an alternative that was far from ideal. The Peronist government worked to overcome many of the major structural obstacles while encouraging manufacturers to search and experiment with new consumer markets beyond the big cities. Different state policies were designed to relocate industrial plants outside of Buenos Aires and to improve and expand commercial redistribution, mainly through roadwork and subsidized transportation. As a result, commercial distribution showed a striking improvement over the past.[39]

Good roads and fleets were important to reach the markets of the interior, but a deep understanding of these markets was no less significant. In 1950, an expert on advertising argued that "it's not enough to know *where* to sell: we require sound knowledge of the desires, needs and lifestyles of those to *whom* we want to sell."[40] While in 1937 an advertising scholar had criticized *Ímpetu* for its lack of attention to the provinces, a decade later, the trade journal was devoting extensive articles, statistics, and editorials to advertising in different regions of the country.[41] Furthermore, specialists affirmed that it was impossible to get to know the market of the interior by looking at a map in a Buenos Aires office. Thus, authorities in the field urged admen to leave Buenos Aires; mingle and talk with working sectors from the provinces; research the traditions, tastes, and needs of this population; and recognize their idiosyncrasies. In fact, according to the experts, not only did industrialists and ad-makers need to consider that the average consumer did not live in a big city; they also had to avoid homogenizing interpretations of the interior that did not account for provincial, regional, and communal variations.[42]

Advertising experts generally agreed that the conquest of markets of the interior depended less on the content of the campaigns than on the advertising means. The top executives in advertising questioned the widely held belief that Buenos Aires newspapers of national circulation were the best medium to reach big cities in the provinces and advised their colleagues to use local newspapers for their campaigns. With print runs that ranged from fifty thousand to eighty thousand copies and covered municipal, regional, national, and international news, local newspapers were destined to become the new trustworthy ally of advertisers. Most importantly, advertising specialists rightly believed that "the further the distance between local dailies and Buenos Aires, the stronger their influence and sales power."[43] Local newspapers actively reinforced this argument. While some like *Los Andes* from Mendoza emphasized its reach—a population of over six hundred thousand inhabitants—others like *Los Principios* from Córdoba reminded possible advertisers of the growing purchasing power of its readers.[44]

In contrast to the recent past, admen encountered manufacturing companies that were much more receptive to promoting their products in these provincial newspapers. Traditionally, business had heavily relied on the two principal Buenos Aires daily newspapers, *La Prensa* and *La Nación*, to reach consumers in the interior. Since the middle and upper classes were the bulk of the consumer market both in the capital and beyond, advertising in these two newspapers was an effective strategy because the overwhelming majority of their readership belonged to those social sectors.[45]

Although manufactures had been running more advertisements in papers in the interior since the 1940s, some made the common mistake of limiting advertisement to only one newspaper in cities that had several dailies. In Buenos Aires, however, the same manufacturers agreed to advertise in six to eight newspapers, in six to eight magazines, on two to three radios, and on innumerable billboards throughout the city. Similarly, in Buenos Aires, manufacturers and stores advertised at length in neighborhood and labor union papers and bulletins to reach potential working-class consumers more effectively. Advertising experts thought that misinformed businessmen underestimated the size of interior markets and overstated the scope of the newspaper they chose for their ads. Experts further argued that advertising in a great variety of dailies in the provinces was even more important than in Buenos Aires because residents in the interior tended to be staunchly loyal to their newspaper of choice. In Rosario, a city of countless local publications and several big and influential newspapers, advertising in only one newspaper was a common and costly error since readers of *Crónica, La Acción,* and *La Tribuna* would necessarily miss the ads published in *La Capital*.[46]

Moreover, numerous specialists insisted on going well beyond large and medium-sized cities and their newspapers to advertise in minor publications from small towns, a clear example of how the internal market was being redefined by advertising agents. Admen affirmed that although newspapers from large and medium-sized cities were regionally influential, their circulation was limited to a radius of forty to fifty miles. In order to access municipalities that lay beyond these limits, advertisers needed to employ local publications which were especially important in small industrial towns. Advertising specialists maintained that regardless of the shorter length, the lack of sophistication in their layout, and the mediocre printing quality, these publications had consistent printings and a devoted readership among the locals, thus making them extremely useful when it came to advertising consumer goods. The local media, for its part, encouraged advertisers to make more extensive use of its pages. The director of the newspaper *La Libertad* in Avellaneda, one of the largest and most prosperous industrial towns of Greater Buenos Aires, urged manufacturers to reconsider their advertising approach. He argued that ads for goods that were very popular among Avellaneda industrial workers, like low-priced shoes and soccer gear, did not always reach their potential consumers when published in Buenos Aires newspapers because workers favored local papers. He also affirmed that in national newspapers, these ads competed for readers' attention on pages cluttered with ads for many products. In local papers, however, these ads could be centrally positioned and thus rapidly get the attention of Avellaneda's workers-consumers. Major department stores that managed their own advertising departments were well aware of this advantage. In the 1950s, these companies typically published their ads in both national and local newspapers and in smaller publications where they shared the same pages with a few ads for mom-and-pop stores.[47]

Persistent and continuous campaigns were also a key factor for success. Advertising agents complained that manufacturers who invested large amounts of money in ongoing campaigns in Buenos Aires newspapers were reluctant to do the same in the provinces. These advertisers incorrectly believed that a few ads would suffice to get the attention of consumers. When they saw no increments in their sales, businessmen claimed that advertising in the interior was like "throwing a pebble into the river." For advertising companies, however, uninterrupted advertising was crucial to attract consumers from the provinces. Admen stressed that continuity was essential to familiarize shoppers with products, particularly in the case of the working-class consumers who were new to the market.[48]

By and large, admen believed that most advertisers had not yet fully recognized the market potential of many cities and whole regions. Manufacturers still prioritized the national press, favored a few dailies in interior cities, and chose national campaigns with no room for local variation. However, the expansion of advertising beyond Buenos Aires was significant in comparison with the previous decades. By the early 1950s, print advertisements in the provinces had increased not only in the newspapers and magazines of the capitals but also in small and medium-sized cities.[49] Beyond discussions on consumer research, advertising channels, and the duration of the campaigns, the quest to effectively reach low-income consumers all over the country was intrinsically connected with a gendered view of the market in which working-class women were singled out as the entry point into the new consumer constituency. In their role as primary consumers, housewives managed the household budget and did the shopping for the whole family. When higher wages created new consumer alternatives for low-income families, admen promoted advertising as an educative tool that could turn working-class women into knowledgeable and conscientious consumers.

Working-Class Women Consumers

In the 1930s, upper and middle-class women consumers had only recently been allowed to make independent decisions regarding the purchase of goods for personal and household purposes. Until then, Argentine men had personally supervised the acquisition of articles for the use of both women and their families.[50] In 1935, however, the new economic empowerment of women resulting from cultural and social modernization and their new visibility as consumers was evident in an editorial published in *Ímpetu* that argued that women spent eighty-five cents of every peso expended in retail commerce. The writer further affirmed that "she buys food, dresses up to the nines; she—God forgive her—buys our ties and chooses the fabric for our suit; we buy a house, a car, and furniture for her and go heavily into debt for her."[51] The witty remark reveals not only the upper-class status of the couple in the example—in a context in which admen focused on the A and B groups of high-income consumers—but also the gender division of consumption in which the husband made the most expensive and socially significant purchases. Still, 1930s women from the high-income sectors had a say in these types of purchases. Ninety-two percent of car dealers reported that women influenced purchasing decisions and were present more than half the time when fathers or husbands bought an automobile.[52]

By the 1950s, the decisive role of women as consumers was unquestionable. Marketing experts believed that women did between 80 and 85 percent of all shopping, including purchases of food, clothing, shoes, toiletries, beauty and cleaning products, and household items, among numerous other consumer goods. Most significantly, specialists affirmed that the lower the total household income, the more important the role of women as consumers for the whole family. Because of this—and in tune with their new interest in surveying consumers from the two lowest income classifications, the C and D groups—admen paid particular attention to working-class housewives. While most advertising agents were upper-class men, women from the low-income sectors turned into the main source of information to understand domestic expenditure and consumer habits through a variety of research methods, from the general survey of living standards to studies of specific products. The International Advertising Association offered a representative example of the dominant trend at the time. In its 1946 marketing survey of Buenos Aires focused on working-class households, two-thirds of the interviewees were housewives. The report explained that housewives were "the most qualified persons in the household to properly answer the many questions asked."[53]

If admen and manufacturers recognized the major role that working-class homemakers played in the mid-twentieth century consumer market, they also considered that these women, who had had minimal or limited access to many consumer goods until recently, were largely unprepared for undertaking such a major role. Thus as admen and businessmen promoted their interests, they embarked on an active pedagogical crusade to transform working-class women into knowledgeable consumers. This goal was enthusiastically shared by the government, which in the early 1950s, in the midst of the "war on speculation," appealed to the housewife, "the guardian angel of the domestic economy," to revive the national economy through responsible consumption.

While the government popularized the idea that working-class housewives had a "sixth sense" for planning and saving, it also actively urged them to educate themselves on rational spending. According to this argument, women had a natural capacity to manage household budgets but needed further instruction to make conscientious purchases at fair prices. To this end, government pamphlets and manuals were widely distributed to teach homemakers to keep a meticulous record of all expenses in the hope of transforming women into the family's informal accountants. Furthermore, the official campaign urged housewives to be informed about official prices; encouraged them to shop at inexpensive stores; and bombarded audiences with radio shows, articles, ads, and posters on sewing, knitting, and cooking inexpensive meals. Women were also responsible for standing up to merchants who did not comply with fixed prices, boycotting their shops, and reporting fraud to the police. A writer for the magazine *El Hogar* synthesized this mission in her vehement advice to her readers: "Do not be passive. React. Complain. Reporting done with justice is noble work."[54]

Consumption became a highly ethical activity that entailed defending the family's purchasing power. However, dealing with rising prices and cutting down on superfluous spending were not the only challenges for newcomers to the consumer market. Between 1946 and 1950, a group of advertisers, both retailers and manufacturers, launched the vigorous Campaña Pro-Comercio Leal (Honest Commerce Campaign) in popular general interest publications and women's magazines of national circulation. Initially, the campaign coincided with the inauguration of a government package of price controls limiting the cost of food, clothing, and household goods known as the Sixty-Day Campaign.[55] Later, it continued alongside the state's "war on speculation" in the early 1950s. Unlike the government crusades, the focus of the Honest Commerce Campaign was not prices but brands. The main purpose was to fight against stores and salesmen who refrained from selling certain brands to shoppers and pressured them to buy other brands or "household products" whose quality was usually lower. Brands, market experts agreed, functioned as a guarantee for consumers since they allowed them to discriminate between good and bad products, continue buying those that fulfilled their expectations, and denounce fraud. Trademarks also protected manufacturers by distinguishing their products from those of the competitors and especially from low-quality products.[56]

The postwar flourishing of industrialization and retailing led to numerous new factories that aspired to compete with well-established brands by offering second-rate versions of manufactured items. On a prosperous market, the most popular products were often out of stock while their mediocre substitutes were not always easy to sell. Thus, dishonest retail techniques became a frequent practice at some stores. This was especially the case with food and beauty products. Stratagems included lying about the availability of a product of a certain brand in order to sell a different one, recommending a brand without proper information or giving false information about it, and unfairly bad-mouthing a certain product to convince consumers to buy a substitute.[57] The Honest Commerce Campaign denounced a form of commercial duplicity embodied in the figure of the salesclerk who pretended to help consumers but actually misled them.[58] In contrast, honest salespersons sold consumers the product they wanted without criticizing it and never used treacherous arguments to deceive customers. Indeed, the notion of cheating was constantly reiterated throughout the campaign. Ads had flashy headings such as "On How a Woman Was Cheated" or "Other Women Have Also Been Deceived," allusions to disappointment in love but also to women with little experience purchasing certain goods. One ad, for instance, tells the story of a woman who was able to afford a perfume at a "luxurious" store for the first time. The woman knew which brand she wanted, but the salesperson discredited her choice and convinced her to buy an expensive perfume of inferior quality.[59]

Although one significant goal of the campaign was to unmask corrupt merchants, educating women from the low-income sectors to become skillful consumers, particularly of food products and toiletries, was its most important aim. According to the Honest Commerce Campaign, competent consumers had to be assertive. Campaign ads exhorted female consumers to never surrender to the pressure of salesmen and to always defend their personal tastes and favorite brands. With these messages, the Honest Commerce Campaign pivoted on the idealized image of a confident, headstrong woman who was highly motivated and resolved. Campaign ads scolded consumers who acted "like robots without a show of character" and praised women like the one who declared, "I have lots of personality and that's why when I go shopping, I always go to shops that give me the product I want without trying to talk me out of it, discrediting my choice with biased arguments."[60]

If an ad persuaded a consumer to buy a branded product but at the store the salesclerk tricked the customer into buying a different one, dishonest commercial practices defeated the purpose of advertising. Admen explained this problem by pointing to female personal indecision and lack of resolve and to the fact that, until recently, working-class women had not had real consumer choices when buying numerous types of products due to their low budgets. Advertising and market experts argued that now, faced with product choices, it was difficult for new and inexperienced low-income consumers to remember brands and differentiate among products.[61]

LA PIEL DEL CORDERO...

Desconfíe de aquel vendedor, amable y servicial, que con hábiles argumentos, trata de inducirlo a comprar un producto que no es el de la marca de su preferencia.

Para evitarlo, favorezca siempre al comerciante leal que le sirve los productos que Vd. pide, sin desmerecerlos con argumentos interesados.

CAMPAÑA PRO COMERCIO LEAL

FIGURE 4: Under the title "Sheep's Clothing," the Honest Commerce Campaign warned consumers, "Distrust the friendly, pleasing salesman who uses clever arguments to convince you to buy a product different from the one you want." *Aquí Está*, March 9, 1950, 23.

In 1945, the Asociación de Jefes de Propaganda (Association of Advertising Directors) launched an annual advertising campaign in numerous newspapers and especially magazines of national circulation aimed at educating consumers on brands. With very plain layouts, each ad featured a friendly man or a woman asking the readers: "What lotion do you buy?" "What stockings do you wear?" "What cooking oil do you use?" The question was the same for different types of inexpensive nondurable consumer goods purchased by women. All of these ads drew attention to the brand as a guarantee of excellence and portrayed businesses that advertised as sincerely committed to consumer satisfaction. The underlying message of the campaign was that these companies and their products had a well-known name and occupied a solid place on the market. Because they were visible, identifiable, and openly provided information about their products, they were accountable.[62]

In line with the government crusade to monitor the quality of consumer goods, the Association of Advertising Directors advised consumers to choose a branded product over a generic, "anonymous" one "because you know that when you buy a certain brand, you will get the quality product promised by the ad—the product you enjoy."[63] In some cases, branded products were more expensive, but in a context of rising standards of living, more consumers were able to afford them. With this campaign, advertising directors urged low-income buyers who never had to choose among different toothpastes, cigarettes, or stockings to learn the attributes of goods from advertisements and thus make an informed decision before reaching the shop. The campaign reaffirmed the notion of advertisement as an "awareness institution" that, like schools and the media, shapes our understanding of how society operates even at its simplest and most practical level. One ad of the campaign affirmed that trying the numerous toothpastes displayed at the store was not the way to find the one that tasted best. In contrast, by reading advertisements and identifying desirable brands, the potential consumer would find the one with the qualities she was seeking.[64]

With these kinds of campaigns, advertising agents reaffirmed their role as honest mentors in a historical moment marked by the need for advice and the search for guidance. Due to the internal migrations to the city, the disruption of long-established systems of information like families and neighbors, and the transformation of material culture, most new consumers found advertisement to be a helpful and authoritative source of information. This notion was condensed in the motto of the Association of Advertising Directors: "Advertising guides, educates, and helps." Admen defended the argument that advertising was more than a mere instrument to sell a product, portraying it as an instructive channel, a privileged means to develop consciousness by uniquely combining psychology and art. In 1948, an editorial in *Ímpetu* affirmed that "advertising can fulfill an invaluable task since it works more persuasively than compulsively. Only advertising can present convincing arguments time and again until they are understood, since it effectively brings the right arguments to the forefront."[65]

The notions of information as a condition for being smart shoppers and of advertisement as an educative and informative tool were central to mid-twentieth-century market culture. Throughout the campaign for judicious consumption, the Peronist government urged low-income housewives not only to read the newspapers and magazines and to listen to the radio for price announcements, but also to look for deals and product recommendations in ads.[66] In 1955, *Confort*, a well-known magazine on home, architecture, and decoration, aptly synthesized this notion by arguing that

> when the need arises to acquire a certain article—let's say, a home appliance—the buyer must consult advertisements, product features, prices, and warrantees, all of which represent a set of elementary factors that the public considers and values. This is the first step before hitting the street; ads are the preview of the store window displaying the product, with the important addition that this preview reaches the reader's house and allows her to do a detailed analysis and change her opinion when advisable.[67]

This was the central idea behind the extensive campaign of the Asociación Argentina de Editores de Revistas (Argentine Association of Magazine Editors) in 1955 that portrayed print ads as means of education. Highly praised by advertising agents, the campaign consisted in a series of compelling ads published simultaneously in fifty-four magazines that circulated nationwide. The ads were centered on the ideal figure of a knowledgeable female consumer who was educated about consumer products and knew where to get the best deals. With the motto "Read the ads and buy the best," those behind the campaign envisioned new consumers with little experience in collecting information about consumer goods and assured this audience that the task was simple, productive, and fun.[68]

The editors' campaign condensed key premises about the role of advertising in the new expansive market. One of the strongest messages of the campaign, especially relevant to low-income consumers, was that advertised products were less expensive than unadvertised ones. According to this argument, advertising increased sales, reduced production costs, and consequently, decreased the prices of advertised consumer goods. Furthermore, using the same argument of advertising directors, magazine editors also promoted the idea of advertising as a guarantee by emphasizing that manufacturers who advertised were more reliable than those who did not. Beyond positively impacting prices and making companies accountable for their products, advertisements made shopping easier and more cost-effective for consumers. Having information on prices and products in advance led customers directly to what they wanted. This was very important for working-class housewives who had no domestic help and were in charge of shopping themselves.

Still, the principal message of the magazine editors' campaign was that print advertising played a crucial role in educating consumers, one that was especially relevant in a country where 85 percent of the population over the age of fourteen was literate. Moreover, Argentines were avid readers of newspapers and magazines, their principal sources of daily information.[69] Historically, advertising in the print media had been the most common form of publicity in the country and the most thoroughly developed. In the mid-1950s, the Argentine branch of the renowned American advertising agency McCann Erickson allotted close to half of its total advertisements in print media. Advertisements in newspapers accounted for 25 percent while magazine advertisement represented 17 percent; the rest was distributed among street, radio, screen, sales promotion, and other less common advertising channels.[70] Editors pointed to several factors to explain why print advertisement was the privileged medium of mid-twentieth-century ad-makers. To begin with, print ads in the media were more personalized and reached consumers more directly than radio ads and outdoor publicity. In one of the campaign ads of the Argentine Association of Magazine Editors, the main character asked the reader: "Would you leave a letter unopened? Well then don't skip over magazine ads. These are messages directed at you and believe us, those who have written them will do what they promise in order to win you over as a client."[71] Print ads were also most convenient because reading ads was a comfortable and efficient version of window shopping, one that could be done without even leaving home. The women's magazine *Maribel* affirmed that "reading *Maribel*, Elena is buying a pair of stockings.

es un juego de niños!

En efecto, si a usted le brindan varias ofertas
ventajosas, comprar bien es un juego de niños.
Pero, ¿cómo llegar a enterarse de ellas?
Sencillamente, ¡leyendo las revistas!
Contienen centenares de anuncios en los
que se ofrecen los productos
de mejor calidad a los precios más
convenientes, pues la propaganda,
al promover una venta mayor,
abarata los costos.
Por eso le aconsejamos:

LEA LOS AVISOS -
COMPRARA MEJOR !

ASOCIACION ARGENTINA DE EDITORES DE REVISTAS

FIGURE 5: Magazine editors assured the new low-income consumers that "when there are so many excellent deals, being a smart shopper is child's play. But how can you find out about the deals? That's easy: by reading magazines!" *Mundo Argentino*, March 23, 1955, 38.

Without even realizing it, Elena is subconsciously making a purchase. The advertising power of *Maribel* is based on the fact that its ads surprise readers at a good time, when they are willing to read, watch, and pay attention."[72] Beyond reaching consumers when they were well-disposed to learn about advertised products, print advertisement was more available than street and radio advertising since readers could always go back to periodicals they kept at home. This argument was particularly relevant to monthlies. The women's magazine *Chabela* appealed to potential advertisers by asserting that in its pages ads "lasted thirty days" and were reread countless times.[73] Commonly, readers also borrowed magazines and newspapers from friends, family, and coworkers, thus further increasing the circulation of print ads.

Mid-twentieth-century market research suggested that women were the principal readers of magazines and "tireless readers of advertisements." Thus magazines had a bigger advantage over competing forms of advertising channels because they were favored by those who did most of the shopping. In addition to a significant number of popular interest magazines with wide national circulation, women's magazines with monthly circulations oscillating between fifty-five thousand and three hundred thousand monopolized the field. The editors of these publications used the identity of their readership to appeal to prospective advertisers: "To sell in homes, win over women in their intimate sphere. *Maribel* is the confidant of mothers, girlfriends, daughters and sisters."[74] Advertising experts, for their part, lamented the fact that there were no men's magazines to challenge the predominance of women as the main readers of magazines. Yet, some media specialists believed that a men's magazine would be a failure due to a lack of consensus on "male topics" comparable to "female themes" like fashion, love, and cooking.[75]

The understanding that women were "insatiable magazine readers" and that magazines were the most effective channels to reach female consumers went back to the early decades of the twentieth century when advertising agents had focused on the highest-income sectors. With these consumers of prestige goods in mind, advertising agents chose magazines whose "readers are the cream of the upper-middle and upper classes." In the 1920s, for example, advertising men ran sophisticated advertisements of high-class goods in *La Nación* and *La Prensa* but *El Hogar* and *Atlántida*, expensive magazines widely read by upper-class women, were the favorite mediums for promoting these types of products. In the mid-1940s, a larger and more socially inclusive market changed this pattern. Alongside the appearance of new and inexpensive dailies and weeklies that openly targeted working-class readers, advertising published across the editorial spectrum was homogenized. Thus the same ad for an electric refrigerator was seen in both *El Hogar* and *Maribel*, a magazine that cost half the price.[76]

At the same time, expensive publications started to run campaigns for economical goods, especially food products, and more publications explicitly and emphatically pointed to workers as their main readership, promising manufacturers an effective medium to reach these consumers. In its ads in advertising trade journals, the popular magazine *Ahora* identified its working-class audience as its main selling point to attract potential advertisers to its pages: "Don't be out-of-date in advertising. Update your campaigns. The buying power of workers is currently undisputed. Make sure your advertisements reach the working class: run ads in the newspaper most read by the Argentine workers."[77] The strategy was the same that upper and middle-class publications had used in previous decades. In 1938, the magazine *Atlántida* invited advertisers to publish ads in the monthly with "a readership that buys expensive goods" and that was "read by 30,000 well-to-do families."[78] By the late 1940s, appeals to working-class readership prevailed among periodicals that sought to increase their advertisement quotas while arguments stressing circulation among upper-class readers vanished.[79]

For advertising professionals and their clients, the new economically empowered working class was unknown territory but held the promise of a larger and eager market. Because of their traditional focus on targeting upper-class consumers and selling expensive goods, admen had disregarded low-income sectors both because meager wages made them marginal in the consumer market and due to ingrained class prejudice. When full employment, better wages, aguinaldos, and fixed rents substantially increased popular purchasing power and transformed former "inactive" consumers into the enthusiastic purchasers of many goods they had rarely or never enjoyed in the past, admen turned their undivided attention to these newcomers to the market. To effectively reach these consumers, admen underwent a process that involved an equal dose of social discovery and cultural integration. The process entailed not only surveys on living conditions and spending patterns, questionnaires, and observation, but also a new interpretation of the collected information—from how to order a drink to how inexpensive shoes fit—in a variety of commercial messages that put mainstream market culture in tune with the values and practices of the working sectors as never before. For educated and high-income advertising agents "to feel and to think" like working-class consumers was far from an easy task. But, in contrast to foreign admen who had dominated the trade in the previous decades, they shared a common national culture and, most importantly, had a new sense of mission, as advertising was considered essential in the achievement of collective well-being and national progress.

In advancing commerce and industry and obtaining higher profits for their clients, admen promoted a vision of the national market that was not only more socially inclusive but also more comprehensive in geographical terms. Admen fought against the skepticism of many advertisers unwilling to promote their goods actively and systematically beyond the biggest urban centers, educating clients about the benefits of reaching minor cities located in the rich pampeana region. Although the market they pictured was far from a replica of the national territory, admen sought to substantially integrate areas that had been historically overlooked by manufacturers and to intensify the contact with potential consumers. As the economy was transforming and advancements in transportation and communications were increasing the scope of both goods and information, many advertising professionals were confident about the advantages of using smaller local publications, expanding national advertising campaigns, and appealing to the cultural characteristics of the population of the interior to reach consumers whose spending power had grown but who remained unaware of the consumer goods they could actually purchase.

To know and reach these working-class consumers, admen placed women as a focal point in their strategies. Women, in fact, made most consumer decisions, did the shopping for the whole family, and were avid readers of the press and thus highly exposed to advertisements. When the participation of women on the market increased due to a higher standard of living, admen, advertisers, and editors conducted intensive campaigns in the print media to educate them on the many responsibilities of being a rational consumer. To make their job of selling goods easier, advertising professionals advocated female consumers who were knowledgeable, assertive, and used advertisements to make informed choices rather than impulse-driven shoppers. If the goals were ultimately to promote branded products and highlight the role of advertising for the chain effect of prosperity, consumers benefited from the endorsement of honest commercial practices and the dissemination of information that resulted in the process.

In developing the strategies necessary to connect with vaster groups of consumers, satisfy the demands of their clients, promote economic growth, and strengthen the profession, advertising matured into a trade that earned unprecedented praise. In his speech celebrating advertising day at the annual gala of 1948, Minister of Industry and Commerce José Constantino Barro commended advertising for being a technically sophisticated field and pointed to the use of consumer indexes, surveys, and statistics as the perfect measure of the level of complexity it had attained. He extensively discussed the application of these tools on the new consumer market and reminded the audience of advertising's critical role in improving the standard of living of the working class. But instead of closing with research, consumers, or social justice, Minister Barro ended his speech by talking about images and colors, language and style, and illustrations and texts—praising advertising as art and method. Using a military metaphor, Barro referred to these elements as "arrows," an arsenal of tools admen should choose carefully and creatively "to shoot" right on "target." And in fact, advertising agents at the gala knew all too well that the measure of advertising success remained in its convincing power to sell, in closing the gap between manufacturer and purchaser. As admen were adapting their research tools for working-class consumers, revising old assumptions about advertising outside Buenos Aires, and singling out women of low-income sectors as the heart of the consumer family, profound changes were transforming the form and content of advertisement.[80]

CHAPTER 3

Commercial Culture
Becomes Popular

Advertising and the Challenges of a Changing Market

In the mid-1930s, advertising experts believed that there were only a few qualified agencies in Argentina and high-quality advertising in the country was still exceptional. In its evolution, leaders in the field contended, Argentine advertising followed the same trends as the country's productive sectors. In 1945, an article in the advertising yearbook *Síntesis Publicitaria* argued that until the early 1940s, there had been no real national advertising because of the lack of a national industry. An economy dependent on industrial imports was contingent on foreign advertising, especially on the adaptation of imported ads and the reproduction of advertising formulas from abroad, mainly from the United States. Although foreign admen acknowledged that "the Argentine is a very proud national and reacts more favorably to ads written in his own language, with local colloquial-isms and local place-names," they also agreed that early twentieth-century advertising was characterized by deficient translations, inappropriate sales arguments, and a profound lack of information on Argentine traditions and culture.[1]

Still, due to business and personal contacts and to the comparatively undeveloped state of the field in the country, advertisers and particularly foreign companies preferred to employ international advertising agencies. In turn, some of these agencies contributed to this preference by dissemi-nating a truly biased view of local admen that stressed their racial and cul-tural inferiority. In 1929, the managing director of one of the largest U.S. advertising companies in South America spoke to an audience of admen in the United States, stating that "the little I could say about advertising agency methods in Argentina would be similar to someone talking to a group of leading doctors here in New York about witch doctors in Africa."[2] Partly because of these prejudices, up until the late 1930s, agencies in Argentina were inclined to bring their top executives and staff members from abroad, further inhibiting the growth of national advertising and the training of local specialists. In fact, to gain new clients, national advertising companies often masked their origins by adopting foreign names. In 1931, the Argentine founder of Best Agency explained that he and his partner "were familiar with the Buenos Aires market and knew from experience that a new agency with a North American name would be taken more seri-ously than one with an Argentine name."[3]

Less than two decades later, assessments of advertising in Argentina had become highly optimistic. In celebration of advertising day, advertising agencies declared that

> advertising is the flower of contemporary life: it is the affirmation of optimism and happiness, attracting the eye and the mind. It is the greatest manifestation today of the vitality and power of our society, of its gift for invention and its imagination. Advertising is the most outstanding result of the social efforts to modernize the world and its needs.[4]

Advertising experts concurred that the dynamic and expansive post-war industrial economy had fostered national advertising and this, in turn, had played a major role in consolidating a national mass consumer market. As concrete proof of this process, funds devoted to advertising went from an estimated 50 million pesos in 1945 to 2.5 billion in 1954. These growing investments ensured record-high volumes of advertisements in a variety of channels. Confirming this development, by the early 1950s, the number of advertising agencies across the country had increased and the level of professionalization and specialization of admen had improved markedly. Changes were so deep that they reached the very makeup of the profession. Although agencies still employed predominantly middle- and upper-class male executives and staff, these employees were, in contrast to the recent past, born in Argentina. The nationalization of the advertising industry is further manifest in mid-twentieth-century agency names taken from autochthonous animal and plant species like Albatros, Condor, and Irupé, which proves that there was no longer a need to conceal the national origins of the majority of the advertising companies.

The growth and strength of the field was also evident in the rising professional organization within the trade. In addition to the Asociación Argentina de Agencias de Publicidad (Argentine Association of Advertising Agencies) and the Asociación Argentina de la Propaganda (Argentine Advertising Association) founded in the 1930s, a number of solid professional associations emerged in this period. These included, among others, the Asociación de Agencias de Publicidad en la Vía Pública (Association of Street Advertising Agencies, 1939), the Asociación Promotores Publicitarios de la Argentina (Association of Admen of Argentina, 1945), the Federación Argentina de Publicidad (Argentine Advertising Federation, 1953), and the Círculo de Redactores Publicitarios (Circle of Advertising Copywriters, 1953). These organizations held conferences and exhibitions, provided education on advertising, promoted advertisement among manufacturers and the general public, and coped with the needs of their members, encouraging the constant advance of the profession.[5]

The superior quality of advertising placed Argentina on the cutting edge of the trade in Latin America and close to the United States, the leader in the field. Praise for advertisement produced in Argentina emphasized the artistic and technical excellence of ads and the remarkable level of inventiveness of the copywriters in charge of conceiving advertising messages.[6] Most importantly, experts believed that this was the moment in which "a distinctively Argentine advertisement" was emerging. In the 1950s, the director of a major advertising agency in Buenos Aires declared that "there is now a specifically Argentine imagination in advertising that reflects a Latin American concept of creativeness."[7] This idiosyncratic national advertisement was different from past attempts of foreign admen who combined the occasionally incorrect use of Spanish syntax with the national flag and the gaucho (the traditional nomadic inhabitant of the pampeana region) to appeal to upper-class consumers through a reified version of nationalism. It was also different from the early twentieth-century pattern ads created abroad and slightly adapted for their publication in the country.[8]

The emergence of national advertising in the mid-twentieth century was unquestionably a response to the creation of national agencies with local personnel who worked for Argentine advertisers. But most importantly, the local spirit of the 1950s advertisement was dependent on the expansive mass consumer culture that challenged ad-makers to engage with the values and expectations of the low-income newcomers to the market. This chapter demonstrates that working-class consumers influenced the language, the visuals, and the mediums of advertisement, thus giving commercial publicity a distinct flair. Yet advertisement also intervened in culture independent from the dictums of consumers. Thus, the rhetoric and the iconography of ads were more than the propaganda of commodities; they produced what historian Jackson Lears has called commercial fables, that is, dynamic representations and reconfigurations of historical values and attitudes. Scholars have endorsed opposing views of the relationship between advertisement and society. For some, advertisement exclusively expresses the meanings of its creators; for others, it is a reflection of the interests and concerns of the audience.[9] This chapter shows that it is both. Although advertisement is the ideological and technical creation of ad-makers, it is also a historically and culturally determined product. And in contrast to other cultural artifacts, it is forced to engage with the beliefs and views of consumers to be successful. In mid-twentieth-century Argentina, advertisement sanctioned as well as subverted existing meanings; it interfered in the symbolic universe and, in turn, got transformed by culture. The new visual, textual, and argumentative components of ads as well as the boom in outdoor advertisement, which are the objects of the analysis that follows, are evidence of this reciprocity.

Speaking the Language of the People

In 1951, advertising journal *Ímpetu*, widely read in the profession, selected the print advertisements of Lux laundry detergent as an example of a successful campaign. The heading of the ads was *la yapa*, a slang expression that means "the extra," an allusion to the added cleaning power of the soap.

La yapa impeccably exemplifies the speech adopted by copywriters in mid-twentieth-century Argentina. In contrast to the longer, elaborate, and more argumentative advertising copies with formal and flowery language of previous decades, admen adopted a new and simple formula to effectively communicate with the masses. Copywriters favored short arguments and catchy, sometimes infantile rhymes and slogans—"Casa Lamota, donde se viste Carlota" (Carlota buys her clothes at Lamota), "Casa Muñoz, donde un peso vale dos" (At Muñoz, one peso's worth two)—and preferred messages that were scarcely intellectual and required little analysis. In 1950, for instance, the famous men's retail store Costa Grande launched a campaign that highlighted the quality of its clothing by presenting the most preeminent characteristic of different animals. One of the ads combined a camel with the message "¡Usted no querrá un traje con jorobita!" (You wouldn't want a jacket with a "hump"!), a simple and graphic way to point out a common defect in men's jackets. Most importantly, advertisements privileged a language that was uncomplicated and colloquial. This was a form of "ventriloquism"—to use cultural critic Stuart Hall's expression—that effectively mimicked the vernacular that common people spoke on the streets.[10]

In its role of ventriloquist, a famous retail store praised the elegance and good looks of its suits by claiming, "Tienen una pinta bárbara" (They look sharp) in its print advertising campaign. *Pinta* is a popular *lunfardo* term, a jargon resulting from the mixture of Spanish, Italian, and French that emerged in turn-of-the-century Buenos Aires upon the arrival of European immigrants. Similarly, admen employed prevalent conversational sayings that had been uncommon in print ads in the past. "¡Qué flor de heladera!" (What a beautiful fridge!) celebrated an ad with a common expression to signify beauty and excellence (*flor* means "flower" but is also a slang expression of admiration) while a furniture store warned potential clients, "No se deje ahorcar " (Don't let them smother you) by expensive competitors that sold at higher prices.[11] The stylistic changes in ads manifested a broader transformation in the language of public life. Articles and especially headlines in the print media recurrently used informal terms that had been absent in magazines and newspapers just a few years before. The same conversational tone characterized the language of the government in pamphlets, ads, official communications, propaganda, and speeches. Both Juan Domingo Perón and Eva Perón broke with the formalities of the past and conquered their constituency with their unceremonious ways, down-to-earth discourse, and unadorned but passionate oratory.[12]

Although the casual style became increasingly popular among copywriters, the profession was divided regarding this trend. Some leading authorities in the field believed that meager vocabulary and the absence of literary turns was a response to eager but unsophisticated consumers who posed no challenges to the creativity of admen. For many advertising agents, straightforward arguments, colloquial language, and infantile forms of addressing the public were a populist, almost demagogic strategy to reach the worker-consumer based on the assumption that this buyer was ingenuous and easily seduced. But being indolent and underestimating their audiences, experts warned, could be costly for advertising agencies and their clients because consumers were not "stupid" as admen sometimes imagined and they could easily turn their backs on "ridiculous" and dull advertising appeals.[13] For others, unrefined copywriting was less connected with the social and cultural characteristics of the new low-income consumers than with the historical conjuncture of an expansive mass market. According to this view, high demand was the primary cause for poor, plain, repetitive, and sometimes even misleading advertising. An expert in the field lamented the negative effects that a prosperous market had on the quality of advertising by asking, "In a period in which the product is not only selling but is practically fought over as a result of the demand, what need could there be for prestigious advertising?"[14] Others alerted admakers that if high demand was making their task easy, they should not "rest on their laurels" but instead remember that advertisement was the indispensable mechanism that propelled the virtuous cycle of production and consumption.[15]

Seeking to strike the right notes among the new consumer constituency without generating disapproval among purists in the profession, admen went beyond the use of colloquial language. Copywriters boosted calls to working-class consumers with rhetoric tics that reinforced the social inclusiveness of the mid-twentieth-century mass market. Unusual in copywriting to that date, "all" and "everybody" were the universal terms in commercial slogans, ad titles, and ad copies that admen employed to portray consumption as a democratized sphere of unrestricted access. Endlessly repeated, catchphrases like "Manufactured for everyone's budget," "A sale that benefits everybody," "You, us, them: We all have things to buy during the December holidays," "Every woman has the right to be happy," and "All types of people buy on credit at Harrods" continuously evoked the image of a market where all social classes participated equally. This message was impeccably delivered by a famous household appliance store whose motto was "Where no one feels like an ugly duck." In this campaign—which stressed installment plans for all consumers according to their wages and the possibility of buying a domestic appliance without making economic sacrifices—admen combined the figure of an ugly duck as a metaphor of social misplacement with the lunfardo "duck" that literally means poor or indigent.[16]

Based on the same idea, though with a slight twist, admen used rhetoric tics that associated consumer goods and stores with "the popular" and "the people" to bring companies and their products closer to working-class consumers. Therefore, by embedding consumer goods with a popular identity, a well-known men's retailer advertised "El tropical del pueblo" (the people's tropical), a light and inexpensive summer suit; an advertising campaign for cold cuts promoted them as "un plato fuerte y popular" (a strong and popular meal); and one of the biggest food companies in the country marketed "Olímpico, el fideo popular" (Olímpico, the people's noodle). Similarly, while retail stores traditionally carried sophisticated names in the past—with numerous English names like Gath & Chaves, Harrods, and Thompson & Williams that sometimes reflected the origins of their founders—new stores adopted names like *La Popular* (The Popular) while others made the connection to the masses clear with slogans like "Tienda Buena Vista: La que nació del pueblo para el pueblo" (Buena Vista Department Store: Born of the people for the people). Going even further, a company launched Santa Teresita yerba maté and advertised it with the motto "La yerba de los descamisados" in direct allusion to "the shirtless ones," the term for Perón's working-class followers.[17]

New Consumers, New Arguments

As the language of ads changed, marketing strategies changed too. Mid-twentieth-century advertisements of gas stoves and electric refrigerators are eloquent examples of how admen targeted working-class consumers by invoking new values. Production of gas stoves and electric refrigerators expanded dramatically throughout the period, and both household appliances experienced the highest sales in the sector. In a context where consumers belonging to the two lower-income groups of the population were becoming potential purchasers of household technology they could not afford in the past, the volume of ads for electric refrigerators and gas stoves underwent unprecedented expansion and companies made record investments in advertising campaigns. The development was especially impressive for electric refrigerators, with SIAM at the head of the list. The case of SIAM is even more remarkable because during the 1930s and early 1940s, advertising had not been a major concern for a company that considered it only secondary in increasing and maintaining sales. By the mid-twentieth century, however, the firm had completely changed its viewpoint, and, as a result, annual expenditures for advertising went from 104,000 pesos in 1937 to 1 million in 1949, rising to more than 13 million in 1955.[18]

Working-class organizations had traditionally criticized the socially restricted access to a modern household and pointed to the irony of grandiloquent advertising claims about the "cleanliness, comfort, and happiness" achieved through domestic appliances while the working population was miserable and hungry. In the mid-1930s, the Communist paper *Orientación* illustrated this argument with a drawing titled *The Modern Family* showing a skeletal, tired, ragged, and shoeless family surrounded by a variety of household artifacts.[19] Indeed, throughout the 1920s and 1930s, advertisers depicted gas stoves and electric refrigerators as embodiments of modernity, but as communists had suggested, it was a form of modernity only affordable to the upper classes. Furthermore, in a context in which the local upper classes admired foreign goods as symbols of progress and sophistication, the equation between appliances and modernity was redoubled by the fact that most of these goods were imports.

In the case of gas and electric stoves, ads associated modernity with the achievement of comfort, the aim of hygiene, and the goals of simplicity and speediness. In targeting high-income consumers, ads portrayed stoves as a means for reaching a state of well-being, especially women's, characterized by the absence of physical exertion. This attribute was in marked opposition to the arduous tasks of carrying, chopping, manipulating, and cleaning coal and wood, tasks primarily performed by women from the working classes who cooked with the *cocina económica*, or "economic stove," a cast iron box with a stovetop and a combustion chamber where charcoal, coal, or wood burned. A 1929 Primitiva ad for gas stoves, portraying an exhausted and weeping housewife who is being comforted by her spouse, warned husbands that "cuddles can cure emotional discomforts but not physical ones." The ad urged men to buy a gas stove to make sure their wives got the rest they needed, a pitch that targeted middle-class consumers who could afford the gas stove but who probably could not fit a maid into their budget.[20]

Generally, ads omitted any mention of the taste, quality, and texture of food cooked with clean fuels and avoided any portrayal of the stove as a tool for making a meal. In other words, the concrete results of cooking with gas were less important than the actual experience of owning the appliance. The accent, by contrast, was on the safe and easy operation of gas stoves, a response to the popular 1920s belief that gas was a dangerous fuel and that the gas stove was a complicated mechanism prone to explosions. Thus, cooking with a gas stove was "as easy as pushing a button" or "with the ease and safety of turning on a light" that allowed "cooking a whole meal at once."[21] Cleanliness was also a fundamental aspect. According to ads, the lack of smoke, ash, dirt, and odors allowed housewives to cook wearing "white gloves" or "their finest dresses." In reality, many prospective consumers did not personally use the stoves; their domestic workers did. Consequently, ads emphasized the effects that modern stoves had on the quality of life, that is, the airy, pristine, and salubrious home they ensured their residents.[22]

During the early twentieth century, advertisements for electric refrigerators also pivoted on the argument that "there is no modern home without an electric refrigerator." In this case, modernity represented the enjoyment of technology, the attainment of health, and the access to leisure and moments of pleasure. As most ads and refrigerators were imported from the United States, these arguments were not specific to Argentina.[23] While ads for stoves lacked in-depth specifications on technical characteristics, ads for electric refrigerators informed potential consumers of the performance, materials, equipment, finishing, and conveniences in extreme detail. Ads for the electric fridge particularly emphasized the novelty of the appliance on the national market, portraying it as a sophisticated mechanism on the verge of technological advancement. One of the most significant benefits of enjoying this type of technology in the household was a healthy family. Ads almost always depicted children as the most likely victims of food poisoning and promoted the fridge as "the armored watchtower." Appeals to science provided an authoritative discourse to frame statements about physical strength, the battle against microbes and bacteria, and the right temperature to conserve dairy products.[24]

Both technology and health were recurring aspects that justified the electric refrigerator as a pricey artifact. In 1926, for example, Servel asked potential buyers, "How much is your baby's health worth?" to endorse a costly investment in what the company represented as a priceless asset.[25] A General Electric ad used a similar strategy to explain to consumers that technological innovation was, in fact, expensive: "Why does a refrigerator cost so much? Because of its technical equipment, which represents three-quarters of its worth and is responsible for its advantages." These types of arguments reinforced the characterization of the electric refrigerator as "aristocratic" and a true "seal of honor," a prestigious good only accessible to a few.[26] In fact, in 1929, advertising company J. Walter Thompson conducted a market study for Frigidaire that showed that it was impossible for the two lower-income groups, including industrial workers, taxi drivers, servants, and clerks, to purchase a refrigerator. Only the two highest-income sectors, the A and B groups—generally car owners—were a potential market. These sectors represented less than a quarter of the national population.[27]

Accordingly, refrigerator ads depicted richly dressed people in evening dresses, furs, and tuxedos as they relaxed, entertained, and dined. By highlighting a hedonistic and wealthy life-style, ads portrayed the electric refrigerator as a means to convey social status. One advertisement argued that the electric refrigerator was essential to throwing parties and treating guests to cocktails "chilled to perfection" while stressing the flavor, freshness, tempting aroma, and attractive appearance of food preserved in an electric refrigerator.[28] By focusing on the sensual features of cold food and on socializing, ads gave fridges the ability to make life more pleasurable. However, this ability did not result from its status as a labor-saving domestic tool like stoves and washing machines. Beyond its functionality, descriptions based on its "elegance," "modern beauty," and "distinguished appearance" made the electric refrigerator a "delightful artifact," a beautiful piece of furniture that was a source of gratification and symbolized prestige.[29]

Beyond the exceptional increase in the quantity of advertisements for gas stoves and electric refrigerators and in the funds that companies invested to promote their products in the mid-twentieth century, the most important consequence of the emergence of an eager new market was the remarkable change in the content of advertising. Some aspects associated with the early twentieth-century ideals of modernity, mainly the promises of cleanliness for stoves and of health for refrigerators, still played a role in advertising discourses. However, nationalism, economy, and durability appeared as the new values that monopolized advertisements in the 1950s. The trend was extensive among ads for different products but especially evident in the case of household appliances. In line with the "nationalization" of ad-making, these principles largely suited working-class consumers who were newcomers to the market of domestic technology and whose purchase of a household artifact was not only the result of careful planning, financing or thoughtful use of savings, but also an investment for life. Consequently, signs of wealth and high social standing disappeared from ads and with them the notion of the household appliance as a prestige good. In its place, ads emphasized functionality and utility. Mentions of parties and cocktails gave way to less sophisticated conveniences, such as enjoying a sandwich in the middle of the night. Furthermore, in opposition to previous decades when gas stove and electric refrigerator ads each had their own set of differentiated principles, the topics that dominated advertising discourses in the mid-twentieth century were common to both appliances.[30]

Nationalism, one of the components of the thematic triad, was an ideology that further permeated every aspect of life in 1950s Argentina. It was a value that Peronism fervently promoted in all facets of its administration, from food policies and transportation to communications and fuels, and that opportunistically coupled with an exacerbated anti-imperialism.[31] Nationalism was intrinsically and noticeably connected with the very nature of both stoves and refrigerators. In the case of gas stoves, the potent nationalistic connotations of the expansive natural gas service—advanced by the Peronist government through subsidized gas rates and the development of a national piped distribution system—made an immediate case for urging consumers to buy only stoves that worked with the "most Argentine" fuel. In contrast to ads from previous decades that made no references to the origins of the stoves, mid-twentieth century ads firmly stated that stoves were made in Argentina. CATITA (Compañía Argentina de Talleres Industriales, Transportes y Anexos), for example, promoted its stove as an "Argentine conception."[32]

Nationalistic appeals were even more prominent in the case of electric refrigerators, the products of a newer industry of unparalleled growth. Interestingly, at the same time that refrigerators were becoming "Argentine" because they were entirely manufactured in the country, their names were also "nationalized." Ads massively adopted the term *heladera* while the Anglo-inspired terms *refrigerador* and *frigidaire* fell into disuse. Beyond conceptual subtleties, refrigerator companies made use of patriotic discourses by highlighting the contribution of the manufacturers to the industrial progress of the country.[33] SIAM, for its part, took nationalist arguments to the level of an advertising credo. A 1955 ad, for example, affirmed that "every SIAM product inspires trust because it is Argentine, noble, and good. SIAM: An Argentine industry run by Argentines." Although it often operated under a foreign license, SIAM was proud to be a firm whose profits were reinvested in the country. In 1953, an ad made this point explicit by affirming that "the benefits that SIAM receives from the country are used to manufacture products that improve the population's well-being."[34]

FIGURE 6: "Argentine, Noble, and Good!" The relation between nationalism and
SIAM is evident in this ad, in which a statue of the republic holds a refrigerator in the palm of her hand. *Mundo Peronista*, November 15, 1954, 37.

The strong self-identification of SIAM as an Argentine company producing Argentine artifacts was a strategy particularly defiant of the preferences of the upper classes. Consumer studies had shown that the elites

paradoxically combined a political type of anti-Americanism with a strong fascination with American technology, brand names, and household appliances. A study of public attitudes toward SIAM conducted in Buenos Aires showed that its products did not convey the prestige of foreign trademarks or the social status of owning a foreign appliance. Consequently, upper classes did not favor SIAM appliances and strongly disapproved of the company's mass-market orientation. In order to attract these high-income consumers, some firms adopted an advertising approach that opposed that of SIAM, stressing the fact that they operated under a foreign license and that their refrigerators were "Argentine but as good as one imported from North America." On the contrary, the working classes had a marked preference for SIAM products they praised as reliable and strong, an aspect addressed in chapter 6.[35]

As significant as nationalism, economy was a new crucial characteristic emphasized in advertising campaigns. With a working-class audience in mind, admen focused on the aguinaldo in ads published over the holidays when sales of refrigerators tended to rise because of the hot weather and the Christmas celebration. In some cases, ads argued that a fridge was the best way to invest one's aguinaldo; in others, they claimed that "the aguinaldo is for saving it since you have worked so hard to earn it," highlighting that the appliance was so inexpensive that workers could buy one with only part of their monthly wages.[36] While earlier ads had explained why refrigerators were so expensive, mid-twentieth-century ads underlined low prices and financing plans that made refrigerators and stoves accessible to all. SIAM, for instance, used its ads to explain that a high volume of production and sales, modern manufacturing techniques, and new factories and advanced equipment allowed the company to keep prices low and constant over the years, even in a context of inflation. In a typical 1950 ad, which echoed the Peronist Second Five-Year Plan, SIAM announced, "The SIAM Plan: 600 percent more units than in 1940. Natural law: more production, lower prices. The SIAM Plan is the People's Plan."[37] Furthermore, to better appeal to consumers with tight budgets, electric fridge ads stressed the low consumption of electricity and the savings on groceries thanks to a longer conservation of food while gas stoves ads put the accent on the economy of cooking with the "cheapest fuel." Aurora, for its part, argued that its stoves "don't make you waste a cent more [on gas]."[38]

Finally, durability was the third value that monopolized ads for gas stoves and electric refrigerators. At the same time that admen conveniently minimized the fact that for working-class consumers the purchase of these appliances represented one of their biggest investments, ads implicitly substantiated the large disbursement by drawing attention to the strength and resilience of the artifacts. These characteristics were critical for potential consumers who needed the appliances to last a lifetime and then be passed on to the next generation.[39] Therefore, the mottoes of several of the most popular gas stoves on the market engaged with these expectations. Longvie had "long-life" stoves; Orbis promoted theirs as "long-lasting" and "worthy of rounds of applause, cooking for many years;" and Domec defined its gas stove as "eternal." This was also a feature that advertisers constantly highlighted for refrigerators with arguments such as "SIAM is a purchase that lasts forever."[40] Endurance was intrinsically related to quality, one of the biggest concerns among manufacturers, admen, the government, and consumers during the industrialist boom in the postwar years. Thus beyond pretentious claims about the company's reputation, reliability, and industrial record—the Sigma company was, for example, "at the peak of quality"—ads for electric refrigerators emphasized the high quality of the artifact by offering convenient warranty and technical support. In fact, these two features became a source of competition among companies that promised consumers longer and more comprehensive protection plans at no cost and expert assistance whenever and wherever it was required.[41]

Workers in Ads

The characters of advertisements changed alongside the promises advertisers made to consumers. In the early twentieth century, department store ads had centered on the testimony of women from local high society who promoted expensive and commonly imported goods and highlighted the sophistication—the ambiance, architecture, and style—of the store. When department stores advertised home goods, the social class of the potential clientele was evident in the figure of uniformed domestic servants who operated the household appliances or cooked for their employers. And when ads publicized evening gowns, rich textiles, or tennis gear, the social class of the target audience was suggested in images of elegant and "modern ladies," always slim, active, exquisitely dressed, and enjoying free time. By the mid-1940s, these types of advertisements had become very infrequent. While advertising characters that gave products and retailers a high-class image were generally fading away, workers took the leading role in advertisements.[42]

With the exception of maids in supporting roles to enhance the prestige of both the product and the potential consumer, the absence of workers as characters in ads had been a persistent characteristic in the early decades of the twentieth century. This trend was inherited from American advertising which, with its focus on promoting products in upscale settings and with an upper-class audience in mind, had a strong influence on Argentine advertising during the first decades of the century. In the mid-twentieth century, however, this "high-class advertising pattern" mostly disappeared and maids, the most common and gendered index of class and social subordination, vanished from local ads. The series of changes was completed when admen cast workers in one of the largest roles in advertising. The new trait was a clear sign of the commercial culture a decade into a "labor government" whose strongest support lay in unions and in a leader who proudly referred to himself as the country's "first worker." In a striking difference with the past, Peronism effectively appropriated the multifarious identities of the working population—the young, muscular, and diligent industrial laborer; the heroic *descamisado*; and the underprivileged *cabecita*, among others—and made them into pervading icons of social empowerment and national progress. This progress was heavily based on the country's industrialization, which the government and the industrialist sectors promoted as the undisputable path to modernity and economic independence. In marketing consumer goods, admen greatly contributed to disseminating this notion. And although they could have done it exclusively by extolling industrial technology, modern shop floors, and the figure of prominent factory owners, as their counterparts in the United States and Mexico had done, they chose the worker as their preferred messenger.[43]

Advertising men coined a production ethos that connected the potential consumer to the advertised good through the worker who manufactured it. The worker in ads made industry humane, personal, and close to the consumer constituency and, most relevantly, attested to the fair treatment that workers received to an audience of working-class consumers. The advertising strategy of Alpargatas offers an excellent example of this trend. One of the oldest and largest textile and shoe companies in the country, the firm was famous for its alpargatas, rope-soled canvas shoes generally worn by working men. In its massive campaign *Cosas de Alpargatas* (Alpargatas Stuff), the company appealed to consumers by publicizing information that made it a model employer that was caring, thoughtful, and fair. In the ads, a young and good-looking lady—a sort of spokesperson for a factory that employed mainly female workers—revealed a wide range of colorful facts about Alpargatas that included the especially appointed pastry chef who made the desserts for the workers' cafeteria, the stylish uniforms provided by the company, and the bonuses for new parents, newlyweds, and workers with children under the age of fourteen. A producer of inexpensive goods for low-income consumers, Alpargatas publicized its products by highlighting their low cost and high quality while categorically emphasizing how the company contributed to the working-class standard of living through good wages. The ads synthesized the appeal to the twofold identity of the worker-consumer by concluding that "since 1885, Alpargatas has had two goals: to produce more and better articles for a greater number of consumers and to continuously increase the standard of living of its workers."[44]

As the mediators between consumers and manufacturers, workers in ads introduced products to audiences while their praise functioned as a warranty delivered by the true maker of the advertised good. The proud worker in overalls who handed over the sewing machine to the excited housewife, the happy mechanic who recommended that consumers purchase the bicycle he had assembled, and the concentrated laborers closely monitoring stoves on the assembly line were some of the images and narrative strategies that portrayed workers—rather than engineers or scientists—as approachable and reliable authorities with practical knowledge about the products they built and endorsed. The strategy proved successful. In the mid-1940s, an advertising campaign for a brand of men's shoes featured the testimonies of the machine operators and inspectors who made the shoes. According to a report by J. Walter Thompson Argentina, the campaign—whose original slogan was "Fits your foot and your pocketbook"—made the men's shoes the most popular brand in the country within two years.[45]

While the leading role of working-class characters in ads broke with a tradition of ignoring them, the most innovative element was their status as consumers, not producers. The new preeminence of working-class consumers in local advertisement was a tool to influence buyers by giving them advice from a peer. Beyond suggesting and recommending the consumer goods they produced, working-class characters sold everything from food and cleaning products to suits and sewing machines by presenting themselves as examples of satisfied consumers. In their new role, they starred in ads that had been previously monopolized by socially indistinguishable figures or stereotyped middle- and upper-class characters, or in advertisements that did not depict any individuals in an effort to not exclude any potential consumers. Now the range of goods endorsed by workers was so wide that, in a true subversion of expectations, admen used a potbellied and good-natured grocer at work to advertise a razor blade while a female customer exclaimed, "¡Qué buen mozo el almacenero!" (That grocer is sure handsome!).[46]

Advertising men even employed working-class characters to sell goods that were not easily or evidently within the reach of working-class consumers. In 1953, SIAM launched a striking campaign in the print media to advertise its washing machine. "If men had to do the wash . . . They would buy a SIAM washing machine," claimed the company. The ads were directly addressed to Mr. Electrician, Mr. Mechanic, Mr. Painter, and Mr. Carpenter and illustrated by men who, dressed with the working clothes typical of these occupations, struggled to wash clothes by hand, clumsily employing their work tools while looking exhausted, sore, and bitter. This type of strategy was risky, as it could potentially have alienated consumers who might not have considered themselves working class or who, due to prejudice and social status, might not have established a positive connection with a product endorsed by a working-class character. But the pervasive use of workers in ads attests not only to the consumer power of low-income sectors, but also to their legitimate status as widely accepted and alluring symbols of trust and respectability with a strong appeal to consumers.[47]

The most famous and stylized male working-class characters in advertising were the legendary *divitos*, a creation of renowned cartoonist Guillermo Divito, founder of the popular comic magazine *Rico Tipo*. Divitos were stereotypical portrayals of men from the popular sectors. Representative of the working class, the divito was not the traditional image of the worker in working clothes but a caricature of a low-income man enjoying life. He was also the counter figure of the *petitero*, a stereotyped version of a middle-class man.[48] Style defined both divitos and petiteros, expressing their class belonging and making them recognizable iconic figures. Unable to reproduce the economic status of the upper sectors, petiteros imitated their style inexpensively and with second-rate results. They commonly wore a very short, close-fitting, single-breasted blue jacket they never took off; straight, tight, gray pants; a tie with a traditional knot; and moccasins. To top off their look, they always used hair cream. In contrast, divitos were distinctive in their brown or blue suits and their long, fitted, double-breasted jackets with very wide and long lapels. They wore long and narrow pants, a waistband and suspenders, a gaudy tie with a wide

LA CAMISA PARA EL HOMBRE QUE TRABAJA!

Aquí tiene una camisa bien cortada, elegante, como hecha "a medida" para usted! Sus colores son firmes, de moda, resistentes al sol y a los lavados. Sí; la camisa OMBU, de Grafa no destiñe, no encoge, sienta bien, y no cuesta más que las camisas comunes.

La Camisa OMBU se ofrece en tres colores distintos: Beige claro, beige oscuro y gris.

CAMISA "OMBU"

de

Grafa

NO ENCOGE - NO DESTIÑE

FIGURE 7: "The shirt for the working man." Working-class men and women became common characters in mid-twentieth-century ads. *Mundo Argentino*, June 30, 1954, back cover.

heart-shaped knot, high-heeled shoes, and a visible handkerchief in the breast pocket. They had long hair, sideburns, a quiff, and a low ponytail.[49]

Divitos—both those sketched by Guillermo Divito and those imitated by other illustrators—became extremely effective cultural mediums in ads that sold innumerable products, but especially merchandise connected with the particular aesthetics of the characters, like hats, men's clothing, and razors. The divito, anachronistically inspired by tango characters and by the *compadrito* or "the tough guy," was the stylistic remnant of a culture that was disappearing. A lower-class man, conceited, quarrelsome, and arrogant, the compadrito was the quintessence of the *porteño* outskirts, which is probably what might have made him appealing to working-class migrants from the provinces striving to assimilate in the big city. By purchasing consumer goods that represented the essence of urban masculinity, these sectors were adopting, on their own terms, an intrinsically porteño style, albeit one that upper-class sectors might have considered outdated and stereotyped.[50]

Working-class female characters also played an unprecedented role in advertisements. Yet, the advertising of diverse consumer goods— food, cleaning products, toiletries, and garments—echoed the prejudice against women factory workers by relying on female characters in more "reputable" white-collar jobs. The marketing strategy was in tune with the context; even a government proclaimed as the champion of the workers advocated motherhood and domesticity over paid work and employed the nurse as the iconic figure of working women and as the counterpart to the male industrial worker.[51] Also, female characters in advertising mirrored the 1940s and 1950s labor market since women working in the tertiary sector more than doubled those employed in the industrial sector. The new marketing pattern is manifest in ads of products that had previously shown very wealthy women in extremely luxurious settings. Ads for stockings, for example, had traditionally followed the "one-step-up-rule" by which admen considered their consumers' most likely status—middle- and upper-class women—and portrayed the products in use by people in the next higher bracket. As evidence of the changing trend, one of the most important manufacturers launched an advertising campaign based on the testimonies of different working women, including a teacher, a secretary, a sales assistant, and a seamstress who, reinforcing the propriety of their occupations, highlighted how Orea stockings were essential for the elegance and femininity—rather than the professionalism and education— required in their jobs.[52]

Admen clearly refrained from showing women involved in manual labor for pay, including domestic paid labor, as seen in ads for sewing machines. The sewing machine, an appliance whose sales boomed in this period, became an icon of the working-class home and the basis of the domestic industry actively endorsed by the Peronist state. Like the government, manufacturers generally avoided marketing the sewing machine—one of the most heavily advertised goods in the print media—as a source of additional income. Instead, they focused on its indirect contribution to the domestic economy by assisting women in making clothes, curtains, and linen for the family.[53]

Alongside fictional characters, admen employed real working women to endorse consumer goods. This was an innovative approach since testimonial advertisements had customarily featured high-class women, members of the European aristocracy, and cinema and radio stars. In contrast to the Pond's campaign, which continued its international strategy of presenting women from prominent local families, a leading national company chose the beauty queen of the sugar cane harvest, a young lady from Tucumán, to be the face for its Manuelita soap. The campaign profited from the widespread popularity of beauty contests sponsored by the Peronist government to elect the national queen of labor among working-class women. "Working beauty queen" contests greatly contributed to make working women emblems of beauty and style in the popular imagination since winners received extensive publicity and their photos, which openly resembled pictures of Argentine radio and cinema female stars of the day, showed them modeling stylish outfits in numerous magazines.

Remarkably, in 1930, J. Walter Thompson had run a campaign for Pond's face cream with a royal dignitary but of a different pedigree, Princess Eulalia of Spain. Ad-makers considered that if an European princess, with her endless resources, chose Pond's to boost her self-image, Argentine upper-class women, who were "very beauty conscious," would be moved by the example of a high-status figure and not even hesitate to buy the cream. Almost two decades later, admen for Manuelita soap subverted the equation of attractiveness and charm with upper-class women by choosing a modest young woman who worked on her parents' farm and studied domestic economics as an icon of national beauty. With this move, ad-makers abandoned appeals to prestige in favor of product endorsement by a familiar and accessible working woman with whom low-income consumers could easily identify.[54]

These innovations notwithstanding, women in ads still complied with gender expectations that tied them to the domestic sphere and reinforced traditional nurturing roles such as cooks, mothers, and housekeepers. And when admen portrayed women at work, female characters performed "unproblematic" occupations that were either extensions of those traditional roles or "reputable" jobs that posed no apparent challenges to femininity, decency, or conventional female responsibilities. Thus, both female workers and housewives in ads remained obedient to gender rules, at least in words and actions. As images, however, mid-twentieth-century female characters transformed the visual canon of advertising by serving as motifs of an alternative feminine aesthetic: the pretty, sexy woman.

Pretty, Sexy Women

While copywriting was changing by mimicking the vernacular, it also became shorter and image prevailed over text. Beyond advertising, market experts agreed on the importance of visual culture in all aspects of commercial life, from the design of labels and product packaging to the proper exhibition of merchandising in stores and the creation of attractive window displays. The influence of images was not unique to commerce, though. Imagery deeply pervaded the 1940s and 1950s Argentine popular culture in new and exhilarating ways. Better wages greatly enlarged movie spectatorship while the successful boom of tabloids like *Aquí Está*, *Esto Es*, and *Ahora* imposed a journalistic style characterized by the vast and unprecedented use of photography. The same trend that reinforced the relationship between audiences and images was evident in the richly illustrated articles and stories of women's magazines and in comic books, whose sales skyrocketed in these years. Even politics became more visually satisfying with Peronism in power. Strongly inclined to spectacle, the Peronist government was a local pioneer of the art of staging exhibitions and massive parades of floats, and of creating and distributing copious memorabilia and ubiquitous visual propaganda in the print media, public buildings, and the streets.

For advertising men, images provided what they viewed as a universal and one-dimensional comprehensive language that could convey dense messages. Admen praised images as a powerful device to instantly grab the attention of consumers, with no reading skills or concentration required. In addition to its merits, good images were now more available for advertising. In the 1940s and 1950s, advertising agencies had access to local artists who were better trained and more professionalized than in previous decades. Although critics concurred that advertising images were still inferior to foreign graphics—especially in the case of photography, which was not employed as extensively as in the United States—they also agreed that the quality of illustration in Argentina was the best in Latin America and that local illustrators were unquestionably inventive and skilled.[55]

From the growing battery of images that dominated advertisements in the mid-twentieth century, the pretty, sexy woman appeared so often and with so many recurring characteristics that it became what historian Roland Marchand has described as a "visual cliché". This cliché was an idealized representation of female beauty defined by the clarity of line and shape, positioned in uncluttered scenarios where she was frequently the only human character. The female visual cliché in advertisements responded to the idea that images of women were very successful in grabbing the attention of both women and men, an argument that has become familiar in studies of visuality. Admen employed female images to generate identification among female viewers, anticipating that women, who did most of the shopping, would establish a relation with their print counterparts and would see them as trustworthy and inspirational peers. With men, admen used female images as "bait," believing that they were a simple and efficient way to rapidly attract a man's eye. It is impossible to assess the reception of the predominant female visual cliché in the mid-twentieth century, but its historical continuity and pervasiveness are evidence of its success in attracting all consumers but, most importantly, the women who did most of the shopping.[56]

The pretty, sexy woman was the result of the persistent repetition of a set of visual conventions. She had fair skin; an adorable face with large sparkling eyes; long, thick eyelashes; delicate, flowing hair; and a big mouth that generally opened into a wide, white smile. Her figure was an imaginative reinterpretation of the body promoted by postwar fashion. In the late 1940s, there was a return to the "womanly silhouette" that had become popular in the 1930s, replacing the chest-flattening boyish figure of the 1920s. After the Second World War, French designer Christian Dior's "New Look," the epitome of the new figure, rapidly spread around the world, moving quickly from the catwalk to fashion magazines and the street. The "New Look" meant "a return to femininity" by imposing an exaggerated silhouette created by the reemergence of the corset and the popularization of the girdle. Both restrictive garments highlighted the bust and cinched the waist to broaden the hips, a body shape linked to a traditional expression of womanhood explicitly rooted in both sexuality and fertility.[57]

The pretty, sexy woman in Argentine ads was tall and had a small frame, long and willowy arms, beautiful thin hands with long fingers, and manicured long nails. Exceptionally curvaceous, the pretty, sexy woman was busty and had an astonishingly slim waist and generous but proportionate hips and buttocks. Her legs were always long and extremely toned, with small ankles and tiny, delicate feet with beautiful insteps exquisitely enhanced by pumps. Her measurements were perfect and unrealistic, making her body unattainable for real women. The cliché was always vivacious, friendly, inviting, and assertive. A prescriptive version of young womanhood, the advertising visual cliché was exceptional within the plethora of female images circulating at that time. The pretty, sexy woman who advertised everything from canned food to gas stoves was an alternative to the stylized and ethereal mannequins of the fashion departments, the modest and self-effacing housewives and strict-looking nurses of the Peronist propaganda, and to both the plump and glamorous Eva Perón of the first years, and her fragile and unpretentious figure right before her death in 1952. Female characters in ads, however, echoed the "glamorization" of working-class women in articles about affordable fashion styles, season trends, or the working beauty queens and in magazines like *PBT* that published full-page photos of ordinary female workers walking down the streets as if they were catwalk models.[58]

Although women in ads were sexy, the images were not too revealing or provocative. They undoubtedly had a family resemblance to the 1940s American pinup girls with their perfect faces, long legs, and firm and uplifted breasts, epitomized by *Esquire* magazine's "Varga Girl," the popular creation of Peruvian-born artist Alberto Vargas. But the pinup's typical postures of raised elbows with hands held behind the head and jutting breasts or hips conveyed far more erotic messages of sexual invitation, exhibitionism, and submission to spectators.[59] Female ad characters in Argentina were unquestionably defined by their exaggerated sexual attractiveness and unrealistic beauty but remained within the social universe of the housewife next door.

A notable exception was the "Divito girl," who, like her male counterpart, was the creation of cartoonist Guillermo Divito. The Divito girls gained such popularity among female audiences that without abandoning the pages of *Rico Tipo*, they also became the leading characters in *Chicas*, a magazine aimed at young women. The aesthetics of the Divito girls were extremely pervasive and profoundly inspired advertising imagery. In fact, most of the pretty, sexy women in ads mimicked Divito's girls to a varying degree. But the true Divito women were more exuberant and sexual, the bombshell rendering of the visual cliché. In their many incarnations, the Divito girls advertised numerous products but especially goods related to beauty, such as swimsuits, suntan lotions, and the extremely popular girdle that promised women the curvaceous body that made the characters famous. In all cases, manufacturers recognized the power of the Divito girls as trendsetters and capitalized on it, both before and after the characters had made some goods fashionable. An eyeglass company, for example, hired Divito to illustrate its ads after his characters had adopted butterfly-shaped sunglasses, turning them into a must-have accessory of the season.[60]

FIGURE 8: The curvaceous Divito girl advertised numerous products including swimsuits. *Rico Tipo*, December 13, 1945, back cover.

While ads featuring Divito girls portrayed humorous interactions between the sexes, the majority of ads with pretty, sexy women did not usually include men. In most cases, the women's partners were the products, which were as prominently depicted as they were. In the case of food products, for example, both La Campagnola and Armour ran paradigmatic advertising campaigns of this kind. In their ads, canned and packaged foods were the same size as a person and physically interacted with the pretty, sexy women like human characters. The women were always affectionately touching, kissing, caressing, cuddling, showing off, embracing, and holding the advertised goods, but rarely used them. In fact, most ads did not show women actually cooking with the products. The pretty, sexy woman functioned as a metaphor, representing and increasing the appeal of the advertised good with which she posed.[61] In this regard, the product in the ad absorbs the attributes of the woman and becomes eroticized and humanized, a process that, as Walter Benjamin has argued, is meant to deny the fact that advertised products are a commodity.[62] This is particularly remarkable in the case of food, which was traditionally considered a female responsibility as well as a privileged means for women to show love. Occasionally, advertised goods were not even displayed in the ads. This is the case of voluptuous women wearing bathing suits and striking suggestive poses in ads of household appliances containing only the picture of a woman and the brand name. While commodities are humanized in these advertisements, women are commodified.[63]

The eroticization and humanization of advertised goods extended beyond advertising visuals to include other elements of commercial culture. In the 1940s and 1950s, a large number of brands, companies, and products had female names. The trend reached different types of goods and many were new to the market, especially in the case of domestic appliances. Still, female names were especially frequent among food products. As a consequence, product logos displayed women who adhered to the visual conventions of the female cliché. In the 1940s, two of the most important canned food companies in the country, La Campagnola and La Marplatense, updated their emblematic characters. Now the peasant from the small town of Campagna in southern Italy had bigger breasts and longer and more toned legs, and her new wardrobe featured an audacious white top with a low neckline worn carelessly loose to expose her right shoulder and chest. The female bather from Mar del Plata, a traditional beach destination in Buenos Aires Province, adopted a new cheerful and amusing body posture—one arm extended festively in the air, the other bent behind her head—and her bathing suit was done in a new, more revealing style.[64]

CABALLA EN SALSA DE TOMATE

CABALLA AL NATURAL

La Campagnola

La Campagnola

RESUELVE EL MENU DEL DIA !

FIGURE 9: The pretty, sexy woman in advertisements promoted a wide array of
goods, including food. *El Hogar*, July 22, 1949, back cover.

Although they were extensively featured in mid-twentieth-century
advertisements, bare shoulders, exposed legs, and voluptuous silhouettes
sparked criticism. Some advertising professionals along with members of
the public and the media condemned these images as immoral, inappropriate, or distasteful. Disapproval was not widespread, and the level of tol-
erance varied, but for this very reason, even minimal amounts of nudity
and sensuality could draw condemnation. This was the case in 1952, when
the street ads of a famous label of beach garments illustrated with women
wearing swimsuits were anonymously censured with signs that read, "Don't
Support Immoral Advertising."[65] Detractors believed that market competition and the advertising boom encouraged advertising agents and their clients to eagerly exceed the limits of decency and propriety in their fervent
desire to get the attention of consumers. In 1949, a female reader wrote to
Ímpetu complaining about an ad of nylon stockings published in a women's
magazine. The woman said that she was offended by the image, a cross-
legged woman whose stockings were revealed. The reader stated that she

was not a "prude" and maintained that "it is all right for them [the admen] to want to get your attention [the ad title reads 'Constant attraction']. That is one of the roles of advertising. But attention to ads should not be confused with morbid attraction. Or bad taste."[66]

Experts believed that this was an overreaction, especially because advertising illustrations were less realistic than pictures and thus potentially less provocative. However, *Ímpetu's* editor agreed with the upset reader and praised the municipal government for confiscating the magazines still in circulation where the ad had been printed. Still, as chapter 1 shows, admen called for advertising agencies and the media to control the content of ads themselves in order to avoid the "intrusion" of the state. In 1946, for example, *Ímpetu* publicly opposed a law in Córdoba that proposed to prohibit advertising "that threatens moral, decency and good manners," on the basis that, rooted on ambiguous criteria, this type of propositions would indiscriminately censor any type of publicity.[67]

Selling with Laughter

As changes in the language and imagery of advertisements provoked controversy among some sectors of the profession and beyond, other transformations occurred with fewer disagreements. The use of humor to sell consumer goods was a new strategy formulated by advertising agencies and favorably received by advertisers and audience alike. By boosting positive emotions and liberating repressed feelings, humor in advertisements was an expression of a market that was open and joyful. In 1950, a Spanish advertising scholar attributed the amusing nature of Argentine advertising to the current social prosperity and to the promising prospects of the country:

> A young people, with countless possibilities for the future and a high standard of living—a people with their whole lives ahead of them— must see the world through rose-colored glasses and naturally, this is evident in the way advertising is done. As a result of the sunny disposition of the Argentines, advertising is light-hearted, funny, and with plenty of illustrations.[68]

In previous decades, manufacturers had generally avoided humor, considering that it damaged the reliability and prestige of advertised products. In this view, sober advertisement conveyed an image of companies as serious enterprises and represented trustworthy products. Besides, humorless ads presupposed an audience of thoughtful and sophisticated consumers. For their part, advertising agents abided by the decisions of their clients based on the belief that humor reduced the argumentative power of ads and could obscure sales messages. The exception was advertisements for children's products, considered by ad-makers to be suitable for humor. In addition to the viewpoints of admen and advertisers, the use of imported advertisement patterns also played a key role in the absence of humor in 1920s and 1930s. American advertisement avoided funny ads in this period while pivoting on different versions of the "scare approach" that dramatically stressed personal fears, weaknesses, and challenges—from bad breath to undernourishment—that the advertised products promised to overcome.[69]

In the 1940s, columnists writing for *Ímpetu* still recommended that colleagues be judicious when using humor in ads. This time, though, experts particularly warned ad-makers against humor that drew attention away from the advertised goods; it was the goods themselves, not the comic strip or joke, that should be the focus of the ads. In spite of this reservation, experts amply acknowledged the advantages of humor in advertisement. This change was linked to a new context characterized by the thriving consumption of humor. The commercial boom of comics, which experienced historical record printings during this period, the resounding success of humorous radio shows that dominated national broadcasting, the increasing popularity of comic strips in magazines and newspapers, and the success of new publications of political humor showed the audience's predilection for humor and convinced advertising agencies to make broader use of humorous appeals to potential consumers. The large number of funny publications born in this period further consolidated the use of humor in advertisement by providing a large number of advertising channels suited to witty ads. With a weekly printing of around three hundred thousand in the mid-to-late 1940s, *Rico Tipo*, for example, guaranteed advertisers an extremely vast readership, one often larger than the older and prominent general interest, sports, and women's magazines. Beyond the preferences of the public and the commercial growth of humor in the print media, advertising agencies could now rely on a larger pool of excellent professional cartoonists, most of whom had extensive experience working as advertising agents.[70]

The use of vernacular, puns, rhymes, and infantile slogans that advertising agents chose to speak to the new market were also perfect mediums for the creation of advertising humor. An ad for working clothes manufactured by the Alpargatas company—which stressed the quality of its textiles that never shrank—read, "¡No se achique, Don Enrique!" (Don't chicken out, Don Enrique!). The ad played on the rhyme between the man's name and the lunfardo word for "daunt," which is also a slang expression that means "to shrink." The humorous outcome was achieved with the illustration of an old man in outrageously tiny, tightly fit clothes trying in vain to catch a chicken. Images, more than ad copy, were essential to funny ads since they were the detonator of comic effects. This reiterated the predominance of visuals over text that characterized mid-twentieth-century advertisement and, just as significantly, reinforced images as the most successful means to communicate with a mass market enlarged by working-class consumers.[71]

As a mechanism of persuasion, humor in ads was commonly innocuous. Crafty without being offensive and effective without being sophisticated, advertising humor was not aggressive or provocative. It was simple, tongue-in-cheek humor, gentle and sparkling rather than caustic or insolent. Still, the comic effect depended on an element of incongruity that was historically and culturally determined. Ads produced amusement by diverging from expectations; the more they deviated from expectations, the funnier they were. By mocking reality and toying with absurdity, humor offered a safety net that allowed incongruities to be portrayed without openly challenging social expectations. Still, some topics might not have been suitable to sell a product with humor. Ads rarely poked fun at religion, politics, or class relations, topics that were prominently featured in humorous magazines, witty newspaper columns, and comics. In contrast, the most persistent topic in humorous advertisement was gender roles. Ad-makers might have perceived gender relations as a safe theme for mockery—at least for commercial purposes—and as a more appealing topic among women consumers. Funny advertisements certainly offered a more original outline than humorless ads by frequently releasing female characters from traditional household tasks and disassociating the housewife and the pretty, sexy woman.[72]

To this effect, gender humor in ads had a clear set of visual conventions regardless of the goods advertised. Housewives were heavy, bossy, and unattractive; love interests were pretty and sexy; and husbands were frequently at odds with their female counterparts for being too small, too old, or not handsome enough. Male characters generally produced a comic effect, and thus humorous advertisements pivoted on two contrasting views of masculinity. One was embodied in a man determined to make an advance toward attractive women. Ads ridiculed oversexualized, Casanova-like male characters that chased pretty, sexy women who were not their wives and tried to seduce them with childlike, chaste strategies. An ad for Volcán stoves depicted a housewife taking a pudding out of the oven while her husband exclaimed, "¡Qué budín!" (What a pudding!), referring to the cake but also to a woman passerby—*budín* was a common slang word that alluded to a beautiful woman—he could see through the window of his home. Not even within this ingenuous context were female characters allowed to act in a similar fashion. Single female characters did not pursue their love interests; on the contrary, they were seduced by unattractive men who captivated them by buying the advertised product, a common advertising outline for razors and shaving creams.[73]

Notably, ads invited the audience to laugh at circumstances that the media, religious sectors, and social critics attributed to the damaging effects of consumerism and materialism in gender relations, an issue explored in detail in chapter 5. Concerns about a family-life crisis focused on the images of absent housewives out shopping and gold-digging bachelorettes while critics pointed to consumer culture as the culprit for the challenge to domestic bliss. According to this view, with women supposedly distracted from their domestic responsibilities by consumption, men's roles were destined to change. An interpretation of this new form of masculinity characterized the second pattern of humorous ads. These advertisements continued to invert gender expectations but were further based on the derision of male characters. Ad-makers portrayed men as emasculated, subjugated, and miserable, removed from traditional male occupations, and unprepared to fulfill domestic roles. This form of masculinity produced a comic effect most closely connected to the primal instinct of deriving amusement from the weakness and misfortune of others. These emotions, scholars of humor have argued, are linked to a feeling of superiority experienced by witnessing the ridicule of others.[74]

For example, the ad campaign for SIAM washing machines mentioned earlier pivoted on gender role reversal by mocking different working men— an electrician, a mechanic, a carpenter, and others—ridiculously struggling to wash clothes by hand. The ads suggested that husbands were inconsiderate and thoughtless since they would have bought a washing machine before suffering the physical and emotional exhaustion that women experienced as the result of such a grueling task. Similarly, the campaign of Corimayo preserves entitled "Home Sweet Home" showed men doing traditional women's tasks to produce a comic result. The campaign depicted husbands who were stressed, desperate, and worn out from handling different domestic chores while portraying housewives as authoritarian, indolent, or absent. In one ad, a man is clearly repressing his anger as he polishes the floor while his wife threatens him with a rolling pin. In another ad, an irritated husband is trying to give a bottle to a wailing baby while his wife sleeps peacefully. In a third ad, playful kids tie their exasperated father to the living room chandelier. The slogan of the campaign, "There is only one sweet thing in this home," implied that the man of the house, frustrated by housework and children, found relief from the hardships of home life only by eating the brand's jelly. In searching for the right approach to appeal to women consumers, these types of humorous ads became a recurring strategy. Focused on supposed liberation from housework through situations staged as subtle acts of revenge against men, gender humor in advertisement may have produced a potent mix of imaginary relief and empowerment, striking the right cords with the female audience. Still, success in the art of persuasion required even sharper tools, particularly in the late 1940s, when paper shortages struck print advertising.[75]

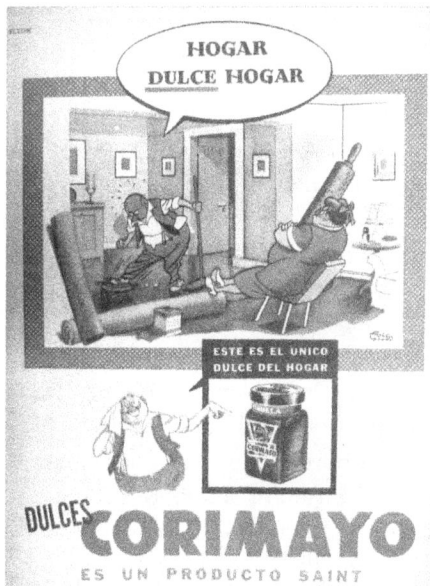

FIGURE 10: Humor in advertising relied on the subversion of traditional gender expectations. *Rico Tipo*, August 5, 1948, back cover.

Outdoor Publicity and the Democratization of Advertising

Paper supply had been problematic since the Second World War, but the shortage and resulting high prices became more acute in the postwar years and extended well into the mid-1950s. In a context in which Argentina needed to invest more foreign currency in supplies to sustain its process of industrialization, several laws decreased expensive paper imports for the print media and limited the number of pages of publications. Because of these measures, several newspapers reduced the size of columns to add one more per page, shrank fonts, altered diagrams, and generally restricted the space devoted to ads. These restrictions posed a serious challenge to the advertising profession. Continuing with a tradition that dated back to the beginning of the century, in the 1940s, manufacturers placed greater emphasis on print ads than on other advertising mediums, including radio, billboards, and direct mail. The preference of print ads was based on the long-standing belief that print advertisement was consistently more effective in attracting consumers and was especially important to obtaining a foothold in the market. Advertisers usually considered that other publicity mediums functioned solely as reminders and were only effective once the product was well known by consumers.[76]

In balancing the limitations in the print media and the preferences of their clients, admen suggested publishing small ads. But the suggestion was not easily accepted, because manufacturers, and even some admen, traditionally believed that larger, more visible ads were more appealing to readers and, consequently, more effective at increasing sales. Giving up on big ads was also difficult for some manufacturers because of a deep-rooted notion that consumers associated big ads with more powerful and reliable companies. As supportive as they were of small ads, admen also had their doubts. Smaller ads were more difficult to design because of the constraints in the length of the copywriting and in the size of drawings and pictures and due to trickier decisions with regard to layout.[77] Furthermore, newspapers reduced the dimensions of their columns, and they all ended up with different sizes. The consequent heterogeneous layouts made the standardization of ads more difficult and required extra work.[78] In spite of these difficulties, the early 1950s witnessed a rise in the publication of smaller ads in which admen compensated for reduced space with eye-catching titles, impressive illustrations, visible logos, regular publication, and systematic campaigns. This trend, rapidly adopted by big, leading companies, especially in the food industry, left a favorable balance for advertising, which reached new levels of creativity.[79]

Apart from the form and content of print ads, the lack of paper contributed to the increase of radio advertisement, which had been growing since the 1930s. In the mid-1930s, Argentina had six hundred thousand radios and ranked first among South American countries with a total of 66 percent of radio receptors in the region. Consequently, its vast influence made radio a traditionally significant advertising channel after newspapers and magazines. In 1933, the two largest advertising agencies in Buenos Aires expended between 20 and 25 percent of the appropriations assigned to them on radio broadcasts. While an estimated half of the hours operated by broadcasting stations were allocated to programs sponsored by businesses, 10 percent of broadcast time was directly devoted to advertising—an important figure considering that 9 percent consisted of theater, 5 percent of news, and almost 2 percent of sports while live and recorded music dominated more than half of broadcast time.[80]

In 1947, around 52 percent of households in the country had a radio, each of which had an average of three listeners. Although radio ads remained significant throughout the 1940s and expanded due to the paper crisis in the early 1950s, the Peronist control over radio contents made advertisement difficult. Some of the radio regulations included the number of advertising words allowed in musical shows and soap operas, the number of times a product could be mentioned, and the number of words permitted—rules that prevented radio publicity from developing more quickly. In the late 1940s, a report by J. Walter Thompson affirmed that regulations made the planning and scheduling of radio advertisement costly and thus less competitive. In addition, many advertisers typically considered radio advertisement as merely a supplement to print ads, a belief based on the premise that "advertising enters through the eyes."[81] This argument was especially persuasive in a country with high rates of literacy and an impressive circulation of magazines and newspapers. Moreover, research suggested that print advertisement was more effective. In 1947, J. Walter Thompson Argentina conducted a survey to identify the best advertising medium to promote toothpaste and concluded that while 75 percent of interviewees recalled hearing ads for the product on the radio, 86 percent remembered seeing ads in magazines and newspapers.[82]

While print advertisement was struggling due to the lack of paper and radio advertisement was growing but remained secondary, there was an impressive rise in street advertising, an alternative that found a unique historical opportunity to fulfill its enormous potential. By the mid-1940s, outdoor displays consisted of an array of billboards that were predominant in big cities and along major roads in the countryside. Displays could be permanently located or changed periodically and included lithographed posters, metal placards, tridimensional boards, electric signs, gigantic hoardings, streetcar and subway cards, lighted billboards, and corner bills. They were positioned in different spots on walls; inside and outside public transportation, subway and railway stations, and stores; or up on buildings. Some of them were affixed to elevated wood and metal structures; others were located on roofs; and several displays were set at the street level. With manufacturers investing more on outdoor advertising, the field became progressively more organized. Professional agencies began to replace "brokers" who had previously controlled the trade and whose only service consisted of managing and selling public spaces to place the signs.[83]

The favorable conditions of development in the mid-twentieth century took the professionalization of outdoor advertising to new heights. From 1945 to 1947, the number of street advertisement companies that operated throughout the country almost doubled. All of them had headquarters in Buenos Aires with branches in the provinces, and one was based in Rosario. With less than a dozen large companies, the field was still small in comparison with print advertising, a fact related to the substantial investment initially required to launch and run this kind of business. After signing agreements with municipal governments and owners to use spaces, outdoor advertising companies leased these locations to advertisers. While some of these companies had permanent staff to design the ads, others hired external admen. In any case, street advertising companies had huge workshops to create and assemble billboards and posters and employed numerous and highly qualified personnel, including sketch artists, photographers, painters, lithographers, electricians, carpenters, and blacksmiths.[84]

An auspicious market, the paper shortage, and the organization and specialization of the trade all played a role in the exponential growth of outdoor publicity. In 1945, advertising yearbook *Síntesis Publicitaria* reported that the biggest outdoor advertising agencies shared more than 9,000 street advertisements nationwide, nearly 2,300 of which were located in the city of Buenos Aires, followed by Rosario, Córdoba, Mendoza, and Tucumán. Two years later, the trade exhibited signs of striking development. Street advertisement had grown to more than 15,000 different types of billboards all over the country, and in 1952, the total number increased to 25,000.

Advertising experts claimed that this number would be higher if the participation of the interior, which lingered behind Buenos Aires, were to increase.[85]

The progress continued throughout the decade in spite of the high prices of street advertisements resulting from costly materials, municipal taxes, qualified specialists and technicians, large workshops, and considerable transportation and installation costs. Regardless of these expenses, several manufacturers like the Coca-Cola Company of Argentina spent more on outdoor displays than on any other form of publicity. The intensive development of the field further undermined the long-established belief among advertisers that street billboards were almost the exclusive domain of cigarettes, beverages, and auto supply companies. In the 1950s, this small list expanded into a large variety of industries, including fish canneries, cosmetic companies, and producers of nylon stockings and household appliances. One major cause for this expansion was that manufacturers began to abandon the common notion that street advertisement was meant to introduce or remind consumers of products and brands. This notion had been linked to the fact that in outdoor publicity, arguments were minimal and images and slogans prevailed. Advertising experts had struggled to convey to advertisers that this did not represent a shortcoming. On the contrary, since billboards had an average of only a few seconds to communicate their message to passersby, the combination of visual accomplishment and a brief written message was key to effectively reaching the audience. Moreover, in terms of their permanence and visibility, outdoor publicity had no competitors. Experts reminded advertisers that posters and displays were "round-the-clock salesmen across the country" working twenty-four hours a day, every day, in plain view of millions of customers.[86]

In 1952, the president of the Argentine Association of Advertising Agencies enthusiastically reflected on this advantage by arguing that "street advertising has proved that it can do much more than introduce a name or a brand: it is also capable of selling it."[87] Much of its sales effectiveness depended on the particularities of the market it served. Street billboards forcefully democratized advertisements while consumer culture was achieving a more inclusive social base. Experts agreed that street displays were the ultimate form of advertising for the masses, a notion that became so persuasive that it was eagerly supported beyond the professional circles and was actively disseminated by the press. For the crowd of working-class consumers who took over the streets, the railway and subway stations, and the parks and squares of major cities, outdoor advertisement

FIGURE 11: The mid-twentieth-century boom in outdoor advertisement transformed the urban landscape. Photo courtesy of Archivo General de la Nación.

had an advantage over print ads in magazines and newspapers: it "was free." In 1952, the owner of one of the biggest street advertisement companies claimed that "a billboard can be seen at any time, in the afternoon and in the morning. It is viewed by the worker, the employee, the student and the housewife, and they see it every time they walk by."[88] With this idea in mind, during the early 1950s, agencies repositioned street advertisements so they could be more easily viewed by pedestrians. Billboards were closer and lower to attract those who walked and relied on public transportation rather than high-income consumers who drove. Simultaneously, street advertisements of auto supplies—one of the main products promoted by these means—diminished considerably while ads for inexpensive and ordinary products with a far vaster market, such as food and textiles, took over the billboards.[89]

As was the case with print ads, some specialists in the field argued that by targeting a popular mass market, the quality and aesthetic value of street advertisements had started to decline. Some voices complained about the artwork, lamenting everything from their lack of detail and the inept choice of colors to inaccurate figure sizes. The director of Eureka, one of the most important street advertising agencies in Argentina and the president of the Association of Street Advertising Agencies, believed that the flourishing conditions for street advertisement had created unprofessional advertising companies that were more eager to make money than a creative contribution. Critics considered that poor artistic standards revealed a gross underestimation of consumers' discern and ability to appreciate ads and that this could eventually hurt the relationship between consumers and brands.[90] Meanwhile, outside the profession, the general public and certain publications joined the disapproving sectors, blaming outdoor publicity for unapologetically "occupying" public spaces and turning cities into "huge magazines of questionable taste." Critics argued that, in contrast to print or radio ads, street advertisement was unavoidable and brutally intrusive, threatening urban landscapes and architecture, surrounding urban dwellers, and "damaging the retina of potential buyers with color, image and the written word."[91] In response to the supposed anarchy of street advertisement denounced by detractors, the national government and several municipal administrations established comprehensive regulations to control the content, dimension, and location of billboards while levying heavy taxes on street advertisement.[92]

Criticism aside, as the perfect sales tool of a socially inclusive consumer culture, outdoor publicity was indisputably linked to the city's identity. Market researchers affirmed that the success of street advertising depended on urbanization and the growth of the urban population. In other words, street advertisement was a true sign of urban development. In this view, outdoor publicity required big, energetic cities to make the most of its potential as a marketing tool. Others took the argument further by pointing out the extreme importance of street advertising as a motor of urbanization. Advertising experts described it as a defining and ubiquitous component of the urban scenery and praised its ability to serve as the ultimate companion of urban dwellers. In 1949, *Mundo Argentino* argued that not only is this advertising essential, it has also become highly useful and entertaining for city dwellers. When someone says that he "is going out for a walk," he knows he won't be alone. He will be accompanied by a series of friends with whom he will have different conversations. Signs and advertisements will demand his attention. Therefore, the pedestrian remembers what has sparked his interest while also enjoying his walk.[93]

No less important than industry, commerce, and internal migration, street advertisement changed the physiognomy of the city and crowned the achievement of modernity.

In a common characterization, advertising is conceived as a distorting mirror that, rather than offering an accurate reflection of the world, alters reality, frequently enhancing it. According to this view, ad creators work on the assumption that most consumers crave images of "life as it ought to be," and thus advertising attempts to engage public aspirations and popular fantasies instead of reality.[94] The use of images of outstanding beauty has been a resilient example of this strategy as characters in ads, and especially female characters, have conventionally been endowed with impressive facial features and body measurements impossible for the audience to obtain. Similarly, mid-twentieth-century ads that portrayed men doing the laundry and wives sleeping soundly while husbands attended to the crying baby, suggesting women's liberation from drudgery through the reversal of traditional gender roles, were idyllic representations rather than the reproduction of current norms of domesticity. Historians of advertising have shown that admen have been particularly inclined to avoid social reality when targeting the upper and middle classes due to the belief that these sectors are more easily attracted by scenes of higher social prominence than by reflections of their lives. Consequently, when selling to high-income consumers, advertisers have tended to follow the "one-step-up-rule," placing their products in upscale settings "a step above" their potential clients and highlighting the achievement of higher status. Thus, in the early twentieth century, refrigerator ads showed them as elegant pieces of furniture surrounded by aristocrats in evening gowns and tuxedos having fun with cocktails in hand.

While in the mid-twentieth-century ads continued to convey a "class image," the content of the image dramatically changed. Naturally, neither wealthy consumers nor high-class goods disappeared. But a new and predominant trend in advertisement began to target the recently economically empowered working-class consumers by employing characters, language, arguments, and advertising mediums that carefully engaged with their needs and characteristics. Advertisement became closer to social reality than it had ever been. Ads continued to be an exercise in cultural interpretation rather than replication, but, driven to sell, ad-makers were required to adapt to the values and expectations of the expansive popular market to successfully accomplish their mission. In so doing, images of workers became predominant in ads, colloquialisms replaced elaborate language, and uncomplicated but concrete contentions substituted lengthy and abstract claims. To further make advertisement accessible and likable, images prevailed over text, "free" outdoor publicity gained unprecedented importance, and humor supplanted the solemnity of the past. Like the consumer market it served, mid-twentieth-century advertisement was fresh and unaffected. And as a commercial fable in tune with the political context, it was imbued with a populist emphasis on "the people" and "the popular" that exalted the worker-consumer as the main protagonist of market culture, subtly echoing the social dichotomization proposed by the Peronist government between the working class and the oligarchy.[95]

At the same time that many celebrated the technical and commercial achievements of mid-twentieth-century national advertising, dissonant voices questioned the quality and the purpose. Critics affirmed that admen, faced with an eager and unsophisticated market, simply suggested products to the consumers and made no efforts to generate needs or develop tastes through innovative appeals. Ventriloquism, critics argued, was not synonymous with creativity; instead, it sounded like demagogy. For others, the debate was less about the properness of jargon and provocative images and more of a general discussion about the definition and aim of advertising. In their desire to characterize their trade as art, the creative elites of advertising confronted the dilemma of the strictly instrumental use of ads to sell goods. Advertisements celebrated for their inventiveness might have had no impact on consumers while ads that successfully appealed to low-income customers could be heavily criticized by advertising experts for being too basic. The dilemma, which was frequent and pervasive among admen around the world, became further complicated in

Argentina because only a decade earlier local admen had often duplicated foreign ads, sparking doubts about the professional honesty and creativity of the country's professionals. Without an easy way out, most local experts agreed on the importance of excellence but highlighted that the true goal of ads was to sell. High-quality advertising that could be placed in art galleries and exhibitions was worthless if it was unable to attract consumers. Experts who endorsed this view believed that those who criticized current copywriting and imagery misunderstood advertising as an end in itself rather than as a means with a clear commercial aim.[96]

Consequently, beyond conceptual and artistic disagreements within the profession, many praised a form of advertising that effectively capitalized on the historical transformations that marked the period. Admen expanded street publicity in line with the explosive urban development, created funny ads in the midst of the commercial boom of comics, and privileged visual appeals to rapidly attract the audience in times in which life had become increasingly hectic. Most importantly, through the billboard for everyone to see, the unadorned message, and the emphasis on quality and low price over prestige, advertising echoed the most noticeable historical changes of all: massiveness and egalitarianism. As some rejected these changes in advertisement, many more resented them in real life.

CHAPTER 4

"How Can a Garbage Collector Be on the Same Level as We Are?"

Upper- and Middle-Class Anxieties over

Working-Class Consumers

A gifted chronicler of the 1930s, the journalist and writer Roberto Arlt contributed an extremely popular column to the daily *El Mundo* in which, with a plainspoken style, he portrayed everyday life in Buenos Aires. In "La tristeza del sábado inglés" ("The Misery of the English Saturday"), Arlt described the weekends of workers as pointless and pathetic, "with no money, no place to go, and no desire to go out." Arlt recounted that

> I was out walking one Saturday . . . when I spotted a worker, stooped shoulders, walking down the sidewalk slowly, on the sunny side of the

street, leading a three-year-old child by the hand. [. . .] Suddenly I had a vision of the rented room where they lived, and the young mother of the child, withered by penury, ironing the ribbons of the little girl's hat. The man walked slowly, sad and bored. Looking at him, I saw the outcome of 20 years inside a sentry box, working 14 hours a day and living on a miserable salary, 20 years of privation, of absurd sacrifice, and the unholy fear of being thrown out onto the street.[1]

For Arlt, the sorrowful worker and his child embodied a gloomy life of exploitation and dissatisfaction, a life without amusement. Life, however, would change for the characters of the story. Almost two decades later, headlines suggested that the penniless boredom and monotony that had characterized the free time of the working-class sectors was a thing of the past. "Buenos Aires has fun," announced *Aquí Está* in a 1947 report on the record-high numbers of spectators of movies, concerts, and sport events; the millions of visitors to zoos, parks, racetracks, and public pools; the animated crowds on streets lined with shops and in restaurants; and the tourists traveling en masse to the beach.[2] The image of vivacious working-class multitudes enjoying their leisure time made a long-lasting impression on historian and journalist Félix Luna, an incisive eyewitness to the mid-twentieth-century transformation. Luna affirmed that high wages "gave people a new and magical purchasing power that was used to acquire many things that had been impossible for them in the past. In many cases, these were unnecessary items: fancy clothes to show off, superfluous or impractical household items, and especially entertainment—entertainment in its myriad forms, from movie theaters to *bailongos* [dance halls]."[3]

The new clothes and the movie tickets that Luna considered superfluous were visible venues of access to mass consumption that gave the Peronist ideal of social justice—solidly grounded in welfare programs— a conspicuous commercial edge. Official propaganda boasted about the good life with statistics that measured happiness through the numbers of suits and tickets to soccer matches that a factory laborer could buy after a day's work.[4] Most significantly, for the first time, a government had recognized that having time and money to devote to recreation and consumption was a legitimate and inalienable right. In 1947, for example, a decree regulating the prices of movie tickets and ordering discounts in movie theaters considered leisure and recreational activities as basic needs and, as such, as indispensable for the well-being of all social classes.[5]

While full employment, minimum wages negotiated through collective agreements, yearly bonuses, and rent freezes made admission to this world of shopping and amusement more affordable, other legal measures ensured workers enough free time. Paid vacations, new public holidays, and the effective observance of the eight-hour working day and the "English Saturday," which let workers out on Saturdays after noon, transformed the working calendar of many occupations, effectively making room for leisure. So much so that industrialists began to complain about the increasing absenteeism of workers who took free days beyond the legally recognized holidays. The practice of the "lunes criollo" (Argentine Monday) became popular among many workers who, according to the business community, took Mondays off after heavy partying over the weekend or because they stayed in recreational facilities outside the city past Sundays.[6]

While absenteeism concerned factory and store owners, the increased participation of workers in consumer culture had broader repercussions among some sectors of the urban upper and middle classes. These sectors encompassed individuals of different levels of affluence and education and commonly involved in nonmanual occupations. This heterogeneous social group included landowners, business proprietors, professionals, university graduates, academics, managers, and housewives who came to perceive the new participation of workers in commercial culture as a threat to their class privileges and identity. Frequently, this assessment had a strong component of anti-Peronism, both from competing political parties and based on personal, noninstitutional stances. Some middle- and upper-class sectors viewed the Peronist government as the promoter of the social and economic transformation that challenged the advantages they had historically enjoyed and as a staunch but manipulative advocate of the *cabecitas negras* (little black heads), a derogatory term commonly equating the working-class migrants from the provinces with Juan Domingo Perón's followers.[7] Although this argument connects the middle and upper classes with anti-Peronism, it does not imply that all members of these sectors were anti-Peronists or that all working-class internal migrants were Peronists. Still, the analysis that follows shows the noticeable correlation between class and political identity. In fact, lending weight to this view, some scholars have highlighted the divisive effects of the Peronist era by suggesting that a self-conscious middle class resulted from the efforts of social sectors who wanted to distance themselves from Peronism.[8]

Yet, the disruptive effects associated with the new worker-consumer exceeded the tensions that grew out of the divisions between Peronists and anti-Peronists. This chapter explores the anxieties of the upper and middle classes when confronted with the new participation of low-income consumers in the urban culture. For those classes, the worker-consumer epitomized a loss of the physical and symbolic monopoly over spaces of consumption and consumer goods they had believed to be for their exclusive enjoyment. Consumption became, then, a site of class conflict over the distribution and appropriation of commodities, spaces, and their meanings. Social mingling with working-class shoppers, diners, and audiences threatened ideals of distinction and social status and provoked bitter accusations of attempted emulation and crass taste. Confronted with a well-dressed worker-consumer enjoying a meal at the same restaurant, the middle sectors particularly resented potential social confusion and feared their own inability to irrefutably assert belonging to their class.

The "Invasion" of Urban Consumer Spaces

In 1947, in a mea culpa for the porteños' conception of the city as "a walled fief," journalist and writer Rodolfo Taboada voiced the frustration of privileged inhabitants of Buenos Aires at the massive arrival of internal migrants looking for work in the booming factories and stores located in and around the city.[9] Taboada explained that "those of us from downtown [Buenos Aires] began to feel as if we were being pushed out. And we began to feel jealous. As if these 'our' streets were being invaded by foreigners. We felt like we were drowning in a human tide that was erasing us from the national map. That we were being diluted in the ever-changing multitude."[10]

The perception of workers as disruptive "invaders" of cities, especially of Buenos Aires, and as social and cultural outsiders, had already surfaced in early interpretations of October 17, 1945, when thousands of people marched on the Plaza de Mayo to demand Perón's freedom after his incarceration by the military regime. Accounts of the historical event, which Peronists canonized as the foundational act of Peronism, stressed how that day the working-class suburbs "had taken" the center.[11] Articulating these feelings, Julio Cortázar's "Casa tomada" ("House Taken Over") (1951) is one of the most striking metaphors of the assault, displacement, and estrangement experienced by the middle and upper classes confronted with the working masses. In the story, unnamed, unseen intruders progressively usurp the home of two upper-class siblings who are finally forced to leave. The brother and sister lose the back of the house first, the library and dining room where they spent most of their time reading, knitting, and indulging in hobbies, the favorite spaces of a leisurely class of landowners. Removed from these quarters, they lock themselves in the front section of the mansion to impede further incursion. But the intruders rapidly move forward into this part of the residence as well, compelling the proprietors to flee and leave their money and precious possessions behind in the seized house. An allegory of upper-class social and spatial dislocation, "Casa tomada" is also a powerful expression of the disorientation of the upper class caught in a historical moment of flux they could not understand or influence.[12]

After the initial confusion and sensation of dispossession of the urban space caused by the founding event of Peronism, the "appropriation" of large cities became massive, continuous, and enduring. During the Peronist administration, Buenos Aires experienced a population boom of enormous proportions, growing from 3,457,000 inhabitants in 1936 to 4,618,000 in 1947. That year, 17 percent of the Argentine population had migrated from the provinces where they were born and 68 percent of these migrants settled in Buenos Aires.[13] Urban elites had found themselves face-to-face with "a foreign and hostile horde" in the past when vast numbers of European immigrants started arriving to the country in the late nineteenth century. Conservative social commentators agreed that this urban crowd of mostly Italian and Spanish origin, which they conceived as a mass of striking workers, anarchists, prostitutes, gamblers, and beggars, was a dangerous source of social disorder, crime, and political unrest. But as alarming as this turn-of-the-century crowd was, it was "contained" in working-class neighborhoods with their run-down *conventillos* (tenements), bordellos, and *boliches* (taverns).[14]

By contrast, for Taboada, as for the mid-twentieth-century upper- and middle-class porteños who lived and worked in the city center, the arrival of internal migrants meant the loss of their previous monopoly over Buenos Aires. The privileged city dwellers were appalled by the "unrecognizable faces" from the suburban neighborhoods that made the "seized city" increasingly impersonal and undecipherable. Feelings of "invasion" and fears of "drowning in a human tide" were more severe on weekends and in the downtown area where the vast majority of theaters, cinemas, department stores, restaurants, cafés, and dance halls were located. Statistics help explain these feelings. In January 1940, for example, theaters and cinemas had a combined audience of 1,607,392 people. Seven years later, monthly audiences reached an impressive 3,147,473 people. In 1952, the average

FIGURE 12: The overcrowded commercial streets of downtown Buenos Aires
reflected the new hectic city life. Photo courtesy of Archivo General
de la Nación.

number of movie theater goers alone was around 4,851,000 people per
month. These numbers illustrate a change that was also affecting boxing
and soccer matches, concerts, horse races, and even the zoo.[15]

While the government and its followers employed these statistics as
a sign of economic prosperity and social bliss, recalcitrant anti-Peronists
severely criticized the patterns of spending of the working classes as a
form of shortsighted and pointless consumption in search of superfluous
joy. In 1950, the editor of the *Atlantic Financial Service* argued in a con-
fidential report that "little of the surplus earning of the workers went into
permanent improvement. Hundreds of millions were lost on racetracks,

in the official casinos and private gambling dens; there appeared almost overnight a multitude of bars and night clubs catering to the taste of the foreman and the typist. . . ."[16] Most detractors abhorred the irresistible attraction that the city, as a locus of plenty and diversion, exerted over multitudes of workers aspiring to a better life. The media made a significant contribution to this process, portraying urban life as exhilarating and prosperous while warning that cities were "baits" that drew in the ingenuous as powerfully and deceptively as siren songs. For residents of small towns in the provinces and the countryside, accounts in the news, government propaganda, and the stories of fellow countrymen who had already moved out transformed the city and particularly Buenos Aires into a "noisy, merry, and tenacious" chimera that, "open to all men of good will, is the paradise of the free."[17]

Beyond tales of naïveté and seduction, most workers carefully assessed what they would gain and lose before moving to the city. In several studies conducted in the late 1950s and early 1960s among migrants who had settled in different shantytowns in Buenos Aires during Peronism, interviewees argued that the lack of well-paid jobs in their places of residence was the first reason to migrate to the metropolis. Laborers expressed that work in the provinces was much more difficult to obtain, less steady, and more strenuous. Because trade union rights were not enforced, hours on the job were harder and longer, especially when performing rural work. In their reasoning, the city was synonymous with more stable jobs and better remuneration, but just as importantly, urban living offered prospects of free time and exciting venues for spending. Indeed, interviewees were vocal about their disappointment with a humdrum existence in their monotonous rural towns and explained how entertainment and consumption had fueled their admiration and craving for urban life. Consequently, it is not surprising that 65 percent of the three hundred interviewees who had moved to Buenos Aires from the western province of La Rioja named the movies as their most frequent form of entertainment.[18]

While working-class consumers were enjoying their shopping and recreational excursions, everyday life became increasingly more inconvenient, chaotic, unpredictable, and disorganized for the traditional privileged urban dwellers. Long waits became common at restaurants, cafés, movie theaters, and stores; there were endless lines to get into jam-packed subways, trains, and buses; and parks and public swimming pools were overcrowded. In addition to congested streets, dangerous traffic, and mobbed sidewalks, food shortages and rising prices also characterized mid-twentieth-century

FIGURE 13: While detractors criticized popular patterns of spending, workers had fun in dance halls and other entertainment venues. Photo courtesy of Archivo General de la Nación.

Argentine cities, especially Buenos Aires. In 1946, the magazine *Mucho Gusto* aptly titled one of the numerous articles reporting on the new problems of overcrowded city life "Buenos Aires: The City of Inhabitants Waiting In Line."[19] Frantic rhythms and congestion deeply permeated all forms of perception of the metropolis. In the 1940s and 1950s, for example, movie directors began to focus on the city streets, looking to realistically depict the hustle and bustle of urban living. Films from this period portrayed the frenzied movement of masses of people and means of transport with visual and sound techniques that conveyed a profound sense of instability and anxiety.[20]

Audiences surely experienced such feelings when stepping into the streets after an afternoon at the movies. Nervousness and unrest infused the account of a contributor to the magazine *Rico Tipo* who comically described a Saturday night in Buenos Aires as "the porteño's martyrdom." Humor, however, cannot disguise the critical commentary on a new form of urban existence characterized by stress, competition, and dissatisfaction. The hassle started just after arriving to a movie theater in the downtown area when "you dive heroically into the stormy human sea that swells in its struggle to buy tickets at the box office. You push, pull, attack, defend yourself, grunt, sweat, advance, swear, fight, make yourself thinner, squeeze in, and you're there! And when you get there, the show is sold out." A generous bribe could barely buy the worst seat in the theater for a film that had already started. Annoyed, the porteño left the movies to "go on a pilgrimage" that involved fighting for room on the sidewalks, visiting dozens of restaurants with no tables, and after finally finding a table, leaving hungry because the waiter announced that the restaurant was closing for the night. Finally, the last stop on "the Saturday calvary" was the subway station where you "pray to the Gods that they blow the winds in your favor so that the subway door opens right where you are standing; otherwise you will be mashed into purée and you may even lose your wife and have to go to the lost-and-found department at the police station to pick her up."[21]

Generally, frustration over the growing inconveniences of urban life took on a less humorous tone. Criticism ranged from candid requests for rural workers to stay in the countryside to serious warnings against the misleading fantasy of "an easy urban life." Some observers stressed that for migrants, coming to the cities entailed a profound deterioration of their standard of living, especially due to higher prices, decrepit and insufficient housing, and increasingly inadequate urban infrastructure. But the same observers affirmed that these aggravations were well masked by the cheap and futile amusements of mass culture. This argument was largely based on an idealization of country life as a wholesome existence free of dangers and troubles, an argument that emphasized an unrealistic freedom of rural dwellers and a naïve version of their communion with nature. In 1952, an expert on agrarian issues and former congressman for the Socialist Party offered an example of this reasoning when he affirmed that

> good salaries conceal difficulties. The noise, the lights, and the fun round off the picture. The rural worker and the son of peasants who have joined the urban masses have unquestionably relegated freedom of movement, space and air, but this doesn't matter to them: they are earning more, they are swept up into the jovial atmosphere of the bars and bask in the sensuality of easy amusements.[22]

Some critics of internal migration and the subsequent uncontrolled process of urbanization, pointed particularly to women as the true "enemies" of life in the countryside. Critics who stereotyped young, poor rural women as materialistic and childlike argued that, eager to escape the countryside, these women dreamed of dance halls and the latest fashions and believed that work in the fields threatened femininity and coquetry. For rural women, detractors affirmed, the city was the place to become "modern ladies" and lead a life of material comfort, beauty, and excitement—a plot line that became popular in explaining the arrival of Eva Perón to Buenos Aires from the countryside to become an actress. Some social commentators maintained that in order to follow their dreams, women left for the city alone or, even worse, fueled desires of city life among entire families, pressuring their parents and husbands to move to the cities with them. But making dreams come true was tricky. Escaping from a life of boredom, a young woman from San Pedro, a small town in Buenos Aires Province, left her family and her job at an orchard to make her fantasies of strolls down elegant city avenues donned in beautiful dresses come true. The journalist who covered the story informed that strolls and dresses aside, the woman had ultimately traded the "paradisiacal" countryside to work as a housemaid in Buenos Aires. The reporter concluded that the young woman had paradoxically succeeded in achieving the reverse of a famous children story. In this case, the princess became Cinderella.[23]

Critics went from aggressively blaming "indolent," "naïf," and "ambitious" working-class migrants for the mounting hardships of city life and for the adversities they brought upon themselves, to identifying the Peronist administration as the true culprit. In fact, anti-Peronists, from socialists and communists to conservatives, charged the government with a poorly planned process of industrialization and urbanization that had serious economic and social consequences for the whole country. Rather than improving the living and working conditions in rural areas, detractors maintained, the government had exaggerated the appeal of the city and the factory, thus encouraging a massive human exodus and sparking a severe crisis in agricultural production. While some opponents downplayed the new benefits for workers, arguing they had traded their freedom for "a dish of lentils," most affirmed that cheap gadgets and amusements only concealed the rising prices of essential goods. Similarly, others pointed to certain aspects of the new participation of workers in the mass consumer culture as a true sign of the overall decline in urban living conditions. Former U.S. Ambassador James Bruce asserted that masses of workers flooded the movies, clubs, and cafés for reasons other than higher wages. Customers and audiences, Bruce affirmed, were escaping the terrible housing they endured in Buenos Aires by taking refuge in public and commercial spaces.[24]

Beyond the differences in their interpretation, critics agreed that the hectic new urban life deeply changed the spirit of both new migrants and long-established city dwellers. For the socialist newspaper *Nuevas Bases*, "this population has become a mass that does not hear or see or feel; it lives beneath the crushing weight of countless inconveniences and difficulties, risking at every turn its physical integrity and chipping away at its spiritual life."[25] Public transportation adequately illustrates how the political opposition used everyday aspects of city life as examples of deteriorated urban living, causes for the wave of socially unacceptable conduct, and finally, proof of the state's incompetence to deal with an unrestrained process of urban growth. In opposition to the Peronist government's claims that it had significantly increased the number of buses, subways, and trains serving major cities and that Argentina had the most inexpensive public transportation system in the world, the Socialist Party argued that prices were exorbitant, fleets were ramshackle, and service and schedules were appalling.[26] Socialists declared that public transportation was "terribly insufficient," forcing people to travel in worse conditions than animals, risking their lives crammed in ancient train cars or hanging from doors and steps. Women bore the worst, suffering from unsolicited flirtations and pawing. Massiveness and impersonality encouraged violence, individualism, and selfishness to the detriment of consideration and good manners. A reporter expressed his dismay at the common sight of avalanches of desperate people violently knocking down women, children, and the elderly to get on the bus or train. The author complained that "the elbow has replaced gentility and the vigor of physical strength has superseded the gallantry that is the trademark of those born into good families."[27]

Still, for the upper and middle classes, the effects of the "invasion" further exceeded the new structural inconveniences of urban life. The new mass market ended the privileged treatment that well-off consumers had traditionally enjoyed. Now, these sectors complained, they had become victims of the unpunished irreverence and disrespect of the social class that was expected to act deferentially and attend to them subserviently. Reynaldo Pastor, a conservative congressman for the National Democratic Party, argued that

> in the deepest depths of Peronism, arrogance, vulgarity and overconfidence extended the same way an oil stain spreads across a marble shelf. A wave of misconduct and brutality covered even the most remote locations of the country, with no respect for morals and no chance to stop it. Field hands, maids, delivery boys, taxi drivers,

streetcar guards, telephone operators, government employees and shop and factory workers in both large and small cities acted with unheard-of haughtiness and insolence; their language was uncouth, their gestures awkward, unfriendly and arrogant.[28]

According to this view, upper- and middle-class customers and passengers became a group "humiliated, jeered, demeaned, begging instead of ordering, smiling at those who had always smiled at them."[29] Socially perceived as the quintessential male cabecitas negras, waiters as well as streetcar, bus, and train conductors especially attracted public attention, followed by barbers, doormen, and newspaper boys. The media covered recurring episodes of vulgarity and rudeness that involved yelling at passengers, using coarse language, addressing customers as *vos* (informal "you") instead of the formal *usted*, and harassing women. In 1948, an *El Mundo* reporter denounced the terrible service in well-known city restaurants where waiters were oblivious to the requests of the customers and even pretended not to hear or see them while diners waited endlessly for them to come to the table. The reporter affirmed that when patrons had complained about the poor service, unabashed waiters had on several occasions hurled insults at them in the middle of the salon.[30] Class politics were clearly at work in arguments about how the government was controlling, persecuting, and even incarcerating store owners for charging high prices while the store employees who abused the public in "moral" and economic ways went unpunished. Stories about customers who discovered that waiters had deliberately overcharged them and bus drivers had cheated them with the change circulated widely, intensifying the tales of distress suffered by upper- and middle-class consumers by adding dishonesty to discourtesy.[31]

The Specter of Interclass Mingling

However, middle- and upper-class consumers resented something more than these episodes of mistreatment and cheating. Working-class consumers had obtained unrestricted access to spaces of consumption that the well-off had previously experienced as socially homogenous and exclusive realms. Exhibiting unprecedented class diversity, those spaces "forced" the middle and upper classes to social mingling with consumers of lower social status. While mass consumer culture was the scenario upon which the government staged the democratization of goods and entertainment, and ultimately working-class well-being, it was also a site of class tensions and upper- and middle-class resentment. Teobaldo Altamiranda recalled that when he was working as a technician at the airbase of El Palomar, an upset captain told him he could not believe he had seen the airbase garbage collector at the prestigious Opera movie theater in downtown Buenos Aires. The captain felt insulted by a form of "class promiscuity" that he equated with the imposition of social disorder. When Altamiranda told him he was glad that a humble worker could enjoy a night at the movies like they both did, the captain exclaimed: "But don't you get it? How can a garbage collector be on the same level as we are? The Peronists are going to drive us into anarchy."[32]

Anecdotes like Altamiranda's became recurring conventions both in the mid-twentieth-century imaginary and later in historical memory, and, as such, they adopted a formulaic mode centered on distressed middle- or upper-class characters and "out-of-place" working-class counterparts. In Julio Cortázar's short story "La banda" ("The Band") (1956), the middle-class main character who enters a prestigious downtown movie theater to see an Anatole Litvak film ends up attending an odd performance of an all-female working-class band. The man senses that "something was not right" and realizes that he is surrounded by a working-class audience that was unsuitably dressed and misbehaved, an audience of "people who were not in their place."[33]

The downtown movie theater was a setting used time and again to portray the class bitterness and confusion sparked by the new social makeup of commercial culture because working-class audiences had traditionally been absent from these sites. The movies had been a popular source of entertainment for workers as early as the mid-1920s, and consequently, working-class neighborhoods like Pompeya and La Boca in Buenos Aires had their own movie theaters. Here, spectators were entitled to a program of three to five Argentine, Spanish, and Mexican films for the relatively low cost of a single ticket. But downtown movie theaters, mostly housed in magnificent buildings, were of a different kind. Tickets were more expensive and programs regularly featured subtitled Hollywood films.[34] Besides the economic and cultural impediments, prejudice and discrimination closed the doors to the working poor, thus maintaining these spaces as the exclusive realm of the privileged. Hipólito J. Paz, foreign minister during Perón's administration, witnessed a paradigmatic episode of exclusion when he was waiting to enter the prestigious Petit Splendid movie house in the exclusive neighborhood of Barrio Norte in Buenos Aires one afternoon in the early 1930s. Paz remembered that it was Sunday and we were waiting in front of the box office for Mr. Chaparra to see us. Just then a dark-skinned girl with jet black hair and a plain dress came up and asked for a ticket. Initially, Mr. Chaparra ignored her. The other people waiting had heard her, which made her even more embarrassed, but she was determined to get her ticket and she raised her voice and asked again. She opened her purse, counted her pesos and extended her hand to pay for the ticket. This time, the box office manager's usual smile disappeared and he feigned surprise. He looked her up and down and emphasized each and every word when he said, "I'm sorry, this show is by invitation only." She got the message and left, looking sad.[35]

Working-class movie goers like this young woman had to wait over a decade to witness the lifting of the barriers that had prevented them from entering the Petit Splendid. While rejecting social discrimination and enthroning the worker as the protagonist of the new era of social justice, the government decreed a reduction of ticket prices all over the country, including downtown Buenos Aires, supported the production of national cinema, and encouraged and monitored the screening of Argentine feature films at all movie theaters. In these scenarios, workers and the privileged reenacted the theme of invasion that, humorously portrayed in "the porteño's martyrdom" and reaffirmed in stories such as Cortázar's and Altamiranda's, exposed a profound sense of dislocation and usurpation among the well-off sectors. Lawyer Luis Sobrino Aranda remembered that high-class ladies considered the presence of working-class women in the elegant movie theaters of downtown Buenos Aires an "absurdity." The women complained with despair, "How can this *chirusa de miércole* (low-class girl) be at our movie theater!"[36]

Mar del Plata, the traditional tourist bastion of the national elites, further illustrates the sense of lost exclusivity. In the 1930s, Mar del Plata had been synonymous with refinement and lineage, the stomping grounds of prominent families and of the middle classes that had gained access to the beach city in the 1920s. In 1930, a local publication highlighted the illustrious pedigree of Mar del Plata by asserting that the city "was founded by a society that dates back to the noble, law-abiding patricians, those with shiny coats of arms whose aristocratic, heraldic past they uphold with gallantry [. . .]; chic, grace, and talent all converge to make this beach a legendary place."[37] By the early 1950s, Mar del Plata had lost its aristocratic aura to become the most popular destination for hundreds of thousands of workers who had never seen the ocean or left their home town for a vacation before. While the city had welcomed 380,000 tourists in the summer of 1940, it witnessed the arrival of one million people in 1950 and 1.4 million five years later.[38] Besides the annual paid vacations, the Peronist government actively introduced numerous reforms aimed at transforming Mar del Plata into "the reflection of Argentina's social democracy."[39] The federal and provincial government built new hotels, expropriated or nationalized existing ones, assisted labor unions in the construction and administration of their own hotels for workers, set affordable transportation tariffs and hotel rates, enhanced the bus and railway systems reaching the coast, and launched programs where tourists paid for transportation and the government covered the lodging expenses. These measures, among others, turned Mar del Plata into "a modern Babylonia, where the rich mingle with the poor."[40]

FIGURE 14: Mar del Plata became a popular destination for working-class tourists. Photo courtesy of Archivo General de la Nación.

To claims of interclass mingling, the Peronist government conveniently added a more radical version that emphasized the almost complete dislodgment of the privileged sectors from the city. In tune with this version, in the inauguration of the International Film Festival of Mar del Plata in 1954, Perón declared that "ten years ago, I visited Mar del Plata and at that time, it was a place of privilege, where wealthy Argentines came to take time off from the leisurely lives they led during the year. [. . .] Today we could say that 90 percent of those who vacation in this marvelous city are workers from across the country."[41] The opening of a center of working-class culture at the well-known Normandie Restaurant in Playa Grande, the most exclusive beach in the city since the 1930s, reinforced the efforts of the government to overtly challenge the past. Playa Grande had a compelling symbolism as the area where the richest visitors moved in the 1930s to escape Playa Bristol, the section that the middle-class tourists had progressively occupied upon their initial arrival into the city a decade earlier. During the Peronist years, Normandie, a former venue of elite socialization, became a tourist club that screened movies, organized dance balls, and staged plays for workers.

Most celebrated these changes, but others looked back with nostalgia at the times when the city had been the privilege of a selected few. In 1947, the author of an editorial published in newspaper *La Prensa* contrasted the happiness of downtown merchants at the amazing increase in sales to avid working-class tourists to the sadness he and his friends felt at the absence, on the same commercial streets, of prestigious people who had bestowed upon Mar del Plata its traditional aristocratic status.[42] The Peronist media responded to these types of arguments by ridiculing the upper classes as spiteful and bitter: "'They're going to Mar del Plata?'—exclaim, scandalized, those who feel that the privilege that has allowed them to enjoy the crystalline shine of the great beach resort is slipping away from them."[43]

In spite of representations of Mar del Plata as a modern Babylonia and the displacement of upper-class visitors, the privileged classes still retained a firm monopoly over the exclusive and expensive clubs, associations, restaurants, stores, and neighborhoods that remained beyond the reach of working-class patrons. In fact, the elites continued to vacation in Mar del Plata but left the downtown area to build their summer homes in the more secluded Los Troncos neighborhood.[44] Beaches continued to have their social standing and unwritten rules of etiquettes. For former U.S. Ambassador James Bruce, Playa Grande remained the ambit of the elites where "even the location of your rented beach cabaña, replete with little wicker chairs, brass-name plate and dressing room, is as much a symbol of acceptance as a listing in the *Social Register*. Placement, in fact, is in hands of a director who has charge of the same protocol for the swank Opera Colón in Buenos Aires."[45]

In the end, whether the upper classes shared the beach with the workers is less intriguing than the fact that in the upper-class imagination as well as in the Peronist imaginary, the workers in Mar del Plata represented an erosion of a past order in which the working poor had only crossed paths with the privileged to serve them. In the imagined new order, by contrast, the low-income patrons, tourists, and spectators challenged the de facto separation of class-based spheres of consumption. Moreover, for middle and upper sectors, this challenge further entailed the decay of those spheres. This transpires in the testimonies of members of the elites that Northwestern University professor of political science George Blanksten collected while conducting field work in early 1950s Argentina. His affluent acquaintances told Blanksten that "now *everybody* has money, and that is bad. *Everybody* can now go to the opera, the night clubs, the fine restaurants. But the new people who go there degrade these places—they do not know how to dress properly, they do not know how to behave in these elegant places."[46]

Commercial streets and department stores were common settings in these types of arguments in which working-class consumers "contaminated" what had once been distinguished spaces. A longtime resident of Buenos Aires remembered that in the 1930s, Florida Street had been "the sweetheart of Buenos Aires, always dressed to the tee and bejeweled with the very best you could imagine."[47] Similarly, as chapter 6 shows in detail, numerous interviewees from Rosario remembered that in the 1930s, working-class consumers bought clothing and home products in small and inexpensive stores in their neighborhoods and refrained from visiting big department stores located in the upscale downtown area and on Córdoba Street. Workers avoided retailers like Gath & Chaves not only because they could not afford the expensive and fashionable textiles and home goods, but also because salesmen mistreated them. Sometimes, store managers even denied working-class customers entrance to the sumptuous shops.

By the 1950s, portrayals of the traditional epitomes of high-class fashion and upscale businesses had changed drastically, focusing on the increasing "vulgarization" of the famous commercial streets. In a cartoon, two gentlemen strolling down Florida comment, "And we porteños can be proud of how chic this street is," while surrounded by boisterous and shabby street vendors selling foodstuffs like cheese and bananas. In another cartoon, a woman tells her friend, "I have always loved shopping on Florida Street. It's so elegant!" while she buys a cheap hairnet from a scruffy street vendor.[48] According to working-class interviewees, high wages rightfully opened the doors of previously exclusive department stores to low-income sectors. While the beneficiaries of the new economic inclusion praised it as a form of market democratization, others lamented that the times when the patrons were "upstanding people" were gone. With the new consumers, the argument went, "the level of the clientele plummeted."[49]

Some observers feared that in addition to the social dynamics taking place in department stores, movie theaters, and tourist towns, lower-class values and aesthetics were rapidly spreading throughout society with far more dangerous consequences.[50] Just as the working sectors were gaining new cultural visibility and recognition as important actors on the consumer market, the upper classes retreated from the public realm. In the context of a government that had made the oligarchy its designated enemy and held it responsible for the country's historic poverty and exploitation, a well-known publication that covered high-class social events claimed that the rich "work hard at mimicry and try to lose themselves in the drab of the multitudes; they prefer to remain unnoticed and aspire to being ignored."[51] For observers who believed that the elites had abandoned their place at the social and cultural forefront, the popular crowd was imposing a downgraded standardization of culture on the rest of society. In an alarming tone, some denounced that all sectors of society were now listening to the music the lower classes listened to and talking the way they did. Similarly, a journalist complained that "the book that everyone now carries is not the one previously read by a select minority, but that generically written for doormen."[52]

This sense of social confusion is ridiculed in a cartoon in the humorous Peronist magazine *Descamisada* that shows an elegant restaurant in which two men dressed in working clothes are happily toasting. At a nearby table, two angry, well-dressed, and heavyset men stare hatefully at the workers. One of the bitter patrons says to his companion: "Have you seen, Mr. Chanchiz [a deformation of *chancho* (pig)], what this dictatorship is doing? Right there at the next table, the riffraff, drinking sparkling wine! And then they deny that they're fascists!"[53] The cartoon mocks the elite's accusation of the Peronist government as an authoritarian regime by showing that the allegation was actually a strategy to oppose the social egalitarianism attained through equal participation in the consumer market. It suggests that one logical aspect of a more egalitarian society was the blurring of fixed class identities and, consequently, the resentment of the upper classes. If they sat side by side at the same restaurant and enjoyed the same wine, how could the well-off clearly differentiate themselves from working-class consumers?

Who's Who? Middle-Class Insecurities and the Assertion of Class

In an article about how workers were now enjoying excursions to parks and the countryside on the weekends, *Mundo Peronista* informed that "it has now become difficult to know the social class of those who head out with picnic baskets on Sunday morning."[54] The alleged difficulty in distinguishing among members of different social classes represented a striking change from the early decades of the century, when unambiguous indicators of class identity made it easy to distinguish among people. Most of these indicators belonged to the realm of consumption, ranging from access to movie theaters and beach resorts to the display of mass-produced goods. Among these, clothing played a prominent role as a code that visibly denoted union and uniformity among members of the same class and the exclusion of all others.[55] Peronist union leader Angel Perelman recalled that in the early 1940s "at dusk, on Callao Street, Avenida de Mayo and other downtown streets, people were divided into two social classes that were easily differentiated: those who walked along the street in a shirt and those who watched from the sidewalk in full suits. The latter were fewer, the representatives of the oligarchy and the middle class."[56]

For Peronists and anti-Peronists alike, dress became one of the earliest and strongest elements in the construction of a distinctive class and political identity and a fundamental component of stereotypes. After Peronists took the streets shouting, "Alpargatas, yes! Books, no!" the espadrille became an enduring symbol of Perón's sympathizers.[57] Peronists appropriated the alpargatas from *lencinismo*, a populist movement in the province of Mendoza that had employed this footwear as an emblem of its humble constituency. Traditionally linked to rural inhabitants, the inexpensive rope-soled canvas shoe came to represent the urban industrial worker, the rural laborer, and the poor. After October 1945, it also symbolized the

Peronist working-class migrant. This is apparent in an anonymous anti-Peronist pamphlet mocking an invitation to a Peronist rally whose only requirements for attendance were "alpargatas, a loud voice, and plenty of sweat."[58] Peronists, for their part, marched on the streets singing, "No top hat and no cane, we're Perón's boys all the way!" The chant targeted the *galeritas*, as Peronists called the opposition in allusion to the top hat, a turn-of-the-century symbol of social prestige.[59]

Still, descamisado (shirtless) was the term that most perfectly expressed the conjunction between dress and political and class identity. Although descamisado applied to both men and women, and anti-Peronists and Peronists occasionally used it as a feminine noun, it refers to a masculine stylistic characteristic, an unbuttoned shirt with sleeves rolled up.[60] The *New York Times* correspondent in Buenos Aires offered an archetypical description of the descamisados: "Judging from the appearance of the crowds that turned out for Perón, his appeal seems to be mainly to the humblest and poorest strata of the population. They almost invariably were hatless, coatless and tieless . . ."[61] Socialist and conservative newspapers used descamisado early on in their accounts of October 17, 1945, to disdainfully refer to Perón's followers congregated in the Plaza de Mayo. For socialists and conservatives, the term was ideologically close to the Blackshirts, Benito Mussolini's paramilitary groups. More generally, the opposition employed descamisado to criticize and mock workers who walked around downtown without a jacket, a violation of a consuetudinary norm of fashion that was also legally enforced. In fact, Buenos Aires had a municipal bylaw that mandated wearing a jacket in public places.[62] Some anti-Peronist representations took the aesthetic characterization well beyond the lack of jacket by emphasizing the miserable and filthy aspect of Perón's supporters. The identification between Perón's working-class sympathizers and scruffiness was so pervasive that the socialist newspaper *La Vanguardia* reported that Peronists insulted and laughed at men who wore polished shoes and clean shirts.[63]

For Peronism, descamisado gave the newborn political movement a name that unintentionally resembled the French *sans-culottes*, the most powerful icon of republicanism, egalitarianism, and popular political extremism. Like its opponents, Peronists also emphasized the shabbiness of Perón's followers who congregated in the Plaza de Mayo while in other instances, Peronist accounts portrayed men in work uniforms. This reaffirmation of working-class identity contradicted claims that Perón represented "the lumpenproletariat" or "the scum of society," an underclass of beggars, gangsters, the unemployed, crooks, and petty criminals.[64]

Despite the sudden popularity of the descamisado, numerous accounts, photographs, and personal testimonies suggest that the great majority of workers did wear jackets at that time. The three young men soaking their feet in a fountain in the Plaza de Mayo, who were immortalized in the most well-known photograph of October 17, might have given the elite reason to claim that Peronists were ill-mannered, but they were certainly wearing suits. In 1996, one of those three workers, Celso Pivida, who had been a twenty-year-old union delegate at a wool factory in 1945, remembered that "back then, people from Greater Buenos Aires who went into the city put on a jacket and tie; otherwise, they were considered riffraff. In fact, that day I went home to change because I had my work clothes on."[65] Corroborating this view, an American reporter argued that on the streets of Buenos Aires, even the newspaper vendors wore ironed suits, clean shirts, and sometimes even ties. He explained that the heat of summer made no difference—men walking around in shirt-sleeve or with an unbuttoned collar were still a rare sight.[66]

Whether or not working-class men wore jackets in public is anecdotic. What makes the anecdote significant is that Peronists and anti-Peronists alike chose the "people in rags" to construct the figure of the suffering and underprivileged worker on the one hand, and the stereotype of the brutish and uncultured working-class Peronist on the other. For the elite, what Peronists wore defined them as poor and vulgar. The attire of the descamisado revealed Peronists' cultural inability to follow the rules of etiquette, suggesting their problematic adaptation to the urban space and exposing their uncouth tastes. In Peronist accounts, by contrast, worn-out dress was proof of the poverty and marginalization endured by workers in the past. Written after 1945, these descriptions were perfectly in tune with the official propaganda that argued how in the "New Argentina," good salaries allowed people to buy new and good-quality clothes frequently. In one of Perón's typical overstatements, he argued that meatpacking workers now showed up to meetings in elegant silk shirts whereas before 1943 they had come to see him poorly dressed and wearing alpargatas.[67] In these interpretations, clothing had been an indicator that made classes recognizable and easy to classify. In other words, people dressed according to the expectations for their social class. For Peronists, clothing was evidence of the social inequality they wanted to eradicate. For the privileged anti-Peronists, clothing represented order, safety, and cultural intelligibility. In 1946, for example, anti-Peronists in charge of polling places did not let men dressed in shirt-sleeve vote because they thought that such attire was evidence of their political sympathies. Tangible style was considered a clear symbol of status that unmistakably conveyed to others what one did for a living and one's political affiliation.[68]

But the new access of low-income consumers to dress changed this perception and inspired hostile feelings. With the new participation of working-class sectors in the consumer market, the descamisado went from being "the ragged poor" to "the well-dressed worker." Thus appearance became a less reliable sign of class identity and more an artifice for disguise, questioning the role of dress to authenticate social status. Comments such as "At a glance, who could tell who is the rich girl and who is the simple worker?" in the fashion section of a magazine not only revealed the improvement of the working-class standard of living, but also hinted at the demise of middle- and upper-class status.[69] This perception of fading visible class distinctions grew palpably in a context of increasing consumer homogeneity. In 1947, a market survey concluded that there was no significant difference in the companies, trademarks, and market products preferred by consumers from different income segments. With higher wages, advertising agents believed, access to many consumer goods—garments included— had also been democratized.[70] With a wink to readers, the magazine *Rico Tipo* echoed the perception of social leveling in a cartoon where two gentlemen in tuxedos admire an elegantly dressed young woman. One of the men exclaims: "What an elegant girl! Imagine what she spent on that dress!" The friend answers: "Oh, nothing at all! Her maid lent it to her!"[71]

In numerous interviews with Peronists and anti-Peronists, middle- and working-class individuals, and members of the elites, the story of the domestic servant who dressed as nicely as her employer is by far the most pervasive example of growing social equality in mid-twentieth-century Argentina.[72] For this reason, the story is also the most powerful index of class tensions born out of a new socially inclusive consumer culture. Given that, as Pierre Bourdieu has shown in his sociological study of taste, "social identity is defined and affirmed in a field of difference," the risk of wearing attire similar to blue-collar workers provoked acute anxieties among the middle classes.[73] Indeed, the duet of maid and mistress represent one of the most extreme cases of social polarization in which low-income women live "in the shadows of affluence." For their part, for most upper- and middle-class women in Latin America, the relationship with a domestic servant was the closest association they had with people of a lower class.[74]

But in the story of the well-groomed maid, the absence of a uniform and her access to the same dress her mistress would wear allegedly reduce the possibility of distinguishing class division. In contrast to the recent past, consumer goods were ineffective in communicating definite social rank and drawing clear boundaries between different income sectors. Violeta Benvenuto, a young militant in the Women's Peronist Party in the 1950s, told me that "the hatred of the oligarchs was very profound. For example, I had an aunt who was very anti-Peronist and I said to her: Auntie, why are you so anti-Peronist? And she answered: Because my maid dresses just like I do."[75] The anecdote recycles a popular belief about feminine concern with clothing and appearance as constituent of women's identity, but most significantly, it illustrates the social perception that the middle classes had lost a traditional sign of prestige and, as a consequence, fervently opposed the Peronist government as the culprit in the new social and economic entitlement of the working sectors.

According to this view, in an extraordinary reversal of social mechanisms, the middle classes struggled to keep up with workers. In *Clase Media*, a theatrical play from 1949 about an impoverished middle-class family, Elvira, the mother, is an anti-Peronist obsessed with advancing the family's social status. Elvira responds to her mother's accusations that the granddaughters were absurdly spending money on clothes when the family had more urgent needs by saying: "Well, what do you expect the poor girls to wear? Nowadays anyone has a fur coat, even the cooks."[76] Reinforcing this imagery, foreign visitors declared they were stunned to see that housemaids spent as much time as their mistresses in beauty parlors and thus "when they serve the table at dinner their coiffures may be as elaborate and shining as the sculptured heads of the guests." Some went as far as to affirm that, judging by the pancake makeup, powder, rouge, and mascara that even the humblest women applied to their faces, the entire female population of Buenos Aires seemed made up of actresses.[77] This representation of working-class women as fashion icons offered a striking contrast with common characterizations circulating in the press, literature, investigative writing, and tango lyrics in the previous decades. Back then, "emaciated, distressed, and disheartened" working women had exploitation marked all over their bodies. With no mention of fine dresses, fruity hues, and hairdos from the salon, early twentieth-century portrayals of women from the low-income sectors exposed lives of disease, backbreaking work, and extreme privation.[78]

The figure of "the maid dressed like us" further conveyed the decline of the middle sectors in a stereotypical argument that, very popular at the time, portrayed domestic workers as one of the major causes of the economic deterioration of middle-class families. The argument was based on the widespread and exaggerated view that domestic service was highly overpaid due to the growing number of women unwilling to do the job and who were turning to the secondary and tertiary sectors for employment. In contrast to housekeeping, these occupations promised higher pay, more stability, and brighter prospects for occupational development.[79] Evidence of the preoccupation with domestic workers is clear in an editorial in the posh magazine *Atlántida* that pointed to the high wages of maids as one of the most serious preoccupations among Argentina's middle-class families in 1951. Giving credence to the view that the incomes of housekeepers were exorbitant, a persistent rumor among the middle classes was that cooks and maids could amass a small fortune over a few years. These women were so affluent—the story went—that they became the easy prey of suitors of questionable reputation. Con men enticed these "ladies of fortune" with promises of eternal love and marriage only to escape with their savings.[80]

Beyond overstatements and rumors, many complained about the high wages of domestic personnel that forced employers to spend more on domestic help and less on clothing, recreation, and other extras that denoted the family's well-being and status.[81] Economic constraints notwithstanding, most middle-class homes did not consider the possibility of renouncing the maid, one of the most powerful symbols of class distinction. Ridiculing this dependency on domestic workers, one cartoon in a series dedicated to housekeepers published in the magazine *Rico Tipo* shows a father who is about to stab himself, a mother on the verge of drinking poison, and their son ready to hit his head with a hammer while a bomb is set to explode. The maid emphatically yells, "Don't you threaten me! I'm quitting. Enough is enough!"[82]

High wages only partly explained new dresses for maids and fewer dresses for mistresses in the middle-class imagination. While living in Argentina, American journalist Ruth Greenup and her husband hired a housekeeper named Lita. Greenup was surprised when Lita bought a new pair of shoes after her first week of work, gloves and hose the second week, and a blouse the third. Greenup noticed that Lita made a weekly visit to the beauty parlor where she had her hair curled and her nails manicured.

After a month, Lita had bought a radio and put on silk stockings every night when she served the table. When Greenup related the events to an Argentine friend, the woman, seasoned in matters of housemaids, immediately asked Greenup how much money she had been giving Lita for staples like eggs and meat. It turned out that Greenup was paying way too much for food and Lita was using a trick commonly employed by maids at that time. Domestic workers struck agreements with butchers, dairymen, and shopkeepers, bringing them the business of the household in return for a 10 percent "cut" that provided the women with extra money for shoes, silk stockings, and manicured nails. Greenup never confronted Lita, and after trying unsuccessfully to track her spending, she decided to leave matters as they were to keep the maid at home. The anecdote reveals the tensions and differences on money administration and consumption between the middle and working classes and perfectly conveys a sort of tug-of-war where the gains of one side—partly trivialized in the story as nonessential consumer goods—resulted in losses for the other side.[83]

The Ostentatious Worker and the Unpretentious Middle Class

The imagery of cooks in fur coats, maids in evening gowns, and Litas in silk stockings fueled the perception that more disposable income—10 percent cuts notwithstanding!—had transformed low-income sectors into feverish shoppers. The Peronist government greatly contributed to the dissemination of these kinds of images. In 1952, when inflation, a negative trade balance, and a drop in industrial productivity prompted an official campaign promoting austere consumption, Perón affirmed that

> in the past five years, we've let everyone do what they want, even squander. Now the people themselves have realized that there is no need to squander. [. . .] The people do not need as many clothes now because everyone's closet is full. In these past few years, people have purchased so many things that buying is no longer as exciting as it was in the past.[84]

The stereotype of the low-income sectors obsessed with unrestrained consumer desires differed greatly from the alleged materialism of turn-of-the-century European immigrants. Fiction, journalistic accounts, and other expressions of nativism portrayed the newcomers as avaricious individuals whose sole purpose in coming to Argentina was to get rich even to the point of enduring extreme deprivation, saving compulsively, and foregoing the most basic needs.[85] In the collective imagination, the goal of European immigrants had been to make money; the purpose of the mid-twentieth-century internal migrants was to spend it. This image was so strong that it became a motif of 1950s working-class culture. In the late 1980s, a working woman and communist militant described the implacable compulsion to buy of her meatpacking women coworkers in Avellaneda, Buenos Aires, when she remembered that

> they'd come running out of the gate as soon as they'd got paid at midday, and across the street in front of the plant would be dozens of vendors who had spread their wares out on the sidewalk. It was mostly cheap things, clothes, scarves, cheap jewelry. But it was as though they couldn't get enough of it, like they had a thirst to buy things . . . And, well, it was logical; they'd never had any money in the provinces, never before in their lives had they had so much money and the chance to buy things for themselves.[86]

The perception of "the craving worker-consumer" coupled effectively with the boom in retail commerce and with the spectacular growth of the textile and garment industries. In 1946, the volume of fabrics produced in the country was twice what it had been in 1939 and the number of workers employed in the industry was 86 percent higher. From the mid- to the late 1940s, production and employment in textile factories increased at a rate exceeding 10 percent annually. The same undisputable growth was evident in the garment industry. Between 1950 and 1953, for example, the manufacture of men's shirts and ties doubled. Alongside the increase in production, general garment sales in retail stores in the city of Buenos Aires almost quadrupled between 1946 and 1952. Indeed, in 1950 the average per capita consumption of textiles in Argentina was twice as high as that of other Latin American countries.[87] Similarly, there was a major boost in the consumption of beauty products. Beauty parlors flourished, false hair and wig merchants were plentiful, and cosmetic shops were so prosperous that according to amazed witnesses, perfume was not only sold by the dram, but "in bottles as big as milk containers."[88] In 1951, an official tourist brochure synthesized the thriving commercial life in Buenos Aires by describing Florida Street, home to the most famous retail stores, as "a street whose luxury, welfare, and abundance proclaim with exuberant prodigality the pride of a people who not only love beautiful things but are also able to pay for them."[89]

Representations of working-class consumers as "starving" for goods degenerated into images of low-income sectors as ostentatious and prone to spending on dispensable and flashy items, especially clothing, shoes, and jewelry. In 2005, the member of a prominent family from Rosario remembered that in the 1950s "working-class women walked around town with gold bracelets." When I expressed my surprise, she responded: "Yes, of course, that was the result of Peronism. Those poor women, who had never had anything, began to have money, and more money; they had jobs. Thousands of factories were opened. And what did those women buy? Gold bracelets!"[90] According to some anti-Peronists, this behavior partly reflected the example set by Eva Perón, whom they depicted as a bitter woman obsessed with wealth and luxury and a model that low-income women eagerly mimicked. In 1951, the Radical Party legislator Ernesto Sammartino expressed this view when he wrote that for "poor maids who dream of being princesses" Eva Perón was the dream come true.[91]

While depicting Eva Perón as tacky, shameless, and resentful, critics employed a moralistic tone to denounce excesses in working-class spending patterns. They targeted working-class men for gambling and alcohol and charged women with "misspending," particularly on garments and cosmetics. Congressman Reynaldo Pastor argued that "workers got used to squandering their income. For such workers, abstinence and sobriety were not virtues, just as laziness and neglect were not vices . . ."[92] To counter these accusations of excessive indulgence, workers provided a very different interpretation in which a higher standard of living included what critics viewed as dispensable expenditures. Along these lines, a housemaid downplayed the importance of the rising cost of living because she could afford a weekly trip to the beauty parlor. Disputing the idea of "unessential" gratifications, the woman related her personal well-being to the expression of femininity: "Before Perón, we servants never enjoyed such luxuries. Now we do. Other things may be costlier. But to us life has always been expensive and we have had nothing to show for it. Now at last we can feel like ladies."[93]

Accusations of frivolity and pretentiousness against working-class consumers stood in stark contrast to the celebration of conspicuous consumption among the elites. In 1946, the editor of the snobbish magazine *Orientación: Modas y Mundo Social* longed for the times when affluence was the measure of good taste and the privileged spared no expense to set the standards of refinement through lavish parties, ostentatious clothing, and expensive cars. The editorial was an expression of frustrated nostalgia for a "golden era" of strident flamboyance. Now, the author lamented, the rich were forced to conceal their status due to the hostility of a government that blamed the oligarchy for amassing their wealth by exploiting the laboring masses and selling off national assets.[94]

Although the elites might have been reducing their superfluous spending and displays of wealth, they still enjoyed an uncontested monopoly over expensive goods and exclusive places. The traditional *gente bien* (the well-off) had been tested earlier in the decade when the most successful children of the European immigrants, "the enriched bourgeoisie," were eager to buy their way up into the higher social sectors. But those parvenus did not rival the elites of *abolengo* (distinguished ancestry); they were looking for approval and integration—which many of them achieved—rather than competition.[95] Quite the contrary, in the mid-twentieth century, the elevation of the working-class standard of living and the new participation of low-income sectors in the consumer market seriously challenged the ability of the middle classes to maintain differentiated signs of status that could effectively distinguish them from blue-collar workers.

In the 1950s, the Argentine middle class had a short history. Loosely defined by their nonmanual occupations, access to education, and disparate levels of property ownership, the middle class was a heterogeneous group of small merchants and industrialists, executive employees, and liberal professionals. In most cases, these groups had started their climb up the social ladder at the beginning of the twentieth century, right after arriving from Europe. By midcentury, they had only secured their middle-class position for a generation or two. For an increasingly larger group of bureaucrats, teachers, white-collar employees, public servants, and independent professionals born in the country, entrance to the middle classes was even more recent, fueled by the rising industrialization, the expansion of the state, and the growth of the tertiary sector in the late 1930s. Such a short collective existence and the social and economic heterogeneity of the middle sectors resulted in the lack of a historically grounded set of norms and traditions and the consequent absence of solid institutional organization and cultural stability.[96]

Furthermore, inflation significantly affected the middle class throughout the Peronist government. Especially after 1950, small merchants suffered government price controls and price ceilings while bureaucrats, public servants, and independent professionals witnessed in frustration how their real salaries were severely reduced due to high prices. In contrast, the standard of living of the working classes was protected through the periodical renegotiation of wages by the unions, while the government monitored factory owners closely to ensure that they honored the collective labor agreements. As a consequence, in the late 1940s, working-class wages tripled, the salaries of white-collar employees doubled, and the income of independent professionals remained unchanged.[97]

Although defining components of middle-class identity such as culture, education, and respectability were quite independent from earnings, another essential aspect of middle-class life was the acquisition of consumer goods, which required a reasonable income. Thus stagnant salaries provoked feelings of dissatisfaction and reinforced the specter of social leveling that, real or imagined, haunted the middle class. In a 1950 study, sociologist Gino Germani concluded that "it is common to observe certain concern among the middle class regarding 'working class pretensions' and this class continues to feel the need to reestablish the differences that correspond to the social hierarchy of each social sector."[98] Anxiety over clear boundaries between classes is evident in the media treatment of working- and middle-class patterns of spending. The fashion expert for the Peronist working-class newspaper *La Época* acknowledged that elegance did not depend on wealth but urged working-class women to invest all their money in clothing to ensure good looks as well as happiness. In contrast, the upper- and middle-class magazine *Para Ti* advised professional women and white-collar female workers to refrain from spending lavishly on clothes, to choose what to buy judiciously, and to focus on looking clean and neat. With the stereotype of the working-class woman as ostentatious and overdone in mind, the *Para Ti* style expert recommended her middle-class readers to express their status through simplicity, frugality, and discern.[99] This is what middle-class families in Germani's study referred to as *decoro* (decorum), which they considered a distinguishing aspect of their style, especially in dress and home decor. Since the early twentieth century, in fact, manuals of good manners identified decoro as a key component of high social standing, exhorting readers to avoid exhibitionism since this was the mark of social climbers.[100]

Clase Media shows how, for the middle sectors, personal appearance was a means to embody decoro and thus a weapon in the struggle for social status. In the play, Elvira expresses her worries in a dialogue with her Peronist son where she complains about his old and ragged jacket, calls him *desharrapado* (shabby)—a term commonly used in anti-Peronist portrayals of the descamisados—and asks him to buy an elegant overcoat:

> Elvira: Buy it [the coat] on credit and then pay it off gradually. Why go around wearing the clothes the workers wear?

> Carlos: I am a worker, too.

> Elvira: You're an engineer.[101]

Peronists, in turn, ridiculed members of the middle class who "put on airs" and considered themselves "the new oligarchy" but suffered severe economic hardship in order to buy clothes they otherwise could not afford: "Composed and elegant, his attire is one of his most legitimate reasons for feeling proud. To perfect it, he forfeits—oh, the cost of vanity!—dire household needs, and credit payments cause him terrible monthly pains!"[102] In fact, sectors of the middle class went to great lengths to maintain a classy wardrobe, a true mark of success. The Greenups recalled that when working in a news agency in Buenos Aires, cable writers and translators changed their elegant street clothes right after entering the office and put on "their work pants." The suits were carefully smoothed on hangers, and the coats neatly draped on top. The American journalists admired how the street clothes were exquisitely tailored and noticed that hues were cautious and somber. Attention to detail and care shows the extremely important role of dress for these white-collar workers as well as the tight budgets that forced them to be overzealous about preserving their clothes. Similarly, journalist Roberto Arlt rightly interpreted the role of dress in the construction of a middle-class identity when he argued that in Buenos Aires, new shoes and a new suit were the best ways to command respect. Arlt recounted with irony that one of his friends categorically recommended dying of hunger before sacrificing these signs of status. Anthropological and sociological studies from the period offer evidence of this mindset by insisting on the middle-class obsession with body cleanliness and impeccable clothing. This obsession, experts believed, resulted from their longing for control and prestige, the exaggerated importance placed on personal appearances, and their fixation on distancing themselves from the lower social sectors.[103]

No one epitomized these characteristics better than Doctor Merengue, the character penned by cartoonist Guillermo Divito. First published in magazine *El Hogar* and later in *Rico Tipo*, the balloon-chested lawyer was impeccably dressed, often with a hat, smoking cigar, and boutonniere. Always an example of professionalism, the poised Doctor Merengue was a principled and decent gentleman committed to righteous actions. But right at a time when psychoanalysis was gaining a place for itself in the popular culture of Argentina and becoming fashionable among the upper sectors, Doctor Merengue offered a hilarious case of split personality. For example, Doctor Merengue was calm and unconcerned after losing a thousand pesos at the Mar del Plata casino, but his other self was desperate and went wild, attempting to bomb the establishment. The good doctor's other half was always mischievous, reckless, and arrogant, and he repeatedly bragged, lied, finger-pointed, and cheated. His alter ego looked tacky and unkempt, reflecting this behavior. On another occasion, the unworried doctor generously lent money to a friend while his alter ego exploded with anger just thinking that the borrower might not return the loan. The relation between the middle class, money, and appearances was indeed at the very heart of the character. Divito recalled that he had drawn inspiration from himself when he lent money to an acquaintance at a racetrack. The man won big that afternoon, and Divito lost all his money. When the overjoyed winner said good-bye forgetting to return the loan, Divito congratulated him and made no attempts to recover the money though he was teeming with fury against the man.[104]

Beyond a means of catharsis for the cartoonist, the extremely popular Doctor Merengue was a critical and poignant observation of the fixation of the middle classes with outward material, emotional, and intellectual appearances; their fears of revealing their true selves; and their concern of being unable to maintain a reputation. In his 1950 analysis of the urban Argentine middle class, sociologist Sergio Bagú seemed to be reflecting on Doctor Merengue and his alter ego when he argued that members of the middle sectors were severely obsessed with economic security and public manifestations of character and well-being. This obsession was "an intangible but powerful force that shapes their souls and determines their existence," Bagú concluded. Under such enormous pressure, the sociologist affirmed, it came as no surprise that the middle classes represented 80 percent of the patients treated by psychoanalysts in Buenos Aires.[105]

Fears of vanishing indicators of class distinction reinforced the need to prevent confusion by forging differences and monitoring them closely. Much of this process of crafting division to avoid class slippage depended on differential access and use of consumer goods. Some thought that polished, high-quality shoes conveyed social difference. Others pointed to well-ironed clothes, and some believed that well-fitting garments unambiguously expressed social belonging. Still others drew attention to details, from pant creases to the texture of women stockings.[106] Along similar lines, the author of a manual for domestic workers thought that makeup on women from the working classes, and especially maids, had a "bad connotation" and could lead to "misunderstandings." The language suggested a possible mix-up between domestics and prostitutes, conveying the idea that the access of women from the lower sectors to certain consumer goods posed a risk of moral decay and the loss of self-control. Beyond this menace, the handbook explicitly referred to the unwelcome confusion between mistresses and maids and urged working women to prevent such confusion by avoiding vanity, dressing modestly, and never wearing cream or makeup. The author believed that the preoccupation of domestic help with their appearance merely replicated a middle-class practice. Thus, in the name of social hierarchy, she warned maids, "Never try to imitate the lady of the house."[107]

The warning was rooted in a "trickle-down" model of consumer hierarchy in which the alleged social confusion resulted from the attempts of working-class consumers to emulate the upper social sectors. A common explanation for the spread of fashion and for the constant search among high-income sectors for new markers of social distinction, the argument on social emulation overlooks the ways in which low-income consumers appropriated goods creatively and selectively, thus transforming styles rather than imitating them.[108] Equally significant, many styles were engendered at the bottom of the social ladder and then moved upward from the working class to higher sectors. The tube skirt, for example, widely popularized by the Divito girls, was a monopoly of factory workers and sales attendants in the late 1940s and early 1950s but became a common staple in the wardrobe of middle- and upper-class women later in the decade. Pants followed a similar trajectory. In the 1940s, working-class women wore pants in the factories because they were a comfortable, practical, and "discrete" alternative to dresses and skirts. Gradually, these women adopted pants as everyday attire, and, from the streets, pants "trickled up," reaching more privileged women.[109]

More broadly, the caveat to maids about mimicking their mistresses was part of defending "good taste" and, ultimately, a reaffirmation of the differences between the haves and have-nots. In many cases, imitation unveiled the difference between taste-makers and poseurs thus serving to effectively restate social distinction. As an effect of emulation, what constituted proper daily attire for the women of the middle classes became wasteful luxury, embodied tackiness, and represented social decadence when donned by working-class women. Detractors bitterly ridiculed low-income women who "dressed above their class" and lambasted their spending on apparel and beauty products as tasteless, pretentious, economically irresponsible, and dishonest. Well-known playwright and radio scriptwriter Nené Cascallar severely criticized working-class women consumers who

> want to appear [rich] but only look ridiculous. They don a fur coat made not of fur but of imitation fur; they add a cheap rhinestone pin that they believe looks expensive; they slip on a "diamond" solitaire that looks like glass ten miles away. [. . .] It's a shame that this erred criterion leads so many people not only to bring ridicule upon themselves in their desire to deceive with false tinsel, but also gets them into debt because they spend more than their budget allows.[110]

Cascallar concluded by affirming that "one cannot bear the absurd pretensions of luxury of certain people who believe they can trick the entire world with their theatrical props."[111] In "Las puertas del cielo" ("The Gates of Heaven"), writer Julio Cortázar instilled similar feelings in his main character, a lawyer who frequented a popular working-class dance hall in Buenos Aires in spite of his aversion to the clientele, whom he refers to as "the monsters." Doctor Hardoy especially disdains the women (many of them maids) and ridicules their appearance as desperate attempts to mask their class, their race, and their bodies:

> Furthermore there's the smell; one cannot imagine the monsters without the smell of damp talcum powder on the skin, of rotten fruit, one thinks of them washing up hastily, the wet washcloth over the face and under the armpits; then comes the important part: creams, mascara, the powder on their faces, a whitish crust and under it dusky patches shining through. They also bleach their hair; *las negras* (the black girls) raise rigid corncobs atop the dark earth of their faces; they even study the expressions of the blonds, wear green dresses, convinced of their transformation and looking down condescendingly on other girls who defend their color.[112]

This and Cascallar's passages suggest a sort of middle-class monopoly of certain consumer goods while denying low-income sectors their unique and independent appropriation of such goods according to personal and collective needs and desires. At the same time, both authors exude a sense of relief when asserting that attempts at emulation failed miserably. In spite of anxieties over imitation and competition, accusations of working-class bad taste, showiness, and vulgarity suggest how commentators ultimately assessed social "passing" as unsuccessful.[113] In this view, rather than being enablers of transformation, goods not only "fixed" consumers' social identity, but also overstated it. For Doctor Hardoy, working-class identity was, in the end, dependent on inescapable racial and physical traits that beauty products and dresses could not disguise. But most importantly, for Hardoy as well as for Cascallar and the author of the manual for domestic servants, working-class identity was marked by the lack of decoro, a deficiency that consumer goods were unable to overcome.

One of the most significant results of the vigorous mid-twentieth-century processes of industrialization, urbanization, and increasing purchasing power was not only the new economic citizenship of the working sectors, but also their social visibility. Working-class consumers, many of whom had left the countryside to live and work in the city, became conspicuous and recognizable figures in the urban marketplace, occupying new physical and symbolic spaces of consumption and participating in new consumer practices. Although the government praised them as a triumph of justicialismo and admen targeted them in their campaigns, for many members of the urban middle and upper classes, the new worker-consumer was an unwelcome presence. Frustrated urban dwellers witnessed how cities had developed into frenetic and rampant spaces of constant, noisy, and chaotic movement. For some, the city was becoming a sparkling and colorful but somewhat vulgar shop window, full of neon signs and street ads of questionable taste. For others, it was mutating into an unrecognizable creature dominated by disturbing massiveness and depersonalization in which indifference, insolence, and hostility were replacing previous codes of conduct based on the stricter observation of social hierarchies.

Beyond the complaints of disgruntled patrons who suffered the mistreatment of waiters, moviegoers upset for sold-out shows, and irritated passengers of jam-packed trains, concerns went well beyond the problems arising from urban growth and population displacement. In those times of flux, certainties about self and others became weakened and new and expanding forms of consumption among low-income sectors suggested that the boundaries of social distinction had been destabilized. A fluid, more open, and socially inclusive market challenged the ways in which middle- and upper-class consumers claimed social membership. These groups equated the new economic entitlement of the working sectors with a lost monopoly over consumer practices, goods, and spaces which they believed existed for their sole enjoyment. As the affluent considered that the realms of former exclusivity were now unlocked, their sense of place and belonging was jeopardized. With it, the perception of the new consumer as a ubiquitous character aroused fears of social mingling with individuals of lower status and intensified the view of these sectors as intruders. While the prospects of forced interclass socialization threatened ideals of incontestable social standing, the apparent unrestricted access to consumer goods became a menace to the ability of the middle classes to irrefutably assert class belonging. The collective imagination emphasized the stereotype of the housemaid dressed like the lady of the house as a potent symbol of a higher standard of living but, most significantly, as a sign of the cultural and economic deterioration that disgraced the prosperous sectors, and as an example of social homogeneity and cultural deterioration.

In spite of fears of class confusion, widely circulated stereotypes of the worker-consumer powerfully reinscribed class distinction. Low-income sectors were portrayed as emulative, superfluous, spendthrift, and showy—obsessed with diversion and cheap goods for display rather than what critics considered practical and respectable investments in lasting betterment. The needs, wants, and tastes that triggered their spending decisions were ignored, and thus their style and consumer practices were minimized as downgraded replicas of the upper social sectors. In this characterization, low-income consumers were always imitators and appropriators rather than creators. This role, in fact, fell to middle- and upper-class consumers who, endowed with means, grace, and decoro, presented themselves as true tastemakers. But as important as this role was, they fulfilled it hesitantly, fearful that their consumer choices would make their way down the social ladder too rapidly. When the threat was imminent, then, the stereotypes of the worker-consumer reestablished the difference between the housemaid and the lady of the house. Yet consumption was a multivalent and complex phenomenon that was more than a site for the creation, reaffirmation, and contestation of class identities. Since both men and women eagerly shopped, used, and displayed their new possessions, consumption also sparked mounting tensions about gender roles and expectations.

CHAPTER 5

Love in the Time of Mass Consumption

In 1950, an article in the women's magazine *Nocturno* discussed the five lies
that couples should never tell each other while dating. One of those lies was
"I love housework," while the other four were about spending: "You will
have a car and jewels," "Nobody influences my financial decisions," "*Contigo
pan y cebolla*," [1] and "We will spend everything we make." [2] The prospects
of a happy marriage, the columnist made clear, depended on reaching a
mutual agreement on frugal or conspicuous consumption, economic independence, and the administration of money. The article illustrates how the
mid-twentieth-century discussions about gender roles and expectations
were closely linked to patterns of consumption. The new public interest
on how much money couples made, who earned it, and how they spent it
revealed not only a preoccupation with everyday household economics, but
also a profound transformation in the ways in which men and women dated,

tied the knot, and enjoyed a happy marriage. The combination of industrialization, an expansive mass market, increasing numbers of women working in the secondary and tertiary sectors, and the liberalization of rules and mores made the mid-twentieth century ripe for change.

This chapter explores the role of consumption in the creation of gender stereotypes that manifested the tensions that arose between men and women in relation to working for a living, spending, and doing housework. It shows that the participation in a socially expansive consumer market created new social types like the materialistic housewife and the "domestic husband" that challenged traditional definitions of proper womanhood and manhood. It is well known that stereotypes are simple and easily grasped forms of representation whose effectiveness resides in the way they invoke apparent consensus. One of the most important functions of stereotypes is to maintain clear-cut classifications while marking the differences between acceptable and unacceptable behavior.[3] In contrast to an idealized past in which men and women had given up comforts for family, relinquished their independence for love, and dutifully played their roles as breadwinners and housekeepers, the new generation—detractors maintained—opted to fulfill hedonistic ambitions at the cost of marriage and parenthood. Although single men were sharply criticized for this choice, in the popular imaginary, young working-class women represented a particularly disturbing force of change as capricious beings who, moved by overblown acquisitiveness and loose principles, bled their parents and husbands dry, entered into relationships of convenience, and spent more time in the beauty parlor than at home. Critics believed that in their quest for small luxuries and pleasure in their different material incarnations—from dresses and manicured nails to furniture and domestic appliances—women not only gave up conventional responsibilities as frugal and diligent homemakers and compliant partners, but also forced men into a contrived and damaging position of personal weakness and social futility.

In analyzing these stereotypes, the chapter particularly focuses on the popular media, especially women's and home magazines, for their significant contribution to creating and circulating gender classifications and prescriptions. As the media alternatively praised and condemned different forms of consumer acts, it both reflected gender behavior and modeled it into stereotypes that would, in turn, affect women's and men's self-perception. Against a one-dimensional view of the media, this chapter underlines its role as an articulator of both clashing stereotypes and disparate messages about gender expectations. By focusing on editorials, nonfictional and fictional articles, advice columns, and advertisements, the analysis delves into the contradiction of promoting consumption as a source of happiness and personal fulfillment while reproving the pernicious effects that consumer culture had on traditional gender roles. A motor that fueled consumer desires as much as a conformist institution that censored change, the press denounced the tensions resulting from consumer culture while openly causing these tensions by promoting a myriad of consumer goods as indispensable means to satisfy aspirations that ranged from physical beauty to marital bliss.

Enjoying the Single Life

In 1952, the newspaper *La Tribuna* published a heated debate among its readers that began with the letter from a married father of five demanding that legislators tax single men. The man was offended by the selfishness and materialistic impulses of men who preferred a life of material comfort and personal indulgence over the economic sacrifices required to feed a family and fulfill a higher, sacred obligation: "While we hardworking fathers and providers seriously undertake to following the Christian mandate to 'be fruitful and multiply,' the bachelor lives for himself and only for himself."[4] The upset married man shared a position common among Catholics who viewed consumption as a threat to a righteous life defined by spirituality, rectitude, and unquestioning obedience of traditional gender roles. Innumerable letters by supporters of the initiative pivoted on the importance of family both as personal achievement and patriotic duty and on the bliss of companionship for life and highlighted the social significance of taking on the role of provider. Bachelors, for their part, responded with arguments on the difficulties of finding true love and assertions of personal freedom. Most importantly, single men were as hardworking as married men and played a crucial economic role as consumers that critics had overlooked. By spending their money in theaters, racetracks, dance halls, and other recreational venues—the epitome of self-indulgence and squandering, according to detractors—bachelors patronized businesses that employed married men. The debate is revealing because in spite of the contrasting opinions, all arguments acknowledged the impact of consumer culture on traditional male roles. Contributors to the discussion recognized that staying single was about choosing personal independence over commitment, looking for the right woman, and avoiding responsibility, as well as about hedonist consumption.[5]

This argument resonated with the stereotyping of the single man in popular culture as prosperous, happy, and economically independent—a true bon vivant who spent generously on fine suits, expensive ties, and leisure. The stereotypical dandy concerned with his appearance had different historical class and racial incarnations in the Americas, from the Dominican *tíguere* to the Mexican-American pachuco. In Argentina, the *bacán* (playboy) was the long-standing archetype of the well-dressed bachelor who led an extravagant life-style. The early twentieth-century bacán was usually well-off, probably born into a rich family, and infamous for his sexual licentiousness.[6] By the mid-twentieth century, the image of the bachelor had been significantly sanitized. He was now more socially innocuous, undisruptive and sexually restrained, more a consumer of goods and recreation than of sex. He was also admired by his married peers. In one episode of the popular radio show *Los Pérez García* about a middle-class family, the father expressed, with a tinge of envy, his high regard for his enchanting single friend by claiming that "Alfredo is a man of the world. He knows what to eat, what to drink . . . It's lovely to go with him anywhere. One feels—I don't know how to say it—one feels . . . distinguished and well-regarded!"[7]

In opposition to the easygoing and carefree personality of the bachelor, the media presented the married man as a victim of his wife's economic misjudgments, continually distressed about the household finances even though he worked round the clock. This is the type of representation in a story published in the humor magazine *Cascabel*, in which a gloomy husband tells his fortunate single friend that, after thorough consideration, he had handed over his annual bonus to his wife with a shopping list that included an inexpensive suit, a pair of shoes, two shirts, and a tie. The man then recounts that the woman had bought herself a dress, two hats, six pairs of stockings, shoes, and a purse. For him, she had only purchased the tie from the list, and with a pained gesture, the mortified man points out the tacky yellow polka-dot bow tie he is wearing while his friend is unable to keep from laughing.[8] The husband, emasculated for relinquishing his income to his wife and with no say over his personal expenses, was commonly the butt of the joke. In comics, ads, fiction, and journalistic writings, exhausted and distressed husbands play attendants, carrying dozens of heavy packages while their wives shop cheerfully, pay exorbitant bills for female whims, and suffer "women's shopping tantrums" stoically.[9]

If keeping control over their finances and consumer indulgence were compelling reasons for men to stay single, they were even more attractive to women. In 1952, a writer for the women's magazine *Maribel* argued that young ladies shared a self-gratifying view of life. Even those from the lower-income sectors believed that "you must enjoy the present, have fun, dress well, go to the salon, go shopping; in short, get as close as possible to the ideal of someone who can have everything."[10] The columnist warned that for women, especially for working-class women, marriage was not a ticket to this kind of life-style but a road to domestic responsibility and economic dependency. Married women struggled with tight budgets and coped with postponed desires, commonly sacrificing a new dress or makeup to buy shoes for the children or shirts for the men. Marriage was no "nonstop party," and women were forced to give up the "luxuries" that they had enjoyed in their parents' house.[11] The press frequently blamed permissive parents of modest means, especially mothers, for encouraging a materialistic outlook among young women and indulging "expensive tastes" at the cost of tremendous economic stress for the family.[12] In reality, parents only occasionally paid for the kind of life-style one Catholic writer defined as "a life of selfishness and immediate personal satisfaction."[13] More frequently, consumer indulgence was possible due to the economic independence of increasing numbers of working women, around 1.2 million in 1947. As a result of industrialization, urbanization, and the crisis of agro-export activities, more women worked outside the home than in the past decades. Fifty-nine percent of these women were employed in the tertiary sector and 27 percent in the industrial sector.[14] Occupations in factories, offices, and commerce gave working women greater social visibility and magnified female participation in the job market. Also, women generally earned better salaries than they had in the past, especially in the industrial sector.[15]

While in the mid-twentieth century the number of married women who worked outside the home was increasing, there was still a strong social consensus that wage labor should be for single women. In the popular imagination, working outside the home allowed single women to contribute to the family budget while giving them a source of pocket money and a means to save for wedding expenses. Many commentators viewed remunerated female occupations as a hobby and a way to practice one's profession before getting married. But even the accomplishment of these well-intentioned ends put women in a problematic position since critics associated female waged labor with a variety of social evils, from

FIGURE 15: Women working in the packaging sector of a candy and cookie factory in Rosario in the late 1940s. Photo courtesy of Museo de la Ciudad de Rosario.

promiscuity, sexual predation, and the erosion of the patriarchal order to the emasculation of men, the masculinization of women, and decreasing birth rates. Consequently, Catholic and conservative sectors fervently opposed female participation in the job market at all stages of a woman's life and grudgingly approved of it only in cases of extreme poverty.[16]

Social disapproval of working women notwithstanding, for these young ladies, economic independence and the ability to afford many consumer pleasures were very difficult to decline. In 1952, a young female factory worker maintained that she and her co-workers "live well and even allow ourselves small luxuries: the movies, the theater, a trip to the café."[17] The media insisted that given the choice, many women preferred a singlehood of "small luxuries" to a married life without them. In 1953, a survey published in the magazine *PBT* showed that although single working-class women contributed to their family budgets, they spent most of their incomes on themselves, disbursing 36 percent of their wages on beauty products. This percentage, observers agreed, would be unthinkable if these women were married. Fathers in particular disapproved of the way their daughters splurged on what they considered superfluous objects and unnecessary expenses. After witnessing his working daughter spend lavishly on new clothes that far exceeded her needs, a frustrated father commented with resignation, "I've worn the same suit for three years and I've worn the same shoes for eleven months and twenty-one days."[18]

In their quest for a good life, young working women drew on numerous sources of inspiration. Widely read magazines dedicated to Argentine cinema and radio glamorized singlehood in articles on young single starlets who boasted elegant apartments with exquisite decoration, remarkable record and book collections, expensive furniture and chandeliers, and impressive wardrobes, all carefully documented with innumerable pictures. In its popular section "How the Stars Live," the radio magazine *Antena* showed the single stars relaxed, blissful, and affluent. One example is a piece on the renowned Elina Colomer, who "renounced marriage to be able to attain her grand ideal life." In one of the ten photos that illustrates the article, a fashionably dressed Colomer, with an expensive necklace and stylish hat included, gazes undecided upon two elegant handbags, one clutched in each hand. Behind her, an open closet reveals an impressive number of dresses, coats, and meticulously arranged chic shoes. In another picture, Colomer poses with her record player; in yet another, she stands before a grand piano. Interestingly, beyond the large assortment of clothes, accessories, and gadgets, the photos of the opulent living and dining room highlight the material splendor of single life by displaying spaces traditionally related to family domesticity. This combination successfully plays down a message of self-indulgence and excess with a halo of propriety and cultivation.[19]

While young starlets in the media stimulated dreams of a comfortable life-style, working-class women found consumer aspirations increasingly achievable due to the rising demand for workers and higher remuneration. Commonly, these women, who had been previously employed as domestic and agricultural workers and earned miserly wages, saw their standards of living improve dramatically. Thus they had no intention to renounce their new lives. In 1947, *Aquí Está* illustrated this trend by reporting on a young office employee who demanded that his fiancée give up her job in a cigarette factory as a condition for marriage. She earned more money than he did and had left her previous job in a store because of the better industrial wages that allowed her to enjoy a more affluent life. When he confronted her, insisting that she decide between "the factory or me," she indubitably chose the factory and the life-style she had as a single woman. The determination of this young working woman defied the role of men as providers and questioned the idea of an instinctive, almost biological connection between women and marriage, motherhood, and romantic love.[20]

Her decision, in fact, challenged a common argument that suggested that marital life was women's exclusive source of happiness. The young factory worker who broke off her engagement was the complete opposite of the *bella pobre* (the beautiful poor girl), the fictional main character of the avidly consumed serial novels from the 1910s and 1920s. The bella pobre was only moved by heterosexual love, passion, and emotions even when this brought her shame and affliction. In her quest for prince charming and a home with children, she embarked upon perilous adventurous against all odds, from challenging mores to overcoming class differences.[21] By contrast, her mid-twentieth-century working-class equivalent, who disobeyed social expectations of female sacrifice for love, offered an alternative path to personal gratification that involved resisting economic dependence on men and rejecting home life.

If the bella pobre was romantic, pious, and dreamy, the recurrent stereotype of the 1950s working-class woman was materialistic, selfish, and frivolous. This characterization was based on the idea that women had a "natural" psychological and biological predisposition to all forms of "consumer misconduct." Indeed, squandering was commonly interpreted as a trait that women "carried in their blood" and developed into an irresistible impulse related to the search for pleasure.[22] Still, "culture" molded "genetic" female patterns of spending. In a 1947 article in the general interest magazine *¿Qué sucedió en siete días?*, a journalist compared the spending of French, American, and Argentine women. He concluded that, unlike the French who were thrifty and had few material aspirations, Argentine women—particularly those from the low-income sectors—were incapable of saving money and always resolved to fulfill even their loftiest consumer ambitions. In this regard, Argentine women, the reporter added, were comparable to the unrestrained, determined, and acquisitive American female consumers.[23]

Mid-twentieth-century magazines persistently warned female readers that men disliked these types of women. Among the female defects that men could not tolerate, a penchant for amusement, frivolity, uncontrolled spending, a lack of financial organization, and excessive independence topped the list. Instead, men were looking for a woman who did not live exclusively for pleasure and who administrated money judiciously.[24] This message was clear in the popular column "Psychoanalysis Will Help You" published in *Idilio*, a magazine that primarily addressed a lower-class female public. A mix of sentimental counseling and dream analysis, the column asked readers to send in letters recounting their dreams. Sociologist Gino Germani and psychologist Enrique Butelman interpreted the dreams under the pseudonym Professor Richard Rest while avant-garde photographer Grete Stern illustrated the column with her creative photomontages. In one case, for instance, a young lady described a recurring dream in which she was picking up money off the floor. The woman, Professor Rest told the readership, was a squanderer and her fiancé criticized her continually for her behavior. The dream, the psychoanalytic expert argued, was a warning to help her save their relationship, a conciliatory response to the man's criticisms. Through her dream, the woman was unconsciously making a promise: "From now on my attitude towards money will be different. Not only will I stop being a spendthrift, but I will even pick up the coins I see on the ground."[25] In contrast to the archetype of the loveless vain woman, most dreams analyzed by Professor Rest revealed that women were torn between fulfilling their consumer desires and the consequences that this had for their finances, for their roles as obedient daughters, and most significantly, for their love lives.

Individual conscience-pricking aside, many believed that consumer self-indulgence had serious moral consequences for young women. The image of the respectable low-income woman who worked to afford small luxuries easily metamorphosed into that of a wicked girl who employed her sexuality, affluent friends, or even a convenient, loveless marriage with an elderly man as suitable tickets to a wealthy life. This 1950s representation echoed common turn-of-the-century female stereotypes especially popularized in tango lyrics, literature, political texts, and theatrical plays. The cocottes (mistresses), *mantenidas* (kept women), and *milonguitas* (cabaret women) were women of modest means whose thirst for luxuries led them to abandon their poor neighborhoods and families, their honorable occupations, and their true loves to live as prostitutes and wealthy men's lovers. These women were also responsible for the "fall" of honest men, a life marked by delinquency, imprisonment, or bankruptcy resulting from their attempts to afford a luxury life-style for their materialistic companions. For the women, the moral of their stories was frequently the same: after the initial fascination with pimps and *bacanes*, greed led to a life of exploitation, isolation, and misery.[26]

By contrast, in line with the current celebration of consumer culture and the working class as the main protagonist of a new era of social justice, the mid-twentieth-century image of the materialistic woman from the low-income sectors was associated with a less tragic destiny. In a context in which the material aspirations of the working class were understood as social rights, they led to redemption rather than disgrace. Also, as a character of the collective imaginary, the mid-twentieth-century materialistic woman inhabited popular newspapers, radio shows, and women's magazines, less somber and less moralizing genres than the tango songs and anarchist writings that had popularized the poignant fate of her older sister a few decades earlier. And unlike her predecessor, the new acquisitive woman was less naïve, more determined, and manipulative. In her radio show scripts, for example, Nené Cascallar severely criticized a new common practice among young working-class women who passed off as affluent to befriend wealthy women. In this way, the poseuses were able to enjoy amusements they could not otherwise afford. Their misled friends paid for restaurants and night clubs, lent them jewelry and clothing, and gave them expensive gifts. Equally important, they introduced these girlfriends to their rich brothers, uncles, and male acquaintances.[27] The mid-twentieth-century acquisitive woman was, indeed, less a victim of deceitful men and more of a *conquistadora* (seductress). Recalcitrant anti-Peronists saw Eva Perón as the epitome of this type. A young, poor, and mediocre actress—the story went—Eva had been the mistress of several older men, unsuccessfully scrambling her way up the social ladder, when she met Perón. As the concubine of the ascending and increasingly powerful colonel, Eva reaped professional and economic benefits before becoming an influential figure on her own.[28]

The media humorously popularized "the seductress" through the Divito girls who were sexy, money-oriented, and immersed in a cutthroat world of women competing for male attention and, principally, their wallets. Either as a sarcastic commentary or as a celebration of the women they mimicked, the Divito girls were appealing and popular enough to be chosen by many advertisers when marketing their products, as chapter 3 shows.[29] The attributes that made the Divito girls famous were also evident in Olga, a well-known comic-strip character in the newspaper *Democracia*. Olga was a voluptuous, egocentric, independent, single, working porteña with a taste for expensive things. She became prominent, though was also occasionally abhorred by readers, for reflections like "Love is an optical aberration that makes us see things through rose-colored glasses. In acute cases, an operation called 'marriage' is recommended. This causes the illness to gradually subside."[30] It was typical for Olga to make comments such as "Have you ever seen such nerve, saying I love him for his money: 556,395 pesos and 22 cents."[31]

The fact that *Democracia* had chosen Olga was peculiar. The newspaper had a massive working-class readership and fervently endorsed the Peronist gender ideology by publishing stories of scrupulous, honorable, and hardworking girls. Consequently, Olga defied readers who felt insulted by a character who was insensitive, hedonistic, and unprincipled and who openly contested the Peronist female role models. One offended male reader argued that "this woman Olga who spends her time seducing old rich men might be the typical film extra but in no way does she portray the porteña woman, much less the Peronist woman."[32] In contrast, one of Olga's admirers congratulated the director of *Democracia* "for running a comic strip that is so human, so natural, the perfect mix of simplicity, thoughtful observation of daily life and clear expression." The reader also praised the artist "for his fine sense of humor and sharp psychological insight."[33] Followers, in fact, enjoyed Olga's witty remarks and appreciated the fact that she was the amusing reflection of a great number of real young women.

¿"Contigo Pan y Cebolla"?

Olga may have been cynical about marriage while reinforcing images of fun-filled singlehood, but most men and women, demographic information shows, were not easily discouraged from getting married. After the declining numbers of weddings in the previous decade, marriage rates started to increase in the early 1940s and became remarkably high between 1945 and 1952. Scholars have explained this development by pointing to the steady prosperous economic conditions that prevailed until the early 1950s and the new arrivals of European immigrants. Still, the same booming market conditions that persuaded couples to marry significantly altered the economic and material expectations of married life and how men and women consumers planned to set up a home and reach and maintain a satisfactory standard of living.[34]

Men had commonly argued in favor of pushing back the wedding date until they got a raise. Whether this was a sensible reason with the couple's best interests in mind or an unconvincing excuse to avoid further commitment, women had traditionally resisted it. However, in the mid-twentieth century, the popular press particularly singled out women as the ones responsible for delaying marriage. Women cited financial and material reasons, including what they perceived as insufficient funds, the longing for household items, the aspiration for a nice house, and a number of other cravings that some observers considered excessive, especially among low-income sectors. One commentator writing in *El Hogar* maintained that the romantic "contigo pan y cebolla," a promise to be happy together in spite of sharing an austere life-style, was a thing of the past. Now brides conclusively and cruelly uttered a very different phrase: "I'm not getting married to be miserable." The writer affirmed that "while the brides of yesterday were satisfied with a union that would guarantee food and a home, today's fiancées have other requisites related to leisure and glitz: a house, food, a car . . . and nights out at the club."[35]

In the late forties, critics signaled a crisis of values and conduct among young people who postponed starting a family and extended courtship with the consequent moral dilemmas related to premarital sexuality and intimacy. In fact, between 1900 and 1960, the average age of men who got married in Buenos Aires went from twenty-nine to thirty-one years and the age of women went from twenty-three to twenty-eight, a considerable change.[36] Foreign observers remarked this was true all the way down to the lower-income sectors of the population: "Even poor families like to stage elaborate church weddings. [. . .] Sometimes the family may postpone the wedding a year or more in order to scrape up enough money to provide a big church ceremony with white tie and tails for the groom and a wedding dress with a train for the bride."[37]

Scriptwriter Nené Cascallar recounted the story of a young couple who had been dating for three years and were madly in love but continuously postponed their wedding because "they won't resign themselves to live modestly or because they want a house with all the comforts and conveniences." Cascallar affirmed that the young man earned enough money to provide for a family of four but that he and his fiancée had a long list of material requirements for their home. Cascallar thought that deferring the wedding to accumulate household possessions was an unfortunate, widespread tendency among young couples that illustrated their increasing materialism, greediness, and social exhibitionism. She claimed that this resulted from the seduction of consumer goods and advertising promises of a comfortable life that prompted couples to prioritize acquisitiveness over love and thus to jeopardize the continuity of the relationship. In this view, the high ambitions of contemporary couples contrasted with an idealized past in which men and women had endured privation and sacrifice in the name of love. Cascallar admired the previous generations that "had no aspirations for an elegant wedding gown, an apartment downtown, or this or that style of furniture."[38]

In contrast, the extensive list of goods couples now wanted for their future home included a great variety of the latest household appliances—from the electric refrigerator to the food processor and the electric blender—along with furniture, a radio, tableware, cooking sets, cutlery sets, chinaware, upholstery, home décor, and some extremely popular 1950s kitchen items like the pressure cooker. Observers maintained that although some of these commodities may have been essential, others were superfluous items that in no way prevented couples from marrying or establishing a home. A columnist in *Nocturno*, for instance, argued that "there are couples that are so set on a certain home aesthetic that they won't get married for anything in the world unless they can have not only the bedroom set but also the dining room set. And not the everyday dining room set, but the other one: 'the deluxe' to receive guests in a separate room that they open just to prove it's there."[39]

Although *Nocturno* criticized the high material ambitions of young couples, the popular press and especially women's and home magazines played a key role in shaping those ambitions, sometimes in articles with pompous titles like "An Electric Blender in Every Home Would Be Ideal."[40] Their pages were full of detailed advice, recommendations, and tips that delved into the particulars of planning, selecting, and shopping for everything from sofas, beds, and lamps to kitchen cabinets, carpets, and electric gadgets and then arranging them in an aesthetic and functional way throughout the house. These were not the traditional decorating tips for married women intending to renovate or update a room, sections that had been a common feature mainly in high-class publications like the magazine *Atlántida*. Instead, new columns pivoted on suggestions specifically directed to couples and most particularly to young women across the economic spectrum who were about to wed.[41] In the lengthy article "The Bride Furnishes Her Home and Kitchen" in *Mucho Gusto*, a popular monthly about home, housework, and cooking with a working-class and lower middle-class readership, the writer explained that thoroughly planning the purchases for the future residence was of crucial economic and emotional significance. She also urged women to persistently seek the collaboration and input of their partners:

Your home will be what you make of it. But it must be done with all your heart. That's why a perfectly furnished home, big or small, is not a matter of chance. It's the result of carefully studied plans. [. . .] Don't make your plans alone. Try to get your fiancé to participate in everything down to buying the last ashtray. We know it's hard to drag him from store to store; but it's worth a try, so your future home will be an adorable space and the clear expression of both of your tastes.[42]

These types of pieces were new in long-standing periodicals and central in the myriad of new women's and home magazines. Also, they were fundamental in special editions of popular magazines dedicated to newlyweds and brides as well as in new publications dedicated to home furnishing, appliances, and decoration that prospered in the mid-twentieth century. These new magazines included *Confort* (Comfort) (1940) and *Nuestro Techo* (Our House) (1955), popular and unpretentious versions of traditionally upper-class magazines like *Casas y Jardines* (Homes and Gardens) (1933), which was also undergoing a process of adaptation to a lower-class readership. *Confort* is an excellent example of the spread of particular consumer practices centered on setting up a home and an illustration of the development of specific literature aimed at providing advice on this matter.[43] From 1940 to 1949, *Confort* mainly focused on general interest topics with cooking as the aspect that received the most coverage over the decade. But in 1949, the magazine experienced a profound transformation, becoming a guide for consumers eager to obtain practical commercial and technical information on appliances along with insider tips on decoration and furniture. In accomplishing this change, the editors of *Confort* drew inspiration from the increasing democratization of household technology in the country. One editorial writer argued that

the window displays [at appliance stores] indicate that the public knows how to live and, furthermore, aspires to live better; that household technology exists because it has a very broad consumer market. And that market is made up of the same public who is becoming increasingly convinced that comfort is not a superfluous luxury, but a need that can't be put off.[44]

In 1951, *Confort* started a lengthy section called Confortlandia (Comfortland) that, in keeping with the popular tone of the magazine, recommended, advertised, and informed readers about "everything new and essential for the modern home"—particularly, electric appliances. Less reachable but still inspirational was the "New Homes" section featuring the stylish houses of newlyweds, frequently from well-off sectors. Still, both *Confort* and *Nuestro Techo* were responsive to the demands of readers of modest means. In their sections on residential construction, articles like "Model of an Economic House" or "Working-Class Home" suggested austere floor plans of less than 900 square feet that accommodated a small but well-appointed two bedroom home with a living and dining room area, a kitchen, and one bath.[45] Similarly, home specialists writing in women's and home magazines gave readers on different budgets choices about decoration, furnishing, and design, and numerous articles offered consumer and creative guidance exclusively for working-class consumers.[46]

Particularly for low-income sectors, experts emphasized quality and durability when shopping for anything for the home even if it meant spending more. Equally important, they advised those who were about to walk down the aisle to be farsighted and predict future needs despite the additional expenses these might involve. The advice resembled a common marketing argument that advertisers employed when promoting their products. An ad for the department store Gath & Chaves publicized its accessible consumer credit by arguing that "staying one step ahead of things is what today is all about."[47] The ad showed a couple at different moments of their lives—the wedding ceremony, the birth of a child, the smiling toddler, and the child at school—promoting consumption in relation to the socially high-regarded ideals of family and children. Similarly, a furniture maker equated a long and solid marriage with first-rate and durable products in an ad that reminded potential customers that "you are also getting married to the furniture."[48] In tune with ads published in their pages, home magazines exhorted couples to save patiently and to invest generously in well-made consumer goods if they wanted to make the home of their dreams a reality:

> Make your first home the first step toward the home you've always dreamed of. [. . .] What matters is that the furniture and possessions last for years and are in tune with decoration and room changes. Comfort, distinction and hospitality must be the guiding points. [. . .] The flatware, silverware, and glassware are what set the tone of your gatherings. Even if you can't afford a great number of pieces, aim for a quality that you can be proud of.[49]

Targets of home magazines and their lengthy sections on consumer advice, newlyweds and, above all, brides—embodied in the figure of the pretty, sexy woman examined in chapter 3—became a new and widespread character in advertisements for everything related to home life, from floor polish and canned food to dining sets and domestic technology. Typically, advertisers argued that women needed the advertised consumer good as a prerequisite to marriage while stressing the prominent role of such goods in creating women's identities as newlyweds. In the ads, products are as central to defining the bride as the iconic wedding dress that women repeatedly don in advertising pictures and illustrations. Along these lines, the main argument in a series of ads for a popular inexpensive sewing machine was that "one can hardly imagine a bride or a wife without an Elna, the essential machine in every well-appointed home."[50] More generally, ads focused on the supposed insecurities and inexperience of young women assuming a new role in life that they would fulfill successfully only by incorporating countless market goods into the household. Even food manufacturers that made familiar and ordinary consumer products played on recently married women's alleged lack of self-confidence in how they performed as homemakers. In one of La Campagnola's ads for its "What a Big Help in the Kitchen" campaign, the young newlywed declares that "I admit that when I got married, I was so scared of cooking on my own that I was shaking. But . . . it's been so much easier than I thought. Thanks to La Campagnola's mackerel in water, I whip up a delicious dish in no time. Even I am surprised how easy it is. And on top of that, it's scrumptious!"[51]

The pressure cooker was one of the latest kitchen gadgets that most intensely invoked newlywed women's supposed anxieties over preparing meals in advertisements. The young, single woman who was a terribly bad cook, had no experience, and frequently hid her lack of culinary knowledge and abilities from her future husband while dating was an iconic figure in the popular imagination. This is, for example, the character evoked in an Anbar pressure cooker ad announcing that "the specter of the newlywed bride who burns the food has disappeared thanks to the new Anbar pressure cooker." Advertisers stressed the idea that women who were young and inexpert especially needed to cook easily, economically, and rapidly. Although they had no kitchen skills, these young women were more familiar with technology and more eager to incorporate it into the household than older housewives. Also, they were particularly able to follow precise technical directions to optimize the performance of the cooker in a context in which the general public tended to see it as a complicated and unsafe device prone to explosions.[52]

Una legítima satisfacción

"Yo misma bordé mi vestido de novia"

PAÑUELOS Y ECHARPES. *Vistosos echarpes y elegantes pañuelos que pondrán un toque delicado y alegre en sus vestidos los hallará en los Centros de Costura Singer.*

"Llegó por fin el momento soñado... ¡Con qué amor bordé este vestido y cuánto cariño puse al preparar mi ajuar!... ¡Cuánto debo al Centro de Costura Singer donde aprendí a cortarme mis propios vestidos, bordar y prepararme para este delicioso momento!"

Usted también, amiga, puede seguir un Curso de Corte y Confección en el Centro de Costura Singer más cercano a su casa. Sólo 8 lecciones bastarán para aprender a hacerse un vestido. En el breve curso básico (dura 36 horas) aprenderá a diseñar, preparar moldes, cortar, coser y bordar. Si lo prefiere, puede llevar sus propios moldes y le ayudaremos a cortar y hacerse sus vestidos!

MÁQUINAS SINGER A PEDAL. *Lleve a su casa una moderna y práctica Máquina Singer a pedal. Le respaldan cerca de 100 años de experiencia. Cose, borda y zurce a perfección. Funciona suavemente.*

Singer Sewing Machine Co.

CENTROS DE COSTURA
SINGER ———

Hay uno cerca de su casa

SUCURSALES EN LA CAPITAL FEDERAL Y PRINCIPALES CIUDADES DEL INTERIOR DEL PAIS
EN EL URUGUAY:
Gral. Flores 3443, 18 de Julio 1101 y Cipriano Miró 2552, Montevideo, y en las ciudades uruguayas más importantes.

MUY ÚTIL PARA SU HOGAR. *Este libro, editado por Singer, pondrá a su alcance la manera más fácil de hacer fundas, cubrecamas, cortinas y muchas otras útiles prendas. Su precio es reducido.*

FIGURE 16: "I embroidered my wedding dress myself." Ads targeted young women consumers through the figure of the bride and a discourse based on the idea that home appliances like the sewing machine were as important for marriage as the wedding gown. *El Hogar*, August 19, 1949, 45.

Ads also stressed that the acquisition of a given consumer good was not only crucial to being the perfect bride, but also a condition for future marital bliss. In a 1949 ad, a smiling young woman in a simple wedding gown expressed her joy because her groom had satisfied the two desires of any happy bride: a nice ring and a Philips stove.[53] Based on this premise, advertisers put forward the idea—which scriptwriter Nené Cascallar and others energetically opposed—that consumer goods for the new house were indispensable requirements for marriage. In a popular advertising campaign for a well-known furniture maker, the bride responds to the priest's question: "I do. But under one condition: the furniture must be Eugenio Diez." The ad, just like magazine columns, reminded women who were about to marry that material well-being was important to a happy marital life: "It's understandable that you choose Eugenio Diez furniture: when you're starting off you might as well start off right. And as you're starting a new life, you want furniture that contributes to making your house a comfortable, pleasant, tasteful home, the home you've dreamed of: a warm home filled with hope to harbor your newlywed love and dreams."[54]

FIGURE 17: Consumer culture and a successful marriage are intertwined in this ad in which the man proposes with "an effective argument" by promising his girlfriend a stove. *Rosario*, February 12, 1955, 1.

Home Sweet Home

While advertisers promised newlyweds their products would bring marital bliss, consumption posed serious challenges to a happy marriage. Consumer culture, many agreed, had a profound alluring and hypnotic effect over women: "The street is a continuous invitation to spend. The window displays tempt you, the posters tempt you."[55] Similar to the common stereotype of working-class single women as materialistic, self-centered, and obsessed with shopping and personal appearance, the "uncontrolled spender" was a widespread characterization of married women, especially those without children. The male counterpart to this stereotype was a man who worked very hard but, emasculated by his controlling wife, had no say in purchasing decisions. This is the main character in the story published in *Cascabel* about the husband who gets only an ugly bow tie after his wife spends his entire annual bonus on things for herself.[56] Echoing this depiction, an upset husband argued that women should understand that a man "is not a money-making machine, but a flesh-and-blood being who suffers and sweats, who has to break his back all day to earn a salary."[57] In 1952, a reporter from the women's magazine *Para Ti* lamented that this figure of the exploited husband who worked exclusively to indulge his wife's whims enjoyed broad consensus: "Many married men are convinced that their respective wives suck their blood like leeches and live parasitically off their work."[58] This view hinged on the ideal division of labor between Mr. Breadwinner and Mrs. Consumer and on a traditional bias against consumption as a feminized, unproductive, and irrational sphere.[59]

The mid-twentieth-century image of the overindulgent housewife represented the reversal of gendered consumer stereotypes that had been popular in earlier decades. Until the 1940s, the popular press drew attention to married men's tendency to splurge especially on activities involving male friends and homosocial leisure. Commentators agreed that this was a prolonged habit from the days when these men had been economically independent bachelors. Socially accepted, men's personal spending on drinks, sports, and clubs apparently posed no conflicts with their financial responsibilities toward family and household, or, most likely, the media disregarded the negative opinions of unhappy wives. Social condemnation was directed toward working-class men though. In their case, critics stigmatized recreational activities as leading to drinking, gambling, and crime and thus as dangerous distractions that prompted lower-class men to evade their economic responsibilities as the breadwinners to the moral detriment of their abandoned women and children.[60]

By the 1950s, the perceived locus of conflict had changed. The allegations of excessive female spending on personal effects, particularly clothing, shoes, and cosmetics, became a well-known source of tension between spouses. In a 1947 article about couples' "number-one enemy," a woman declared that the way she spent money was a constant cause of arguments with her husband and that she hated "his general grumbling" over her spending. Living together had become harder due to the quarrels that broke out when the man reproached his wife for spending more on makeup than on food. The common belief was that women's spending on personal consumer goods damaged the household budget and reduced the funds available for the husband's expenditures.[61] These women lacked one of the traditionally highest-valued traits of women, that of being an efficient household administrator. A selfish and spendthrift housewife went against what was expected of women in terms of financial organization and discipline, savings, and consumer restraint, the cardinal principals of household economy, particularly among working-class women whose families had smaller incomes and tighter budgets.[62]

However, the perception of married women consumers was far from monolithic, and contrasting popular images that praised housewives for their purchasing decisions and ridiculed husbands for their incompetence also circulated widely in the collective imaginary. As chapter 2 shows, during the campaign for frugal consumption in the early 1950s, the Peronist government emphatically praised working-class housewives as prudent consumers and penny-pinching family managers while chastising men for their wasteful habits. Like the government, the feminine press underlined how men who accused their wives of being poor household administrators would be a complete failure if put in the same position. In a typical interpretation of the conflict between spouses over the household economy, *Nocturno* published an amusing short story of a man who took a day off work to stay at home and "teach" his wife how to shop wisely and save money. The experiment turned out to be a total fiasco since he was unprepared, unknowledgeable, and disorganized. The wife witnessed in dismay how her husband threw away the daily allowance when shopping, and destroyed cookware and spoiled food with his attempts to cook cheaply.[63]

Women were in a difficult position that demanded balancing household and personal expenses in a context in which social expectations of female appearances were unrealistic. In 1955, a *Para Ti* columnist affirmed that "whatever your occupation, you must never forget that you are a woman before all else and you have the obligation to be attractive."[64] Besides being time-consuming and psychologically stressful, this "obligation" was costly. However, even the working-class press compelled female readers to fulfill it no matter the price. In its popular column for women "Aquí, entre nosotras" ("Here, Between Us"), the newspaper *La Época* urged its working-class readers to splurge on hair salons, beauty products, manicures, and fashion accessories and to even change dressmakers—even though the new seamstress might have charged twice as much as the old one. The goal of attractiveness was pricey but clear; it was "the certainty that you look good every time you leave the house. The certainty that puts a shine in your eyes, confidence in your step, and satisfaction in spending the last cent in pursuing your best appearance."[65]

Women's magazines argued that beauty and image were the keys to success for all women regardless of their age or marital status, but they especially highlighted the importance of appearance for recently married women. Columns continuously advised female newlyweds that dressing elegantly, being attractive, and looking pretty were essential to marital happiness for they contributed to ensuring devoted husbands. While appeal had served as a weapon to find a man—the argument went—it continued to be a useful instrument to keep him. In support of this claim, Nené Cascallar urged women to avoid looking like a *fregona* (drudge) even if they had been scrubbing rooms all day. With unkempt looks, women instigated dispassion, indifference, and, ultimately, unfaithfulness in their husbands. The message to housewives was that a pleasant appearance should effectively conceal physical exertion and scruffy looks. Thus, the main recommendation for married women was to look better than when they were dating. Some even advocated wearing nice clothes and makeup for dusting, mopping the floors, washing clothes, and cooking. One columnist, for example, warned female readers: "Don't dress like an ugly slob with the excuse that you have to clean. [. . .] You must look nice for your husband and not just to go out window shopping or to see your friends."[66] In a context in which men reproved women's patterns of consumption for weakening the household economy, the article suggested that spending that boosted women's attractiveness ultimately strengthened marriage and kept husbands content.

Despite male complaints about women's overspending on personal items, the friction between spouses was not only about money. Husbands believed that consumer activities kept women outside the house for too long and thus challenged the traditional gendered division of public and private spheres. The image of multitudes in stores, movie theaters, cafés, and commercial streets that, as chapter 4 shows, had a strong class component also offered a new gendered representation of city life. More than one irritated man accused women of "taking over" all spaces of consumption: "Go to a movie theater: almost all women. Go to a café: three women for every man. And at the shops? Oh well!"[67] This image noticeably contrasted with portrayals of everyday life a few decades earlier that had depicted young working-class women leading a boring life marked by the monotony of the run-down neighborhood, a tedious social life, and a striking lack of distractions.[68] In the early twentieth century, in fact, men almost monopolized public spaces and participation in recreational activities, while women and especially married women, tended to avoid going out alone or spending too much time shopping, a result of their fear of what literary critic Adriana J. Bergero has called the equation of the woman in the street with the woman of the street.[69]

FIGURE 18: Women "invaded" consumer spaces like the department store La Piedad in Buenos Aires. Photo courtesy of Archivo General de la Nación.

But the mid-twentieth-century crowd of female consumers that flooded shopping districts also differed from current feminine images, most notably, from the traditional Peronist iconography in which women appeared sitting in front of the sewing machine, greeting husbands and children at home, or as working women, stereotypically represented by the self-abnegated nurse confined to the hospital.[70] When applied to working-class women, the famous Peronist motto "From home to work and from work to home" suggests the lack of government endorsement of unaccompanied shopping incursions or stops at the cafés. Most importantly, although women were among the newly entitled workers and consumers, Peronism believed they belonged first and foremost to the domestic sphere—especially if they were married. Indeed, the government was careful to never challenge traditional gender roles when celebrating the new consumer bliss enjoyed by the working sectors. In the Peronist iconography, working-class women always put the consumer needs of their families first, managed the household budget judiciously, and devotedly fulfilled their housekeeping responsibilities.

However, beyond Peronist ideals, the image of married women who felt more at home in the department store than in the kitchen was ubiquitous. The media labeled these women *las callejeras* (street women) and maintained that their aversion to domesticity was so strong that "it seems they're afraid the roof will cave in on them, so few are the hours they spend at home."[71] The term *callejera*, which could also refer to a streetwalker or a homeless woman, implicitly suggested the dangers faced by women who rejected domesticity as well as the stigma attached to it. But for callejeras, the derogatory label was less important than the exciting alternatives that spaces and practices of consumption, as roads to female independence and the modernization of gender conventions, offered to domestic life and housework. The consumer market was indeed the opposite of the home: it was public, social, convivial, entertaining, and alluring. It was an escape from a way of life that "has no consequence, glitz or reward." Nené Cascallar unsuccessfully advanced arguments for personal fulfillment through domesticity to married girlfriends who hated home chores and preferred spending hours window-shopping, at the hair salon, or in the movie theaters. One of her friends exclaimed, "I can't believe you don't have a nervous breakdown shut up between four walls," when Cascallar confessed she had not left her house in a week. A young housewife agreed: "I can assure you that I'm tired, apathetic, depressed. It seems that by always doing the same thing, I'm not doing anything, at least not anything important."[72]

The same feelings of emptiness and boredom were common among many working-class women who described their dreams to Professor Rest in *Idilio*. In one case, photographer Grete Stern imaginatively represented those emotions of tedious and exhausting imprisonment and the desire for escape through the image of a young woman desperately climbing out of a washbowl full of soapy water up a slippery washboard.[73]

Critics argued that in the pursuit of distractions and entertainment, married women severely neglected household tasks. Cascallar claimed, for example, that she could identify such women by merely glancing into their houses from the doorway.[74] Similarly, the main columnist of "Charlas Femeninas" ("Women's Talks"), the women's section in magazine *Mundo Argentino*, argued that "the callejeras are the ones who are never home, and where there's no woman, of course there's no order or cleanliness."[75] While in the early twentieth century, the anxieties over consumption had been almost exclusively related to "lascivious and despotic" upper-class ladies, the mid-twentieth-century concerns were centered on lower-class housewives who neglected housework—a responsibility that upper- and middle-class women lacked.[76] More generally, by relinquishing traditional domestic tasks, mid-twentieth-century women contributed to redefining womanhood as critics equated their conduct with traditional male behavior, that is, public behavior, on the streets, and in the market: "They're like those men who are a shadow in their own homes and who only show up to eat and sleep."[77] In this sense, as women who were corporeally and emotionally disconnected from domesticity, the callejeras embodied a form of masculine femininity.[78]

The male counterpart of the callejera was the man who spent more time at the sports club, the bar, or the café than he did at home. In the 1950s, men spent most of the day away from their families and women habitually wrote to counselors in women's magazines complaining about loneliness and seclusion while husbands had fun. Reflecting on this issue, a writer affirmed that "as men aren't in the habit of reading and they don't enjoy music, they never open a book or listen to the radio. The club or the café is thus their second home."[79] There was a consensus that while men protested against women's prolonged shopping excursions, their own absence from home gave wives a compelling reason to go out. Why should women stay in the house alone and frustrated when commercial streets offered so many distractions?[80]

But the "absent husband" was not the only counterpart to the callejera. In the popular imagination, the figure of the hardworking husband who took on all types of domestic chores was the prevalent male complement to the married woman who spent more time shopping for clothes than at home. The "domestic husband," the man who cooked, cleaned, ironed, and mopped while his wife was having a good time, was more fictional than real. The mid-twentieth-century press frequently reported that men hated household tasks and disliked helping their wives in even the smallest and easiest chores. According to the media, women alone were responsible for housework and mothers instructed little girls in household responsibilities from a very young age. For their part, female labor activists constantly complained about the "double burden" on women working both at the factory and at home while men offered their wives no assistance with the household chores.[81]

The figure of the "domestic husband" occupied a prominent place in the social imagination because regardless of the fact that he was rare among real men, he perfectly embodied the supposed reversal of gender expectations that happened when women left home for the department store. In other words, "masculine women," defined as those who rejected their domestic role, contributed to the reinvention of male masculinity. By enjoying financial freedom, making their own consumer decisions, and spending substantial time in commercial and recreational spaces, married women challenged a female identity based on economic dependency, emotional vulnerability, social isolation, and alienation from public spaces. The challenge equally destabilized a characterization of men as intrinsically autonomous and self-sufficient, as subjects physically unrelated to and emotionally detached from the domestic world. In disputing established gender conventions, the stereotypical "domestic husband" combined the traditional male provider with an unpaid domestic servant. This character became ubiquitous. He was the leading figure in several advertising campaigns and the main subject of numerous editorials, investigative reports, and comics; a photo of him wearing a white apron illustrated the cover of a famous cooking magazine for women; and his misadventures were the central theme of a popular daily radio show. Famous cartoonist Oski mocked the fears of emasculation, feminization, and weakness associated with the "domestic husband" by depicting men in typically feminine behaviors and wives acting in ways traditionally considered masculine. A weeping and distressed man sees his wife getting ready to leave while exclaiming, "Always going out with your friends, Laura, and you never remember to take me to the movies!" Another man, a feather duster in hand, gets angry at his wife and yells: "I'm telling you for the last time,

Sara! You keep sweeping your cigarette ashes under the rug and I'm going to my mother's!"[82]

But female consumption contested traditional gender expectations way beyond housekeeping. Consumer desires pushed women to get a job to be financially independent and active economic contributors to the household. An occupation—the argument frequently went—would ultimately make women overlook their domestic responsibilities while triggering the dreaded reversal of gender roles. Beyond the amusing portrayal of the "domestic husband," the media got serious when warning women about the emasculating effects that their decisions to work for a salary might have on their partners. Traditionally, female economic independence had been portrayed as a profound attack on the role of men as economic providers. In the 1950s, the attack went to the very core of the marital relation, at home—a danger different from the perceived competition of women on the job market that had threatened family men with unemployment in the mid-1930s.[83] Columnists in women's magazines reminded readers that a man's purpose was to sustain their families and that, stripped of that goal, men would feel inferior, insecure, and useless. A columnist in *Rosalinda* affirmed that "female labor is gradually weakening men. It's known that men put out an effort in proportion to the burden they bear. [. . .] Working women wrench from men's hands the possibility to struggle and triumph for themselves. By removing their natural burdens, women debilitate men mentally and morally."[84] This situation damaged the male character, affected conviviality, and generated a rivalry between spouses. Even worse, in some cases men would fully relinquish their work responsibilities, leaving wives with the unsolicited burden of becoming the main providers.[85]

In contrast to potentially emasculated husbands, women who worked were differentiated according to the type of consumption that compelled them to find a job. First, there was the greedy and acquisitive woman who was obsessed with the "small luxuries" her husband was unable to afford.[86] This was the kind of woman who offended her husband by shouting: "Deal with it, Juancho! I bought this myself! I don't need you!" The media considered that her aims were superfluous, selfish, and frivolous and that her independence posed serious threats to marital bliss and male self-confidence. However, this image concealed the fact that it was neither materialism nor spousal competition that prompted many women to work, but the honest goal of financial independence to cover personal expenses. A young woman lamented that she had to explain all her expenditures to her husband and envied working women who managed their own money and freely decided how to spend it:

There are some things I'd rather not have to tell my husband that I buy, for example, the powders, certain perfumes, a blush or a lipstick. Basically, little beauty supplies that lose all their charm and value if they're mentioned before they're used. It's odd that Luis, like so many husbands, doesn't understand this. [. . .] Sometimes I think how lucky those women are who have their small income or monthly allowance. Those women don't need to say to their husbands: Dear, I need ten pesos . . . Do you have five pesos, dear? I need to buy something.[87]

The second type of working woman was the one who accepted a job out of alleged material necessity or, more generally, with the well-intentioned goal of improving her family's standard of living. The purpose was socially perceived as respectable, generous, and reasonable. María Roldán explained that when she took a job in a meat-packing plant in the 1940s, she told her husband that "it would be for a while," but she remained at the plant for ten years. She justified her decision by arguing that she prioritized the well-being of the household and the fulfillment of basic needs: "You had to continue and continue because we were improving our house and though it seems not so, an extra pay packet every two weeks improves the home, buys you sheets, an extra bed, a mattress, eat a little better."[88]

The reasons explaining why married women like María Roldán worked may have enjoyed increasing acceptance in the 1950s, but the relationship between female employment and consumption was still extremely problematic. The same anxieties over uncontrolled female sexuality, the deterioration of patriarchy, and the decline of the family that challenged single women's right to get a job were even more potent in the case of married female workers. In this regard, a magazine columnist categorically affirmed that "the callejeras were not born to raise a family."[89] In his description of life in mid-1940s Buenos Aires, physician Florencio Escardó reinforced this argument by noting that "for those who observe the Buenos Aires crowds, two features are noted immediately: the clear and striking predominance of women and the almost total lack of children."[90] Escardó was implicitly drawing attention to the declining birth rate among the working-class sectors, a serious concern of the time. Between the mid-1940s and late 1950s, the birth rate grew among the urban middle classes and the European immigrants who had arrived to the country right after the war. However, the birth rate among internal working-class migrants was declining, and, in contrast to the past, their families were shrinking and becoming as small as middle-class families. To counteract this tendency, the Peronist government articulated a gender ideology that encouraged married women to stay at home while appealing to them as housewives and mothers rather than workers. Eva Perón directly asked women to decide the "home or factory dilemma" in favor of the former and thus to choose motherhood over work.[91]

Catholic sectors, for their part, which had traditionally been against female work and, especially in the case of married women, were also a strong force of opposition to female labor and consumption. Although some Catholics believed that women only worked when poverty forced them to, most Catholic thinkers manifested that, in truth, women from the low-income sectors got jobs to pay for unnecessary consumer goods rather than to feed their families. Most significantly, Catholics were appalled at the case of young working-class couples who, in their search for self-indulgence and comfort, postponed parenthood or rejected it altogether. In 1949, one of the presenters at the "Social Restoration of the Argentine Family Conference" organized by the Acción Católica Argentina (Argentine Catholic League) asked the audience, "Who hasn't heard of working-class men and even working-class women boldly stating that they are going to get married but they aren't going to have children?"[92] Catholics attacked this choice as the triumph of acquisitiveness over family responsibilities and, most particularly, over what they considered the sacred obligation of motherhood.

While pointing an accusatory finger to the working-class sectors, Catholics charged the Peronist government with the destructive consequences of popular consumption. Even before the violent clashes with the government in 1954 and in spite of the Peronist defense of traditional gender roles and the implementation of numerous policies assisting families with children and promoting a higher birth rate, the Catholic Church blamed the government for the corrupting hedonism of the lower sectors. Catholic commentators maintained that the state had carelessly instigated burning consumer desires among the working classes without demanding ethical conduct or warning about the pernicious effects of materialism. In a direct attack on the official rhetoric of social well-being, a writer from the Catholic magazine *Criterio* affirmed that, in the end, a country was dignified by the moral virtues of its people and not because "all its inhabitants have an electric washing machine, a gas stove, and can go to the movies every week."[93]

In the midst of concerns over a declining population, accusations of self-indulgence, and the menace of male emasculation, some sympathetic commentators took pity on women who stayed at home and depended on their husbands' paychecks but suffered greatly because of this decision. In its many different versions, the stereotype of the acquisitive and egotistical wife went hand in hand with the archetype of the generous, tolerant, and resigned husband or, in less positive terms, of the dominated and powerless one. However, these widely circulating images did not reflect the fact that innumerable wives were married to stingy husbands and that, in a context in which employment was still taboo for many married women, they were unable to change their poor economic situation. Indeed, a columnist in *Para Ti* asserted that "the number of unfair, selfish husbands is infinitely greater than the number of spendthrift, inconsiderate wives."[94] In contrast to the images of the enthusiastic consumer wife, the unfortunate woman who married this type of man had no time for leisurely shopping, was constrained by a very tight household budget, had no personal funds, suffered strict control over personal and household expenses, and endured the most strenuous domestic chores only to save money:

> There are perhaps no women more unfortunate than the wives of men who protect their money with their lives, because these men deny their wives even the right to dress and feed themselves. They are the men who force their wives to do the work of three maids without even giving the poor woman money to spend as she pleases, the same men who give their wives a sum for household expenses every morning and every night demand a detailed list of her purchases, the same men who accuse their wives of spending too much and who make the first days of the month a living hell for them.[95]

Women's magazines recommended that readers pay increasing attention to the prospects of the future couple's household economy and budget before getting married: "You know what he has, what he makes. Are his standard of living, his habits, and his education in line with the kind of life you expect? Don't try to fool him or yourself by affirming that love is more than enough."[96] Due to inexperience, lack of ambitions, or romantic ideals, women in the past had tended to ignore potential financial complications and ended up marrying in spite of limited means. Now marriage was about companionship and children, but it was also about making and managing money. Social commentators argued that in contrast to their mothers, for mid-twentieth-century women, the resources of the couple were a priority and how men administered money was a matter of serious consideration. In 1951, *Para Ti* covered the story of a young lady who broke off her engagement when her fiancé refused to leave a tip because, he argued, he "did not throw money away." The woman realized that "he wasn't the man for me" and thought that "if he kept his money under lock and key I would do better to stick with my single life and the economic independence that my well-paid job brings."[97]

The fact that single women carefully assessed men's views on money and their financial decisions must have been quite widespread, noteworthy, and puzzling provided that, in 1955, it was a topic of discussion in publications like the newspaper edited by the predominantly male union of insurance sellers. One author asserted that he was not completely unsympathetic toward women who prioritized economic concerns and closely assessed men's patterns of spending, especially when such women had a job and were financially independent. Still, the columnist negatively described these women as "pretentious" and affirmed that lofty ambitions would only grant them a gloomy future as *solteronas* (spinsters). In a publication for a male readership, men were reassured that the independent woman paid a high price for her materialistic stance by becoming bitter and "incomplete." However, this traditional stereotype of the solterona was a far cry from the cheerful Divito girls or the exultant Olga for whom self-indulgent singlehood was a personal choice rather than a punishment.[98]

Most women's magazines did not openly encourage these role models as suggested by their photographic covers showing young couples cuddling romantically, exciting love stories, and articles on how to find the "man of your dreams." But contributors did celebrate acts of female self-assertion that prevented women from entering an unhappy marriage. The *Para Ti* women's consultant applauded the young lady's determination to call off the engagement after her fiancé refused to tip and urged women to follow her example. Women, the writer reflected, should pay attention to even the smallest clues as to how husbands-to-be acted as consumers. The caution was dire, pivoted on female fears of privation, servitude, and oppression after marriage, and challenged idealizations of marital life as idyllic. The anecdote about the tip made clear that "if ever a humble coin has saved a woman from disappointment and disenchantment, this was the time."[99] Indeed, more often than not, instead of urging women to work and gain financial independence, the media prompted them to select their husbands carefully and exhorted men to be generous and comprehensive to make wives happy and to keep peace at home. Beyond these exhortations, women's magazines ridiculed and openly detested stingy husbands because they were "the worst curse that could befall a family."[100] In 1953, a contributor to *Rosalinda* argued that these men were the most irrefutable proof that "every man carries inside him the faint marks of a potential dictator."[101] Along with open rejection, the press conveyed the idea that these men were unsuitable for married life: "These egomaniacs should stay single and spend their money on themselves, since it's so hard for them to let go of it."[102] Just as social commentators believed that women obsessed with consuming and spending were unfit for bringing up a family, miserly men did not make good husbands either.

The new forms of consumption and a more inclusive consumer market in the mid-twentieth century altered the way in which men and women related to each other, the decisions they made regarding their marital status, the material standards they set in establishing a home, as well as the roles they played in the household. Consumption was crucial to creating gender stereotypes that reflected the tensions between men and women who increasingly disagreed in key aspects of married life including working for a living, expenses, and domestic duties. Patterns of spending and consumer decisions were essential in redefining stereotypes of dedicated homemakers and virtuous husbands and, ultimately, in transforming the meanings of what a happy marriage was across social classes, but especially among the working-class consumers who experienced exceptional wage increases. Public debates about household economy showed the mounting anxieties over the social effects of consumption, effects that challenged ideas as enduring as women's "natural" predisposition to housework, married women's financial dependency on husbands, and men's responsibility as sole economic providers. Those debates also revealed how consumption pervaded even less predictable aspects of everyday life, from concepts of female beauty and appearance to definitions of male power and men's righteousness.

The popular media, especially women's and home magazines, greatly contributed to the circulation of images, prescriptions, warnings, and arguments about the transformations that mass consumer culture fueled in gender relations. The role of the press was problematic, as the messages it delivered were significantly inconsistent, a clear manifestation of a process of change in which old gender beliefs were superimposed with new viewpoints. In this way, while many social commentators warned women against stingy men, they advised married housewives to stay at home rather than work to secure their personal financial independence. Similarly, columnists criticized young couples for delaying their wedding because of their high material expectations while magazines bombarded audiences with advertisements that set increasingly high comfort standards for newlyweds and made domestic bliss contingent upon ownership of a wide array of consumer goods. In addition, magazines condemned homemakers who neglected their households and felt better shopping than they did cleaning but recognized that husbands were uncooperative and spent most of their time away from home.

Although male social types like the bon vivant were the object of disapproval, stereotyped female consumers were particularly perceived as socially disruptive. Materialistic women who valued economic independence and small luxuries over marriage as well as ambitious fiancées obsessed with the latest gadgets for their new residences challenged traditional ideals of family, motherhood, and even morality. In reality, aside from allegations of exaggerated materialism and frivolity, young female consumers were average working women who were gaining new and significant roles on the job market and clearly understood the changes that marriage would bring to their finances and standard of living. For their part, the stereotypes of hedonistic housewives defied expectations of complete devotion to home and children and resisted compliance with male control over the household economy. Images of pleasure-seeking women disobeyed traditional icons of frugal and dutiful homemakers who were ready to sacrifice their consumer wants for the needs of their families. While the collective imagination depicted these characters as unruly, the moralizing condemnation of women was toned down by pointing to men as culprits. Magazine columnists, radio personalities, and newspaper journalists openly disapproved of men whose absence, aloofness, and tightfistedness contributed to distancing women from the gendered norm. Writers in women's magazines claimed that self-indulgent bachelors, selfish fiancés, and miserly and indolent husbands ultimately got what they deserved.

Beyond stereotypes and anxieties, participation in the mid-twentieth-century mass consumer culture heightened the sense of personal freedom and expanded individual and collective choices, frequently positioning consumers in conflict with traditional gender and class expectations. Through consumption, young working-class men and women found new forms of individual and collective expression that allowed them to employ consumer goods and practices to communicate who they were and to understand the social relationships they developed with others. The impact of this experience was so strong that it survived for many decades in the memories of a generation.

CHAPTER 6

Tales of Consumers

Memory and Working-Class Material Culture

One of the most remarkable components of the mid-twentieth-century imagination was the powerful awareness among Peronists, anti-Peronists, and those outside the great political divide that the historical process they were part of was both unique and unrepeatable. In 2005, Amelia Foresto, who worked in a small pharmaceutical factory in the 1950s, conveyed to me that sense of historical exceptionality. In remembering her past as a young working woman, Amelia suggested how the expansion of the consumer market that fascinated advertising agents, industrialists, government officials, and journalists was a transformative collective and individual experience for the newly incorporated working-class consumers. Amelia recalled that the first time I went in to Gath & Chaves [a chic department store in downtown Rosario], I couldn't believe it. What a place! I had seen the ads in *La Capital* and I thought it would be nice to be able to buy something there, but it was impossible. And well, the day finally arrived and I spent my first Christmas bonus there. It was probably 1949 or 1950. I can't remember what I bought, but it was the first time I had gone into a shop downtown.[1]

Amelia Foresto's recollections evoked relative affluence, purchasing choices and new consumer goods as vividly as feelings of spatial and social inclusion, the satisfaction of long-term material desires, and a profound sense of personal achievement. Much has been said about the irretrievability of the subaltern voices as a consequence of archival dearth and authorial and power issues, but the quest of making history more inclusive continues to be so enticing that scholars have persevered in their attempts to do so.[2] Among these different attempts, oral history offers one of the most promising entry points into the "everyday side of culture," that is, the lives of ordinary individuals but, most importantly, the way in which they made and make sense of the world around them.[3] Although oral historians may gaze hopefully through this window, they also now know, as historian Daniel James has put it, that "the view it affords is not a transparent one that simply reflects thoughts, feelings as they really were/are. At the very least the image is bent, the glass of the window unclear."[4] This notion emerged when oral historians, influenced by postmodern ethnography and the "linguistic turn," began to debate the purposes and tensions of their craft including the differential power in terms of gender, racial, class, and cultural capital between the interviewer and the interviewee; the moral and ethical dilemmas arising from interpretation of oral sources and the allocation of authorship; the relationship among factual information, errors, and inventions; and the role of memory. Central to this discussion was the realization that the typical product of an oral interview is a text that poses intriguing questions about meanings and coherence.[5]

Meanings are, in fact, at the core of this chapter, which is primarily based on the testimonies of working-class consumers who, more than fifty years later, remembered and interpreted their experiences in mid-twentieth-century Argentina. The analysis is an attempt to connect life to times, uniqueness to representativeness.[6] The interviewees, who defined themselves as *trabajadores*, were a diverse group of wage-earners that included industrial, construction, and railroad workers, sale clerks, secretaries, and seamstresses, as well as housewives. Most of the interviewees were born in the 1920s and early 1930s and a minority in the 1910s, and lived in Buenos Aires and mostly in Rosario in the following decades. The period that I asked them to particularly focus on corresponded to the time of their lives when they were young men and women, generally ages twenty-five to thirty-five. For the most part, the interviews started with my questions, but I found that many respondents had their own interests and agendas and felt strongly about what was important to discuss. So I followed their lead, and most times, I discovered fascinating issues that expanded my initial perspective, enriched the terms of inquiry, and became important to me as well. In some cases, enthusiastic and fascinating narrators encouraged me to collect their life stories, which went beyond the theme and historical period of my study. This placed consumption within a historical continuum, thus accentuating the specific changes of consumer power in the mid-twentieth century. Most important, since life stories express people's sense of self—who they are and how they came to be that way—they added valuable insights to the understanding of identity construction.[7]

Based fundamentally on oral history, this chapter is about memory as much as it is about history. Memory refers to the mental faculty by which we retrieve the past as well as to the past itself, or better yet, the versions of the past we recover. Historian Pierre Nora has argued that memory is alive, a product of the present that is in constant evolution through the dynamics of remembering and forgetting, appropriation and manipulation. Personal and individual, memory is at the same time inherently collective since we express it through language, a social construction that sets the standards of plausibility and authenticity of what we recall and how we express it. As a narrative, then, the form of memory is as important as its content.[8] Thus, this chapter analyzes the narrative choices of working-class interviewees in order to show how linguistic patterns in their testimonies were crucial to the construction of working-class agency and identity. If language defines a "field of expressive possibilities," so do cultural scripts, specific past and present public discourses that subjects use, though not always consciously, to make sense of their past experiences and articulate their memories. As pervasive as the influence of cultural scripts may be, it is not completely restrictive. While analyzing the testimonies of interviewees, I realized that the most intriguing issue was not the presence of cultural scripts, but the question of why respondents chose the scripts they employed and, most significantly, how and why they rejected others. In other words, although memory is socially shared and culturally and historically shaped, it still needs the individuals, in all their uniqueness and exceptionality, to come alive.[9] In this regard, since it is formed at the juncture of subject and process, oral history alters the traditional criteria of representativeness in the social sciences, acknowledging that the individual both represents and departs from the historical process. This tension is there for the oral historians to interrogate and include as part of their interpretations; it is more of an asset than an epistemological shortcoming.[10]

Through the analysis of working-class testimonies, this chapter explores the role of consumption as an arena of subjective self-creation and representation. As oral history is an exercise involving a social and individual reconstruction of the past as well as personal self-construction, remembering is crucial for the creation of identity both past and present. Interviewees used memories of consumption to reaffirm their working-class identity by contesting public discourses that both have downplayed the agency of workers in attaining a better standard of living and have interpreted greater consumer power as a means of social emulation. When remembering the 1940s and 1950s, interviewees reproduced conventional wisdom about the transcendental role that Peronism played in the material bonanza and yet, rather than assuming the passive role of recipients, working-class folks reinscribed themselves as active participants in the consumer market. Higher levels of consumption did not mean abandoning traditional practices like thriftiness and shopping at neighborhood stores, but adapting to new opportunities and selectively incorporating new goods. Consumption, interviewees suggested, was not a channel for rising class aspirations or a marker of a higher class standing that placed individuals outside their social group. Instead, workers interpreted consumer goods and practices in terms of social achievement and personal gratification that reinforced their class belonging. Furthermore, the memories of consumption pivoted on a broad array of 1950s consumer goods like sewing machines, electric refrigerators, and garments. Through an analysis of the recollections of consumer goods, this chapter reminds us of the materiality of culture and reveals the significance of ordinary objects not only in the reconstruction of one's personal past, but also in structuring collective memory.

Working-Class Consumption and the Role of Peronism

In 1951, in her Christmas message, Eva Perón declared that

> I know that many years from now, when Argentines slip back into their memories and fly back into the past on this same night in the future, they will come back to these years of their lives and nostalgically say, "We were happy then. Perón was with us." Because the truth, the unassailable truth is that we are all happier now than we were before Perón.[11]

Evita synthesized the idea of Peronism as a historical rupture, as the peak of social well-being, inexistent before Peronism and unrepeatable afterwards. As Evita had predicted in her 1951 Christmas message, many decades later, working-class Argentines continued to believe that life during Peronism had been one of the happiest times of their lives and that collective bliss, equated with a better standard of living and the acquisition of goods, was associated with Perón's leadership. When retelling her life story to Daniel James in the late 1980s, María Roldán, a Peronist meat-packing worker from Berisso, fifty miles from Buenos Aires, enthusiastically voiced this version of the past:

> In Perón's time Berisso was one of the happiest places on the face of earth. I have seen people happy, shopping, going on their vacations because we got paid vacations too. [. . .] Everyone was happier. There were dances every Saturday and Sunday. There were two cinemas in Berisso. People could dress better. There were people who didn't know Buenos Aires before Perón.[12]

The idyllic days of Peronism when wages were high and entertainment, food, and goods were abundant and accessible to all is a story I heard many times myself. The troubles that occurred in those prosperous times, like periodic shortages of foodstuffs and fuel, inflation, and long lines at stores, were not part of the narratives. It is likely that, in the memories, these inconveniences were overshadowed by the serious economic difficulties that these working-class consumers would confront in the following decades, most notably the hyperinflation of the 1980s. Occasionally, respondents mentioned *pan negro*, the low-quality bread that resulted from the disastrous 1952 wheat harvest, or the government prohibition to sell beef one day a week, which also started that year, as the most common nuisances faced by consumers during the period. However, neither threatened the persistent memories of bliss. Any conversation about the 1950s, as unrelated as the initial topic might have been, always involved stories of high standards of living and material well-being, and, as in the case of María Roldán's, most times they closely resembled Peronist propagandistic scripts as well as the commonplace anti-Peronist protestations analyzed in chapter 4. During Peronism, Luis Ricardo Romero was a worker and a Peronist union delegate in Estexa, the biggest textile factory in Rosario:

> Before Perón, no one taught people how they should live. When Perón and Evita took power, they taught people to live; for example, people stopped wearing alpargatas and started wearing shoes; they exchanged their old ripped sweaters for nice ones. So the high-society people just couldn't believe that they would be walking along Córdoba Street [in downtown Rosario] and they would walk by workers wearing nice sweaters and decent shoes. Then they would say: "We can't wait for the alpargata to return." But the alpargata had disappeared.[13]

When recounting the changes in mid-twentieth-century Argentina, Luis combined prototypical elements of Peronist and anti-Peronist ideology: the role of the Peróns as civilizing providers, clothing as a marker of newly acquired comfort and as a means of social leveling, and the rejection of the upper classes during a social transformation that Luis deemed both unique and irrevocable. The presence of available cultural scripts in personal accounts does not reduce the legitimacy of individual perceptions or make the Peronist bonanza illusory, but it does show how established discourses found their way into the narratives of individuals and societies through "vehicles of memory" like the media, schools, and institutional histories.[14] It also demonstrates that although it commonly materializes through individual minds and voices, memory is a social construction and, to borrow historian Pierre Nora's definition, a generational paradigm that grows out of social interactions and a common collective history that subjects later internalize.[15] The reinscription of available scripts is evident in the case of committed Peronist militants politically loyal to the Peronist cause. These militants, who were more or less formally indoctrinated, may have reflected on these issues and rehearsed these narratives before. But the incorporation of official discourses and formulas is also manifest among Peronist supporters, a group that includes workers who identified themselves as nonmilitant Peronists or who expressed their approval of Peronism without establishing political identification. For these interviewees, the available ideological repertoire was useful in maintaining and strengthening their political sympathy for Peronism while functioning as evidence that "authenticated" their versions of the past. Both groups of interviewees may be considered part of the same "mnemonic community" that shares common mnemonic traditions, commemorations, and socialization and, as a result, a common past they all seem to recall.[16]

Although they proudly defined themselves as "Perón's Peronists," "Peronists from the start," and "Peronists until death," because "Peronism is like a religion that you never abandon," most interviewees aimed to convey their stories as neutral accounts and rarely admitted that their political identity or inclinations might influence their recollections. This was evident in my conversations with Héctor Acosta who defined himself as a "Peronist sympathizer." Héctor held several occupations in his youth, from a job at a Swift food plant in Rosario to a cleaning post in the Santa Fe Provincial Bank, jobs that allowed him to finish his studies and land a clerical position at the bank in the 1950s. Héctor argued that

> I liked Perón because he fought for the poor, for the descamisados. With Perón, people purchased their first homes and went on vacation. Young working men walked around in nice clothes and earned a very, very good salary during Perón's administration. I'm not saying this because I liked Perón: I saw it for myself. I saw it in the bank, where working folks got loans to buy their home. There were long lines! They would never have been able to get a loan in the past, not in their wildest dreams.[17]

By using "I saw it," a common expression among respondents, Héctor Acosta invoked the language of spectatorship to highlight the historical evidence in his account and to dispute the potential conclusion that his recollections might have been the result of political propagandism. In their attempts to convey a sense of impartiality and credibility, interviewees strived to provide "proof," examples or arguments that substantiated the Peronist repertoire and their own political views. This interest in "validation" illustrates the pervasiveness of a version of professional positivist history among common people who associated their collaboration in a project of oral history with an obligation of accuracy and truth. But it also shows the centrality of reliability and consistency in self and social perception.

By emphasizing their identities as witnesses, interviewees produced and articulated a high standard of historical veracity. For interviewees, observation, participation, and "having been there" sanctioned their authority as sources of information and validated their individual experiences as representative of the past. As historical observers, they embodied the collective experience of a generation.

In Héctor Acosta's and other testimonies, the Peronist government appears in the role of enabler and provider of the good things in life, an aspect frequently stressed through the use of "con Perón" (with Perón), a discursive choice that not only refers to the times of the Peronist government, but also suggests Perón's personal guidance and companionship. The recurrence of "con Perón" and its role in the accounts points to what oral historian Marie Francoise Chanfrault-Duchet has termed a "key phrase," a formal marker that accents the narrative and aims to define the type of relation between the self and the social sphere.[18] In this case, "con Perón" commonly prefaces the exclusion of the narrator from the collective. Indeed, there is a noticeable and reiterated reference to "the people" and "the workers" in these types of accounts, but interviewees do not directly incorporate themselves as subjects belonging to these social entities. Workers did reflect extensively on the changes in their own standard of living but avoided framing those reflections in a version of Peronism as a provider. This is evident, for example, in an exchange with Juan Carlos Legas, a textile worker who considered himself a supporter of Peronism:

> With Perón, workers fixed up their houses and discovered the gas stove, the electric refrigerator, the washing machine, and countless other things. They used to have coal irons and then they found out what the electric iron was. Everyone purchased home appliances, which weren't as good as the ones available today, but they were still good.
> *You too?*
> Yes, I built my house, I bought an electric fridge . . . But I was always hardworking and independent, and I worked very hard to buy everything, spent years at the factory.[19]

When interviewees needed to reflect on consumerism from personal experience and far from grandiloquent political statements about affluence during Peronism, they discursively removed the Peronist government and repositioned themselves as the main characters in the acquisition of goods and the attainment of a comfortable life. This was particularly evident in connection to the purchase of expensive household appliances, mainly refrigerators and stoves, which represented one of the biggest expenditures for low-income households and were acquired by working-class consumers in installment plans. Besides hard work and self-sufficiency—the factors that Juan Carlos Legas mentioned when explaining how he purchased his home and refrigerator—most interviewees invoked a culture of rational saving that allowed them to invest in consumer durables, and referred to financial planning over a lifetime with a focus on family needs. Violeta Benvenuto, who worked as a secretary and was an activist in the Women's Peronist Party, offers a good example of these types of rationales. In her account, her family, their work, and the careful attention they devoted to the household budget are what drove the satisfaction of material needs— not Perón or the government:

> We never lived better than we did under Peronism. There was always extra money, great salaries, good retirement plans . . . There was never another leader like Perón but I also have to say that my family was always struggling. We are hardworking, people who know the value of savings. We knew how to live, how to manage our money, even before Perón, when there wasn't so much. We had a slogan: no credit. We always paid in cash.[20]

Like in these examples, many interviewees placed themselves, the working-class consumers, at the center of the personal stories of material comfort while situating Peronism in a secondary position, that of a propitious historical context. Here, Peronism set the structural conditions for progress but lost direct intervention. In this way, interviewees moved their narratives from a political level in which Peronism was eulogized as a catalyst for material well-being for "the people" to a personal level that allowed them to reposition themselves as accomplishers. Oral historian Alessandro Portelli has shown that most narrators try to make their stories coherent by placing their memories and their meanings in three different mnemonic modes: the sphere of politics, the life of the community, and personal experiences. Furthermore, Portelli has argued that shifts between modes, which for my interviewees is the move from politics to personal life, is a strategy to handle problematic matters.[21] In this case, I believe that this strategy is a tacit response to cultural and historical assumptions created and promoted by both the Peronist government and anti-Peronists alike that have erased working-class agency in the search for a better standard of living.

By shifting the narrative modes, respondents do not reject the tale of Peronist bonanza, but when confronted to position themselves within the story, they attributed the accomplishment of consumer bliss—through hard work, savings, and rational spending behavior—to themselves, the workers. In so doing, working-class interviewees challenged problematic cultural scripts that have traditionally casted workers in the role of recipients rather than consumers of goods.

The role of workers as recipients is clear in the Peronist discourse of happiness based on metaphors of prodigality and images of prosperity in which Perón functioned as a historical redeemer and his government emerged as a provider of material benefits. This conception extended well beyond Peronist welfare services, including public works and infrastructure, to fully encompass consumer goods that workers purchased on the market. In recounting an exchange with some members of the upper sectors, Perón offered a typical example of his identification with a supplier who defied the greed of the oligarchy and bestowed upon the workers the right to indulgence through the enjoyment of nonessential goods:

In 1947 and '48, they used to say to me, "Don't give them so much, those people spend it all on wine." I responded, well, they're poor! They haven't had wine in so long! They [the oligarchy] always had another way of looking at things: "We don't give to the poor so they don't spend and will learn to be thrifty." Thrifty, for what? They didn't have anything.[22]

Perón used the self-image of an openhanded father repeatedly in stories about meat-packing workers who came to see him wearing silk shirts, statements that the beef ration in Argentina doubled the recommended daily intake, and portrayals of everyday living of the working class characterized by weekly visits to entertainment venues.[23] Anti-Peronists, for their part, reinforced this image by considering that the working class had sold off their liberty, autonomy, and rights in exchange for consumer goods. Thus, material benefits represented the basis of an unequal and exploitative relationship, an idea that writer Ezequiel Martínez Estrada vividly condensed by arguing that "Perón used money like a drug: it was the opium that he gave the people; it was a superstitious spell he cast."[24] In this widespread view, the attraction toward goods transformed workers into a manipulated mass rather than into conscientious actors pursuing a realistic path to the overdue satisfaction of their material needs.

Cartoonist José Antonio Ginzo, aka Tristán, a militant of the Socialist Party and a frequent illustrator of party publications, portrayed this argument in *Old Trick*, the drawing of a donkey—the "thoughtless workers" as it reads on its side—excitedly running after a carrot marked as "promises" and attached to a stick over its head. In Argentina the burro is both a symbol of hard physical work and exploitation and a slang term that refers to an obstinate, stupid, or ignorant individual. In its careless and ultimately fruitless race, the donkey in the illustration proves true to these features by obliviously running toward a precipice. Below, a tiger marked with swastikas—product of the common association between Peronism and Nazism—lies in wait for its prey.[25]

In spite of their clearly different assessments on state paternalism and Perón as its incarnation, both the Peronist discourse of goods as gifts and the anti-Peronist discourse of goods as bait circumvented workers, labor, and hard-won wages in order to present goods as offerings rather than as commodities. The magazine *Mundo Peronista* conveyed this notion in an article about "happy" textile worker Aída Rojas. In her testimony, Aída addresses the sacrifice and exploitation before Peronism and recalls with sadness that her two small children were "filled with shame, ragged and hungry." Then she turns to praise her new comfortable life, which makes her "fanatic about Perón and Evita." In closing, Aída thanks the president for the radio, the full closet, and the nights at the movies that she now enjoys.[26] Similarly, the short story "¿Esto occurría antes?" ("Did This Happen Before?") combines working-class indulgence, social leveling, and Peronism as enabler in a conventional piece of didactic propaganda about popular consumption. In the story, an iceman named Antonio takes his girlfriend to the luxurious restaurant Tabarís in Buenos Aires to celebrate his birthday. When they are leaving the restaurant, the couple runs into Don Carlos, a rich businessman and one of Antonio's customers. When Don Carlos' wife recognizes Antonio and after the two couples exchange greetings, Antonio tells them that he had delivered ice to Tabarís with his father since he was a child and that he had always dreamed of being able to come to the restaurant as a customer. But life was hard, and his family had constantly struggled to make ends meet. This, Antonio reflected, changed after 1946 when higher wages and Perón made his dream come true: "Thanks to Perón, I was finally able to come to Tabarís and pay 25 pesos for a drink. [. . .] It's no longer a desire that can never be satisfied." The story ends with the couples happily toasting to Antonio's birthday and to Peronism, which "allows them to celebrate without social differences."[27]

By articulating the participation of working-class consumers in the market culture through a language evocative of gifts, the government highlighted the figure of Perón as a benefactor while downplaying the historical struggle of the labor movement for a better standard of living, the economic conditions that made it possible, and most significantly, those who toiled to be able to afford what the market had to offer. Similarly and in a succinct fashion, the ubiquitous slogan "Perón cumple" ("Perón delivers") not only reminded Argentines of the generous and dependable leader who kept his promise of making the working people happy, but also obliterated the individual and collective efforts that were fundamental for personal and national progress. These are the efforts that the working-class interviewees highlighted in their narratives while challenging the portrayal of workers as self-indulgent, childish, dependent, and spendthrift, portrayals implicit in both the paternalist Peronist and anti-Peronist rhetorics. For example, Norma Mordini, a housewife married to a railroad worker, contested this notion by arguing that

> it's true that people had great lives during Peronism. Perón increased wages, people bought a lot of new things, I don't know . . . People did well . . . but it was also up to you. We were cautious. We didn't say, "Oh, I've got money, I'll go out and spend it," because you had to earn the money, and you had to work to buy things. [. . .] I always sewed my children's clothes and saved the annual bonus payment.[28]

With their reinstatements of consumer agency, working-class interviewees also implicitly defied official narratives in which the enjoyment of material prosperity imposed an associated duty. Indeed, the official language and imagery of the gift implied the generation of a debt that the government skillfully employed when in need of popular support. This was particularly evident in times of elections, the implementation of economic packages to fight inflation, and the campaign to increase industrial productivity.[29] In times of crisis, the government made it clear that the consumers played a more important role than the state in the successful return to abundance and summoned these consumers as responsible parties. Thus the government highlighted its role as provider in good times but made consumers accountable for material well-being in less advantageous conditions. On the verge of the implementation of the 1952 economic plan, designed to fight an unfavorable trade balance and rising prices, the government persistently called upon consumers to cut back on spending and avoid wasteful consumer behavior. In this context, Eva Perón eloquently shifted the responsibility and informed women, her intended interlocutors, of their obligations toward their "generous leader":

> Perón has again proven that our well-being is owed to his extraor-
> dinary leadership, which allows us to live as happy people in a world
> filled with uncertainty and concern. General Perón has presented us
> his Economic Plan; he has told us what we have to do . . . We cannot
> relieve the Argentine woman of her social responsibility—especially
> Peronist women, since we represent the living, fecund essence of the
> true Argentine people.[30]

No other Peronist institution reinforced the notion of gift and consequent debt in the popular imagination more unmistakably than the Eva Perón Foundation. A charitable organization founded by the first lady in 1948, the foundation became renowned for rapidly constructing and opening schools, hospitals, homes for orphans and single mothers, vacation resorts for workers, grocery stores, and working-class restaurants that were usually housed in sumptuous buildings and provided first-rate services. Most importantly, the foundation became legendary for the direct distribution of food, mattresses, medicine, clothes, toys, and sewing machines to the poorest sectors of the population amid allegations of coercion to obtain money and goods from industries and stores.[31] In 1951, the foundation distributed two million sweetbread loafs or pan dulce, a traditional Christmas treat; the same amount of bottles of *sidra*, the alcoholic cider also traditionally consumed during the holidays; and four million toys.[32] In addition to these annual donations, the foundation responded to written requests sent to Eva Perón and granted interviews with the first lady or with foundation employees to ask people what they needed. This form of communication personalized the donation, strengthened the sense of indebtedness of the beneficiary, and reinforced the image of Evita as a gift-giver or the *hada buena* (good fairy).[33]

Just as they rejected explanations of personal prosperity based on the benefactor state, interviewees reasserted their status as consumers by affirming that they had never received any goods from the foundation. However, almost all of them remembered a neighbor or an acquaintance who had. Interviewees stressed hard work, savings, and economic planning in order to implicitly differentiate themselves from the poorest and most marginal social groups that, according to conventional wisdom, were the foundation's beneficiaries.[34] Familiar stories of sewing machines offer a fine example of this strategy of distinction and show that if memory converts public events into idiosyncratic personal experiences, the most intriguing question to ask is how.[35] All the women I interviewed fondly remembered their sewing machines, the brand they owned, the savings and economic sacrifices they made in order to afford them, and the stories surrounding the purchase. The machine is particularly salient in women's memories because sewing was a major component of mid-twentieth-century working-class womanhood:

> At that time, when young women finished sixth grade—and even if they would be going on to high school—the first thing their mothers would do was to send them to learn to sew. This was a very good thing because most of us sewed our own clothes. I learned to sew at the age of 12 and I always sewed.[36]

Women categorically conveyed how central the sewing machine was for their role as productive working-class housewives who contributed to the household budget. In addition, the appliance reinforced their identities as devoted mothers who expressed love for their children by making their clothing. For many of these working-class women, the sewing machine was also a means of economic independence from parents and husbands and a source of instruction because it required the formal or informal acquisition of technical skills. Women learned at home, with friends, or took lessons, a common venue for sociability and, in many cases, the only form of formal instruction they had after primary school. Furthermore, the sewing machine expanded these women's social networks since even those who did not engage in *coser para afuera* (sewing for other people for pay) as an occupation were able to establish and strengthen relations with neighbors through sewing, often doing small jobs as favors to them.[37]

The sewing machine was also a powerful icon in the Peronist imaginary. It was a symbol of the Peronist home, the working-class woman, and the Eva Perón Foundation. *The Sewing Machine*, an illustrated pamphlet published by the foundation, fairly represents the Peronist gendered labor ideology centered on women's productivity in the domestic realm. After they got married, Andrés sold Marta's old sewing machine because he did not want her to work, but after he was the victim of an accident on the street, the young couple's only income was the money contributed by the labor union. Marta's mother, "an old criolla who was used to bad luck baring its teeth and who fought back fiercely," wrote to the foundation for help, and Marta received a new modern sewing machine shortly after. This time, Andrés was happy and supported his wife's new job as a seamstress. In the story, an older generation that had known suffering and privation in the past plays the enlightened mediator, the foundation takes on the role of the redeemer, and the sewing machine is the true instrument of salvation. Many other official pamphlets, photos and short stories in the print media, posters, and even economic policies promoting the production and commercialization of this appliance immortalized the sewing machine as a pivotal component of the mid-twentieth-century imagination. In fact, the government considered the sewing machine the core of the Peronist-sponsored domestic industry aimed at making women industrious workers while reinforcing their belonging at home. Close to half a million women received credits from the Peronist government to purchase a sewing machine, a fact that has remained buried under the resonance of the massive distribution of around half a million sewing machines annually by the Eva Perón Foundation.[38]

The powerful symbolism of the sewing machine as an icon of 1950s femininity and domesticity as well as its centrality to the memories of working-class women shows what ethnologist Orvar Löfgren has called a process of cultural condensation by which a certain object becomes part of the folklore of a decade.[39] Margarita Rubani was one of the many working-class Peronist housewives with loving memories of her sewing machine. She sewed the clothes and diapers of all her children, and used this as an example to argue that both clothes and mothering were better at that time. When I asked her if she had received the sewing machine from Eva Perón, we had the following exchange:

> No, no . . . My husband bought the sewing machine for me, and with a lot of sacrifice. Luckily we never got anything from Evita. We never needed to because he had a job that allowed him to buy everything we needed.
>
> *But at that time it was common . . . Evita's foundation gave away a lot of sewing machines, isn't that right?*
>
> Yes, of course, but that's different. Those went to other people. I knew a girl who had four or five children. She was so, so poor—you know, those girls who have a husband but he doesn't act like a husband and you don't know whose children they are? Well, my sister taught her to sew and she started sewing pants on order for a store downtown, but she had to borrow the sewing machine because she didn't

have her own. She was very poor. So a neighbor who was a staunch Peronist wrote a letter to Eva. She told Eva the truth and a week later the girl had her own sewing machine. [. . .] With that sewing machine, she brought up her children and sent them to school.[40]

Margarita's story follows Peronist convention, evoking the key motifs of Marta and Andrés's story published by the Eva Perón Foundation. In Margarita's narrative, the foundation is an efficient and responsive institution and Evita redeems the poor woman, enabling her, through the gift, to make an honest living and to raise her children properly. But Margarita differentiated the worker-consumer who purchased the goods from the beneficiary of goods distributed by the foundation. The former was a masculinized and industrious figure represented by her husband; the latter was a feminized and dependent indigent of dubious morality. The fact that "true" workers purchased goods instead of taking donations was, in fact, a common argumentative thread in many accounts, and once again, it was a means by which working-class folks separated themselves from the recipients of Peronist benefaction:

I did not agree with the gifts, toys and other things that were given away because I don't like charity; I think it's much more respectable to work for what I need. But it's important to keep in mind that the people are the people, and the people need things and they don't care whether they get them through charity or of their own accord. The issue is to have them and through that medium [the foundation], they were able to get them.[41]

Interestingly, many stories also addressed the difference between the working-class consumer who purchased the sewing machine and the donee who received it from the foundation by contrasting the relationship that each group established with the goods. While the respondents stressed their emotional attachment to the sewing machines, which they kept for life or bequeathed to their children, several of them affirmed that, in contrast, many women rapidly sold the sewing machines they had received from the foundation, suggesting that people only cherished goods they had worked hard to get. As commentaries on class identity, gender roles, and Peronism, tales of sewing machines reveal that memories of consumption always involve a plethora of meanings that consumers bestowed upon market culture and goods.[42]

The Meanings of Consumption

Some historians have argued that Peronist images of popular domesticity were closer to idyllic representations of middle-class life-style than to conventional portrayals of working-class everyday life. Official propaganda reproduced the image of a family lounging in a simple but well-kept living room that frequently included a nice table lamp, sometimes a bookcase, and almost always a radio. The father, dressed in a suit and tie, is comfortably sitting on a sofa, reading a newspaper or a book, while the neatly groomed wife, wearing a pretty dress and heels, is hand-embroidering, and the two immaculate, well-dressed children work enthusiastically on their homework or read. These graphic representations used consumer goods such as clothing, furniture, and reading materials to reproduce a formulaic version of middle-class aesthetics characterized by clean minimalism and inconspicuous refinement. Moreover, the scenes pivoted on privileges and values stereotypically associated with the middle classes, including the free time to devote to recreational activities and family, access to education and culture, respectability, and the likely existence of a housemaid who is cooking dinner or cleaning while the (full-time) mother embroiders. These images challenged anti-Peronist characterizations of Peronists as vulgar, tacky, and showy while sending the message that workers shared the life-style, consumer patterns, aesthetic choices, and values of the middle sectors. At the same time, this type of government propaganda had pedagogical value, encouraging workers to emulate middle-class taste and probably contributing to middle-class anxieties of social leveling. As chapter 4 shows, emulation permeated the anti-Peronist imaginary that portrayed working-class consumers as tasteless imitators of upper and, especially, middle-class sectors.[43]

Many decades later, in contrast to official propaganda and anti-Peronist claims, working-class folks explicitly avoided a conceptualization of consumer culture as a means to upward mobility. According to the interviewees, higher levels of consumption brought benefits and pleasure but were not connected to the striving for status. In other words, aspiration to a better life did not equal aspiration to become middle class. While workers affirmed that social change was profound, they also believed that class division had remained still and that they proudly belonged to the same social ranks: "They say 'The middle class ended with Perón.' No! The fact is, the working class rose up a notch."[44] However, if a higher working-class standard of living did not alter social standing—as some official propaganda may have suggested—it undoubtedly transformed understandings of self and class.

Railroad worker Rodolfo Di Marco offers a fine example of this argument in an anecdote he used to exemplify the new level of prosperity experienced by workers in the 1950s. The story revolves around a version of working-class masculinity based on the role of men as providers and, most importantly, as consumers of nonessential goods. The anecdote also reveals a subtle strategy of self-representation since the main character of the story was a young marriageable railroad worker like Rodolfo. Rodolfo recalled that in the late 1940s, he overheard a conversation between two neighbors who were happy that the daughter of one of them had started dating one of Rodolfo's co-workers. The women remarked how a few years earlier, the girl would have had to avoid such a boyfriend but that now, the family was excited about the prospects of the marriage as a "true salvation." The boyfriend's wages would guarantee a comfortable life for the couple with nice modern gadgets; in addition, they would have the trust and respect of local shopkeepers, who extended generous credits to workers. The anecdote articulates the new living conditions of workers through social perception and praise. In the story, the remarkable standard of living of railroad workers, who were already considered one of the most prosperous working sectors, is evident through the high opinion of neighbors, the deference of merchants, and the admiration of women. In other words, the story suggests that new levels of consumption secured different forms of social esteem for working-class men.[45]

This anecdote strikingly condenses the meanings of consumer power for most of the interviewees, that is, a sense of newly gained collective and individual status embodied in the figure of an "affluent worker," and a means to reaffirm working-class identity rather than an instrument to subvert it.[46] In their testimonies, working-class interviewees spoke of different practices of consumption that showed a conscientious choice to continue rather than change their life-style. The "affluent worker," who was able to comfortably raise a family, obtain credit, and purchase new gadgets, experienced consumer goods and consumption selectively, reinforcing rather than altering conventional working-class practices and cultural values. The most evident example of this argument is the geography of shopping that shows how modest wage earners accommodated new forms of consumption to their budget and life-style instead of imitating middle-class consumer patterns. Most interviewees shared stories from the 1930s when poverty, the mistreatment of salesclerks, and feelings of embarrassment turned downtown commercial streets and stores into "banned territories." They argued that this changed in the following two decades, when better wages literally opened the doors of renowned shops that had traditionally been monopolized by upper-class customers. Interviewees recalled the magnificent buildings that housed the stores, the marble staircases to the upper floor, and the immaculate presentation of merchandise while others framed their memories in the language of newcomers fulfilling a long-overdue aspiration.

But these incursions, working-class testimonies suggest, were milestones rather than routine visits. Working-class consumers had more disposable money than before, but they continued to buy most of their clothes, shoes, and household appliances in neighborhood shops that they either had traditionally patronized in the past or had begun frequenting when

FIGURE 19: Prestigious department stores like Harrods had been the privileged realm of upper-class consumers in the early twentieth century.
Photo courtesy of Archivo General de la Nación.

larger budgets allowed it. In fact, interviewees visited prominent down-town shops during sales, for special occasions, or to purchase expensive household appliances or goods that were unavailable in local shops. This does not necessarily contradict Peronist and anti-Peronist images of over-crowding on Florida Street in Buenos Aires and Córdoba Street in Rosario, but it certainly challenges facile conclusions about the meanings of new consumer practices that both the government and its opponents linked to emulation. Most women, for example, remembered turning to downtown stores for high-quality wool and fabrics to knit and make clothes for the family, especially for themselves and their children. This experience took working-class consumers into traditional middle- and upper-class sce-narios, but they continued to make most of their clothes while middle- and upper-class women did not. The goods working-class consumers bought and the way they used them did not subvert class difference and class identity but reinscribed them.

Interviewees from Rosario, for instance, remembered that buying in Gath & Chaves brought an additional benefit since the store offered free knitting classes for customers who had bought wool. The material was imported and thus high-priced, but many women remembered that they saved to be able to perfect their abilities and improve the quality of the garments they made for both their families and their customers. When I suggested that maybe downtown stores were still beyond the reach of working-class shoppers, most interviewees agreed that they were places for "rich people" and more expensive than local shops, but most answered with a question: why would you go out of your neighborhood to buy stuff if you could buy it closer to home, help local commerce, or contribute to the growth of the vicinity?[47]

Respondents explained that choosing local merchants over downtown retailers involved more than price considerations and linked the decision to convenience and a sense of responsibility and pride in their neighbor-hood. Commerce was indeed central in memories of the neighborhood; shopkeepers and stores mapped out the layout of the district in detail:

> Arroyito was a nice neighborhood. You could get whatever you needed, nothing was missing . . . We bought our food at the railroad workers' coop on Alberdi Avenue, we bought our clothes at Sastrería Martín and our shoes at Casals and at another store . . . Dayton. [. . .] And at the Arroyito branch of Banco Nación, we had a savings account where we would make a deposit every two or three months.[48]

The fact that women did most of the shopping, even for men's items, played an important role in the geography of consumption since working-class housewives recognized that they were disinclined to leave the neighborhood too often, citing lack of time and distances. In addition, they argued that they could find what they needed in the *negocios muy surtidos del barrio* (well-stocked neighborhood shops). Moreover, some women asserted that parents and husbands only allowed excursions to downtown commercial areas with a chaperone, so they depended on female family members or friends. Beyond issues of women's mobility, consumer practices involved other types of considerations that reveal that consumption was as much a choice among different kinds of relationships as it was a choice among different kinds of goods.[49] Interviewees remembered that in some cases, such as local tailors and men's clothing stores, buying or having a suit made in the neighborhood was generally more expensive than buying it in downtown where even costlier garments were accessible through installment plans. However, personal and family relations as well as neighbors' references kept working-class customers loyal to the local shops.

Furthermore, many working folks affirmed they tried to avoid installment plans because they disliked incurring costly debts. Therefore, purchases at pricey stores that required this type of payment were less common or were reserved for special acquisitions. Working-class consumers did keep the *libreta* for groceries, a small notebook where storekeepers wrote down what clients purchased each day and that customers were expected to pay when they received their salary. When I asked whether the libreta resembled, on a smaller scale, installment payments in department stores, working-class consumers explained the difference by arguing that the debt was smaller but, most importantly, that the libreta was an old custom based on trust (*"una costumbre basada en la confianza"*), acquaintance, and proximity. If one could not repay, local creditors were sympathetic and deferred the debt.[50]

Parallel to the adaptations and continuities in consumer practices that show the significance of learning and unlearning consumer skills, memories vividly evoked the transformation of low-income consumers.[51] Both for newcomers to the city and for workers who were long-time urban dwellers but had been historically relegated to the fringes, access to downtown and its attractions was a revealing experience that many of them voiced with language evocative of a discovery. Adelma Martínez remembered that she and her family had never left their barrio on the outskirts of Rosario. They did not have any compelling reasons to do so since her family could

FIGURE 20: La Unión, a typical grocery store in the Alberdi neighborhood, Rosario, where consumers could use a libreta. Photo courtesy of Museo de la Ciudad de Rosario.

just barely afford the neighborhood movie theater once in a while. When she began working as a maid in the 1940s, she started to explore the city, shop in new stores, and visit downtown attractions. Adelma recalled this experience as a true revelation, the realization that outside the confines of her working-class neighborhood and the harshness of everyday life laid a captivating city with many things to offer which she could now afford. Adelma affirmed that at that time

> you start going out, you start seeing there is another world, another life, other places that are much more important and more attractive.

I opened my eyes to another reality that was not just the world with mud floors, with unkempt rooms, with bathrooms that were usually located at the end of a long hall in the very back of the house.[52]

Just like consumer excursions, consumer goods were landmarks in the memories of working-class interviewees as well as symbols of social and personal transformation. Cultural anthropologists have shown that objects are "the set and props on the theatrical stage of our lives" and thus new objects signal a passage into a different condition.[53] In their stories of things of the past, interviewees conveyed this new condition as a combination of working-class achievement and gratification rather than as an experience of upward mobility. Tales of accomplishment were eminently collective. Even in anecdotes like Rodolfo Di Marco's about his fellow railroad worker, the main character stands for the improvement of the class. But in remembering goods, as in disputing the role of the state in the accomplishment of a higher material standard of living, the sense of achievement among working-class consumers was also decidedly personal. This is evident, for example, in many accounts in which working-class consumers stressed they were the first in their families or neighborhoods, or among their friends, to purchase certain goods: "When we bought our first pressure cooker, we told absolutely everyone. It was a real occasion. I remember when we bought our first blender. Every little thing was a heroic deed."[54]

Interviewees employed cherished possessions to organize their memories, associating goods with particular events or situations both collective—the annual bonus for workers or a historic salary raise—and personal, like getting a job, having a baby, or moving in to a new house. Goods literally marked trajectories in the past, an aspect that some researchers have interpreted as the inclination of older adults to represent social history in objects.[55] Because of their visibility, cost, and profound association with a higher standard of living, household appliances appear as the most prominent embodiment of attainment and the most salient status-granting goods among peers. In fact, testimonies reveal that consumer goods were important because they evoked prestige and admiration among the group and not because they took owners outside of it:

In 1950, I built my house on Lamadrid Street, two bedrooms, a kitchen and bathroom, and first I bought a Carú drip stovetop (it didn't come with an oven) and then I bought a kerosene stove just like the modern ones but powered by kerosene instead of gas. The kerosene tank was right next to it, you pumped the bellows and the oven heated up. It was an Istilar, not a Simplex. And my brother-in-law really envied us because he couldn't buy new appliances like those.[56]

Among all household appliances, and comparable to the sewing machine, the electric refrigerator was ubiquitous in memories of mid-twentieth-century material culture, thus reinforcing its status as one of the strongest components of the folklore of the period. The demand for electric refrigerators was the highest, most elastic and unsatisfied of all electric appliances, including "new" artifacts, such as washing machines and vacuum cleaners almost exclusively purchased by upper-class consumers, and "old" appliances, such as irons, electric fans, and radios that were affordable for low-income sectors.[57] The embodiment of well-being, the refrigerator was one of the highest material aspirations of low-income households. In 1951, for example, a popular magazine informed that "a few days back, at an Argentine factory, the plant's 1,500 workers gave a coworker an electric refrigerator. This gift is a symbol. It represents the dream of all Argentine families: to own a refrigerator."[58]

For its part, the Peronist government supported this dream, especially because the electric refrigerator was an emblem of industrialization and, consequently, of national progress and economic independence. As it had done with other consumer goods, official propaganda appropriated the electric refrigerator as an icon of wealth evenly distributed among social classes.[59] This message engaged a long-standing tradition in which technology, as chapter 3 analyzes, had been considered the privilege of the rich and a marker of the unequal access to modernity. While the government employed the refrigerator as an emblem of working-class consumer power, its opponents used it to question the achievements of justicialismo. In contrast to official statistics that highlighted the material advantages of living in the "third position," Communists argued that while a Soviet worker could afford an electric refrigerator with only half of his monthly income, the same appliance would cost an Argentine worker his annual salary.[60]

Similarly, socialist thinker Alicia Moreau de Justo enthusiastically supported the mechanization of homework through domestic appliances and praised its liberating effects especially for women who toiled both at home and at the factory. However, she deeply regretted the fact that beyond the official glorification, the access to household technology among working-class homemakers was still limited.[61] Other political opponents, in contrast, acknowledged the new access of working-class sectors to domestic technology but employed it to illustrate what they considered as ill-chosen priorities. Writer Jorge Luis Borges, for instance, commented: "That's the way people were here during Peronism. They piled on all the clothes that they owned. Five of them lived in a single room and they owned a Frigidaire [a brand name–turned–Americanized generic term for refrigerator]."[62] For Borges, the electric refrigerator in the working-class home represented the vulgar kitsch style, ostentation, and foolishness of the low-income sectors.

As the 1950s electric refrigerator is now a relic for collectors, its meanings outlived in the memories of a generation. Interviewees remembered electric refrigerators as a technological conquest that showed the progress of the industry and as a social achievement because "in the past, the rich man had a refrigerator and we poor people used an icebox."[63] Interviewees voiced the convenience of electric refrigerators over iceboxes in the language of modernization, remembered the savings and economic planning that went into purchasing their first appliance, and shared a sense of unfulfilled aspiration when other, most urgent needs led them to postpone the acquisition of an electric refrigerator. Others, in contrast, prioritized it over other buys:

> The SIAM fridge was the best one. It had a reinforced motor and it never broke. We saved up and bought it in six installment payments . . . or something like that. We had a coal oven and it was really dirty because of the ash but I didn't care because I had my refrigerator, which was a big advantage.[64]

For most interviewees, the 1950s electric refrigerator was synonymous with *la Siam*, one of the most affordable electric refrigerators in the market produced by SIAM, the largest national manufacturer of electric refrigerators. Among respondents, SIAM served as a memory cue and was the ultimate symbol of national industry. In spite of some nuisances that characterized the early technology, SIAM products have remained in the popular imagination as the epitome of sturdiness and durability:

> SIAM fridges had a very important feature: they were extremely durable because they never needed repairs . . . The bad thing was that they were noisy and the ice trays didn't make enough ice. They also accumulated a lot of frost and then stopped cooling. [. . .] So then you had to unplug it, be patient, wait a few hours until the

frost melted, and then clean it up, dry it off and start over again. We all learned to open and close the door quickly so it wouldn't accumulate frost as quickly.[65]

Women in particular remembered the electric refrigerator, a symbol of modern technology, as a true accomplishment. Clean, safe, and convenient, the electric fridge reduced the number of trips to the market, saved money, and made fresh food available at home daily. When asked which appliance had had the greatest impact on everyday life in the 1950s, Violeta Benvenuto did not hesitate to answer:

No question about it: the electric refrigerator. Before that, we used a fridge that was cooled by chunks of ice that the iceman delivered to your door. It was a mess and you always depended on the iceman. So the electric refrigerator was a true relief. . . We bought a SIAM in the mid-1950s. That was a change! It was less work and more comfort.[66]

As Violeta's testimony suggests, by invoking the advantages of new goods, memories of consumption revolved around a novel sense of indulgence, that is, the experience of buying and enjoying something unique. This was evident in the case of expenditures that respondents remembered as exceptional like investments in household technology and particularly in an electric refrigerator that, unlike other appliances, was more a sign of modern comfort than a means of liberation from drudgery. Yet the sense of indulgence was even more prominent in the case of goods interviewees not only deemed infrequent and expensive, but also "unnecessary." Working-class consumers characterized these expenses as *darse un gusto* (to treat oneself):

At that time, we began to treat ourselves in ways that would have been unthinkable a few years earlier. We wore imported cashmere, English cashmere. A tailor from Pehuajó made me a suit, pants, a coat and a vest, all sewed by hand, a magnificent piece of handiwork. I wore it for 20 years and then I gave it away. It was beautiful. It cost me 90 pesos, and that was a ton of money.[67]

Interviewees recalled a good pair of leather shoes, a pricey dress, a piece of jewelry, or a high-quality suit, which did not replace alpargatas or inexpensive outfits, as unique and cherished indulgences. They had no utilitarian value for working men and women who spent most of their days in their working outfits; instead, they were symbols of satisfied desires, and most importantly, they reminded their owners and bystanders of the actual possibility of gratification. But consumer indulgence did not entail a trade-off between working-class identity and material aspirations. Nice clothes and shoes functioned as representations of work and consumer ethics, that is, embodiments of both toil and careful spending rather than of middle-class style. In fact, the meanings that interviewees assigned to their attire are directly dependent on the widespread frugality with which they characterized their life in those years.[68] I felt embarrassed by the present-day culture of excess and "disposable" garments—inexpensive due to the brutal exploitation of workers around the world—when most working-class interviewees fondly recalled they owned no more than two suits and a pair of shoes at a time and that these lasted a very long time. These purchases were indeed *un acontecimiento* (an occasion):

> I wore a suit with a hard neck and cufflinks, double cuffs and starchy dress shirts. Since I liked a curved heel, I had my steer shoes made in the Delgado system. It was expensive, of course, but it was one of those exceptional purchases that you could afford back then; plus, I got credit and paid it monthly.[69]

This kind of attire made working-class interviewees proud and symbolized the notion of proper elegance and formality they craved. A neat appearance has historically been a common means for the unprivileged to contest demeaning characterizations that have equated unkempt looks with poverty or racial otherness.[70] Still, it was as if for some respondents, expensive garments contradicted working-class identities and tales of hard work, so many of them "justified" these expenses with certain humbleness, detailing how formal clothes were the norm for all men in the 1950s regardless of their occupation. In contrast to the current casual fashion of jeans and sneakers, interviewees linked 1950s working-class masculinity to formal outfits. Some of them remembered that this attire was expected even at labor union meetings: "All of us at the union were descamisados, but when we went to the meetings, we wore a suit and tie."[71] This kind of testimony pivoted on a definition of working-class masculinity that combines labor activism—in the context of unparalleled power of labor unions—with a sense of competence and authority obtained through the suit and the tie, clothes that traditionally symbolize these features.[72] Similarly, a

combination of thriftiness, working-class respectability, and sense of fulfillment was evident in the accounts of working-class women who remembered stockings and hats as "must-haves" for public outings.[73]

But darse un gusto was more than buying special goods. The expression evokes an occasional change in habits, the transformation of everyday
routines. Eloisa Pozzi remembered with emotion how she and her husband
set aside money for a couple of monthly visits to a popular pizza parlor in
downtown Buenos Aires where they often met friends. The restaurant was
not expensive, but they were saving every penny for a house, so the cost of
the food and transportation had an impact on their budget. Still, it was a
gusto they could afford:

> Going to Las Cuartetas was so nice! It wasn't an elegant place, but it
> was an expense for us. But that's what I remember most about living
> in Buenos Aires, *esos gustitos* [small pleasures]. . . Being able to go
> out with friends, go to the *confiterías* [cafés], which was something
> that we had only done rarely in the past. Nowadays, it sounds silly, but
> for us it was so important . . . Saturdays were such great days![74]

The remembrance of a trivial act of consumption triggered a spiraling
memory effect that elicited a narrative about working-class aspirations,
blue-collar leisure, and deep personal feelings that I witnessed many times.
This memory effect is owed to the capacity of consumer goods and consumer practices to operate as "nostalgic time machines."[75] Similarly, in this
capacity, the memories of wool purchased at Gath & Chaves prompted tales
of new geographies (downtown and the store), friends, abilities acquired in
the knitting classes, and goods produced thanks to those newly acquired
abilities. Stories of wool were also accounts of gender relations (the encouragement or discouragement of husbands), motherhood and housewifery
(contribution to the household economy and knitting for their children),
and working-class material culture. As anthropologist Barbara Myerhoff
argued, moments of recollection may be so enlightening, compelling, and
moving that "memory may offer the opportunity not merely to recall the
past but to relive it, in all its original freshness, unaltered by intervening
change and reflection."[76]

Memories of consumption were consistently happy memories and therefore provoked a special yearning for times past. In the accounts, life was simpler and fuller, goods brought joy, and people were content, a characterization of the 1940s and 1950s that contrasted starkly with the grim portrayal that interviewees offered of the earlier decades. But nostalgia, many have argued, also arises from the mistrust of the future, and, most notably, from a present that individuals perceive as unsatisfactory. In fact, the memories of an idyllic past differed greatly from the mid-2000s when the interviews took place and these retirees struggled to survive on meager pensions while still suffering the consequences of the appalling economic crisis that devastated Argentina in 2001. Former textile worker Juan Carlos Legas, for example, contrasted the congested and bustling commercial streets of the late 1940s with a gloomy and desolated depiction of the present day:

> You can't even imagine what Córdoba Street was back then. There were so many people you couldn't make your way down the street. And the holidays . . . the shops were just crazy. It was great! And now? No way! With all this poverty. It's awful, there's no one there.[77]

Yet nostalgia was more than craving for full pockets and crowded stores; it was the result of assessing one's personal life and reviving people, experiences, and meanings, most of them long gone. This evaluation is no easy endeavor. Although it reconnects the elderly with their previous selves, thus reinforcing a sense of identity, remembering confronts them with the realization that they are frequently more fragile and lonely, less confident, and more vulnerable than they were in the past. However, nostalgia can also "shore up self-esteem, reminding us that however sad our present lot we were once happy and worthwhile."[78] The sense of worth was no minor issue when conducting interviews with older people in a society that worships youth, openly disregards the past as inconsequential, and makes the elderly and their needs invisible. It is no surprise then that many of the working-class interviewees were skeptical about what they could contribute to my project, affirming that they were unimportant individuals and that their lives had been ordinary "just like many others." In her study of French and German working-class autobiographies, Mary Jo Maynes interpreted this tendency among narrators as a resistance to heroic self-presentation and individualism, both at the core of the construction of traditional "Western" autobiographical selves.[79] To this inclination, working-class women added a greater sense of irrelevancy. They wondered why housewifery and other traditional women's chores like shopping and budgeting might be of any interest to a historian, evidence of the historical invisibility and social neglect of housework as well as of the women who performed it.

Still, the threat of extinction, stronger among the elderly, generates a drive toward self-scrutiny that triggers an affinity for reminiscence and provokes a desire to evaluate the past and to manifest a valuable identity. In this context, and "without natural audiences to be witness of their life," old interviewees truly appreciated a supportive listener and initial skepticism and surprise turned into genuine enthusiasm. The fact that I could have been their granddaughter further persuaded interviewees to tell their stories and recall the past since our exchanges allowed them to fulfill what they perceived as a social responsibility, only occasionally undertaken, of instructing and counseling a younger generation.[80] In fulfilling this role, interviewees drew upon conventional scripts and employed standard plots and recurrent motifs that, while in harmony with their political sympathies, solidified their belonging to a generation. But in an effort to manifest a valuable identity, individuals created alternative routes amid inherited socialization and ideological positioning. These routes, still rarely framed by narratives of their own making, led working-class consumers to construct a past in which, in a context of relative well-being, they desired, shopped, and displayed goods on their own terms, according to their own needs, and remained proud to belong to the laboring masses.

Epilogue

Consumer Culture Today

Looking back at the almost six decades that have passed since Perón was ousted in 1955, one has the uncomfortable feeling that the collective search for a better life has suffered many setbacks for most of the population and that the recurring promises of social and economic inclusion, made by political candidates with questionable degrees of commitment and credibility, remain unfulfilled. After a brief overview of the period that followed the coup that toppled Perón, these final pages discuss some of the most significant aspects of consumer culture in contemporary Argentina, particularly among the low-income sectors. The story of Argentine working-class consumers in the last decade evokes the phoenix myth, a social group reborn from the ashes of a catastrophic crisis that sent half of the population below the poverty line. Sadly, unlike the myth, many are still awaiting resurgence. For these sectors, the story actually involves the unmaking of the mid-twentieth-century definitions of worker and consumer.

In spite of Argentina's numerous national idiosyncrasies, the events that began to unfold in the mid-twentieth century and then continued on into the present have occurred worldwide, a process in which government authorities have radically reduced the form and obligations of the state, disposed of the welfare system, and sacrificed the well-being of workers and the future of local industries in the name of integration into the global economy. In the end, the devotees of neoliberalism emerged triumphant, but most nations and their people around the world have little to show for it. In Argentina, the 1970s military dictatorship experimented with the first neoliberal reforms and a democratically elected government completed the implementation of *el modelo* ("the model") twenty years later. Globally, the antistate and free market proposals, the twenty-first-century technological and scientific advancements, and the extraordinary levels of corporate and individual wealth have not made income redistribution any fairer, nor is society any less polarized or violent as a result. The assaults on the environment are ever more dramatic; new forms of exploitation and slavery are common; the illegal movement of people and goods is a prevailing practice; and the provision of food, health, and education fails to reach those who need them the most.[1]

In the ten years after the fall of Peronism, foreign investment grew significantly, especially in automobiles, petrochemicals, and steel, creating a modern and efficient sector that produced for high-income consumers. In contrast, traditional industries like shoes and electric appliances, which had led growth in the previous decade, stagnated or declined as the wages of their main consumers, the workers, deteriorated as the result of industrial rationalization, the recovery of management's authority on the shop floor, and most importantly, the fall of labor unions' bargaining power.[2] During this decade, the goals of democracy, modernization, and development dominated the debates over the national future but remained hindered by the proscription of Peronism—which extended until 1973— and the continuing dependency of industry on the agricultural sector for the foreign exchange necessary to purchase capital goods and inputs. Argentines knew the limits of this model all too well, but this time the successive administrations, unlike Peronism, had fewer incentives to remedy the situation. When the international market for agricultural exports contracted, foreign debt grew, and the state launched stabilization plans that significantly reduced employment and wages, introduced sharp devaluation, and implemented deflationary policies.[3]

In the decade that began in 1966 with the repressive regime of General Juan Carlos Onganía, new international markets for Argentine oils and grains produced notable growth in the agricultural sector, prompting a mild but steady overall economic expansion. These favorable conditions began to change in the early 1970s, which coincided with the political and social debacle following the death of Perón in 1974, a year after returning to the country from exile and winning the presidential elections. In the midst of growing violence between the right and left factions of the Peronist party, it became apparent that much had changed in the country since Perón had implemented his political and social project thirty years earlier. The once powerful and charismatic leader of the 1940s who had taken the political scene by storm had lost his impetus, his clear vision, and, most significantly, his control over his own ranks.[4]

The military dictatorship that took power in 1976 was one of the bloodiest in Latin America, employing systematic violence to control society and impose new economic rules that made the financial sector the heart of the model. During its first year in power, the military junta interdicted unions and the Confederación General del Trabajo (CGT, General Confederation of Labor), occupied factories, eliminated collective bargaining negotiations, and prohibited strikes. Based on the belief that the market was the most efficient mechanism in ordering all economic actors, the military regime began dismantling the interventionist and welfare state that the Peronist government had consolidated in the 1940s. In this new and highly speculative financial climate, the government lifted traditional mechanisms that protected local industries—tariffs, the regulation of credit, exchange controls—and thus many sectors succumbed to the flood of cheap imported goods. In the new scenario, economic power became highly concentrated among a few national and transnational businesses with great political influence. During the first five years of the military regime, industrial production and its workforce declined twenty percent while real incomes fell dramatically, a trend exacerbated by rising inflation. By the time the military government called for democratic elections in the early 1980s after the defeat in the Malvinas war against England, the country was utterly depleted: society was torn and exhausted and the harmful economic policies had seriously deteriorated the standard of living.[5]

The democratic government of Raúl Alfonsín, the candidate of the Radical Party who took power in 1983, inaugurated a period of great disappointments—from a declining commitment to justice for the victims of human rights violations committed in the previous decade to the hyperinflation that submerged the country into chaos. The economy was stagnant, the external debt continued to grow, the state's deficit rose, and welfare initiatives like the Programa Alimentario Nacional (PAN, National Food Program) were ineffective in providing sustained relief to deprived low-income sectors. To better control the economy, the Alfonsín administration froze prices and wages, changed the national currency, and finally devalued it. But the combination of inadequate measures and the powerlessness of the government resulted in an economy that was out of control. As consumers suffered the systematic shortages of numerous basic goods, price tags were updated every day, frequently more than once a day. Hyperinflation destroyed real wages and paralyzed many productive activities. A dramatic episode revealed the extreme deterioration of the living conditions among low-income consumers for whom food continued to be the most important expense in the household budget. In May 1989, thousands of people in Rosario, Córdoba, and Greater Buenos Aires broke into supermarkets and small grocery stores and the government repressed rioters violently.[6]

In this anarchic context, president-elect Carlos Menem took power in July 1989, six months before the constitutionally established date. That month, inflation reached 200 percent. Menem, a charismatic caudillo from the interior province of La Rioja who promised a "productive revolution" and a *salariazo* (a huge salary increase), represented old-style Peronism.[7] However, when the presidential campaign was over, he became the obedient implementer of the neoliberal reforms promoted by the International Monetary Fund (IMF) and the World Bank. Glossing his platform with the cherished Peronist ideals of social justice and economic independence, Menem finished what the military dictatorship had started in the 1970s. As government corruption and impunity reached unprecedented levels, the goal was to demolish the welfare and interventionist state. To this end, Menem's administration reduced state spending, suspended state subsidies, authorized layoffs of public employees, privatized state-owned companies—from telephones, railways, and television to oil production, the postal system, and airports—and opened up the market to foreign competition.[8]

Paradoxically, while the government gave transnational companies carte blanche to raise prices, cut services, and diminish quality, Congress approved the law for consumer defense in 1993, and it was incorporated to the Constitution a year later. Given the neoliberal context, the law was not part of a systematic government effort to protect consumers as had occurred with the regulations on advertising, labels, and packages established by

Perón's administration more than forty years earlier. In fact, the comparison suggests the pioneering nature of those past regulations. The 1950s Food Code, for example, remained the principal articulator of all the laws and institutions for food control created in the past fifty years. The compliance of companies, however, is problematic as evident in the fact that, as late as 2008, research found that 80 percent of a widely consumed product like tomato sauce did not meet the requirements imposed by the Food Code and was unhealthy.[9]

Central to Menem's administration was the convertibility law, which established a fixed exchange rate making the dollar equivalent to the peso. For a few years, *el uno a uno* (the one-to-one) created the illusion—which played a role in Menem's reelection in 1995—of a revitalized economy and greater consumer power enhanced by wide access to imports and new installment plans in dollars. Consumption became consumerism, a sort of raging fever that compelled society to possess and, most importantly, to display. In this period, Argentines turned into global consumers, each social sector according to its income. Most were proud to show off foreign brands purchased in recently inaugurated shopping malls as markers of individual and collective participation into globalized cities. As the president donned ultraexpensive imported suits and revved his red Ferrari, Miami became the tourist and shopping mecca of the upper middle classes and Nike shoes the new symbol of status among low-income youth.[10]

In reality, gratification was fleeting and increasingly limited since growing numbers of workers were losing their jobs. Unemployment began to rise when local industries started to cut costs to compete with imported products and many companies, without state protection or subsidies, went bankrupt. By the last year of Menem's second term, it was evident that "the consumer paradise" was a mirage and official discourses of bonanza were nothing more than a facade to hide the cataclysmic consequences of the economic reforms. The foreign debt almost doubled between 1992 and 1996, sales taxes grew exponentially, export prices fell, and the country underwent a profound recession. A reflection of the times, unemployment became structural while the country was frequently paralyzed by strikes and citizens were increasingly frustrated. Still, at the very bottom of the social ladder, in the poorest neighborhoods and shantytowns, loyalty to the government remained strong and was sustained by local Peronist patronage networks. In these poor communities where participation in the labor and consumer market was reduced to a minimum, the personalized political mediation of "brokers" effectively solved the needs of residents providing items from food and medicines to construction materials and creating a strong sense of obligation among "clients."[11]

Fernando De la Rúa, the candidate of an electoral alliance between the Radical Party and the new Frente País Solidario (FREPASO, Front for a Country in Solidarity), assumed the presidency in 1999 amid hopes of true change that would rapidly be shattered. De la Rúa's campaign pivoted on social justice and honesty without questioning the peso-dollar convertibility, the privatizations, or the shrinkage of the state implemented by his predecessor. By De la Rúa's second year in power, Argentina's recession had aggravated and the country was on the verge of default. Unemployment reached 20 percent, and 40 percent of the population was living below the poverty line. Social protest became explosive. In addition to the unions, which organized numerous general strikes, and the Peronists, who were openly hostile to the government, the *piqueteros* (pickets), a social movement of the unemployed, demanded state-funded jobs and better living conditions. The piqueteros were responsible for mass road blockages and bonfires, successfully stopping urban traffic and shutting down highways in many parts of the country—even the access roads from Greater Buenos Aires to the capital city.[12]

In December 2001, after capital flight and a run on the banks, the government froze all bank deposits, a measure known as the *corralito*. As the poor and unemployed ransacked grocery stores, multitudes of workers and the middle class took to the streets of Buenos Aires and gathered in the Plaza de Mayo to protest the corralito as a confiscation of their savings and to demand the resignation of all political authorities. When groups of protestors destroyed cars and shop windows, the police repressed with unparalleled brutality and De la Rúa, unable to control the rabid situation, presented his resignation. In the following two weeks, there was a succession of five presidents and Argentina recorded the biggest debt default in history. In January 2002, Peronist Eduardo Duhalde was appointed interim president to finish De la Rúa's term and the peso-dollar parity was abandoned.[13]

Forty-seven years after Perón was overthrown, the mid-twentieth-century "New Argentina," based on the premises of national industrialization, high consumer power, and social integration, had turned into a country impoverished and chaotic, one marked by violence and political ineptness, and immersed in its worst economic and institutional crisis in the past century. A breaking point, the 2001 crisis crystallized the profound transformation of social identities and ways of life that had been fermenting in the last decade. The social function, cultural meanings, and rights of wage earners were shaken to the core since workers became unemployed or joined an informal economy whose ranks ranged from *changarines* to *cartoneros*.[14] In 2002, families below the poverty line—18 million people, a figure that represented half of the population—survived on slightly more than one dollar per day. While the recently unemployed lamented the loss of a job, many others were afraid they would never have one. As factories and businesses closed, a new generation of young men and women who had reached working age joined the victims of endemic unemployment and exploitative underemployment or left the country in search for a better future. Between 2000 and 2001, 140,000 Argentines left mainly for Spain, Italy, and the United States.[15] Many of those who migrated were part of the middle class, a social sector that had drastically lost the cultural and material signs of social standing due to unemployment and underconsumption. The press, economists, and researchers began to refer to this group as "the impoverished middle class," a concept that reaffirmed the belonging of such individuals to the middle class but highlighted that, in economic terms, they were as poor as the working class and the unemployed.[16]

Evidence of the assaults on the identity of the worker-consumer is clear in one of the most moving scenes of *The Take*, a 2004 documentary that vividly chronicles the aftermath of the 2001 crisis. The film focuses on the experience of the recuperated businesses, companies abandoned by their owners after bankruptcy and taken over and put back to production by the workers. In the midst of the judicial and political struggle to operate an auto-parts factory closed by its owners, worker Freddy Espinoza, one of the leaders of the newly created workers' cooperative, reflects on the onerous costs of losing his job in a language of consumption. With pain, Espinoza and his wife recount canceling their credit cards, no longer going to stores, suspending meals with their children at McDonald's (a sign of status in Argentina as it targets and serves middle-class consumers), and choosing to pay for food over debts when forced to administer the small amount of money they had left.[17] Their testimony conveyed the debacle of the male provider, the end of the illusion of global consumption for all, and the termination of a life-style sustained on credit. It also expressed the return of disciplined spending and the reordering of material priorities. Indeed, the decline of the working-class standard of living was so precipitous that it affected even the most basic needs like food and medicine, polarizing society between the "haves" and the "have-nots." Over the past decade, research shows, low-income sectors restricted by small budgets and high prices have been suffering from an extremely inadequate and unhealthy diet. This represents a striking contrast with the mid-twentieth century when all classes achieved access to equivalent foods and thus nutritional levels were high across the social pyramid.[18]

Beyond desperation and disillusionment, workers actively looked for alternatives to overcome the crisis. By the mid-2000s, there were 180 recuperated businesses from manufacturing plants to hotels that employed more than ten thousand workers.[19] While worker-run enterprises—many organized as cooperatives whose profits are equally distributed among workers—defied the logics of capitalist production, the *clubs del trueque* (barter clubs) challenged the principles of capitalist consumption. An unconventional path to economic inclusion and social integration, barter clubs grew independently from the state, which, weakened and undersized, remained dedicated to economic orthodoxy even when consumers hit rock bottom. When in 2001, the factory where Pedro Pérez worked began to pay the labor force with shoes and sneakers due to the lack of funds, Pedro took the goods to one of the many barter clubs to exchange them for food and clothing. At the clubs, organized by neighbors and publicized by word of mouth and the Internet to announce schedules and locations, new members received fifty "credits." The currency, whose names and logos varied from club to club, was exchanged alongside goods—everything from homemade pizzas and sweaters to toys and skin products—and services ranging from a haircut and plumbing to a computer lesson.[20]

In Argentina, barter clubs began in the mid-1990s but remained small and marginal. Between late 2001 and mid-2002, at the peak of the crisis, the numbers grew exponentially, reaching around six thousand clubs in twenty out of twenty-four provinces. Called *nodos* and organized in networks like the pioneering Red Global de Trueque (Global Barter Network), clubs had around 1.2 million members who with their families represented a total close to 6 million people in a country of 35 million inhabitants. Club members set their prices through supply and demand and according to their own needs, making the nodos into an original experience that mixed competition with collective solidarity. Barter clubs showed that "consumption is good for thinking," a site for civic reflection, experimentation, and organization with the potential to renew social life.[21] Beyond the politics of consumption, and in a context of cash shortages and an inflationary consumer market, the barter clubs offered people the unique space for fulfilling basic needs and socialization. Most importantly, they provided individuals with an opportunity for regaining a sense of self as useful and valuable workers and as entitled and enthusiastic consumers. The barter clubs called this subject the *prosumidor* (prosumer), a balanced and integrated producer and consumer. In contrast to the mid-twentieth-century worker-consumer, the epitome of market inclusion through industrialization, full employment, and high purchasing power, the prosumer emerged out of deindustrialization and unemployment. The prosumers bartered goods and services mostly produced in the informal and domestic realms, independently from the traditional monetary exchanges of the mainstream economy. They are then a clear example of the unmaking of the traditional working class—and the middle class for that matter—shaped by deproletarianization and the neoliberal assault on economic rights.[22]

In spite of its abrupt reduction, cash consumption remained central. However, in an economy that the state had left to its own devices, new types of markets surfaced as an experimental response forcing vulnerable social sectors to generate new recourses. La Salada aptly illustrates this process. A true representative of the new global economy, the market is the result of a devastated national garment industry and the lack of viable alternatives for disfranchised immigrants, the unemployed, and low-income consumers. La Salada was founded in the early 1990s by a group of Bolivian workers and small entrepreneurs who had come to Argentina in search for work and prosperity and ended up jobless and marginalized. The market is located in Lomas de Zamora, a poor district of Greater Buenos Aires, and sits on the banks of the polluted Riachuelo River. Here, Perón's government had inaugurated a beach resort that was closed in the early 1960s due to the high levels of contamination. Ironically, a symbol of working-class entitlement turned into an emblem of pauperized workers and the impoverished middle class.

What started as a group of twenty stalls selling mainly food and clothes became the largest informal and illegal market in Latin America, one where merchants pay no sales or property taxes and systematically violate copyright laws. Not surprisingly, the growth began in the aftermath of the 2001 crisis. La Salada specializes in selling knockoff brand-name merchandise at very low prices, especially clothing but increasingly shoes, CDs, DVDs, and electronics. Most clothing is manufactured in clandestine sweatshops that labor activists have denounced for holding workers in conditions of semislavery. Opened only on Wednesdays and Sundays, the fifteen thousand makeshift stalls in La Salada support around six thousand families who serve the forty thousand consumers that arrive weekly from all over the country. In addition to individual customers, La Salada became the supplier of around three hundred smaller markets distributed in different provinces as well as an exporter to bordering countries. This "vicious cycle" of second-rate counterfeited goods, exploited workers, poor merchants, and low-income consumers currently generates around 9 million dollars a week.[23]

The growing presence of middle-class consumers in La Salada shows how the crisis made consumer practices uniform. This became evident in the explosive commercial success of the *autoservicios chinos* (Chinese grocery stores) that began to spread in the neighborhoods of big cities as well as in shantytowns. There are now close to seven thousand of these stores in the whole country, and they specialize in selling food at very low prices to clientele from all social classes. In the 1990s, the middle classes, following the highest-income sectors, favored big foreign chains (*hipermercados*), where they shopped for expensive, high-quality brands. But in 2006, middle-class consumers represented 38 percent of the customers who patronized Chinese grocery stores, a percentage equal to that of low-income patrons. The rest were high-income consumers. In fact, more than La Salada and the barter clubs, the Chinese grocery stores located in central and fancy neighborhoods are a quintessential commercial space of interclass mingling. In the mid-twentieth century, this had resulted from an upward movement, as working-class consumers visited the department stores that had been exclusive in the past. Now the affluent and, most significantly, the middle sectors push their shopping carts in the modest supermarkets of low-income sectors.[24]

For their part, companies and their advertising agents needed to come to terms with this new consumer market. While economic growth had revitalized advertising in the 1940s and 1950s, economic decline similarly renewed the profession and their strategies at the turn of the twenty-first century. In the early 2000s, most consumers had the budgets and spending patterns of low-income sectors that ad-makers had almost systematically overlooked in the previous decade. In this context, prominent businesses cut costs, introducing inexpensive packages and ingredients, which prompted the complaints of many consumers; offered second and even third brands inspired by their leading products; and launched numerous limited-time promotions and deals. Still, in spite of the fact that the consumer market was more homogeneous, the lowest-income sectors remained a particular type of consumer profoundly marked by economic and geographical marginality. New entrepreneurs understood how difficult it was for these low-income consumers to afford mainstream products and popular brands, particularly in the case of food. Therefore, as the crisis triggered new types of commerce that survive until this day, it also prompted the production of new types of enduring goods. With catchy, popular, and sometimes inelegant names (Pirulo ice cream, Alfajores Cachafaz, Fierita bubble gum), simple packaging, and costing up to two-thirds less than leading brands, abundant new food products became favorites among poor consumers. These products have given low-income areas, like many districts in Greater Buenos Aires, an unprecedented cultural singularity, since carbonated drinks, cookies, salty snacks, and other goodies that are widely consumed within these communities are impossible to find outside their borders.[25]

In 2003, with the economy in tatters, Néstor Kirchner, the little known left-wing Peronist governor of the southern province of Santa Cruz, became president. With a strong hold of the government and a combination of populism and fiscal discipline, Kirchner refused to bend to the IMF and foreign creditors and steered Argentina out of its crisis by forcing debt holders to accept far less than they had loaned. His administration increased state control of the economy and intervention in the financial and commodity markets while taking advantage of a boom in soybeans and beef that stimulated domestic spending. Kirchner's government expanded social programs and public infrastructure, nationalized previously privatized enterprises, and reversed amnesty laws, allowing prosecutors to charge former military officers for human right violations. In 2007, Kirchner's wife, Cristina Fernández de Kirchner, became the first woman to be elected president of Argentina. A year later, Fernández de Kirchner's administration raised export taxes for agricultural products, provoking a nationwide lockout by farming associations, extensive social protests, and food shortages. The relationship between political authorities and the agro sectors improved, but the government has struggled to maintain economic growth and control inflation.[26]

Both Kirchner's and Fernández de Kirchner's administrations have celebrated a marked economic improvement across social classes, a claim they have substantiated with the positive figures provided by the government-intervened INDEC (the National Institute of Statistics and Censuses). However, in 2008, while the INDEC maintained that close to 18 percent of the population was under the poverty line, independent economists affirmed that the real percentage was 32 percent.[27] In fact, many sectors, particularly the middle classes, continue to experience what researchers have called "subjective poverty," a profound state of dissatisfaction anchored in their inability to afford the goods they crave. Although these families are not poor according to indexes that determine poverty levels, their members perceive themselves as impoverished because they cannot access what they believe they rightfully deserve.[28]

These perceptions are exacerbated in a context of consumer homogeneity that occurred because inflation and tighter budgets have forced middle-class consumers to go into commercial spaces and buy consumer products favored by the low-income sectors and also because these groups are purchasing consumer durables equal or equivalent to those the middle classes buy. There are a series of causes behind this phenomenon, including higher levels of employment, the lack of access or participation of the low-income consumers in the banking system, which incline them to spending more than saving, and new marketing strategies that have been intensively targeting these consumers in the past few years. When the purchasing power of their usual middle- and upper-class customers fell abruptly after 2001, many companies realized that, in order to survive, they needed to expand the market to include consumers whom they had traditionally disregarded. Interestingly, while in Perón's Argentina the higher wages of working-class consumers made them attractive to business, in the 2000s, it was the overall declining income that sparked corporate interest in those at the bottom of the consumer pyramid. Electronic stores, for example, opened numerous branches even in the poorest districts of Greater Buenos Aires offering the same products they marketed in high-income neighborhoods but with more flexible installment plans. The strategy was a success and a revelation since the consumer patterns of low-income sectors showed that, in contrast to previous assumptions, these customers spend more than other groups on certain durables and privilege well-known and high-quality brands.[29]

Like detractors more than five decades ago, critics fault low-income consumers for "squandering" their money rather than investing in long-term improvements. However, marketing research proved them wrong, showing that the purchases are mostly based on rational decisions rather than frivolity, social mimicry, or the search for status. Like working-class consumers in the 1950s, low-income consumers today favor brands that they associate with durability. In contrast to middle- and upper-class consumers who can afford to throw away a lemon or buy a new TV or DVD player, low-income sectors cannot go wrong. Even symbols of status like cell phones are purchased based on reasonable evaluations of needs and lacks. For example, low-income consumers spend 5 percent more than middle- and upper-class buyers on cells. The reason is that they opt for more sophisticated devices with a built-in camera, web browser, and MP3 player because, in contrast to wealthier buyers, low-income sectors do not have Internet at home, a separate MP3 player, or a camera.[30]

At first sight, cell phones, autoservicios chinos, and Nike shoes suggest that present-day consumer culture in Argentina bears little resemblance with its counterpart more than five decades earlier. Yet, in all their differences, both contexts prove the centrality of consumption for modern life. Consumption occupies a privileged position at the intersection of private and public life and, as such, is as central in defining the obligations of the state as it is in shaping popular understandings of what constitutes luxury and who deserves it. For this reason consumption is a means in the exercise of power. Companies crave profits, advertising agents want to persuade, the media circulate recommendations and stereotypes, and governments look for control and legitimacy, and, more often than we would like, they all have done so at the expense of consumers. Many critics argue that consumers barely notice it as dreams of abundance can blur perception. But beyond discussions of the political risks, social dangers, and cultural deterioration of consumption, consumer practices continue to be, as they were in the past, a crucial mechanism in creating consciousness and solidarity.

NOTES

INTRODUCTION

1. Juan Carlos Legas, interview by author, Rosario, December 21, 2005.

2. Fernando Rocchi, "La americanización del consumo: Las batallas del mercado argentino, 1920–1945," in *Americanización: Estados Unidos y América Latina en el Siglo XX; Transferencias económicas, tecnológicas y culturales*, ed. María I. Barbero and Andrés M. Regalsky (Buenos Aires: EDUNTREF, 2003), 154.

3. For a general history of Argentina, see Luis Alberto Romero, *A History of Argentina in the Twentieth Century* (University Park: Pennsylvania State University Press, 2002).

4. Robert G. Dunn, *Identifying Consumption: Subjects and Objects in Consumer Society* (Philadelphia: Temple University Press, 2008), 1–14.

5. Jean Baudrillard, *For a Critique of the Political Economy of the Sign* (St. Louis, MO: Telos Press, 1981). Classic examples of this scholarship are Mary Douglas and Baron Isherwood, *The World of Goods: Towards an Anthropology of Consumption*, 2nd ed. (New York: Routledge, 1996); Pierre Bourdieu, *Distinction: A Social Critique of the Judgement of Taste*, trans. Richard Nice (Cambridge, MA: Harvard University Press, 1984); Arjun Appadurai, ed., *The Social Life of Things: Commodities in Cultural Perspective* (New York: Cambridge University Press, 1986); Daniel Miller, *Material Culture and Mass Consumption* (Oxford: Basil Blackwell, 1987); and Grant McCracken, *Culture and Consumption: New Approaches to the Symbolic Character of Consumer Goods and Activities* (Bloomington: Indiana University Press, 1990).

6. Dunn, *Identifying Consumption*, 13.

7. Examples of this scholarship are Neil McKendrick, John Brewer, and J. H. Plumb, eds., *The Birth of a Consumer Society: The Commercialization of Eighteenth-Century England* (Bloomington: Indiana University Press, 1982); and John Brewer and Roy Porter, eds., *Consumption and the World of Goods* (New York: Routledge, 1993). For a discussion about consumption and periodization, see Peter Stearns, "Stages of Consumerism: Recent Work on the Issues of Periodization," *Journal of Modern History* 69, no. 1 (March 1997): 102–17.

8. See, for example, Erika Diane Rappaport, *Shopping for Pleasure: Women in the Making of London's West End* (Princeton, NJ: Princeton University Press, 2000); and Gary S. Cross and John K. Walton, *The Playful Crowd: Pleasure Places in the Twentieth Century* (New York: Columbia University Press, 2005).

9. Seminal works are Roland Marchand, *Advertising the American Dream: Making Way for Modernity, 1920–1940* (Berkeley: University of California Press, 1985); and Jackson Lears, *Fables of Abundance: A Cultural History of Advertising in America* (New York: Basic Books, 1994). See also Pamela Walker Laird, *Advertising Progress: American Business and the Rise of Consumer Marketing* (Baltimore: John Hopkins University Press, 1998); and Katherine J. Parkin, *Food Is Love: Advertising and Gender Roles in Modern America* (Philadelphia: University of Pennsylvania Press, 2006).

10. A classic work on gender and consumption is Victoria de Grazia and Ellen Furlough, eds., *The Sex of Things: Gender and Consumption in Historical Perspective* (Berkeley: University of California Press, 1996). For a historiographical assessment of gender and consumption, see Mary Louise Roberts, "Gender, Consumption, and Commodity Culture," *American Historical Review* 103, no. 3 (June 1998): 817–44.

11. See, for example, Ellen Furlough, *Consumer Cooperation in France: The Politics of Consumption, 1834–1930* (Ithaca, NY: Cornell University Press, 1991); and Landon R. Y. Storrs, *Civilizing Capitalism: The National Consumers' League, Women's Activism, and Labor Standards in the New Deal Era* (Chapel Hill: University of North Carolina Press, 2000). For an analysis of consumption regimes, see Victoria de Grazia, "Changing Consumption Regimes in Europe, 1930–1970: Comparative Perspectives on the Distribution Problem," in *Getting and Spending: European and American Consumer Societies in the Twentieth Century*, ed. Susan Strasser, Charles McGovern, and Matthias Judt (Cambridge: Cambridge University Press, 1998), 59–83.

12. Representative studies are Martin Daunton and Matthew Hilton, eds., *The Politics of Consumption: Material Culture and Citizenship in Europe and America* (New York: Berg, 2001); Lizabeth Cohen, *A Consumers' Republic: The Politics of Mass Consumption in Postwar America* (New York: Vintage, 2004); Meg Jacobs, *Pocketbook Politics: Economic Citizenship in Twentieth-Century America* (Princeton, NJ: Princeton University Press, 2005); and Charles F. McGovern, *Sold American: Consumption and Citizenship, 1890–1945* (Chapel Hill: University of North Carolina Press, 2006).

13. In fact, historians are paying increasing attention to the relation between children and consumption. See, for example, Daniel Thomas Cook, *The Commodification of Childhood: The Children's Clothing Industry and the Rise of the Child Consumer* (Durham, NC: Duke University Press, 2004).

14. Victoria de Grazia and Lizabeth Cohen, "Class and Consumption," *International Labor and Working-Class History* 55 (Spring 1999): 1–5.

15. Gary Cross, "Consumer History and the Dilemmas of Working-Class History," *Labor History Review* 62, no. 3 (Winter 1997): 261–74.

16. See, for example, Lizabeth Cohen, *Making a New Deal: Industrial Workers in Chicago, 1919–1939* (New York: Cambridge University Press, 1990); Gary Cross, *Time and Money: The Making of Consumer Culture* (New York: Routledge, 1993); Lawrence B. Glickman, *A Living Wage: American Workers and the Making of Consumer Society* (Ithaca, NY: Cornell University Press, 1997); and Susan Porter Benson, *Household Accounts: Working-Class Family Economies in the Interwar United States* (Ithaca, NY: Cornel University Press, 2007).

17. Craig Clunas, "Modernity Global and Local: Consumption and the Rise of the West," *American Historical Review* 104, no. 5 (December 1999): 1506.

18. On consumption in Canada, see, for example, Joy Parr, *Domestic Goods: The Material, the Moral, and the Economic in the Postwar Years* (Toronto: University of Toronto Press, 1999); and Donica Belisle, *Retail Nation: Department Stores and the Making of Modern Canada* (Vancouver: University of British Columbia Press, 2011). On consumption in Africa, see Timothy Burke, *Lifebuoy Men, Lux Women: Commodification, Consumption, and Cleanliness in Modern Zimbabwe* (Durham, NC: Duke University Press, 1996); and Jeremy Prestholdt, *Domesticating the World: African Consumerism and the Genealogies of Globalization* (Berkeley: University of California Press, 2008). On consumer culture in Asia, see, for example, Karl Gerth, *China Made: Consumer Culture and the Creation of the Nation* (Cambridge, MA: Harvard University Press, 2003); and Penelope Francks, *The Japanese Consumer: An Alternative Economic History of Modern Japan* (New York: Cambridge University Press, 2009). On consumption in the borderlands, see Alexis McCrossen, ed., *Land of Necessity: Consumer Culture in the United States–Mexico Borderlands* (Durham, NC: Duke University Press, 2009). On consumption and communism, see, for example, Sheila Fitzpatrick, *Everyday Stalinism: Ordinary Life in Extraordinary Times; Soviet Russia in the 1930s* (New York: Oxford University Press, 1999); and Julie Hessler, *A Social History of Soviet Trade: Trade Policy, Retail Practices, and Consumption, 1917–1953* (Princeton, NJ: Princeton University Press, 2004).

19. Jean-Christophe Agnew, "Coming Up for Air: Consumer Culture in Historical Perspective," in *Consumer Society in American History: A Reader*, ed. Lawrence B. Glickman (Ithaca, NY: Cornell University Press, 1999), 373–97; and David Steigerwald,

"All Hail the Republic of Choice: Consumer History as Contemporary Thought," *Journal of American History* 93, no. 2 (September 2006): 385–403.

20. Arnold J. Bauer, *Goods, Power, History: Latin America's Material Culture* (New York: Cambridge University Press, 2001); and Julio Moreno, *Yankee Don't Go Home! Mexican Nationalism, American Business Culture, and the Shaping of Modern Mexico, 1920–1950* (Chapel Hill: University of North Carolina Press, 2003).

21. See, for example, John Soluri, *Banana Cultures: Agriculture, Consumption, and Environmental Change in Honduras and the United States* (Austin: University of Texas Press, 2005); Marcy Norton, *Sacred Gifts, Profane Pleasures: A History of Tobacco and Chocolate in the Atlantic World* (Ithaca, NY: Cornell University Press, 2008); and Paul Gootenberg, *Andean Cocaine: The Making of a Global Drug* (Chapel Hill: University of North Carolina Press, 2008).

22. See, for example, Benjamin Orlove, ed., *The Allure of the Foreign: Imported Goods in Postcolonial Latin America* (Ann Harbor: University of Michigan Press, 1997); and Brian Owensby, *Intimate Ironies: Modernity and the Making of Middle-Class Lives in Brazil* (Stanford, CA: Stanford University Press, 1999).

23. Illustrative examples of this trend are Marie Eileen Francois, *A Culture of Everyday Credit: Housekeeping, Pawnbroking, and Governance in Mexico City, 1750–1920* (Lincoln: University of Nebraska Press, 2006); Lauren Derby, *The Dictator's Seduction: Politics and the Popular Imagination in the Era of Trujillo* (Durham, NC: Duke University Press, 2009); Micol Seigel, *Uneven Encounters: Making Race and Nation in Brazil and the United States* (Durham, NC: Duke University Press, 2009); and Dina Berger and Andrew Grant Wood, eds., *Holiday in Mexico: Critical Reflections on Tourism and Tourist Encounters* (Durham, NC: Duke University Press, 2010).

24. See, for example, John D. French and Daniel James, eds., *The Gendered Worlds of Latin American Women Workers: From Household and Factory to the Union Hall and Ballot Box* (Durham, NC: Duke University Press, 1997).

25. Two studies that represent this new scholarship are Mirta Zaida Lobato, *La vida en las fábricas: Trabajo, protesta y política en una comunidad obrera, Berisso (1904–1970)* (Buenos Aires: Prometeo, 2001); and Hernán Camarero, *A la conquista de la clase obrera: Los comunistas y el mundo del trabajo en la Argentina, 1920–1935* (Buenos Aires: Siglo Veintiuno, 2007).

26. See, for example, Jennifer Scanlon, "Mediators in the International Marketplace: U.S. Advertising in Latin America in the Early Twentieth Century," *Business History Review* 77, no. 3 (Autumn 2003): 387–415; and James Woodard, "Marketing Modernity: The J. Walter Thompson Company and North American Advertising in Brazil, 1929–1939," *Hispanic American Historical Review* 82, no. 2 (May 2002): 257–90.

27. A few scholars of Argentina, particularly literary critics, have incorporated the analysis of consumption as part of broader themes. See, for example, Laura Podalsky, *Specular City: Transforming Culture, Consumption, and Space in Buenos Aires, 1955–1973* (Philadelphia: Temple University Press, 2004); Adriana J. Bergero, *Intersecting Tango: Cultural Geographies of Buenos Aires, 1900–1930*, trans. Richard Young (Pittsburgh: University of Pittsburgh Press, 2008); and Regina A. Root, *Couture and Consensus: Fashion and Politics in Postcolonial Argentina* (Minneapolis: University of Minnesota Press, 2010). For an example of business and economic history that considers issues of consumption, see Fernando Rocchi, *Chimneys in the Desert: Industrialization in Argentina During the Export Boom Years, 1870–1930* (Stanford, CA: Stanford University Press, 2006).

28. Juan Carlos Torre and Eliza Pastoriza, "La democratización del bienestar," in *Nueva Historia Argentina*, vol. 8, *Los años peronistas (1943–1955)*, ed. Juan Carlos Torre (Buenos Aires: Sudamericana, 2002). See, for example, Patricia Berrotarán, Aníbal Jaúregui, and Marcelo Rougier, eds., *Sueños de bienestar en la Nueva Argentina: Estado y políticas públicas durante el peronismo, 1946–1955* (Buenos Aires: Imago Mundi, 2004); Anahí Ballent, *Las huellas de la política: Vivienda, ciudad, peronismo en Buenos Aires, 1943–1955* (Buenos Aires: Universidad Nacional de Quilmes/Prometeo, 2005); and Rosa Aboy, *Viviendas para el pueblo: Espacio urbano y sociabilidad en el barrio Los Perales, 1946–1955* (Buenos Aires: Fondo de Cultura Económica, 2005).

29. Eduardo Elena, *Dignifying Argentina: Peronism, Citizenship, and Mass Consumption* (Pittsburgh: University of Pittsburgh Press, 2011) and "Peronism in 'Good Taste': Culture and Consumption in the Magazine *Argentina*," in *The New Cultural History of Peronism: Power and Identity in Mid-Twentieth-Century Argentina*, ed. Matthew B. Karush and Oscar Chamosa (Durham, NC: Duke University Press, 2010), 209–37. See also Natalia Milanesio, "Food Politics and Consumption in Peronist Argentina," *Hispanic American Historical Review* 90, no.1 (February 2010): 75–108 and "The Guardian Angels of the Domestic Economy: Housewives' Responsible Consumption in Peronist Argentina," *Journal of Women's History* 18, no. 3 (Fall 2006): 91–117.

30. For examples of new scholarship on Peronism, see Mariano Ben Plotkin, *Mañana es San Perón: A Cultural History of Perón's Argentina*, trans. Keith Zahniser (Wilmington, DE: SR Books, 2003); Karina Inés Ramacciotti and Adriana María Valobra, eds., *Generando el Peronismo: Estudios de cultura, política y género (1946–1955)* (Buenos Aires: Proyecto Editorial, 2004); Marcela Gené, *Un mundo feliz: Imágenes de los trabajadores en el primer peronismo, 1946–1955* (Buenos Aires: Fondo de Cultura Económica, 2005); and Mark A. Healey, *The Ruins of the New Argentina: Peronism and the Remaking of San Juan After the 1944 Earthquake* (Durham, NC: Duke University Press, 2011).

Chapter 1

1. Corporación para la Promoción del Intercambio, *La estructura económica y el desarrollo industrial en la Argentina* (Buenos Aires: Corporación para la Promoción del Intercambio, 1944), 29, 56–61.

2. "El nivel de vida de los trabajadores argentinos es el más alto del mundo," *Mundo Argentino*, September 29, 1951, 10–11; and "La Argentina es el país donde la vida cuesta menos y el obrero gana más," *Ahora*, January 30, 1947, 10–11.

3. Daniel James, *Doña María's Story: Life History, Memory, and Political Identity* (Durham, NC: Duke University Press, 2000), 71.

4. On industrial growth in Argentina in the early twentieth century, see Rocchi, *Chimneys in the Desert*; and Yovanna Pineda, *Industrial Development in a Frontier Economy: The Industrialization of Argentina, 1870–1930* (Stanford, CA: Stanford University Press, 2009).

5. Pineda, *Industrial Development in a Frontier Economy*, 4–6; and María Inés Barbero and Fernando Rocchi, "Industry," in *A New Economic History of Argentina*, ed. Gerardo Della Paolera and Alan Taylor (Cambridge: Cambridge University Press, 2003), 275–77.

6. Secretaría de Asuntos Técnicos, *Índices Estadísticos, 1954* (Buenos Aires: Secretaría de Asuntos Técnicos, 1954), 55; and Barbero and Rocchi, "Industry," 277.

7. Quoted in Cristina Lucchini, *Apoyo empresarial en los orígenes del peronismo* (Buenos Aires: CEAL, 1990), 45.

8. Romero, *A History of Argentina in the Twentieth Century*, 100–102. For an analysis of the Pinedo Plan, see Juan José Llach, "El Plan Pinedo de 1940, su significado histórico y los orígenes de la economía política del Peronismo," *Desarrollo Económico* 23, no. 92 (1984): 515–57.

9. Pablo Gerchunoff and Lucas Llach, *El ciclo de la ilusión y el desencanto: Un siglo de políticas económicas argentinas* (Buenos Aires: Ariel, 1998), 161–65; and James P. Brennan and Marcelo Rougier, *The Politics of National Capitalism: Peronism and the Argentine Bourgeoisie, 1946–1976* (University Park: Pennsylvania State University Press, 2002), 26–28, 47–48.

10. "Las industrias en el pensamiento vivo de Perón," *Mundo Peronista*, October 15, 1952, 45. Also, "La transformación económica argentina," *Hechos e Ideas*, July 1948, 13–20.

11. *Bolicheros* comes from *boliche*, a colloquial term to refer to a small shop or a tavern.

12. Brennan and Rougier, *The Politics of National Capitalism*, 37, 62–63; and Romero, *A History of Argentina in the Twentieth Century*, 102.

13. Claudio Belini, *La industria peronista* (Buenos Aires: Edhasa, 2009), 136–37, 166; and "La expansión fabril argentina," *Dinámica Social*, February 1955, 38–40.

14. Dirección Nacional de Estadísticas y Censos, *IV Censo General de la Nación: Censo de Vivienda* (Buenos Aires: Dirección Nacional de Estadísticas y Censos, 1947), 12, 15–16.

15. Carlos Volpi, *El problema energético argentino* (Buenos Aires: Editorial de Autores, 1954), 49–50; José Constantino Barro, "Fomento industrial del país por la electrificación del mismo," *Agua y Energía*, October 1947, 9; and Adolfo Dorfman, *Cincuenta años de industrialización en la Argentina, 1930–1980: Desarrollo y perspectivas* (Buenos Aires: Solar, 1983), 207–14.

16. Thomas Cochran and Ruben Reina, *Entrepreneurship in Argentine Culture: Torcuato Di Tella and S.I.A.M.* (Philadelphia: University of Pennsylvania Press, 1962), 72–111, 172–255.

17. Noemí Girbal-Blacha, *Mitos, paradojas y realidades en la Argentina Peronista (1946–1955): Una interpretación histórica de sus decisiones político-económicas* (Bernal, Argentina: Universidad Nacional de Quilmes, 2003), 42–48.

18. On the IAPI, see Susana Novick, *IAPI: Auge y decadencia* (Buenos Aires: CEAL, 1986).

19. Gerchunoff and Llach, *El ciclo de la ilusión y el desencanto*, 195–99, 205; and Barbero and Rocchi, "Industry," 280.

20. "Las industrias en el pensamiento vivo de Perón," *Mundo Peronista*, October 15, 1952, 45.

21. Gerchunoff and Llach, *El ciclo de la ilusión y el desencanto*, 218–20; and "La productividad del trabajo en el pensamiento vivo de Perón," *Mundo Peronista*, September 1, 1954, 47.

22. Gerchunoff and Llach, *El ciclo de la ilusión y el desencanto*, 235–37; and Romero, *A History of Argentina in the Twentieth Century*, 122.

23. Juan Domingo Perón, *Obras Completas* (Buenos Aires: Docencia, 1997), 6: 479.

24. Juan Bialet Massé, *Informe sobre el estado de la clase obrera* (Buenos Aires: Hyspamérica, 1985); and Pedro Escudero, *Alimentación: Colaboraciones publicadas en La Prensa* (Buenos Aires: Hachette, 1934), 252.

25. On underconsumption, see Emilio Llorens, *El subconsumo de alimentos en América del Sur* (Buenos Aires: Sudamericana, 1942); and Moisés Poblete Troncoso, *El subconsumo en América del Sur* (Santiago de Chile: Nascimento, 1946).

26. Paulino González Alberdi, *Cómo abaratar la vida* (Buenos Aires: Anteo, 1942), 5–6.

27. Quoted in Camarero, *A la conquista de la clase obrera*, 55.

28. Elena, *Dignifying Argentina*, 59–60; and Cochran and Reina, *Entrepreneurship in Argentine Culture*, 159.

29. Elena, *Dignifying Argentina*, 39–40.

30. The phrase was coined by Antonio Cafiero, minister of foreign trade between 1952 and 1954. Antonio Cafiero, *Cinco años después* (Buenos Aires: El Gráfico, 1961), 126.

31. "El salario en el pensamiento vivo de Perón," *Mundo Peronista*, January 1953, 44.

32. David Tamarin, *The Argentine Labor Movement, 1930–1945: A Study in the Origins of Peronism* (Albuquerque: University of New Mexico Press, 1985), 191, 209.

33. Quoted in Juan Carlos Torre, *La vieja guardia sindical y Perón: Sobre los orígenes del peronismo* (Buenos Aires: Sudamericana, 1990), 99.

34. Gerchunoff and Llach, *El ciclo de la ilusión y el desencanto*, 181; and Peter Ross, "Justicia social: Una evaluación de los logros del Peronismo clásico," *Anuario del IEHS*, no. 8 (1993): 114.

35. "Piden la abolición de la propina," *La Época*, July 18, 1946, 5.

36. Alejandro Unsaín, *Ordenamiento de las leyes obreras argentinas* (Buenos Aires: El Ateneo, 1952), 295–311; "O laudo o propina," *¡Extra!*, March 5, 1948, 5; and Rubens Iscaro, *Historia del movimiento sindical* (Buenos Aires: Fundamentos, 1973), 2:260.

37. "Buenos Aires de hoy," *Continente*, December 1951, 91; and "Veinticinco restaurantes y hoteles en dos manzanas," *Caras y Caretas*, March 1952, 132–34.

38. "Apuntes de economía peronista," *Hechos e Ideas*, August/September 1954, 241.

39. Gerchunoff and Llach, *El ciclo de la ilusión y el desencanto*, 182; Ross, "Justicia social," 112; and Girbal-Blacha, *Mitos, paradojas y realidades en la Argentina Peronista (1946–1955)*, 48.

40. Aníbal Jáuregui, "Prometeo encadenado: Los industriales y el régimen peronista," in *Sueños de bienestar en la Nueva Argentina*, Berrotarán, Jáuregui, and Rougier, 47–71.

41. Dirección de Estadística Social, *Condiciones de vida de la familia obrera, 1943–1945* (Buenos Aires: Dirección de Estadística Social, 1946), 75; Casa Beige ad, *La Capital*, December 17, 1947; and Roveda ad, *La Prensa*, January 7, 1947, 6.

42. Susana Torrado, *Estructura social de la Argentina, 1945–1983* (Buenos Aires: Ediciones de la Flor, 1992), 272.

43. Belini, *La industria peronista*, 138–39; La Piedad ad, *El Mundo*, October 14, 1945, 9; Costa Grande ad, *Clarín*, October 13, 1949, 3; and Gath & Chaves ad, *La Prensa*, July 5, 1945, 14.

44. "Humanizar el capital," *La Nación Argentina: Justa, Libre, Soberana* (Buenos Aires: Ediciones Peuser, 1950), n.p.

45. On the changing and finally tumultuous relationship between the Peronist government and the Catholic Church, see Susana Bianchi, *Catolicismo y Peronismo: Religión y política en la Argentina, 1943–1955* (Tandil, Argentina: Instituto de Estudios Históricos Sociales, 2001); and Loris Zanatta, *Perón y el mito de la nación católica: Iglesia y Ejército en los orígenes del Peronismo (1943–1946)* (Buenos Aires: Sudamericana, 1999).

46. Enrique Pavón Pereira, *Coloquios con Perón* (Buenos Aires: n.p., 1965), 134.

47. "Lo que va de ayer a hoy," *La Época*, January 15, 1947, 10.

48. Quoted in Tamarin, *The Argentine Labor Movement, 1930–1945*, 193.

49. On labor laws before Peronism, see José Panettieri, *Las primeras leyes obreras* (Buenos Aires: CEAL, 1984).

50. Juan Domingo Perón, *Principios doctrinarios de política social* (Buenos Aires: Subsecretaría de Informaciones, 1947), 20.

51. Brennan and Rougier, *The Politics of National Capitalism*, 56; and "El paraíso no queda ni a la derecha ni a la izquierda," *Mundo Peronista*, May 15, 1952, 21.

52. Brennan and Rougier, *The Politics of National Capitalism*, 51.

53. Elena, *Dignifying Argentina*, 95–99.

54. Elena, *Dignifying Argentina*, 176–78; Secretaría de Asuntos Técnicos, *Índices Estadísticos, 1954*, 76; Jorge del Río, "En defensa del consumidor," *Hechos e Ideas*, December 1951, 319–38; and Fundación Eva Perón, *Proveedurías Eva Perón* (Buenos Aires: Fundación Eva Perón, 1950).

55. Elena, *Dignifying Argentina*, 175. On appeals to citizenship and nationalism in connection to food consumption, see Milanesio, "Food Politics and Consumption in Peronist Argentina." On consumerism as patriotic duty in the United States, see Cohen, *A Consumers' Republic*.

56. "Consumo y Derroche," *Mundo Peronista*, February 13, 1952, 3.

57. Gerchunoff and Llach, *El ciclo de la ilusión y el desencanto*, 211.

58. Academia Nacional de Ciencias Económicas, *Estadísticas Históricas Argentinas: Compendio 1873–1973* (Buenos Aires: Academia Nacional de Ciencias Económicas, 1988), 147; and Ministerio de Agricultura y Ganadería, *Producción Pesquera de la República Argentina: Años 1946–53* (Buenos Aires: Ministerio de Agricultura y Ganadería, 1955), 58, 445.

59. "Inaudito: Caramelos Tóxicos," *Democracia*, July 9, 1949, 7.

60. Congreso Nacional, Cámara de Diputados de la Nación, *Diario de Sesiones de 1949*, 1:650.

61. Emilio Schleh, *La alimentación en la Argentina: Sus características y deficiencias; Anotaciones para resolver un gran problema* (Buenos Aires: Ferrari, 1930), 2: 223–31. On food adulteration in the provincial interior, see Fernando Remedi, *Consumo de alimentos, condiciones sanitarias y políticas públicas en la ciudad de Córdoba en las primeras décadas del siglo XX* (Córdoba, Argentina: Municipalidad de Córdoba, 2003), 23–42.

62. Fred Motz, *The Fruit Industry of Argentina* (Washington, D.C.: Office of Foreign Agricultural Relations, United States Department of Agriculture, 1942), 71.

63. "Contra los que envenenan al pueblo," *Aquí Está*, March 18, 1948, 2–3; "Pan Criollo contesta a Don Rudecindo," *Panadería Argentina*, December 1, 1951, 4; and "El comercio no es una aventura: Es mejor vender buenos productos," *Ímpetu*, April 1948, 26–27.

64. Jorge Mullor, *Por un alimento mejor: Bases para un código bromatológico nacional* (Santa Fe, Argentina: Castelvi, 1949), 19–21, 32–33; and "Inspecciones Industriales," *Veritas*, January 15, 1940, 4.

65. "Abastecedores inescrupulosos juegan con la salud de la población ante la pasividad consciente del jefe de la comuna, Agustín Repetto," *Rosario Norte*, June 1, 1942, 5.

66. Schleh, *La alimentación en la Argentina*, 293–99.

67. Ramón Carrillo, *Organización general del Ministerio de Salud Pública: Obras Completas* (Buenos Aires: Eudeba, 1974), 3:355–65.

68. "Para que no se engañe al público es vigilada la pureza y la calidad de los alimentos," *La Época*, December 24, 1949, 4.

69. "Contralor sanitario de artículos alimenticios," *Revista de la Asociación de Fabricantes de Dulces, Conservas y Afines*, May 1949, 15. In contrast to provinces, "national territories" had less than sixty thousand inhabitants and no representatives in Congress. By the early 1940s, the *territorios nacionales* were Misiones, Chaco, Formosa, La Pampa, Chubut, Río Negro, Santa Cruz, and Tierra del Fuego. All were transformed into provinces during the Peronist administration with the exception of Tierra del Fuego.

70. Ministerio de Salud Pública y Asistencia Social, Provincia de Buenos Aires, *Memoria 1949–1950* (La Plata, Argentina: Ministerio de Salud Pública y Asistencia Social, Provincia de Buenos Aires, 1950), 45.

71. "Serán sometidos a proceso los fabricantes de productos Mu-Mu," *Democracia*, July 20, 1949, 7; "Fue levantada la clausura impuesta a la fábrica de productos Mu-Mu," *Democracia*, January 2, 1953, 5; and "Se decomisan todos los productos Mu-Mu," *Noticias Gráficas*, July 14, 1949, 7. In 1966, Samuel Groisman, one of the owners of Mu-Mu declared that the factory had been closed down because the company had attempted to collect a debt from the Eva Perón Foundation. Groisman also argued that the reopening of the company was due to "voluntary" donations to the foundation that were to be paid by the company once every three months. Hugo Gambini, *Historia del Peronismo: El poder total (1943–1951)* (Buenos Aires: Planeta, 1999), 182.

72. Specific regulations that responded to the needs of different sectors of the food industry were also slowly appearing in the late 1930s and the 1940s. For example, sanitary measures for the canned fish industry were passed for the first time in 1939. Mullor, *Por un alimento mejor*, 19–21; Ministerio de Gobierno de la Provincia de Buenos Aires, *Reglamento Bromatológico de la Provincia de Buenos Aires: Codex Alimentarius*, 2nd ed. (La Plata, Argentina: Ministerio de Gobierno de la Provincia de Buenos Aires, 1937); and Italo Carrara, *La industria de las conservas de pescado en la República Argentina* (Buenos Aires: n.p., 1941), 47–74.

73. The members of the committee were important figures from national and provincial agencies related to food production and commercialization; they included Carlos Alberto Grau, head of the Buenos Aires Chemistry Department and the author of the Buenos Aires Food Code of 1928 (which served as a model for the new set of rules), and Jorge Mullor, director of the Santa Fe Institute of Bromatology. "El Código Bromatológico Nacional," *La Industria Lechera*, September 1950, 449–50.

74. The sophistication of the 1953 code was also evident abroad when, in the late 1950s, it served as the model for the first Latin American Food Code. Ministerio de Salud Pública, *Reglamento alimentario aprobado por decreto no. 141/53* (Buenos Aires:

Ministerio de Salud Pública, 1953); and Carlos Alurralde, *A Statement of the Laws of Argentina in Matters Affecting Business* (Washington, D.C.: Pan American Union, 1963), 310.

75. Mullor, *Por un alimento mejor,* n.p.; "Comisión de Higiene Alimenticia," *El Mundo,* March 10, 1948, 4; and "Provisión de providencias a adoptar por la Municipalidad de Mar del Plata para asegurar un abasto racional de leche a la población," *La Industria Lechera,* January 1949, 44–49.

76. Carlos Ángel Zavala Rodríguez, *Publicidad comercial: Su régimen legal* (Buenos Aires: De Palma, 1947), 247–48; and "¿Debe decirse 'industria nacional' o 'industria argentina'?," *Ímpetu,* May 1937, 18–19. On elite and middle-class preference for imports, see Bauer, *Goods, Power, History,* 1–14; and Arnold J. Bauer and Benjamin Orlove, "Giving Importance to Imports," in *The Allure of the Foreign,* Orlove, 1–31.

77. "Calidad de los productos que usamos o consumimos," *El Tranviario,* June 1941, 3; and Mullor, *Por un alimento mejor,* 31–33.

78. Congreso Nacional, Cámara de Diputados de la Nación, *Diario de Sesiones de 1949,* 1:651.

79. República Argentina, Ministerio de Industria y Comercio, Resolución No. 1141, Archivo General de la Nación, Secretaría de Asuntos Técnicos, Industria, Legajo 477.

80. Congreso Nacional, Cámara de Diputados de la Nación, *Diario de Sesiones de 1949,* 1:653; "Recuérdese disposiciones sobre rótulos de mercaderías y formas de hacer publicidad," *Revista de la Asociación de Fabricantes de Dulces, Conservas y Afines,* July 1947, 17–18; and "Modifícase la ley No. 11.275," *Revista de la Asociación de Fabricantes de Dulces, Conservas y Afines,* August 1949, 5–6.

81. "Las revistas aumentaron su volumen publicitario en 1948," *Ímpetu,* March 1949, 17–21; and "Clientes y cuentas," *Ímpetu,* December 1947, 99–127.

82. "Buenas campañas," *Ímpetu,* March 1951, 20–22, 31; *Ímpetu,* February 1952, 20–2; and *Ímpetu,* April 1954, 34–36.

83. Aníbal White, *La industria cervecera por dentro* (Buenos Aires: Americana, 1946), 165–67; and "Calidad de los productos que usamos o consumimos," *El Tranviario,* June 1941, 3.

84. Zavala Rodríguez, *Publicidad comercial,* 243–53.

85. Congreso Nacional, Cámara de Diputados de la Nación, *Diario de Sesiones de 1950,* 5: 4076.

86. "Fiscalización de la propaganda de los artículos de consumo," *Revista de la Asociación de Fabricantes de Dulces, Conservas y Afines,* May 1949, 16; and "La aprobación previa de la propaganda oral, gráfica o escrita de los productos alimenticios," *Ímpetu,* May 1949, 14–17.

87. "Advertising—International: Argentina," *Tide: The Magazine of Advertising, Marketing, and Public Relations,* December 1, 1947, 20.

88. "La propaganda engañosa," *Ímpetu*, January 1950, 32; and "La acción de la mala propaganda redunda en perjuicio del anunciante honesto," *Ímpetu*, October 1947, 3, 27.

89. Instituto Alejandro E. Bunge de Investigaciones Económicas y Sociales, *Soluciones argentinas a los problemas económicos y sociales del presente* (Buenos Aires: Kraft, 1945), 186; and "La competencia no debe estar reñida con la honestidad comercial," *Ímpetu*, May 1946, 6–7.

90. "Algo sobre publicidad de productos alimenticios," *Ímpetu*, December 1949, 118–21.

91. "La Cámara del Café solicita la reglamentación del contenido de los envases," *Revista de la Federación Gremial del Comercio e Industria de Rosario*, February 1945, 17–18.

92. "Oportunidad para perfeccionar los envases," *Ímpetu*, June 1942, 33; and "Cómo la Guerra ha influído en la industria del envase en la Argentina," *Ímpetu*, April/June 1943, 120–21.

93. Olímpico ads, *Radiolandia*, July 6, 1946, n.p., and *El Hogar*, August 4, 1950, 74; and Lactal ad, *El Mundo*, June 18, 1946, 8.

94. Archivo General de la Nación, Secretaría de Asuntos Técnicos, Industria, Legajo 477 and Legajo 471; and "Normas para envasar dulces," *Ímpetu*, November 1952, 28.

Chapter 2

1. *Argentina*, October 1, 1949, 22–24.

2. Subsecretaría de Informaciones de la Presidencia de la Nación, *Perón: Anécdotas, recuerdos, relatos* (Buenos Aires: Subsecretaría de Informaciones de la Presidencia de la Nación, 1950), 82; Juan Domingo Perón, "La Política Alimentaria Argentina," *Hechos e Ideas*, May/June 1949, 353; and Juan Domingo Perón, "El consumo y la especulación," *Hechos e Ideas*, August 1950, 428.

3. Gerchunoff and Llach, *El ciclo de la ilusión y el desencanto*, 182–83; and Secretaría de Asuntos Técnicos, *Índices Estadísticos, 1954*, 76.

4. Frank Montgomery Dunbaugh, *Marketing in Latin America* (New York: Printers' Ink Book Company, 1960), 9.

5. *La Razón: Medio siglo de vida del país y del mundo, 1905–1955* (Buenos Aires: Alea, 1955), n.p.; *Ímpetu: Muestra Guía de publicidad y sus clientes*, December 1947; "Las revistas y diarios del interior mantuvieron su volumen publicitario en 1949," *Ímpetu*, February 1950, 26–27; "Como trabajan las agencias de publicidad," *Ímpetu*, June 1948, 22–25; and "Clarín aumentó en su tercer año el 140% de su publicidad," *Ímpetu*, December 1948, 19.

6. Ministerio de Industria y Comercio de la Nación, *Economía Publicitaria* (Buenos Aires: Ministerio de Industria y Comercio de la Nación, 1949), n.p.

7. Ysabel F. Rennie, *The Argentine Republic* (New York: MacMillan, 1945), 310. On the relation between J. Walter Thompson and General Motors, see Jeff Merron, "Putting Foreign Consumers on the Map: J. Walter Thompson's Struggle with General Motors'

International Advertising Account in the 1920s," *Business History Review* 73, no. 3 (Autumn 1999): 465–502. For an analysis of J. Walter Thompson in Brazil, see Woodard, "Marketing Modernity," 257–90.

8. J. W. Sanger, *Advertising Methods in Argentina, Uruguay, and Brazil* (Washington, D.C.: Department of Commerce, 1920), 30. On the J. Walter Thompson company in early twentieth-century Argentina, see Ricardo Salvatore, "Yankee Advertising in Buenos Aires: Reflections on Americanization," *Interventions* 7, no. 2 (2005): 216–35; and Scanlon, "Mediators in the International Marketplace," 387–415.

9. "El pueblo argentino vive mal alimentado," *Orientación*, October 8, 1936, 4.

10. Ruth Greenup and Leonard Greenup, *Revolution Before Breakfast: Argentina, 1941–1946* (Chapel Hill: University of North Carolina Press, 1947), 120.

11. Schleh, *La alimentación en la Argentina*; "Así está hoy la plaza publicitaria argentina," *Ímpetu*, January 1934, 12–13; Dirección de Estadística Social, *Nivel de vida de la familia obrera: Evolución durante la Segunda Guerra Mundial, 1939–1945* (Buenos Aires: Dirección de Estadística Social, 1945); and Dirección de Estadística Social, *Condiciones de vida de la familia obrera, 1943–1945*. Starting in the 1930s, the *Revista de la Asociación Argentina de Dietología* conducted studies on working-class budgets to assess food habits. For a historical analysis of the evolution of state statistics and research on standards of living in Argentina, see Eduardo Zimmerman, *Los liberales reformistas: La cuestión social en la Argentina, 1890–1916* (Buenos Aires: Sudamericana, 1995); and Hernán González Bollo, "La cuestión obrera en números: La estadística socio-laboral en la Argentina y su impacto en la política y la sociedad, 1895–1943," in *El mosaico argentino*, ed. Hernán Otero (Buenos Aires: Siglo Veintiuno, 2004), 331–77.

12. Scanlon, "Mediators in the International Marketplace," 406–7.

13. "Nuestro limitado mercado interno y el bajo poder adquisitivo de la clase media son escollos que prohíben un mayor progreso publicitario," *Ímpetu*, July 1939, 30.

14. Belini, *La industria peronista*, 139.

15. "Cómo vemos 1949," *Ímpetu*, January 1949, 33 (emphasis in the original).

16. Ibid. and Salvatore, "Yankee Advertising in Buenos Aires," 216–35. American advertising companies introduced the letter classification of consumers in the late 1920s, and it was rapidly adopted by all advertising agencies in the country.

17. "Análisis de mercado," *La Reforma Comercial*, November 30, 1946, 19–25; and "Cómo determinar el nivel de vida en las encuestas," *Investigaciones de Mercado*, April 1952, 2–3.

18. International Advertising Association, *Consumer Study of the Buenos Aires Market* (New York: Export Advertising Association, 1947). On national statistical trends in mid-twentieth-century Argentina, see Hernán Otero, "El concepto de población en el sistema estadístico nacional," in *Población y bienestar en la Argentina del primero al segundo centenario*, ed. Susana Torrado (Buenos Aires, Edhasa, 2007), 1:171–73.

19. Gino Germani's lectures were compiled in a series of articles titled "El Consumidor" that appeared in *Ventas*, June 1954, 11–16; July 1954, 8–16; and August 1954, 6–12, 38–42.

20. Russell Pierce, *Gringo-Gaucho: An Advertising Odyssey* (Ashland, OR: Southern Cross, 1991), 215.

21. "La propaganda y la investigación de mercado," *La Reforma Comercial*, November 30, 1946, 11–12; "El estudio de mercado ofrece garantías de éxito a las campañas," *Ímpetu*, special edition 1950, no. 198, 42–44; and International Advertising Association, *Consumer Study of the Buenos Aires Market*, 172–87.

22. "Frente al nuevo mercado," *Ímpetu*, December 1949, 128 (emphasis in the original).

23. "Argentina," *Tide: The Magazine of Advertising, Marketing, and Public Relations*, December 1, 1947, 22; and JWT Company Archive, Information Center Records, Box 9. *The JWT Weekly News* 5, no. 21, May 22, 1950, 3, JWT Company Archive, Newsletter Collection, Box 5.

24. "Cómo determinar la capacidad de consumo del mercado argentino," *Investigaciones de Mercado*, May 1954, 3–4.

25. "Buenas Campañas," *Ímpetu*, March 1951, 20–22.

26. "La acción conjunta en la investigación de mercado," *Investigaciones de Mercado*, March 1952, 1; Salvatore, "Yankee Advertising in Buenos Aires," 226; and International Advertising Association, *Consumer Study of the Buenos Aires Market*, 5.

27. "Aplicación social de la investigación de mercado," *Investigaciones de Mercado*, June 1952, 3; Instituto Lanús ad, *Ventas*, September/October 1950, 8; and "Los actuales hábitos de consumo revelan un mayor bienestar," *Esto Es*, December 14, 1954, 3. In addition to traditional economic publications like *Veritas* (1919) and *Ímpetu* (1933), the field of market studies journals grew to include *Síntesis Publicitaria* (1945), *Ventas* (1947), *Síntesis Económica Americana* (1948), *Economía y Finanzas* (1949), and *Investigaciones de Mercado* (1951), to name a few of the most important periodicals.

28. "En la Capital se gasta el 31.1 % del dinero de todo el país," *Ímpetu*, April 1941, 40; and George Wythe, *Industry in Latin America* (New York: Columbia University Press, 1949), 120–22.

29. Alejandro Bunge, *Una Nueva Argentina* (Buenos Aires: Kraft, 1940), 222–28; Poblete Troncoso, *El subconsumo en América del Sur*, 175–78; and Llorens, *El subconsumo de alimentos en América del Sur.*

30. "Geografía del nivel de vida," *Panorama*, June 1958, 177–95.

31. "Hagamos algo por los 10.000.000 millones de olvidados . . . ," *Ímpetu*, August/September 1937, 4–8.

32. J. Walter Thompson Company, *The Latin American Markets* (New York: McGraw Hill Book Company, 1956), 13–23.

33. "No será una novedad . . . pero es una gran verdad," *Ímpetu*, July 1949, 14.

34. "Conozcamos el interior del país," *Ímpetu*, May 1955, 20–23; and "Capacidad económica total," *Síntesis Publicitaria*, 1946, 293.

35. "Geografía del nivel de vida," *Panorama*, June 1958, 177–95; "Conozcamos mejor nuestros mercados," *Ímpetu*, March 1950, 32; and "Una zona descuidada por los jefes de propaganda," *Ímpetu*, June 1939, 6–7.

36. Alfredo Lattes, "Esplendor y ocaso en las migraciones internas," in *Población y bienestar en la Argentina del primero al segundo centenario*, ed. Susana Torrado (Buenos Aires: Edhasa, 2007), 2:11–46.

37. "El periodismo del interior," *Ímpetu*, special edition, December 1950, 36–38; "Un proyecto de estatutos," *Ímpetu*, November 1946, 18–19; and "Naturaleza jurídica de los contratos de las llamadas Agencias de Publicidad," *Ímpetu*, March 1951, 23–27. On how manufacturers changed their perception of advertising after the 1940s, see Cochran and Reina, *Entrepreneurship in Argentine Culture*, 97–104, 239–42.

38. "La distribución geográfica de las ventas," *Ventas*, April 1955, 44–45; and "Oiga hablar a los números," *Ímpetu*, December 1953, 72–81.

39. "El interior argentino," *Ímpetu*, October 1947, 32; Robert Woodward, *Advertising Methods in Argentina* (Washington, D.C.: Department of Commerce, 1935), 5; and Rocchi, "La americanización del consumo," 174.

40. "Conozcamos mejor nuestros mercados," *Ímpetu*, March 1950, 32 (emphasis in the original).

41. "El mercado consumidor," *Ímpetu*, November 1947, 32; and "Conozcamos el interior del país," *Ímpetu*, 20–23.

42. "El poder adquisitivo de la población," *Ventas*, November 1954, 108–12.

43. "El periodismo del interior," *Ímpetu*, special edition, December 1950, 36–38; and "No será una novedad . . . pero es una gran verdad," *Ímpetu*, July 1949, 14.

44. *Los Andes* ad, *Ímpetu*, July 1949, 9; and *Los Principios* ad, *Ímpetu*, special edition, December 1950, 9.

45. Because of the high concentration of the population in the pampeana region around Buenos Aires, readers in this area had access to these two dailies within twelve hours of publication.

46. "Con seis medios capitales no se absorbe el interior del país," *Ímpetu*, September 1949, 22–25.

47. Woodward, *Advertising Methods in Argentina*, 8; Sanger, *Advertising Methods in Argentina, Uruguay, and Brazil*, 21–22; and "Una zona descuidada por los jefes de propaganda," *Ímpetu*, June 1939, 6–7.

48. "Los mercados del interior no se conquistan con un aviso," *Ímpetu*, August 1949, 28–31; and "Importancia de la prensa regional, *Ímpetu*, November 1953, 4–6.

49. "El periodismo del interior," *Ímpetu*, special edition, December 1950, 36–38; "Y hablemos ahora de la indiferencia periodística regional," *Ímpetu*, October 1949, 40–41; and "Necesidad imperiosa: Prensa interior," *Ímpetu*, November 1949, 12–16.

50. Woodward, *Advertising Methods in Argentina*, 11.

51. "Hablemos de mujeres . . . y de dinero," *Ímpetu*, November 1936, 11.

52. Sanger, *Advertising Methods in Argentina, Uruguay, and Brazil*; Merron, "Putting Foreign Consumers on the Map," 489; and "El delicado arte de vender a las damas," *Ímpetu*, June 1935, 38–39.

53. International Advertising Association, *Consumer Study of the Buenos Aires Market*, 17, 104; Gino Germani, "El Consumidor," *Ventas*, June 1954, 8–16; "Buenas Campañas," *Ímpetu*, January 1951, 20–21; "En el 83,4 % de los casos, las amas de casa de la Capital Federal que consumen pescado fresco, prefieren merluza," *Investigaciones de Mercado*, September 1952, 6–10; "A buena compradora, pocas palabras," *Mucho Gusto*, April 1955, 42–43; and "Se festeja en nuestro país el día de la propaganda," *Mundo Argentino*, November 30, 1949, 42.

54. "Hemos adquirido el derecho y el deber de ser buenas ciudadanas," *El Hogar*, May 16, 1952, 30. On the role of housewives during the Peronist government, see Milanesio, "The Guardian Angels of the Domestic Economy."

55. In a context of rising wages and economic development, the Sixty-Day Campaign was shorter, less dramatic, and much less significant in political and economic terms than the 1952 campaign. Another important difference is that the housewife was not such a central character of the 1946 campaign. On the Peronist politics against "unjust" commerce, see Eduardo Elena, "Peronist Consumer Politics and the Problem of Domesticating Markets in Argentina, 1943–1955," *Hispanic American Historical Review* 87, no.1 (2007): 111–49.

56. "La marca de fábrica protege tanto al que produce como al que consume y trafica mercancías," *Investigaciones de Mercado*, September 1953, 34–35.

57. "El comercio no es una aventura: Es mejor vender buenos productos," *Ímpetu*, April 1948, 26–27; and "Industria Argentina debe ser símbolo de calidad," *Ímpetu*, February 1951, 3–4.

58. Campaña Pro-Comercio Leal ad, *Aquí Está*, March 9, 1950, 23.

59. Campaña Pro-Comercio Leal ads, *Maribel*, October 1, 1946, 80, and *Rosalinda*, October 1946, 50.

60. Campaña Pro-Comercio Leal ads, *Aquí Está*, March 29, 1948, 28; *Aquí Está*, April 6, 1950, 9; and *Rosalinda*, February 1950, 2.

61. "Es mucha la gente aún que desconoce la marca de lo que consume," *Investigaciones de Mercado*, February/March 1954, 12.

62. *Síntesis Publicitaria*, 1945, 360–63.

63. *Síntesis Publicitaria*, 1945, 362.

64. On advertisement as an "awareness institution," see Michael Schudson, *Advertising, the Uneasy Persuasion: Its Dubious Impact on American Society* (New York: Routledge, 1993), xix; and "Campaña de propaganda de la propaganda 1945," *Síntesis Publicitaria*, 1945, 360–63.

65. "La propaganda y la seguridad en el tránsito," *Ímpetu*, February 1948, 32.

66. Perón, "El consumo y la especulación," 426–30; and "Vamos a terminar con los ladrones," *Mundo Peronista*, May 1, 1953, 18–22.

67. "La función económica y social del aviso," *Confort*, February 1955, 2.

68. "Buenas Campañas," *Ímpetu*, January 1955, 30–31.

69. Asociación Argentina de Editores de Revistas ads, *Caras y Caretas*, February 1955, 75; *Caras y Caretas*, March 1955, 71; *Esto Es*, February 15, 1955, 45; *Mundo Argentino*, March 16, 1955, 22; and *Rico Tipo*, February 9, 1955, 17; and Dirección del Censo Escolar de la Nación, *IV Censo Escolar de la Nación* (Buenos Aires: Dirección del Censo Escolar de la Nación, 1948), 1:150.

70. Dunbaugh, *Marketing in Latin America*, 87.

71. Asociación Argentina de Editores de Revistas ad, *Mundo Argentino*, March 9, 1955, 39.

72. *Maribel* ad, *Ímpetu*, July 1950, 18–19.

73. *Chabela* ad, *Ímpetu*, January 1949, 18–19.

74. *Maribel* ad, *Ímpetu*, May 1948, 18–19.

75. "Se festeja en nuestro país el día de la propaganda," *Mundo Argentino*, November 30, 1949, 42; "El arte publicitario argentino en los últimos años," *Ímpetu*, special edition, December 1950, 18; "Quién se anima?," *Ímpetu*, June 1953, 3–4; and *Atlántida* ad, *Ímpetu*, July 1947, 13.

76. Woodward, *Advertising Methods in Argentina*, 8–12; and Sanger, *Advertising Methods in Argentina, Uruguay, and Brazil*, 21–25.

77. *Ahora* ad, *Ímpetu*, December 1947, 41.

78. *Atlántida* ad, *Ímpetu*, April 1938, 17.

79. "Tarifas y precios de venta por ejemplar de las publicaciones argentinas," *Ímpetu*, July 1947, 28–30.

80. Ministerio de Industria y Comercio de la Nación, *Economía Publicitaria*, n.p.

Chapter 3

1. "Argentina," *Tide: The News Magazine of Advertising, Marketing, and Public Relations*, December 1, 1947, 20; "La actual situación mundial" and "La propaganda argentina," *Síntesis Publicitaria*, 1945, 76–81, 129–32; "Opinan sobre publicidad los expertos," *La Voz Argentina*, January 19, 1935, 3; and "Mr. Pierce, actual director de J. Walter Thompson Argentina, contesta la encuesta de prensa panamericana," *La Voz Argentina*, March 9, 1935, 4.

2. Quoted in Denise H. Sutton, *Globalizing Ideal Beauty: How Female Copywriters of the J. Walter Thompson Advertising Agency Redefined Beauty for the Twentieth Century* (New York: Palgrave Macmillan, 2005), 138.

3. "Falta solidaridad entre las agencias de publicidad," *Atlántida*, April 23, 1931, 54.

4. "Día panamericano de la publicidad," *Rosario*, December 4, 1953, 4.

5. Woodward, *Advertising Methods in Argentina*, 4–6; "Argentina," *Tide: The News Magazine of Advertising, Marketing, and Public Relations*, December 1, 1947, 20; *Ímpetu: Muestra Guía de publicidad y sus clientes*, December 1947; and *La Razón: Medio siglo de vida del país y del mundo, 1905–1955* (Buenos Aires: La Razón, 1955), n.p.

6. "Un aviso no publicado es una venta que no se hace," *Ímpetu*, May 1951, 3–4.

7. "El arte publicitario argentino en los últimos años," *Ímpetu*, December 1950, 18.

8. Salvatore, "Yankee Advertising in Buenos Aires," 229–31; "La propaganda argentina debe tener una personalidad nacional," *Veritas*, November 15, 1949, 1410; and Merron, "Putting Foreign Consumers on the Map," 498.

9. On different perspectives about the relation between advertisement and society, see Walker Laird, *Advertising Progress*; and Lears, *Fables of Abundance*.

10. Casa Lamota ad, *El Mundo*, June 10, 1946, 25; Casa Muñoz ad, *Democracia*, March 31, 1947, 3; "Buenas Campañas," *Ímpetu*, September 1950, 20; and Stuart Hall, "Notes on Deconstructing 'the Popular,'" in *People's History and Socialist Theory*, ed. Raphael Samuel (London: Routledge and Kegan Paul, 1981), 233.

11. Thompson and Williams ad, *Ahora*, September 19, 1946, 7; Frigolita ad, *Rico Tipo*, February 6, 1952, 27; and SADIMA ad, *La Época*, April 15, 1948, 5.

12. "Buenas Campañas," *Ímpetu*, January 1951, 20–21.

13. "Enfoques vulgares pero siempre vendedores," *Ímpetu*, November 1951, 54–55; and "Qué se anuncia y cómo se anuncia," *Ímpetu*, March 1949, 6–8.

14. "Los mercados actuales y la propaganda," *Ímpetu*, January 1949, 20–23.

15. "Siempre habrá algo nuevo," *Ímpetu*, February 1947, 36.

16. Orleans ad, *Mucho Gusto*, April 1955, 2; Harrods ad, *Nativa*, May 31, 1943, n.p.; El Pozo ad, *Para Ti*, September 2, 1947, 40; La Piedad ad, *El Mundo*, July 29, 1946, 10; Gath & Chaves ad, *La Época*, December 21, 1947, 10; and Mirvill's ad, *La Razón: Medio siglo de vida del país y del mundo, 1905–1955*, n.p.

17. La Mondiale ad, *El Mundo*, November 16, 1953, 8; CAP ad, *Revista de la Sociedad Rural de Rosario*, May 1946, n.p.; Olímpico ad, *El Hogar*, July 14, 1950, 19; La Popular ad, *La Capital*, July 14, 1946, 17; La Buena Vista ad, *La Capital*, June 24, 1946, 13; and Gambini, *Historia de Peronismo*, 90–91. Yerba refers to the dry leaves of the yerba maté plant which is used for a traditional Argentine drink, maté. Yerba is placed in a gourd with hot water, and the infusion is drunk with a metal straw.

18. "Cómo vemos 1949," *Ímpetu*, January 1949, 33; "A 103 mil pesos alcanzó en Agosto último la cifra de lo que se invirtió en diarios y revistas para anuncios de cocinas a gas,"

Investigaciones de Mercado, December 1952, 9–10; "Medio millón de pesos por mes se invirtieron en 1953 para anunciar heladeras eléctricas," *Investigaciones de Mercado*, April 1954, 12; "Estadística Publicitaria," *Investigaciones de Mercado*, May 1956, 52; and Cochran and Reina, *Entrepreneurship in Argentine Culture*, 103, 246–47.

19. "La familia moderna," *Orientación*, April 27, 1939, 3.

20. Primitiva ad, *Para Ti*, March 26, 1929, 2.

21. General Electric ad, *Para Ti*, July 5, 1932, 83; Primitiva ad, *El Hogar*, August 17, 1934, 87; and CADE ad, *El Hogar*, June 11, 1937, 2.

22. Senking ad, *El Hogar*, October 10, 1924, 21; Goli ad, *Para Ti*, January 15, 1929, 2; Primitiva ad, *Para Ti*, March 12, 1929, 111; and CIAE ad, *El Mundo*, February 10, 1931, 25. On cooking with gas in the 1920s, see Rebekah Pite, "Creating a Common Table: Doña Petrona, Cooking, and Consumption in Argentina, 1928–1983," (PhD diss., University of Michigan, 2007), 63–65.

23. On electric refrigerator advertisement in the Unites States, see Daniel Delis Hill, *Advertising to the American Woman, 1900–1999* (Columbus: Ohio State University Press, 2002), 45.

24. Crossley ad, *La Prensa*, December 14, 1930, 22; General Electric ad, *El Hogar*, October 12, 1928, 56; and Kelvinator ad, *El Hogar*, October 12, 1928, 68.

25. Servel ad, *La Razón*, December 17, 1926, 10.

26. General Electric ad, *La Nación*, October 22, 1939, 10; and Frigidaire ad, *La Prensa*, December 16, 1930, 13.

27. Salvatore, "Yankee Advertising in Buenos Aires," 227.

28. General Electric ad, *La Prensa*, December 18, 1930, 20; and CHIADE ad, *La Prensa*, December 22, 1930, 13.

29. General Electric ads, *El Hogar*, January 22, 1932, 43; *El Hogar*, February 5, 1932, 49; and *La Prensa*, December 18, 1930, 20; SIAM ad, *La Prensa*, January 20, 1935, 16; and Servel ad, *La Razón*, December 9, 1926, 9.

30. Flamex ad, *El Hogar*, April 28, 1950, 61; Carú ad, *Confort*, May 1951, 16; Warrens ad, *La Prensa*, May 26, 1955, 7; and Saccol ad, *Rico Tipo*, June 8, 1955, 23.

31. On nationalism and Peronism, see Cristián Buchrucker, *Peronismo y nacionalismo: La Argentina en la crisis ideológica mundial (1927–1955)* (Buenos Aires: Sudamericana, 1987).

32. Inelga ad, *Chabela*, May 1953, 18; CATITA ad, *El Hogar*, May 30, 1952, 84; and Flamex ad, *Revista de Arquitectura*, March 1949, 50. On the use of nationalism in advertising in the 1950s, see "Nuestro país y la publicidad," *Ímpetu*, December 1952, 32.

33. SANNA ad, *El Hogar*, October 21, 1949, 5; and Frigolita ad, *Rico Tipo*, February 6, 1952, 27.

34. SIAM ads, *Clarín*, February 9, 1953, 8; *Mundo Peronista*, January 15, 1952, 52; and *Mundo Peronista*, May 15, 1955, 30.

35. Salvatore, "Yankee Advertising in Buenos Aires," 228; Cochran and Reina, *Entrepreneurship in Argentine Culture*, 240–41; and Crossley ad, *Vea y Lea*, February 3, 1955, 27.

36. Lisma ad, *Clarín*, December 12, 1954, 5.

37. SIAM ads, *La Nación*, November 3, 1955, 3; *La Nación*, March 15, 1950, 3; and *La Tribuna*, September 14, 1955, 3.

38. Patrick ad, *El Hogar*, January 11, 1952, 102; Frigotec ad, *El Hogar*, January 4, 1952, 60; Inelga ad, *Chicas*, November 1952, 15; and Aurora ad, *Mundo Argentino*, February 2, 1955, 25.

39. On the expectations of consumers from the popular sectors regarding refrigerators and stoves, see testimonies compiled by Roxana Garbarini in "Relatos fríos" (paper presented at the 4th National Conference of Oral History, Buenos Aires, 1999); and Pablo Ungaro, "El confort viene marchando: La recepción de artefactos de cocina en el ámbito doméstico de la Argentina, 1930–1960," (paper presented at the 5th National Conference of Oral History, Buenos Aires, 2001).

40. Longvie ad, *Confort*, December 1952, 3–4; Caeba ad, *Confort*, September 1951, 67; Orbis ads, *El Hogar*, March 21, 1952, 63, and *El Hogar*, March 1948, 20; Domec ad, *Para Ti*, May 13, 1952, 77; and SIAM ad, *La Prensa*, September 29, 1954, 3.

41. CATITA ad, *Para Ti*, September 30, 1952, 15; Longvie ad, *Revista de Arquitectura*, October 1949, 298; Sigma ad, *Antena*, January 27, 1953, n.p.; SIAM ad, *La Nación*, January 17, 1955, 3; Patrick ad, *Rico Tipo*, July 13, 1955, 2; and GAL ad, *El Laborista*, November 24, 1952, 5.

42. Gath & Chaves ad, *La Nación*, March 3, 1920, 26; Harrods ad, *La Prensa*, July 13, 1925, 30; and Casa Tow ad, *La Prensa*, January 9, 1935, 15.

43. On representations of the working class during Peronism, see Natalia Milanesio, "Peronists and *Cabecitas*: Stereotypes and Anxieties at the Peak of Social Change," in *The New Cultural History of Peronism*, Karush and Chamosa, 53–84; and Gené, *Un mundo feliz*. On the production ethos of U.S. and Mexican advertisements, see Walker Laird, *Advertising Progress*, 118–37; and Moreno, *Yankee Don't Go Home!*, 113–29.

44. Alpargatas ads, *La Época*, January 21, 1948, 7, and *La Época*, March 17, 1948, 3.

45. IMPA ad, *El Laborista*, October 16, 1948, 22; Aurora ad, *Rosalinda*, May 1953, 28–29; Elna ad, *La Prensa*, March 20, 1947, 9; and *The JWT Weekly News* 5, no. 21, May 22, 1950, 3, JWT Company Archives, Newsletter Collection, Box 5.

46. Cruz de Acero ad, *La Razón*, January 13, 1946, 3.

47. SIAM ads, *Clarín*, November 22, 1954, 6; *El Mundo*, February 10, 1953, 7; *El Mundo*, February 17, 1953, 9; *El Mundo*, December 7, 1953, 6; and *El Mundo*, December 17, 1953, 7.

48. Petiteros took their name from the Petit Café in the elitist Barrio Norte neighborhood, a place they regarded as a social and cultural mecca. However, they did not belong to the elites but to the anti-Peronist middle classes.

49. Ernesto Goldar, *Buenos Aires: Vida cotidiana en la década del 50* (Buenos Aires: Plus Ultra, 1980), 50–60; "Modas," *Rico Tipo*, January 30, 1947, 3; and "Sastres," *Rico Tipo*, May 13, 1948, 3.

50. Gon-Ser ad, *Rico Tipo*, July 5, 1945, 13; Julio Mafud, *Argentina desde adentro* (Buenos Aires: Américalee, 1971), 183; and Pablo de Santis, *Rico Tipo y las chicas de Divito* (Buenos Aires: Espasa Humor Gráfico, 1994), 68–73. Attempts at acculturation might have been a reaction to the fact that some members of the upper sectors saw the lack of "urban clothing" among recent internal migrants as a sign of misery and backwardness comparable to the lack of electricity and gas among rural dwellers. See, for example, "Ingenio barato," *Fortaleza*, October 28, 1949, 3.

51. On the figure of the nurse in Peronist imagery, see Gené, *Un mundo feliz*, 130–40. On Peronist gender ideology and concepts of motherhood, see Susana Bianchi, "Las mujeres en el Peronismo (Argentina, 1945–1955)," in *Historia de las mujeres en Occidente, Siglo XX*, ed. George Duby and Michelle Perrot (Madrid: Taurus, 2000), 313–23.

52. Orea ads, *El Hogar*, October 10, 1947, 58; *El Hogar*, October 17, 1947, 68; *Para Ti*, July 15, 1947, 39; and *Para Ti*, May 18, 1948, 35. On the historical use of the "one-step-up-rule," see Walker Laird, *Advertising Progress*, 94.

53. Singer ads, *El Hogar*, March 21, 1947, 32, and *El Hogar*, May 11, 1948, 59; Godeco ads, *La Nación*, June 24, 1953, 3, and *La Capital*, August 22, 1954, 1; and Noemí Girbal-Blacha, "El hogar o la fábrica: De costureras y tejedoras en la Argentina Peronista (1946–1955)," *Revista de Ciencias Sociales*, no. 6 (September 1997): 217–30.

54. Sutton, *Globalizing Ideal Beauty*, 159–60. On beauty queens during Peronism, see Mirta Zaida Lobato, María Damilakou, and Lizel Tornay, "Las reinas del trabajo bajo el peronismo," in *Cuando las mujeres reinaban: Belleza, virtud y poder en la Argentina del siglo XX*, ed. Mirta Zaida Lobato (Buenos Aires: Biblos, 2005), 92.

55. "El ilustrador argentino es completamente imaginativo y recurre ocasionalmente a la documentación fotográfica," *Ímpetu*, July 1949, 16–20; and "El arte publicitario argentino en los últimos años," *Ímpetu*, December 1950, 18.

56. Marchand, *Advertising the American Dream*, 237–38.

57. On the "New Look" in Argentina, see Susana Saulquín, *Historia de la moda argentina: Del miriñaque al diseño de autor* (Buenos Aires: Emecé, 2006), 116–18. On the marketing of the "New Look" in the United States, see Hill, *Advertising to the American Woman, 1900–1999*, 143–46.

58. "Pebetas Porteñas," *PBT*, May 4, 1951, 35; *PBT*, June 1, 1951, 39; and *PBT*, January 25, 1952, 27; "24 horas en la vida de una reina joven, bonita y criolla," *Ahora*, May 6, 1948,

2–5; and "Eva Angélica 1ra invade el sur con su corte de hermosos ángeles," *Ahora*, May 11, 1948, 2–5.

59. María Elena Buszek, *Pin-Up Grrls: Feminism, Sexuality, Popular Culture* (Durham, NC: Duke University Press, 2006). On the appropriation of the pinup style in American ads, see Jill Fields, *An Intimate Affair: Women, Lingerie, and Sexuality* (Los Angeles: University of California Press, 2007), 208–11.

60. Legión Extranjera ad, *Rico Tipo*, April 26, 1945, 21; Sombreros Noelis ad, *Rico Tipo*, April 26, 1945, back cover; Mistinguett ad, *Rico Tipo*, December 13, 1945, back cover; and Santis, *Rico Tipo y las chicas de Divito*, 63–65.

61. La Campagnola ads, *Para Ti*, June 22, 1948, back cover, and *El Hogar*, July 22, 1949, back cover; Armour ads, *Antena*, February 11, 1947, back cover, and *Labores*, January 1948, 123.

62. Susan Buck-Morss, *The Dialectics of Seeing: Walter Benjamin and the Arcades Project* (Cambridge, MA: MIT Press, 1991), 184.

63. Cadei ad, *La Tribuna*, July 2, 1955, 1; Recor ad, *La Tribuna*, July 29, 1955, 2; and "El mejor affiche del mes," *Continente*, May 15, 1947, 50. On the associations between food, women, and love in advertisements, see Parkin, *Food is Love*.

64. "Buenas Campañas," *Ímpetu*, January 1951, 20–21. Other popular products with women names were Santa Teresita, La Criolla, La Blanca, Letizia, Nereida (food products), Aurora, Rolita, Minerva, and Elna (domestic appliances). Several other products did not have female names but had a woman incorporated into their logos, for example, Salus (yerba maté), Puloil (cleaning product), and AFD (fruit preserves), among others.

65. "¿Por qué inmoral?," *Ímpetu*, February 1952, 12–14.

66. "Cartas," *Ímpetu*, May 1949, 12.

67. "Seriedad y moral de la publicidad," *Veritas*, September 15, 1949, 1167–68; and "Un problema inexistente," *Ímpetu*, September 1946, 36.

68. "La publicidad en la República Argentina," *Ímpetu*, December 1950, 10–12, 30.

69. "El auge del humorismo en publicidad," *Ímpetu*, June 1942, 3–4; and Marchand, *Advertising the American Dream*, 206–34.

70. "El texto publicitario y sus variados enfoques," *Ímpetu*, January 1948, 12–20; and "La historieta, sensación del siglo," *Ímpetu*, December 1950, 40–42. On the boom of humor in the printed media, see Andrés Cascioli, *La Argentina que ríe: El humor gráfico en las décadas de 1940 y 1950* (Buenos Aires: Fondo Nacional de las Artes, 2008). On humor in radio broadcasting, see Carlos Ulanovsky, *Días de radio, 1920–1959* (Buenos Aires: Emecé, 2004).

71. Alpargatas ad in Alberto Borrini, *El siglo de la publicidad, 1898–1998: Historia de la publicidad gráfica argentina* (Buenos Aires: Atlántida, 1998), 130.

72. On incongruity theories to explain humor, see Michael Billig, *Laughter and Ridicule: Toward a Social Critique of Humour* (London: Sage, 2005), 57–85.

73. Volcán ad, *La Capital*, March 29, 1952, 1.

74. Billig, *Laughter and Ridicule*, 37–56.

75. See Corimayo ads, *Clarín*, June 10, 1948, 4; *Clarín*, June 24, 1948, 3; *Rico Tipo*, August 5, 1948, back cover; *Rico Tipo*, April 27, 1949, back cover; and *La Razón*, July 8, 1948, 9. The word *dulce* (sweet/sweet thing) in the slogan refers to both jelly and a nice person.

76. "Los proyectos que limitan las páginas de los diarios encuentran la opinión adversa de todos los sectores vinculados al periodismo," *Ímpetu*, July 1947, 12–20; and "Crisis de papel y circulación," *Ímpetu*, December 1950, 32.

77. "Con polleras cortas," *Ímpetu*, December 1950, 16–17.

78. "Una prueba de fuego para la publicidad argentina: El problema del papel y el aviso chico," *Ímpetu*, August 1948, 3–6.

79. "Qué quiere decir un aviso a tres columnas?," *Ímpetu*, July 1951, 3–4; and "Frente a la nueva estructura del mercado local," *Investigaciones de Mercado*, January 1953, 1–2.

80. Dirección Nacional de Estadísticas y Censos, *IV Censo General de la Nación: Censo de la Vivienda*, 17; Woodward, *Advertising Methods in Argentina*, 13; Robert Howard Claxton, *From Parsifal to Perón: Early Radio in Argentina, 1920–1944* (Gainesville: University Press of Florida, 2007), 123; and Andrea Matallana, *"Locos por la radio": Una historia social de la radiofonía en la Argentina, 1923–1947* (Buenos Aires: Prometeo, 2006), 36.

81. "Argentina," *Tide: The Magazine of Advertising, Marketing, and Public Relations*, December 1, 1947, 21; "Qué vimos en publicidad radiofónica en 1950," *Ímpetu*, December 1950, 28–30; and "50 años de propaganda comercial en nuestro país," *La Razón: Medio siglo de vida del país y del mundo, 1905–1955* (Buenos Aires: La Razón, 1955), n.p.

82. J. Walter Thompson Company, *Market for Dentifrices: Mexico, D.F., Buenos Aires, Havana* (New York, July 1947), J. Walter Thompson Archives, John W. Hartman Center for Sales, Advertising, and Marketing History, Duke University, Reel 713.

83. Sanger, *Advertising Methods in Argentina, Uruguay, and Brazil*, 49–52; and Woodward, *Advertising Methods in Argentina*, 14–15.

84. "Cómo trabajan las empresas de publicidad en la vía pública," *Ímpetu*, December 1947, 4–53; and "Adelante, Vía Pública!," *Ímpetu*, December 1952, 9.

85. "Elenco de carteleras en Capital y el Interior de la República," *Síntesis Publicitaria*, 1945, 358–59; and "La importancia de la vía pública," *Ímpetu*, December 1952, 22–28.

86. "Dinamismo actual de vía pública," *Ímpetu*, December 1950, 32–34; "El admirable progreso de vía pública," *Ímpetu*, December 1952, 8; and Enrique Silvetti ad, *Ímpetu*, December 1950, 89.

87. "Valores estéticos de nuestra publicidad en vía pública," *Ímpetu*, December 1952, 16–18.

88. "La importancia de la vía pública," *Ímpetu*, December 1952, 24.

89. "Publicidad en ferrocarriles" and "Divagaciones analíticas sobre la propaganda en la vía pública," *Ímpetu*, December 1952, 28–38.

90. "El Director de Arte y vía pública" and "Valores estéticos de nuestra publicidad en vía pública," *Ímpetu*, December 1952, 16–18.

91. "Los rosarinos enemigos de Rosario," *La Tribuna*, March 8, 1952, 6.

92. "Sobre la publicidad mural en la ciudad," *El Mundo*, March 4, 1951, 4; "Un positivo medio de propaganda," *Ímpetu*, November 1948, 32; "Bases científicas para la publicidad en vía pública," *Ímpetu*, December 1950, 20; and "Fueron aumentadas las tasas de propaganda," *Ímpetu*, December 1947, 173.

93. "Urbanismo y propaganda," *Síntesis Publicitaria*, 1946, 26; "Valores estéticos de nuestra publicidad en vía pública," *Ímpetu*, December 1952, 16–18; and "Se festeja en nuestro país el día de la propaganda," *Mundo Argentino*, November 30, 1949, 42.

94. Marchand, *Advertising the American Dream*, 166.

95. For a classic study of populism, see Ernesto Laclau, *Politics and Ideology in Marxist Theory: Capitalism, Fascism, Populism* (London: NLB, 1977), 143–98.

96. "Una batalla contra los avisos artísticos," *Ímpetu*, April 1950, 4–5; "Los títulos de los avisos," *Ímpetu*, October 1946, 8–16; and "Llamar la atención es un medio pero no el fin del aviso," *Ímpetu*, July 1947, 6–12.

CHAPTER 4

1. Roberto Arlt, "La tristeza del sábado inglés," in *Aguafuertes porteñas* (Buenos Aires: Losada, 2008), 71.

2. "Buenos Aires se divierte," *Aquí Está*, November 10, 1947, 18–19.

3. Félix Luna, *Perón y su tiempo* (Buenos Aires: Sudamericana, 1992), 314.

4. "Cuando el pueblo se divierte," *Mundo Peronista*, December 1953, 39; and "Un privilegio de algunos que ahora es de cualquiera," *Mundo Peronista*, January 15, 1954, 26–30.

5. Archivo General de la Nación, Fondo Agio y Especulación, Series Históricas, Legajo 100.

6. Like indiscipline and inefficiency, absenteeism was associated by manufacturers with the power of labor union representatives on the shop floor and with the new regulations that allowed absence from work without justification. For its part, the Peronist government downplayed absenteeism and other obstacles to productivity until 1955 when it launched the National Congress of Productivity with the objective of increasing and rationalizing production through stricter controls over performance in the factory. "¿Por qué hay más enfermos los lunes?," *Aquí Está*, November 9, 1948, 10–11; "Retorno a una nueva polémica: ¿Sábado inglés o lunes criollo?," *Aquí Está*, March 9, 1950, 8–9; and José Luis Imaz, *La clase alta en Buenos Aires* (Buenos Aires: Universidad de Buenos Aires, 1965), 68–69.

7. *Cabecita negra* referred to the migrants' dark skin and black hair. On cabecitas negras and representations of internal migrants, see Milanesio, "Peronists and *Cabecitas*," 53–84.

8. See Ezequiel Adamovsky, *Historia de la clase media en Argentina: Apogeo y decadencia de una ilusión, 1919–2003* (Buenos Aires: Planeta, 2010); and Enrique Garguin, "'Los Argentinos Descendemos de los Barcos': The Racial Articulation of Middle-Class Identity in Argentina (1920–1960)," *Latin American and Caribbean Ethnic Studies* 2, no. 2 (September 2007): 161–84.

9. *Porteños* are the residents of the city of Buenos Aires.

10. Rodolfo Taboada, "Turismo al centro," *Rico Tipo*, July 31, 1947, 12.

11. Plotkin, *Mañana es San Perón*, 31–32; and Daniel James, "October 17th and 18th, 1945: Mass Protest, Peronism, and the Argentine Working Class," *Journal of Social History* 21, no. 3 (Spring 1988): 456.

12. Julio Cortázar, "Casa tomada," in *Bestiario* (Buenos Aires: Alfaguara, 1995), 13–21; Andrés Avellaneda, *El habla de la ideología* (Buenos Aires: Sudamericana, 1983), 93–128; Podalsky, *Specular City*, 1–7; and Peter Standish, "Julio Cortázar, 1914–1984," in *Encyclopedia of Latin American Literature*, ed. Verity Smith (Chicago: Fitzroy Dearborn, 1997), 224–26.

13. Torre and Pastoriza, "La democratización del bienestar," 262.

14. Julia Rodriguez, *Civilizing Argentina: Science, Medicine, and the Modern State* (Chapel Hill: University of North Carolina Press, 2006), 84–88. In a seminal work, James Scobie has argued that although the Buenos Aires elites moved to the suburbs at the turn of the century, they did not abandon the city center as their counterparts had done in other major cities when immigrant workers moved to tenements. Barrio Norte remained the most prestigious place to live for the porteño elite who tightened their hold on the central district, home to the city's most important political, cultural, and recreational institutions. James Scobie, *Buenos Aires: Plaza to Suburb, 1870–1910* (Oxford: Oxford University Press, 1974), 114–59. On European immigration to Argentina, see José Moya, *Cousins and Strangers: Spanish Immigrants in Buenos Aires, 1850–1930* (Los Angeles: University of California Press, 1998).

15. In fact, in January 1940, the Buenos Aires Zoo received 71,495 visitors. In 1946, the monthly average peaked at 144,732 visitors. "Buenos Aires se divierte," *Aquí Está*, November 10, 1947, 18–19; *Revista de Estadística Municipal de la Ciudad de Buenos Aires*, January–March, 1940, 99; *Revista de Estadística Municipal de la Ciudad de Buenos Aires*, January–March, 1935, 108; *Revista de Estadística Municipal de la Ciudad de Buenos Aires*, January–March, 1940, 99–101; *Revista de Estadística Municipal de la Ciudad de Buenos Aires*, January–March, 1947, 76; and "Cuando se divierte el pueblo," *Mundo Peronista*, December 15, 1953, 39.

16. Walter Schuck, *River Plate Sphinx: Argentina at the Turn of 1949–50* (Buenos Aires, n.p., 1950), 74.

17. "Planteos y soluciones para un gran problema nacional," *Nuevas Bases*, August 5, 1952, 1; and Subsecretaría de Informaciones, *Buenos Aires: Capital City of Justicialism* (Buenos Aires: Subsecretaría de Informaciones, 1951), 6.

18. Mario Margulis, *Migración y marginalidad en la sociedad argentina* (Buenos Aires: Paidós, 1968), 78, 127–30; and Gino Germani, "Inquiry into the Social Effects of Urbanization in a Working-Class Sector of Greater Buenos Aires," in *Urbanization in Latin America*, ed. Philip Hauser (New York: International Documents Service, 1961), 207–33.

19. "Buenos Aires: La ciudad de los habitantes que están en fila y esperan," *Mucho Gusto*, December 1946, 34–35. See also Taboada, "Turismo al centro," 12; and "La ciudad se ahoga en el centro," *Continente*, May 15, 1947, 182.

20. Clara Kriger, *Cine y Peronismo: El estado en escena* (Buenos Aires: Siglo Veintiuno, 2009), 141, 147–48.

21. "La noche del sábado," *Rico Tipo*, August 23, 1945, 4–5.

22. "Planteos y soluciones para un gran problema nacional," *Nuevas Bases*, August 5, 1952, 1.

23. "De cada cinco habitantes que tiene el país, uno vive en la capital," *Mundo Argentino*, November 14, 1945, 3–5.

24. James Bruce, *Those Perplexing Argentines* (New York: Longmans, Green, 1953), 77–78.

25. "Planteos y soluciones para un gran problema nacional," *Nuevas Bases*, August 5, 1952, 1. See also "Éxodo provinciano a la capital," *Aquí Está*, January 12, 1948, 6–7; and "No dejeis el campo," *Vea y Lea*, November 13, 1947, 4.

26. "Desastrosa situación del transporte," *Nuevas Bases*, November 15, 1950, 7; and "Las tarifas y el servicio ferroviario," *Nuevas Bases*, January 1955, 2.

27. "Vivienda y transporte en Argentina," *Nuevas Bases*, July 15, 1950, 6.

28. Reynaldo Pastor, *Frente al totalitarismo peronista* (Buenos Aires: Bases, 1959), 119.

29. "Cuestión de proponérselo," *El Mundo*, April 7, 1948, 4.

30. Ibid.

31. Greenup and Greenup, *Revolution Before Breakfast*, 45.

32. Teobaldo Altamiranda, interview 155A, audio recording, December 12, 2001, Memoria Abierta Archives, Buenos Aires.

33. Julio Cortázar, *Ceremonias* (Buenos Aires: Seix Barral, 1983), 86.

34. On moviegoing and the film industry in the 1930s and early 1940s, see Matthew Karush, "The Melodramatic Nation: Integration and Polarization in the Argentine Cinema of the 1930s," *Hispanic American Historical Review* 87, no. 2 (May 2007): 293–326; Joaquín Calvagno, "El primer cine industrial y las masas en Argentina: La sección 'Cinematografía' del semanario CGT (1934–1943)," *A Contracorriente* 7, no. 3 (Spring 2010): 38–81; and Kriger, *Cine y Peronismo*.

35. Hipólito J. Paz, *Memorias: Vida pública y privada de un argentino en el siglo XX* (Buenos Aires: Planeta, 1999), 19.

36. Luis Sobrino Aranda, interview by author, Rosario, December 27, 2005.

37. *Guía Social de Mar del Plata* (Buenos Aires, 1930), n.p. Quoted in Graciela Zuppa, "Prácticas de sociabilidad en la construcción de la villa balneario: Mar del Plata y el acceso al siglo XX," in *Prácticas de sociabilidad en un escenario argentino: Mar del Plata 1870–1970*, ed. Graciela Zuppa (Mar del Plata, Argentina: Universidad Nacional de Mar del Plata, 2004), 63.

38. Torre and Pastoriza, "La democratización del bienestar," 301.

39. *Continente*, February 1949, 18. Quoted in Elisa Pastoriza and Juan Carlos Torre, "Mar del Plata: Un sueño argentino," in *Historia de la vida privada*, ed. Fernando Devoto and Marta Madero (Buenos Aires: Taurus, 1999), 3:70.

40. "Mar del Plata. Moderna Babilonia del verano," *Caras y Caretas*, February 1953, 83.

41. *Boletín Municipal* (Mar del Plata, 1954), n.p. Quoted in Pastoriza and Torre, "Mar del Plata," 67.

42. Torre and Pastoriza, "La democratización del bienestar," 303; and "Carta de un costumbrista a Bermudez," *La Prensa*, March 15, 1947, 9.

43. "Mar del Plata ya no es la ciudad del privilegio," *Mundo Peronista*, February 15, 1954, 26.

44. On popular tourism during Peronism, see Eugenia Scarzanella, "El ocio peronista: Vacaciones y 'turismo popular' en Argentina (1943–1955)," *Entrepasados* 14 (1998): 65–84.

45. Bruce, *Those Perplexing Argentines*, 219.

46. George I. Blanksten, *Perón's Argentina* (Chicago: University of Chicago Press, 1953), 273 (emphasis in the original).

47. Quoted in Ricardo Llanes, *Historia de la Calle Florida*, (Buenos Aires: Honorable Sala de Representantes de la Ciudad de Buenos Aires, 1976), 2:256.

48. "Paseando por Florida," *Rico Tipo*, November 14, 1946, 11.

49. Elena Murray Lagos, interview by author, Rosario, October 12, 2005; Héctor Acosta, interview by author, Rosario, October 13, 2005; Laura Perera, interview by author, Rosario, December 14, 2005; Juan Carlos Legas, interview by author, Rosario, December 21, 2005.

50. "Claudicación de las elites," *El Mundo*, April 1, 1948, 4.

51. "Cuando los ricos gastaban . . . ," *Orientación: Modas y Mundo Social*, March 1946, 56.

52. "Claudicación de las elites," *El Mundo*, April 1, 1948, 4.

53. "Democracia y dictadura . . . o estamos todos locos," *Descamisada*, January 22, 1946, n.p.

54. "Un privilegio de algunos que ahora es de cualquiera," *Mundo Peronista*, January 15, 1954, 26.

55. On dress and identity construction, see Joanne Finkelstein, *The Fashioned Self* (Philadelphia: Temple University Press, 1991). For a seminal interpretation, see Georg Simmel, "Fashion," [1904] *The American Journal of Sociology* 62, no. 6 (May 1957): 541–58.

56. Angel Perelman, *Como hicimos el 17 de octubre* (Buenos Aires: Coyoacán, 1961), 77.

57. "¡Viva la alpargata!," *Unión Ferroviaria*, January 1946, 1; and "Reivindicación de la alpargata," *La Hora*, November 26, 1945, 4.

58. Anonymous pamphlet, Hoover Institution Archives, Argentine Subject Collection, Box 3, File 4.

59. Pedro Michelini, *El 17 de octubre de 1945: Testimonio de sus protagonistas* (Buenos Aires: Corregidor, 1994), 93; and "Los 'galeritas' son racistas . . . ," *Descamisada*, April 10, 1946, n.p.

60. *Descamisado* was initially used in the title of an anarchist newspaper published in the late nineteenth century. On the use of *descamisada* to refer to women, see Eva Perón, *Discursos Completos* (Buenos Aires: Megafón, 1985–1986), 1:73. On visual representations of the descamisado by the Peronist government, see Gené, *Un mundo feliz*, 65–83.

61. Arnaldo Cortesi, "Portrait of a Rabble-Rouser," *New York Times Magazine*, February 3, 1946, 8.

62. Juan Pérez, *Radiografías de una dictadura (por Argentino Cantinflas)* (Buenos Aires: La Vanguardia, 1946), 32; Félix Luna, *El 45* (Buenos Aires: Jorge Alvarez, 1969), 513; "Anexo documental," in *El 17 de octubre de 1945*, ed. Santiago Senén González and Gabriel Lerman (Buenos Aires: Lumiere, 2005), 279; and "Los descamisados reclamamos el derecho a andar sin saco por las calles de la ciudad," *La Época*, January 18, 1948, 5.

63. "Plan estratégico del Coronel Perón," *La Vanguardia*, October 23, 1945, 3; and James, "October 17th and 18th, 1945," 450.

64. Eduardo Colom, *El 17 de octubre: La revolución de los descamisados* (Buenos Aires: La Época, 1946), 87; Raúl Scalabrini Ortiz, *Los ferrocarriles deben ser del pueblo argentino* (Buenos Aires: Reconquista, 1946), 60; Santiago Nudelman, *El radicalismo al servicio de la libertad* (Buenos Aires: Jus, 1947), 252; and Ezequiel Martínez Estrada, *¿Qué es esto? Catilinaria* (Buenos Aires: Lautaro, 1956), 27–37. Interestingly, *lumpen* originally means "rags" and has been used to refer to "people in rags."

65. "Anexo documental," in *El 17 de octubre de 1945*, Senén González and Lerman, 279.

66. "El obrero tiene en la Argentina comida barata y buenos jornales," *Democracia*, April 9, 1947, 5.

67. "Postales estadísticas," *Mundo Peronista*, September 15, 1953, 2; and Subsecretaría de Informaciones de la Presidencia de la Nación, *Perón: Anécdotas, recuerdos, relatos*, 82.

68. "Salúdelo," *Democracia*, May 23, 1946, 8; "Nuestro hogar obrero," *Democracia* (Rosario), January 25, 1954, 2nd section, 1; and Luis Ricardo Romero, interview by author, Rosario, December 21, 2005.

69. "Las pieles," *Argentina*, June 1, 1949, 56.

70. International Advertising Association, *Consumer Study of the Buenos Aires Market*, 91.

71. *Rico Tipo*, April 11, 1946, 16.

72. Elena Murray Lagos, interview by author, Rosario, October 12, 2005; Ema Lucero, interview by author, Rosario November 3, 2005; Luis Sobrino Aranda, interview by author, Rosario, December 27, 2005; and Amelia Foresto, interview by author, Rosario, October 18, 2005.

73. Bourdieu, *Distinction*, 172.

74. Pierrete Hondagneu-Sotelo, *Doméstica: Immigrant Workers Cleaning and Caring in the Shadow of Affluence* (Los Angeles: University of California Press, 2001).

75. Violeta Benvenuto, interview by author, Rosario, December 5, 2005.

76. Jorge Newton, *Clase Media: El dilema de cinco millones de argentinos* (Buenos Aires: Municipalidad de Buenos Aires, 1949), 29.

77. Greenup and Greenup, *Revolution Before Breakfast*, 217.

78. Roberto Arlt, "La muchacha del atado," in *Aguafuertes Porteñas*, 73; Diego Armus, "El viaje al centro: Tísicas, costureritas y milonguitas en Buenos Aires, 1910–1940," *Boletín del Instituto de Historia Argentina y Americana Dr. Emilio Ravignani*, no. 22 (2000): 101–24; and Mirta Zaida Lobato, *Historia de las trabajadoras en la Argentina (1869–1960)* (Buenos Aires: Edhasa, 2007), 283–320.

79. In 1947, there were around four hundred thousand domestic workers in Argentina that represented the 6.4 percent of the economically active population. Ninety-four percent of these domestic workers were women. The number of domestic workers decreased progressively over a long period. Zulma Rechini de Lattes, *La participación económica femenina en la Argentina desde la segunda posguerra hasta 1970* (Buenos Aires: CENEP, 1980), 57, 109; Héctor Szretter, *La terciarización del empleo en la Argentina: El sector del servicio doméstico* (Buenos Aires: Ministerio de Trabajo y Seguridad Social, 1985), 8; and Lobato, *Historia de las trabajadoras en la Argentina*, 59.

80. "En el año 2051," *Atlántida*, June 1951, 3; and Greenup and Greenup, *Revolution Before Breakfast*, 45.

81. *La Tribuna*, April 15, 1952, 6.

82. "Qué servicio, eh!," *Rico Tipo*, August 5, 1948, 21. Historian Brian Owensby has shown that in the list of aspects that defined the identity of the middle class in Brazil, a social sector very similar to its Argentine counterpart, domestic service was ranked behind homes but came before clothing, reading materials, and formal education. Owensby, *Intimate Ironies*, 107–9.

83. Greenup and Greenup, *Revolution Before Breakfast*, 44.

84. "Política peronista: Consumo y derroche," *Mundo Peronista*, February 13, 1952, 3.

85. Jeane Delaney, "Making Sense of Modernity: Changing Attitudes Toward the Immigrant and the Gaucho in Turn-of-the-Century Argentina," *Comparative Studies in Society and History* 38, no. 3 (July 1986), 448.

86. Quoted in James, *Doña María's Story*, 259.

87. Index numbers for the garment industry (base 1943=100) grew from 118.2 in 1944 to 178.2 in 1948. For general garment sales in retail stores in the city of Buenos Aires, (base 1939=100) the index number also shows an impressive increase from 210.2 in 1946 to 744.5 in 1952. Dirección Nacional de Estadística y Censos, *Índices del costo del nivel de vida, actividad industrial y costo de la producción, Informe B.1*, (Buenos Aires: Dirección Nacional de Estadística y Censos, 1956), 16; United Nations, Economic Commission for Latin America, *La industria textil en América Latina: Argentina* (New York: United Nations, Economic Commission for Latin America, 1965), 45; and Dirección Nacional de Estadística y Censos, *Censo Industrial 1950* (Buenos Aires: Dirección Nacional de Estadística y Censos, 1957), 58–59, and *Censo Industrial 1954* (Buenos Aires: Dirección Nacional de Estadística y Censos, 1960), 183–84.

88. Greenup and Greenup, *Revolution Before Breakfast*, 217; and "Mientras la porteña gasta 36% de lo que gana en su belleza, las otras . . . ," *PBT*, January 30, 1953, 126–28.

89. Subsecretaría de Informaciones de la Presidencia de la Nación, *Buenos Aires*, 15.

90. Elena Murray Lagos, interview by author, Rosario, October 12, 2005.

91. Ernesto Sammartino, *La verdad sobre la situación argentina* (Montevideo: n.p., 1951), 138. Daniel James has suggested that the figure of Evita legitimized feelings of envy and resentment among working-class women and allowed them to express their desires for expensive consumer goods, desires that traditional leftist ideologies either ignored or censured. James, *Doña María's Story*, 240.

92. Pastor, *Frente al totalitarismo peronista*, 330.

93. Quoted in Bruce, *Those Perplexing Argentines*, 50.

94. "Cuando los ricos gastaban . . . ," *Orientación: Modas y Mundo Social*, March 1946, 56.

95. Adamovsky, *Historia de la clase media en Argentina*, 54–55.

96. Gino Germani, "La clase media en la Argentina con especial referencia a los sectores urbanos," in *La clase media en Argentina y Uruguay: Materiales para el estudio de la clase media en América Latina*, ed. Theo Crevenna (Washington, D.C.: Unión Panamericana, 1950), 4–33. For a recent reconceptualization of the history of the middle class, see Adamovsky, *Historia de la clase media en Argentina*. Historians have also suggested that the concept of middle class has even a shorter history given the fact that there is no significant use of the term prior to the 1950s. Garguin, "Los Argentinos descendemos de los barcos," 180.

97. Alfredo Poviña, "Concepto de clase media y su proyección argentina," in *La clase media en Argentina y Uruguay*, Crevenna, 73.

98. Germani, "La clase media en la Argentina con especial referencia a los sectores urbanos," 31.

99. "Ser más elegante," *La Época*, January 20, 1948, 15; and "La mujer que trabaja y la moda," *Para Ti*, June 21, 1955, 38.

100. Germani, "La clase media en la Argentina con especial referencia a los sectores urbanos," 23; and Adamovsky, *Historia de la clase media en Argentina*, 91.

101. Newton, *Clase Media*, 33.

102. "El nuevo oligarca," *Fortaleza*, December 21, 1949, 2.

103. Greenup and Greenup, *Revolution Before Breakfast*, 211–15; Bruce, *Those Perplexing Argentines*, 51; Roberto Arlt, "El tímido llamado," in *Aguafuertes porteñas*, 257; and Alfredo Moffat, *Estrategias para sobrevivir en Buenos Aires* (Buenos Aires: Jorge Álvarez, 1967), 50.

104. De Santis, *Rico Tipo y las Chicas Divito*, 89–93. On psychoanalysis in Argentina, see Mariano Ben Plotkin, *Freud in the Pampas: The Emergence and Development of a Psychoanalytic Culture in Argentina* (Stanford, CA: Stanford University Press, 2001).

105. Sergio Bagú, "La clase media en Argentina," in *La clase media en Argentina y Uruguay*, Crevenna, 57, 61.

106. "La raya del pantalón," *El Mundo*, October 10, 1945, 6; and "Contrapeso de chiquizuela," *El Mundo*, October 24, 1945, 4.

107. María Gallia, *Trabajar con amor: Manual de instrucción para mujeres del servicio doméstico* (Buenos Aires: Difusión, 1943), 114–15.

108. The theory of social emulation was first conceived by Thorstein Veblen and later employed by Georg Simmel in his arguments about fashion. Thorstein Veblen, *The Theory of the Leisure Class* (New York: Macmillan, 1899); and Simmel, "Fashion." Many scholars have challenged the theory of social emulation in their interpretations of the consumer habits and style of the lower social sectors; see, for example, Brent Shannon, *The Cut of His Coat: Men, Dress, and Consumer Culture in Britain, 1860–1914* (Athens, OH: Ohio University Press, 2006).

109. Saulquín, *Historia de la moda argentina*, 149; Goldar, *Buenos Aires*, 49; and "Las obreras argentinas se han puesto ya los pantalones en muchas fábricas," *Mundo Argentino*, November 21, 1945, 3–5.

110. Nené Cascallar, *Esas cosas de mamá: Palabras para otras mujeres y otras mamás* (Buenos Aires: Arcur, 1945), 268–69.

111. Ibid., 270.

112. Julio Cortázar, "Las puertas del cielo," 118–19.

113. Although applied to gender and class identities, "passing" usually refers to racial identities. See Elaine Ginsberg, ed., *Passing and the Fictions of Identity* (Durham, NC: Duke University Press, 1996).

CHAPTER 5

1. *Contigo pan y cebolla* (Bread and onions with you) is a popular declaration of commitment that means "We can live on love alone" and suggests that material privations (bread and onions) are nothing compared to love.

2. "Cinco mentiras que no han de decirse los novios," *Nocturno*, November 13, 1950, 96.

3. Richard Dyer, "The Role of Stereotypes," in *Media Studies: A Reader*, ed. Paul Marris and Sue Thornham (New York: New York University Press, 2000), 245–51. For the classic definition of stereotype, see Walter Lippmann, *Public Opinion* (New York: Macmillan, 1956).

4. "Pido la palabra," *La Tribuna*, November 20, 1952, 5.

5. "Pido la palabra," *La Tribuna*, November 26, 1952, 6; *La Tribuna*, December 17, 1952, 6; and *La Tribuna*, December 26, 1952, 6.

6. On the bacán, see Bergero, *Intersecting Tango*, 318–26. On the tíguere, see Derby, *The Dictator's Seduction*, 173–203. On the pachuco, see Alvarez, *The Power of the Suit*.

7. Luis Grau, *Los Pérez García y yo* (Buenos Aires: Ciordia & Rodriguez, 1952), 129.

8. "La mujer es la verdadera administradora del hogar," *Cascabel*, March 8, 1944, 15.

9. "Anatolio," *La Época*, January 4, 1948, 11; "Vidrieras porteñas," *Rico Tipo*, May 30, 1946, 8; "Hoy gran liquidación de invierno," *Rico Tipo*, August 22, 1946, 20–21; and Corimayo ad, *Rico Tipo*, April 27, 1949, back cover.

10. "La etiqueta de las economías," *Maribel*, April 22, 1952, 34.

11. "Hombres egoístas," *Para Ti*, September 16, 1952, 28.

12. "Madres débiles," *Para Ti*, May 6, 1952, 30.

13. Sara Montes de Oca de Cárdenas, "Fundamentos históricos de la familia argentina: Su estado actual," in *Restauración Social de la Familia Argentina*, ed. Francisco Valsecchi (Buenos Aires: Acción Católica Argentina, 1950), 37.

14. Interestingly, the 1947 national census marked a low point in female participation in the job market, which dropped from 43 percent in 1895 to 23 percent that year. However, the 1895 census did not clearly differentiate between domestic and extra-domestic occupations. Consequently, the figure was inflated because in the late nineteenth century more women worked at home or in small family businesses. In 1947, the percentage of working women was lower but the type of female employment had radically changed. Bianchi, "Las mujeres en el peronismo," 313–14; Rechini de Lattes, *La participación económica femenina en la Argentina desde la segunda postguerra hasta 1970*, 38; and "Postales estadísticas" and "La explotación de la mujer," *Mundo Peronista*, November 1, 1951, 2, 31.

15. The increase in wages for women laborers—an impressive rise from 0.56 pesos per hour for unskilled women workers in 1943 to 3.21 in 1951—was frequently mentioned in Peronist propaganda. For political opponents, especially Communist women, the change was not as profound as the government claimed. They asserted that working

women still earned less than men in identical jobs and toiled without help at home after work. "Ha pasado un día en la vida de una obrera," *Nuestras Mujeres*, July 1, 1948, 13–14; and "La mujer: Factor decisivo en el progreso de nuestro país," *Nuestras Mujeres*, October 1, 1955, 13.

16. Museo Social Argentino, *Primer Congreso de la Población* (Buenos Aires: Museo Social Argentino, 1941), 172–73. On the Peronist gender ideology, see Susana Bianchi and Norma Sanchis, *El Partido Peronista Femenino, 1949–1955* (Buenos Aires: CEAL, 1988); Bianchi, "Las mujeres en el Peronismo"; and Ramacciotti and Valobra, *Generando el Peronismo*. For a historical overview on working women in Argentina, see Lobato, *Historia de las trabajadoras en la Argentina*.

17. "Por la huella de un ejemplo," *Mundo Peronista*, February 15, 1952, 17.

18. "Mientras la porteña gasta el 36% de lo que gana en belleza, las otras . . . ," *PBT*, January 30, 1953, 127.

19. "En pleno centro de la ciudad: Elina Colomer vive el ritmo de su tiempo," *Antena*, February 12, 1947, n.p.; "Sobre las nubes descansa la casa de Irma Córdoba,"*Antena*, April 1, 1947, n.p.; "Cautiva en una casa de ensueño: Elisa Galve es una mujer feliz," *Antena*, April 15, 1947, n.p.; "Mirta Legrand quiere evadirse del molde en que estaban aprisionándola," *Radiolandia*, August 31, 1946, n.p.; and "Amo hasta la fatiga que provoca el cine, expresa Elisa Galve," *Radiolandia*, September 21, 1946, n.p.

20. "260.000 mujeres en las fábricas," *Aquí Está*, March 27, 1947, 2–3.

21. On marriage and love as female ideals in early twentieth-century weekly romantic novels and the figure of the bella pobre, see Beatriz Sarlo, *El imperio de los sentimientos: Narraciones de circulación periódica en la Argentina (1917–1927)* (Buenos Aires: Catálogos, 1985).

22. "La etiqueta de las economías," *Maribel*, April 22, 1952, 34.

23. "Encuesta: Tres tipos de mujer," *¿Qué sucedió en siete días?*, December 18, 1946, 40.

24. "Así opinan los hombres," *Vosotras*, January 7, 1949, 14–15. Also Cascallar, *Esas cosas de mamá*, 304–5.

25. Grete Stern, *Sueños: Fotomontajes de Grete Stern* (Buenos Aires: CEPPA, 2003), 60, 125–26. On the dissemination of psychoanalysis in Argentina through widely read publications, including *Idilio*, see Mariano Ben Plotkin, "Tell Me Your Dreams: Psychoanalysis and Popular Culture in Buenos Aires, 1930–1950," *The Americas* 55, no. 4 (April 1999): 601–29.

26. On early twentieth-century female representations, especially moralistic tales of money-oriented women from the popular sectors, see Donna Guy, *Sex and Gender in Buenos Aires: Prostitution, Family, and Nation in Argentina* (Lincoln: University of Nebraska Press, 1990), 141–74; and Bergero, *Intersecting Tango*, 121–22, 201.

27. Cascallar, *Esas cosas de mamá*, 64–67, 258–59, 304–5

28. For Eva's "black myth," see Julie Taylor, *Eva Perón: The Myths of a Woman* (Chicago:

University of Chicago Press, 1979), 78. For anti-Peronist backlashes against Eva Perón, see Martínez Estrada, *¿Qué es esto?*, 239–61; Bernardo Rabinovitz, *Sucedió en la Argentina (1943–1956): Lo que no se dijo* (Buenos Aires: Gure, 1956), 47; and Pastor, *Frente al totalitarismo peronista*, 80–93.

29. On the Divito girls, see *Rico Tipo*, May 24, 1945, 10; *Rico Tipo*, July 12, 1945, 11; *Rico Tipo*, January 10, 1946, 11; and *Rico Tipo*, September 26, 1946, 19.

30. "Olga," *Democracia*, August 20, 1946, 8.

31. "Olga," *Democracia*, August 18, 1946, 8.

32. "Contra Olga," *Democracia*, August 26, 1946, 2.

33. "Admirador de Olga," *Democracia*, September 11, 1946, 2.

34. Susana Torrado, *Historia de la familia en la Argentina moderna (1870–2000)* (Buenos Aires: Ediciones de la Flor, 2003), 225–319; and Susana Novick, "Argentina (1946–1986): Las políticas de población y los planes nacionales de desarrollo," in *Política, población y políticas de población: Argentina, 1946–1986*, Susana Torrado, Susana Novick, and Silvia Olego de Campos (Buenos Aires: CEUR, 1986), 25–52.

35. "Contigo pan y cebolla," *El Hogar*, June 11, 1937, 7; "El joven chapado a la antigua," *Idilio*, May 3, 1949, 37; and "260.000 mujeres en las fábricas," *Aquí Está*, March 27, 1947, 2–3.

36. "Historia del pasado y del presente del matrimonio en Buenos Aires," *Mundo Argentino*, July 31, 1946, 3–4; and Torrado, *Historia de la familia en la Argentina moderna*, 253–56. For an analysis of dating and gender roles through an exploration of 1950s radio shows, see Isabella Cosse, "Relaciones de pareja a mediados de siglo en las representaciones de la radio porteña: Entre sueños románticos y visos de realidad," *Estudios Sociológicos* 25, no. 73 (2007): 131–53.

37. Bruce, *Those Perplexing Argentines*, 165. See also Greenup and Greenup, *Revolution Before Breakfast*, 211.

38. Cascallar, *Esas cosas de mamá*, 12–13.

39. "Acerca de los muebles," *Nocturno*, December 1951, 1937. Even those who disapproved of delaying marriage agreed that finding and affording a house was a pressing concern and an arduous task for newlyweds in mid-twentieth-century Argentina. Although Peronist housing policies included rent freezes, the legal permission to sell individual units in building blocks, the construction of individual and collective housing, and generous loans for residential construction, adequate urban housing was a critical issue. On Peronist housing politics, see Aboy, *Viviendas para el pueblo*; and Ballent, *Las huellas de la política*.

40. "Lo ideal sería un batidor eléctrico en cada hogar," *Mucho Gusto*, April 1950, 8.

41. "Como comprar muebles," *Rosalinda*, May 1952, 53; "El living room," *Para Ti*, May 31, 1955, 16–17; "Si usted piensa construír, acuérdese de la cocina," *Mucho Gusto*, November 1946, 41; and "Una cocina bien armada," *Mucho Gusto*, March 1948,

42–43. For shopping and decorating advice in upper-class publications, see "En la residencia . . . ," *Atlántida*, December 1946, 93; and "El arte en el comedor," *Atlántida*, April 1947, 54.

42. "La novia equipa su casa y su cocina," *Mucho Gusto*, August 1948, 41–47.

43. Old-standing publications that featured these types of sections included *Para Ti*, *Vosotras*, and *El Hogar*. Good examples of new magazines with a special focus on shopping for the newlyweds' home were *Mucho Gusto* (1946), *Cuéntame* (1948), *Idilio* (1948), *Chicas* (1948), and *Nocturno* (1950), among others.

44. "El confort, índice de cultura," *Confort*, July 1951, 3.

45. "Confortlandia," *Confort*, September 1951, 43–46; "Los nuevos hogares," *Confort*, September 1952, 29–32; "Morada Obrera," *Confort*, July 1948, 14; "Modelo de Casa Económica," *Confort*, May 1950, 48; and "Un plan para un matrimonio de recién consagrados," *Nuestro Techo*, June 1955, 30–33.

46. "La primera casa," *Rosalinda*, July 1950, 50.

47. Gath & Chaves ad, *La Capital*, November 10, 1946, 5.

48. Díaz ad, *Para Ti*, June 29, 1948, 70.

49. "Planeando un hogar para dos," *Mucho Gusto: Número Extraordinario dedicado a las novias*, Winter 1949, 2–3.

50. Elna ad, *Para Ti*, August 19, 1947, 9.

51. La Campagnola ad, *Para Ti*, June 11, 1948, back cover.

52. Anbar ad, *El Hogar*, December 23, 1949, 62; Duilia ad, *Mucho Gusto*, July 1951, 22; Carú ad, *Mucho Gusto*, September 1951, 29; "Si usted es una mujer muy ocupada cocine con una olla a presión," *Mucho Gusto*, September 1951, 14–15; "Olla a presión," *Caras y Caretas*, July 1954, 134; and Marta Beines, *Las recetas de Doña Prestísima* (Buenos Aires, n.p.: 1952). On the stereotype of the single woman as a bad cook who lies to her fiancé, see "Equivocación," *Nocturno*, June 1952, 55.

53. Philips ad, *La Tribuna*, March 19, 1952, 2.

54. Eugenio Diez ad, *Chicas*, June 1954, 25.

55. "Quedarse en casa," *Democracia*, June 17, 1952, 2.

56. "La mujer es la verdadera administradora del hogar," *Cascabel*, March 8, 1944, 15. See also "Hoy, gran liquidación de invierno," *Rico Tipo*, August 22, 1946, 20–21; and "Queremos el aguinaldo," *Rico Tipo*, December 26, 1946, 20–21.

57. "Mientras la porteña gasta el 36% de lo que gana en belleza, las otras . . . ," *PBT*, January 30, 1953, 126.

58. "Esposos injustos," *Para Ti*, September 30, 1952, 30.

59. Victoria de Grazia, "Introduction," *The Sex of Things*, de Grazia and Furlough, 3; and Roberts, "Gender, Consumption, and Commodity Culture," 817–44.

60. "Código Social: La mujer casada," *Para Ti*, February 19, 1929, 69. On the stigmatization of the working sectors, see Rodriguez, *Civilizing Argentina*, 79–93, 131–37.

On different views about social problems related to the working class in early twentieth-century Argentina, see Zimmerman, *Los liberales reformistas*.

61. "¿Cuál es el enemigo número uno de todos los matrimonios?," *Mundo Argentino*, May 21, 1947, 16–17.

62. Marcela Nari, *Políticas de maternidad y maternalismo político: Buenos Aires, 1890–1940* (Buenos Aires: Biblos, 2004), 74–75.

63. "Economía," *Nocturno*, February 1952, 59. On the views of the government, see "Austeridad en el consumo," *Mundo Peronista*, March 1, 1952, 25.

64. "La mujer que trabaja y la moda," *Para Ti*, June 21, 1955, 38.

65. "Ser más elegante," *La Época*, January 20, 1948, 15. See also, "Cuando vaya a la peluquería," *La Época*, January 4, 1948, 11; and "Prendas útiles," *La Época*, January 15, 1948, 15.

66. "Como ser una esposa adorable . . . y adorada," *Mundo Argentino*, November 2, 1949, 57. See also "¿Existen los maridos fieles?," *Vosotras*, June 8, 1951, 24–25; "Consejos a la recién casada," *Nocturno*, February 1951, 14; and Cascallar, *Esas cosas de mamá*, 122–23.

67. *La Tribuna*, October 18, 1955, 6.

68. On the representation of the daily life of young women in the 1910s and 1920s, see Sarlo, *El imperio de los sentimientos*, 26–27.

69. Bergero, *Intersecting Tango*, 202.

70. On women in Peronist iconography, see Lobato, Damilakou, and Tornay, "Las reinas del trabajo bajo el peronismo."

71. "No seas callejera," *Mundo Argentino*, July 2, 1952, 54.

72. Cascallar, *Esas cosas de mamá*, 80–81, 203–4.

73. Stern, *Sueños*, 75, 134–35.

74. Cascallar, *Esas cosas de mamá*, 203–4.

75. "No seas callejera," *Mundo Argentino*, July 2, 1952, 54.

76. Cascallar, *Esas cosas de mamá*, 80–81. On early twentieth-century interpretations about the dangers of consumption for upper-class women and as a threat to maternity, see Bergero, *Intersecting Tango*, 228–29.

77. "No seas callejera," *Mundo Argentino*, July 2, 1952, 54.

78. On interpretations of masculine femininity focused on sexuality and the body, see Judith Halberstam, *Female Masculinity* (Durham, NC: Duke University Press, 1998).

79. "El marido que hace vida de club o de café," *Mundo Argentino*, May 26, 1954, 62.

80. "Esposos desatentos," *Para Ti*, August 18, 1952, 30.

81. "A ponernos el delantal," *El Mundo*, March 16, 1948, 4; "Los maridos y las tareas domésticas," *Para Ti*, February 13, 1951, 39; and "Ha pasado un día en la vida de una obrera," *Nuestras Mujeres*, July 1, 1948, 13–14.

82. "Quehaceres domésticos," *Caras y Caretas*, July 1955, 3–4; *Mucho Gusto*, May 1947, cover; "Carlos Gines, ama de casa," *¿Qué sucedió en siete días?*, August 8, 1946, 41; Corimayo ads, *Clarín*, June 10, 1948, 4; *Clarín*, June 24, 1948, 3; *Rico Tipo*, August 5, 1948, back cover; *Rico Tipo*, April 27, 1949, back cover; and *La Razón*, July 8, 1948, 9; SIAM ads, *Clarín*, November 22, 1954, 6; *El Mundo*, February 10, 1953, 7; *El Mundo*, February 17, 9; *El Mundo*, December 7, 1953, 6; and *El Mundo*, December 17, 7; and Oski, "Estos hombres," *Rico Tipo*, November 14, 1946, 22.

83. On the backlash against women's labor in the 1930s, see Asunción Lavrin, *Women, Feminism and Social Change in Argentina, Chile and Uruguay, 1890–1940* (Lincoln: University of Nebraska Press, 1995), 92–96.

84. "El matrimonio de la mujer que trabaja," *Rosalinda*, September 1953, 17.

85. "El lugar de la mujer casada," *Para Ti*, March 6, 1951, 38.

86. Cascallar, *Esas cosas de mamá*, 276–77.

87. "El matrimonio de la mujer que trabaja," *Rosalinda*, September 1953, 17.

88. Quoted in James, *Doña María's Story*, 42.

89. "No seas callejera," *Mundo Argentino*, July 2, 1952, 54.

90. Florencio Escardó, *Geografía de Buenos Aires* (Buenos Aires: Losada, 1945), 139.

91. In search of a consistent rise in birth rates, the Peronist government actively supported the increase of the national population and promoted parenthood. On mid-twentieth-century population issues in Argentina, see Torrado, *Historia de la familia en la Argentina moderna*, 323–25. On the Peronist view of motherhood, see María Herminia Di Liscia, "'Ser madre es un deber': Maternidad en los gobiernos peronistas, 1946–1955," in *Historia y género: Seis estudios sobre la condición femenina*, ed. Daniel Villar, María Herminia Di Liscia, and María Jorgelina Caviglia (Buenos Aires: Biblos, 1999), 33–49; and Bianchi, "Las mujeres en el peronismo."

92. Harold Darquier, "Ataques morales a la familia argentina," in *Restauración Social de la Familia Argentina*, Valsecchi, 123; and Museo Social Argentino, *Primer Congreso de la Población*, 56.

93. Quoted in Susana Bianchi, "Catolicismo y Peronismo: La familia entre la religión y la política (1945–1955)," *Boletín del Instituto de Historia Argentina y Américana Dr. Emilio Ravignani*, no. 19 (1999): 115–37. On the changing and finally tumultuous relationship between the Peronist government and the Catholic Church, see Bianchi, *Catolicismo y Peronismo*. On the position of Catholics against consumerism in Mexico during the same time period, see Moreno, *Yankee Don't Go Home!*, 207–28.

94. "Esposos injustos," *Para Ti*, September 30, 1952, 30.

95. "Más vale prevenir . . . ," *Para Ti*, February 20, 1951, 37. See also "El hombre ahorrativo," *Idilio*, June 21, 1946, 37; and "Los errores de ellos y los de ellas," *Rosalinda*, April 1952, 14

96. "El hombre ahorrativo," *Idilio*, June 21, 1949, 37

97. "Más vale prevenir . . . ," *Para Ti*, February 20, 1951, 37.

98. "La solterona," *El Compañero*, August 1955, 6.

99. "Más vale prevenir . . . ," *Para Ti*, February 20, 1951, 37.

100. "Hombres egoístas," *Para Ti*, September 16, 1952, 28.

101. "Para casadas solamente," *Rosalinda*, August 1953, 50.

102. "Hombres egoístas," *Para Ti*, September 16, 1952, 28.

CHAPTER 6

1. Amelia Foresto, interview by author, Rosario, October 18, 2005.

2. Rosalind Morris, ed., *Can the Subaltern Speak? Reflections on the History of an Idea* (New York: Columbia University Press, 2010). For the debate in Latin America, see Florencia Mallon, "The Promise and Dilemma of Subaltern Studies: Perspectives of Latin American History," *American Historical Review* 99, no. 5 (1994): 1491–515.

3. Luisa Passerini, *Fascism in Popular Memory: The Cultural Experience of the Turin Working Class* (New York: Cambridge University Press, 1987), 1. For excellent examples of Latin American oral history, see James, *Doña María's Story*; Steve Stern, *Remembering Pinochet's Chile: On the Eve of London, 1998* (Durham, NC: Duke University Press, 2004); and Sandra McGee Deutsch, *Crossing Borders, Claiming a Nation: A History of Argentine Jewish Women, 1880–1955* (Durham, NC: Duke University Press, 2010).

4. James, *Doña María's Story*, 124.

5. For an interesting discussion of these issues from a feminist perspective, see Sherna Berger Gluck and Daphne Patai, eds., *Women's Words: The Feminist Practice of Oral History* (New York: Routledge, 1991). See also Mary Chamberlain and Paul Thompson, eds., *Narrative and Genre* (London: Routledge, 1998).

6. Alessandro Portelli, "Oral History as Genre," in *Narrative and Genre*, Chamberlain and Thompson, 26.

7. Charlotte Linde, *Life Stories: The Creation of Coherence* (New York: Oxford University Press, 1993), 3.

8. Pierre Nora, "Between Memory and History," in *Realms of Memory: The Construction of the French Past*, ed. Pierre Nora (New York: Columbia University Press, 1996), 1–20.

9. Anna Green, "Individual Remembering and 'Collective Memory': Theoretical Presuppositions and Contemporary Debates," *Oral History* 32, no. 2 (Autumn 2004): 35–44.

10. Passerini, *Fascism in Popular Memory*, 11.

11. Eva Perón, *Discursos Completos*, 1:389.

12. James, *Doña María's Story*, 70.

13. Luis Ricardo Romero, interview by author, Rosario, December 21, 2005.

14. I borrow the term "vehicles of memory" from Alon Confino, "Collective Memory and Cultural History: Problems of Method," *American Historical Review* 102, no. 5 (December 1997): 1386–403.

15. Pierre Nora, "Generation," in *Realms of Memory*, Nora, 500.

16. I borrow the term "mnemonic community" from Eviatar Zerubabel, *Time Maps: Collective Memory and the Social Shape of the Past* (Chicago: University of Chicago Press, 2003), 6.

17. Héctor Acosta, interview by author, Rosario, October 17, 2005.

18. Marie Francoise Chanfrault-Duchet, "Narrative Structures, Social Models, and Symbolic Representation in the Life Story," in *Women's Words*, Berger Gluck and Patai, 77–92.

19. Juan Carlos Legas, interview by author, Rosario, December 21, 2005.

20. Violeta Benvenuto, interview by author, Rosario, December 5, 2005.

21. Alessandro Portelli, *The Death of Luigi Trastulli and Other Stories: Form and Meaning in Oral History* (Albany: State University of New York Press, 1991), 21.

22. "Cosas del general," *Mundo Peronista*, April 1952, 42–43.

23. "Consumo y derroche," *Mundo Peronista*, February 1952, 2; Subsecretaría de Informaciones de Presidencia de la Nación, *Perón: Anécdotas, recuerdos, relatos*, 82; and Juan Perón, "La política alimentaria argentina," *Hechos e Ideas*, May/June 1949, 353.

24. Martínez Estrada, *¿Qué es esto?*, 74.

25. Tristán, *150 caricaturas* (Buenos Aires: Gure, 1955), 26.

26. "Historia de una obrera feliz," *Mundo Peronista*, June 1952, 10.

27. "¿Esto ocurría antes?," *Mundo Peronista*, August 1951, 27.

28. Norma Mordini, interview by author, Rosario, October 4, 2005.

29. The classic approach to the gift as generator of debt is Marcel Mauss, *The Gift: The Form and Reason for Exchange in Archaic Societies* (London: Routledge, 2000); "El plan económico para 1952," *Mundo Peronista*, March 1952, 2; and Presidencia de la Nación, *Perón y el Plan Económico 1952* (Buenos Aires, 1952).

30. Eva Perón, *Habla Eva Perón* (Buenos Aires: Partido Peronista Femenino, 1952), 3–4.

31. The foundation distributed over 2.7 million items of aid each year for a population of close to 17 million persons. On the Eva Perón Foundation, see Martín Stawski, "El populismo paralelo: Política social de la Fundación Eva Perón (1948–1955)," in *Sueños de bienestar en la Nueva Argentina*, Berrotarán, Jáuregui, and Rougier, 193–227. For a new approach to the foundation, see Donna Guy, *Women Build the Welfare State: Performing Charity and Creating Rights in Argentina, 1880–1955* (Durham, NC: Duke University Press, 2009), 151–85.

32. Néstor Ferioli, *La Fundación Eva Perón* (Buenos Aires: CEAL, 1990), 1:15.

33. On the "myths" of Eva Perón, see Taylor, *Eva Perón*; and Marysa Navarro and Nicholas Fraser, *Evita: The Real Life of Eva Perón* (New York: W.W. Norton, 1996).

34. These working-class interviewees provide a striking contrast to the socially isolated and extremely poor shantytown dwellers interviewed by sociologist Javier Auyero in the mid-1990s. Dependent on the Peronist patronage system to survive, both in the 1950s as well as in the present, they reaffirmed a Peronist identity based on their participation in clientelistic networks that deliver goods and services. Javier Auyero, *Poor People's Politics: Peronist Survival and the Legacy of Evita* (Durham, NC: Duke University Press, 2001), 182–204.

35. About this role of memory, see David Lowenthal, *The Past is a Foreign Country* (New York: Cambridge University Press, 1985), 195.

36. Ema Lucero, interview by author, Rosario, November 3, 2005.

37. Norma Mordini, interview by author, Rosario, October 4, 2005; and Amelia Foresto, interview by author, Rosario, October 18, 2005. For the relation between femininity and sewing in other geographical and historical contexts, see Barbara Burman, ed., *The Culture of Sewing: Gender, Consumption, and Home Dressmaking* (New York: Oxford University Press, 1999).

38. Fundación Eva Perón, *La máquina de coser* (Buenos Aires, n.d.); "Nuestro hogar obrero," *Democracia* (Rosario), January 25, 1954, 1; and Navarro and Fraser, *Evita*, 118. On government measures to strengthen the sewing machine industry, see Girbal-Blacha, "El hogar o la fábrica," 217–30.

39. Orvar Löfgren, "My Life as Consumer: Narratives from the World of Goods," in *Narrative and Genre*, Chamberlain and Thompson, 123.

40. Margarita Rubani, interview by author, Rosario, October 4, 2005.

41. Juan Carlos Legas, interview by author, Rosario, December 21, 2005.

42. María Rosa Bertea, interview by author, Rosario, October 13, 2005; and Norma Mordini, interview by author, Rosario, October 4, 2005.

43. On analyses of middle-class images in the Peronist propaganda, see Gené, *Un mundo feliz*, 117–29; Torre and Pastoriza, "La democratización del bienestar"; and Elena, "Peronism in 'Good Taste.'"

44. Quoted in Javier Prado, *Aquí están, estos son los muchachos de Perón: El peronismo y su memoria* (Trelew, Argentina: Javier Prado, 2007), 108.

45. Rodolfo Di Marco, interview by author, Rosario, October 13, 2005.

46. I borrow the concept of affluent worker from John Goldthorpe et al., *The Affluent Worker in the Class Structure* (New York: Cambridge University Press, 1969).

47. Irma Salvatierra, interview by autor, Rosario, October 11, 2005; Donata Boso, interview by author, Rosario, November 11, 2005; Nélida Caña, interview by author, Rosario, October 5, 2005; and Eduardo Sosa, interview by author, Rosario, December 7, 2005.

48. Eduardo Sosa, interview by author, Rosario, December 7, 2005.

49. Mary Douglas, *Thought Styles: Critical Essays on Good Taste* (London: Sage, 1996).

50. Filomena Gómez, interview by author, Rosario, October 11, 2005; Hortensia Difilipo, interview by author, Rosario, December 8, 2005; Margarita Rubani, interview by author, Rosario, October 4, 2005; and Ernesto Miranda, interview by author, Rosario, October 14, 2005.

51. The centrality of these skills in how people narrate their lives as consumers is an argument made by Löfgren, "My Life as Consumer," 115.

52. Adelma Martínez, interview by author, Rosario, December 27, 2005.

53. Melanie Wallendorf and Eric Arnould, "'My Favorite Things': A Cross-Cultural Inquiry into Object Attachment, Possessiveness, and Social Linkage," *Journal of Consumer Research* 14, no. 4 (March 1988): 531–47.

54. Dante Zucchini, *Recuerdos de un inmigrante* (Buenos Aires: La Base, 1994), 100.

55. Wallendorf and Arnould, "My Favorite Things," 541; and Joanna Bornat, "Oral History as A Social Movement: Reminiscence and Older People," *Oral History* 17, no. 2 (Autumn 1989): 16–24.

56. Quoted in Ungaro, "El confort viene marchando."

57. United Nations, Economic Commission for Latin America, *Análisis y proyecciones del desarrollo económico: El desarrollo económico de la Argentina* (Mexico City: Departamento de Asuntos Económicos y Sociales, 1959), 243–45; and Dorfman, *Cincuenta años de industrialización en la Argentina*, 207–14. In 1955, there was also a production of twenty thousand kerosene-absorption refrigerators.

58. Dirección Nacional de Estadísticas y Censos, *IV Censo General de la Nación: Censo de Vivienda*, 12, 15–16; and "La riqueza de una nación," *Orientación: Modas y Mundo Social*, June 1951, 12.

59. "Comfort para el pueblo," *Mundo Peronista*, April 1, 1955, 31; and "Cosas que pasan . . . ," *PBT*, May 9, 1952, 125;

60. "Las mujeres a la cabeza de la lucha contra la carestía," *Nuestras Mujeres*, January 1955, 9.

61. Alicia Moreau de Justo, "En defensa de la trabajadora del hogar," *Nuevas Bases*, December 15, 1950, 7.

62. Adolfo Bioy Casares, *Borges* (Barcelona: Destino, 2006), 275.

63. Lilia Fernández, interview by author, Rosario, December 1, 2005.

64. Eloísa Pozzi, interview by author, Rosario, October 13, 2005.

65. G. Mauricio Bulman, *Reminiscencias y algo más . . . : El barrio Florida en la Argentina cotidiana y el mundo entre 1930 y 1950* (Buenos Aires: LOLA, 2006), 61.

66. Violeta Benvenuto, interview by author, Rosario, December 5, 2005.

67. Zucchini, *Recuerdos de un inmigrante*, 81.

68. Rubén Ghioldi, interview by author, Rosario, December 2, 2005; Ernesto Miranda, interview by author, Rosario, October 14, 2005; and Héctor Acosta, interview by author, Rosario, October 13, 2005.

69. Norberto Tomasini, interview by author, Rosario, December 9, 2005.

70. For an example of this argument focused on the zoot-suiters, see Alvarez, *The Power of the Suit*.

71. Juan Carlos Legas, interview by author, Rosario, December 21, 2005.

72. Lee Wright, "The Suit: A Common Bond or Defeated Purpose?" in *The Gendered Object*, ed. Pat Kirkham (Manchester: Manchester University Press, 1996), 153–56.

73. Violeta Benvenuto, interview by author, Rosario, December 5, 2005; and Laura Perera, interview by author, Rosario, December 14, 2005.

74. Eloisa Pozzi, interview by author, Rosario, October 13, 2005.

75. Löfgren, "My Life as Consumer," 123.

76. Barbara Myerhoff, "Life History Among the Elderly: Performance, Visibility, and Re-Membering," in *Remembered Lives: The Work of Ritual, Storytelling, and Growing Older*, ed. Marc Kaminsky (Ann Harbor: University of Michigan Press, 1992), 238.

77. Juan Carlos Legas, interview by author, Rosario, December 21, 2005.

78. Lowenthal, *The Past is a Foreign Country*, 8.

79. Mary Jo Maynes, *Taking the Hard Road: Life Course in French and German Workers' Autobiographies in the Era of Industrialization* (Chapel Hill: University of North Carolina Press, 1995), 32.

80. Barbara Myerhoff, *Number Our Days* (New York: E. P. Dutton, 1978), 143; and Barbara Myerhoff and Virginia Tufte, "Life History as Integration: Personal Myth and Aging" in *Remembered Lives*, Kaminsky, 249–55.

Epilogue

1. Naomi Klein, *The Shock Doctrine: The Rise of Disaster Capitalism* (New York: Picador, 2007); and Joseph Stiglitz, *Globalization and Its Discontents* (New York: W. W. Norton, 2003).

2. On the Peronist resistance, see Daniel James, *Resistance and Integration: Peronism and the Argentine Working Class, 1946–1976* (New York: Cambridge University Press, 1988); and César Seveso, "Political Emotions and the Origins of the Peronist Resistance," in *The New Cultural History of Peronism*, Karush and Chamosa, 239–69. On labor mobilization in this period, see James P. Brennan, *The Labors Wars in Córdoba, 1955–1976: Ideology, Work, and Labor Politics in an Argentine Industrial City* (Cambridge, MA: Harvard University Press, 1994).

3. Romero, *A History of Argentina in the Twentieth Century*, 131–71.

4. Gerchunoff and Llach, *El ciclo de la ilusión y el desencanto*, 243–87.

5. Klaus Veigel, *Dictatorship, Democracy, and Globalization: Argentina and the Cost of Paralysis, 1973–2001* (University Park: Pennsylvania State University Press, 2009).

6. Jorge Schvarzer, *Implementación de un modelo económico: La experiencia argentina entre 1975 y 2000* (Buenos Aires: A-Z Editora, 1998).

7. In this context, *caudillo* refers to a political boss or leader.

8. On Menem's government, see Alberto Bonnet, *La hegemonía menemista: El neo-conservadurismo en Argentina, 1989–2001* (Buenos Aires: Prometeo, 2007). On the impact of neoliberal reforms in Argentina, see Maristella Svampa, *La sociedad excluyente: La Argentina bajo el signo del neoliberalismo* (Buenos Aires: Taurus, 2005).

9. "Qué culpa tiene el tomate," *Crítica*, March 7, 2008.

10. For an analysis of global consumers and globalized cities focused on Mexico City, see Néstor García Canclini, *Consumers and Citizens: Globalization and Multicultural Conflicts* (Minneapolis: University of Minnesota Press, 2001).

11. For an analysis of Peronist clientelism in the 1990s, see Auyero, *Poor People's Politics*.

12. On piqueteros, see Maristella Svampa and Sebastián Pereyra, *Entre la ruta y el barrio: La experiencia de las organizaciones piqueteras* (Buenos Aires: Biblos, 2003).

13. José Ángel Di Mauro, *¿Qué se vayan todos? Crónica del derrumbe político* (Buenos Aires: Corregidor, 2003).

14. Changarines are handymen who work sporadically, and cartoneros are scavengers who pick recyclables out of the trash and sell them.

15. "Cuando emigrar se convierte en una cuestión cultural," *Página/12*, February 25, 2002.

16. "La mitad de los argentinos ya está bajo la línea de pobreza," *Clarín*, May 5, 2002.

17. *The Take*, directed by Avi Lewis (Canada: First Run Features / Icarus Films, 2004). On factory take-overs, see Esteban Magnani, *El cambio silencioso: Fábricas y empresas recuperadas por los trabajadores en la Argentina* (Buenos Aires: Prometeo, 2003).

18. Patricia Aguirre, *Ricos flacos y gordos pobres: La alimentación en crisis* (Buenos Aires: Capital Intelectual, 2007).

19. Peter Ranis, "Factories Without Bosses: Argentina's Experience with Worker-Run Enterprises," *Labor: Studies in Working-Class History of the Americas* 3, no. 1 (Spring 2006): 11–23.

20. "To Weather Recession, Argentines Revert to Barter," *New York Times*, May 6, 2001.

21. The expression belongs to García Canclini, *Consumers and Citizens*, 47.

22. "La híper le ganó la pulseada al trueque," *La Nación*, August 17, 2003. On barter clubs in Argentina, see Susana Hintze and Daniel Casanno, *Trueque y economía solidaria* (Buenos Aires: Prometeo, 2003). The term *prosumer* was coined by American writer and journalist Alvin Toffler. In his study of the rise of a postindustrial society, Toffler employed *prosumer* to refer to consumers who actively participate in customizing the goods they buy. Alvin Toffler, *The Third Wave* (New York: Bantam Books, 1981).

23. "La Salada ya es la mayor feria ilegal de América Latina," *La Nación*, January 21, 2007; and "La Salada ya se parece a un shopping," *La Nación*, February 7, 2010.

24. "Impulsan el consumo los sectores de menores recursos," *La Nación*, October 14, 2003; and "Los híper para los ABC1: Los chinos son para todos," *Página/12*, October 18, 2006.

25. "Las empresas quieren venderles más a los sectores de bajos recursos," *La Nación*, December 4, 2003; and "El consumidor menos pensado," *La Nación*, July 19, 2009. On successful new companies that target low-income consumers, see Alfredo Sainz, *Negocios exitosos argentinos* (Buenos Aires: Planeta, 2009).

26. Julio Godio and Alberto José Robles, *El tiempo de CFK: Entre la mobilización y la institucionalidad; El desafío de organizar los mercados* (Buenos Aires: Corregidor, 2008).

27. "Credibilidad intervenida: Claves para entender la crisis del INDEC," *La Nación*, August 10, 2008; and "Ya hay tantos argentinos pobres como en 2001," *La Nación*, November 10, 2008.

28. On "subjective poverty," see Victoria Giarrizzo, "Pobreza subjetiva en Argentina: Construcción de indicadores de bienestar económico" (PhD dissertation, Universidad de Buenos Aires, 2007).

29. "El consumidor menos pensado," *La Nación*, July 19, 2009; and "El auge del consumo llega a más sectores," *La Nación*, December 31, 2006.

30. "Los celulares más caros, preferidos por los pobres," *La Nación*, August 22, 2008.

Selected Bibliography

Archives and Libraries

Buenos Aires, Argentina

Archivo del Partido Comunista
Archivo General de la Nación: Biblioteca Juan Domingo Perón, Colección del Ministerio
    de Asuntos Técnicos (MAT), Archivo Intermedio, Departamento de Fotografía
Archivo SIAM, Biblioteca de la Universidad Torcuato Di Tella
Biblioteca del Congreso Nacional: Colección Peronista
Biblioteca del Ministerio de Economía
Biblioteca del Ministerio de Trabajo
Biblioteca del Museo Evita
Biblioteca y Hemeroteca Nacional
Centro de Documentación e Investigación de la Cultura de Izquierdas en la Argentina
    (CEDINCI)
Instituto Juan Domingo Perón
Memoria Abierta

Rosario, Argentina

Archivo Fotográfico del Museo de la Ciudad
Archivo y Hemeroteca del Museo Provincial Julio Marc
Biblioteca de la Bolsa de Comercio de Rosario

Biblioteca de la Facultad de Economía, Universidad Nacional de Rosario
Biblioteca y Archivo de la Sociedad Rural de Rosario
Biblioteca y Hemeroteca Argentina

United States

Herman B. Wells Library, Indiana University
Hoover Institution on War, Revolution and Peace Archives and Library,
    Stanford University
J. Walter Thompson Company Archives, Rare Book, Manuscript, and
    Special Collections Library, Duke University
M.D. Anderson Library, University of Houston
New York Public Library

PERIODICALS
(PLACE OF PUBLICATION IS BUENOS AIRES UNLESS NOTED)

Agua y Energía	*El Mundo*	*Mucho Gusto*
Ahora	*El Pueblo*	*Mujeres Argentinas*
Antena	*El Socialista*	*Mundo Argentino*
Aquí Está	*El Tranviario*	*Mundo Peronista*
Argentina	*Esto Es*	*New York Times* (U.S.)
Atlántida	*¡Extra!*	*New York Times Magazine*
Caras y Caretas	*Fortaleza*	(U.S.)
Cascabel	*Hechos e Ideas*	*Nocturno*
Chabela	*Idilio*	*Noticias Gráficas*
Chicas	*Ímpetu*	*Nuestras Mujeres*
Clarín	*Investigaciones de Mercado*	*Nuestro Techo*
Confort	*La Capital* (Rosario)	*Nuevas Bases*
Continente	*La Época*	*Orientación*
Crítica	*La Hora*	*Orientación: Modas y*
Crónica (Rosario)	*La Industria Lechera*	*Mundo Social*
Cuéntame	*La Nación*	*Página/12*
Democracia	*La Prensa*	*Panadería Argentina*
Democracia (Rosario)	*La Razón*	*Panorama*
Descamisada	*La Reforma Comercial*	*Para Ti*
Dinámica Social	*La Tribuna* (Rosario)	*PBT*
Economía y Finanzas	*La Vanguardia*	*Publicidad Argentina*
El Hogar	*La Voz Argentina*	*¿Qué sucedió en siete*
El Laborista	*Maribel*	*días?*

Radiolandia
Revista de Arquitectura
Revista de Estadística
  Municipal de la Ciudad
  de Buenos Aires
Revista de la Asociación
  Argentina de Dietología
Revista de la Asociación de
  Fabricantes de Dulces,
  Conservas y Afines
Revista de la Federación
  Gremial del Comercio e
  Industria (Rosario)

Revista de la Sociedad Rural de Rosario
  (Rosario)
Rico Tipo
Rosalinda
Rosario (Rosario)
Rosario Norte (Rosario)
Síntesis Publicitaria
Unión Ferroviaria (Rosario)
Vea y Lea
Ventas
Veritas
Vosotras
Washington Post (U.S.)

PRINT PRIMARY SOURCES

Academia Nacional de Ciencias Económicas. *Estadísticas Históricas Argentinas: Compendio 1873–1973*. Buenos Aires: Academia Nacional de Ciencias Económicas, 1988.

Alurralde, Carlos. *A Statement of the Laws of Argentina in Matters Affecting Business*. Washington, D.C.: Pan American Union, 1963.

Arlt, Roberto. *Aguafuertes porteñas*. Buenos Aires: Losada, 2008.

Bagú, Sergio. "La clase media en Argentina." In *La clase media en Argentina y Uruguay: Materiales para el estudio de la clase media en América Latina*, edited by Theo Crevenna, 36–75. Washington, D.C.: Unión Panamericana, 1950.

Beines, Marta. *Las recetas de Doña Prestísima*. Buenos Aires: n.p., 1952.

Bialet Massé, Juan. *Informe sobre el estado de la clase obrera*. Buenos Aires: Hyspamérica, 1985.

Blanksten, George I. *Perón's Argentina*. Chicago: University of Chicago Press, 1953.

Bruce, James. *Those Perplexing Argentines*. New York: Longmans, Green, 1953.

Bunge, Alejandro. *Una Nueva Argentina*. Buenos Aires: Kraft, 1940.

Cafiero, Antonio. *Cinco años después*. Buenos Aires: El Gráfico, 1961.

Carrara, Italo. *La industria de las conservas de pescado en la República Argentina*. Buenos Aires: n.p., 1941.

Carrillo, Ramón. *Organización general del Ministerio de Salud Pública: Obras Completas*. 2 vols. Buenos Aires: Eudeba, 1974.

Cascallar, Nené. *Esas cosas de mamá: Palabras para otras mujeres y otras mamás*. Buenos Aires: Arcur, 1945.

Colom, Eduardo. *El 17 de octubre: La revolución de los descamisados*. Buenos Aires: La Época, 1946.

Congreso Nacional, Cámara de Diputados de la Nación. *Diario de Sesiones*, 1949–1950.

Corporación para la Promoción del Intercambio. *La estructura económica y el desarrollo industrial en la Argentina*. Buenos Aires: Corporación para la Promoción del Intercambio, 1944.

Cortázar, Julio. *Bestiario*. Buenos Aires: Alfaguara, 1995.

———. *Ceremonias*. Buenos Aires: Seix Barral, 1983.

Darquier, Harold. "Ataques morales a la familia argentina." In *Restauración Social de la Familia Argentina*, edited by Francisco Valsecchi, 120–26. Buenos Aires: Acción Católica Argentina, 1950.

Dirección de Estadística Social. *Condiciones de vida de la familia obrera, 1943–1945*. Buenos Aires: Dirección de Estadística Social, 1946.

———. *Nivel de vida de la familia obrera: Evolución durante la Segunda Guerra Mundial, 1939–1945*. Buenos Aires: Dirección de Estadística Social, 1945.

Dirección del Censo Escolar de la Nación. *IV Censo Escolar de la Nación*. Buenos Aires: Dirección del Censo Escolar de la Nación, 1948.

Dirección Nacional de Estadísticas y Censos. *IV Censo General de la Nación: Censo de Vivienda*. Buenos Aires: Dirección Nacional de Estadísticas y Censos, 1947.

———. *Censo Industrial 1950*. Buenos Aires: Dirección Nacional de Estadísticas y Censos, 1957.

———. *Censo Industrial 1954*. Buenos Aires: Dirección Nacional de Estadísticas y Censos, 1960.

———. *Índices del costo del nivel de vida, actividad industrial y costo de la producción, Informe B.1*. Buenos Aires: Dirección Nacional de Estadísticas y Censos, 1956.

Dunbaugh, Frank Montgomery. *Marketing in Latin America*. New York: Printers' Ink Book Company, 1960.

Escardó, Florencio. *Geografía de Buenos Aires*. Buenos Aires: Losada, 1945.

Escudero, Pedro. *Alimentación: Colaboraciones publicadas en La Prensa*. Buenos Aires: Hachette, 1934.

Fundación Eva Perón. *La máquina de coser*. Buenos Aires, n.d.

———. *Proveedurías Eva Perón*. Buenos Aires: Fundación Eva Perón, 1950.

Gallia, María. *Trabajar con amor: Manual de instrucción para mujeres del servicio doméstico*. Buenos Aires: Difusión, 1943.

Germani, Gino. "Inquiry into the Social Effects of Urbanization in a Working-Class Sector of Greater Buenos Aires." In *Urbanization in Latin America*, edited by Philip Hauser, 207–33. New York: International Documents Service, 1961.

———. "La clase media en la Argentina con especial referencia a los sectores urbanos." In *La clase media en Argentina y Uruguay: Materiales para el estudio de la clase media en América Latina*, edited by Theo Crevenna, 4–33. Washington, D.C.: Unión Panamericana, 1950.

González Alberdi, Paulino. *Cómo abaratar la vida*. Buenos Aires: Anteo, 1942.

Grau, Luis. *Los Pérez García y yo*. Buenos Aires: Ciordia & Rodriguez, 1952.

Greenup, Ruth, and Leonard Greenup. *Revolution Before Breakfast: Argentina, 1941–1946*. Chapel Hill: University of North Carolina Press, 1947.

Imaz, José Luis. *La clase alta en Buenos Aires*. Buenos Aires: Universidad de Buenos Aires, 1965.

Instituto Alejandro E. Bunge de Investigaciones Económicas y Sociales. *Soluciones argentinas a los problemas económicos y sociales del presente*. Buenos Aires: Kraft, 1945.

International Advertising Association. *Consumer Study of the Buenos Aires Market*. New York: Export Advertising Association, 1947.

J. Walter Thompson Company. *The Latin American Markets*. New York: McGraw Hill Book Company, 1956.

La Nación Argentina: Justa, Libre, Soberana. Buenos Aires: Ediciones Peuser, 1950.

La Razón: Medio siglo de vida del país y del mundo, 1905–1955. Buenos Aires: La Razón, 1955.

Llorens, Emilio. *El subconsumo de alimentos en América del Sur*. Buenos Aires: Sudamericana, 1942.

Margulis, Mario. *Migración y marginalidad en la sociedad argentina*. Buenos Aires: Paidós, 1968.

Martínez Estrada, Ezequiel. *¿Qué es esto? Catilinaria*. Buenos Aires: Lautaro, 1956.

Michelini, Pedro. *El 17 de octubre de 1945: Testimonio de sus protagonistas*. Buenos Aires: Corregidor, 1994.

Ministerio de Agricultura y Ganadería. *Producción Pesquera de la República Argentina: Años 1946–53*. Buenos Aires: Ministerio de Agricultura y Ganadería, 1955.

Ministerio de Gobierno de la Provincia de Buenos Aires. *Reglamento Bromatológico de la Provincia de Buenos Aires: Codex Alimentarius*. 2nd. ed. La Plata, Argentina: Ministerio de Gobierno de la Provincia de Buenos Aires, 1937.

Ministerio de Industria y Comercio de la Nación. *Economía Publicitaria*. Buenos Aires: Ministerio de Industria y Comercio de la Nación, 1949.

Ministerio de Salud Pública. *Reglamento alimentario aprobado por decreto no. 141/53*. Buenos Aires: Ministerio de Salud Pública, 1953.

Ministerio de Salud Pública y Asistencia Social de la Provincia de Buenos Aires. *Memoria 1949–1950*. La Plata, Argentina: Ministerio de Salud Pública y Asistencia Social de la Provincia de Buenos Aires, 1950.

Moffat, Alfredo. *Estrategias para sobrevivir en Buenos Aires*. Buenos Aires: Jorge Álvarez, 1967.

Montes de Oca de Cárdenas, Sara. "Fundamentos históricos de la familia argentina: Su estado actual." In *Restauración Social de la Familia Argentina*, edited by Francisco Valsecchi, 31–40. Buenos Aires: Acción Católica Argentina, 1950.

Motz, Fred. *The Fruit Industry of Argentina*. Washington, D.C.: Office of Foreign Agricultural Relations, United States Department of Agriculture, 1942.

Mullor, Jorge. *Por un alimento mejor: Bases para un código bromatológico nacional.* Santa Fe, Argentina: Castelvi, 1949.

Museo Social Argentino. *Primer Congreso de la Población.* Buenos Aires: Museo Social Argentino, 1941.

Newton, Jorge. *Clase Media: El dilema de cinco millones de argentinos.* Buenos Aires: Municipalidad de Buenos Aires, 1949.

Nudelman, Santiago. *El radicalismo al servicio de la libertad.* Buenos Aires: Jus, 1947.

Pastor, Reynaldo. *Frente al totalitarismo peronista.* Buenos Aires: Bases, 1959.

Pavón Pereira, Enrique. *Coloquios con Perón.* Buenos Aires: n.p., 1965.

Paz, Hipólito J. *Memorias: Vida pública y privada de un argentino en el siglo XX.* Buenos Aires: Planeta, 1999.

Perelman, Angel. *Como hicimos el 17 de octubre.* Buenos Aires: Coyoacán, 1961.

Pérez, Juan. *Radiografías de una dictadura (por Argentino Cantinflas).* Buenos Aires: La Vanguardia, 1946.

Perón, Eva. *Discursos Completos.* 2 vols. Buenos Aires: Megafón, 1985–1986.

———. *Habla Eva Perón.* Buenos Aires: Partido Peronista Femenino, 1952.

Perón, Juan Domingo. *Obras Completas.* 29 vols. Buenos Aires: Docencia, 1997–2008.

———. *Principios doctrinarios de política social.* Buenos Aires: Subsecretaría de Informaciones, 1947.

Pierce, Russell. *Gringo-Gaucho: An Advertising Odyssey.* Ashland, OR: Southern Cross, 1991.

Poblete Troncoso, Moisés. *El subconsumo en América del Sur.* Santiago de Chile: Nascimento, 1946.

Poviña, Alfredo. "Concepto de clase media y su proyección argentina." In *La clase media en Argentina y Uruguay: Materiales para el estudio de la clase media en América Latina,* edited by Theo Crevenna, 68–75. Washington, D.C.: Unión Panamericana, 1950.

Presidencia de la Nación, *Perón y el Plan Económico 1952.* Buenos Aires, 1952.

Rabinovitz, Bernardo. *Sucedió en la Argentina (1943–1956): Lo que no se dijo.* Buenos Aires: Gure, 1956.

Rennie, Ysabel F. *The Argentine Republic.* New York: MacMillan, 1945.

Sammartino, Ernesto. *La verdad sobre la situación argentina.* Montevideo: n.p., 1951.

Sanger, J. W. *Advertising Methods in Argentina, Uruguay, and Brazil.* Washington, D.C.: Department of Commerce, 1920.

Scalabrini Ortiz, Raúl. *Los ferrocarriles deben ser del pueblo argentino.* Buenos Aires: Reconquista, 1946.

Schleh, Emilio. *La alimentación en la Argentina: Sus características y deficiencias; Anotaciones para resolver un gran problema.* Vol. 2. Buenos Aires: Ferrari, 1930.

Schuck, Walter. *River Plate Sphinx: Argentina at the Turn of 1949–50*. Buenos Aires: n.p., 1950.

Secretaría de Asuntos Técnicos. *Índices Estadísticos, 1954*. Buenos Aires: Secretaría de Asuntos Técnicos, 1954.

Subsecretaría de Informaciones de la Presidencia de la Nación. *Buenos Aires: Capital City of Justicialism*. Buenos Aires: Subsecretaría de Informaciones de la Presidencia de la Nación, 1951.

———. *Perón: Anécdotas, recuerdos, relatos*. Buenos Aires: Subsecretaría de Informaciones de la Presidencia de la Nación, 1950.

Tristán. 150 caricaturas. Buenos Aires: Gure, 1955.

United Nations, Economic Commission for Latin America. *Análisis y proyecciones del desarrollo económico: El desarrollo económico de la Argentina*. Mexico City: Departamento de Asuntos Económicos y Sociales, 1959.

———. *La industria textil en América Latina: Argentina*. New York: United Nations, Economic Commission for Latin America, 1965.

Unsaín, Alejandro. *Ordenamiento de las leyes obreras argentinas*. Buenos Aires: El Ateneo, 1952.

Volpi, Carlos. *El problema energético argentino*. Buenos Aires: Editorial de Autores, 1954.

White, Aníbal. *La industria cervecera por dentro*. Buenos Aires: Americana, 1946.

Woodward, Robert. *Advertising Methods in Argentina*. Washington, D.C.: Department of Commerce, 1935.

Wythe, George. *Industry in Latin America*. New York: Columbia University Press, 1949.

Zavala Rodríguez, Carlos Ángel. *Publicidad comercial: Su régimen legal*. Buenos Aires: De Palma, 1947.

Zucchini, Dante. *Recuerdos de un inmigrante*. Buenos Aires: La Base, 1994.

ORAL INTERVIEWS (IN ROSARIO, ARGENTINA)

Acosta, Héctor. October 13 and 17, 2005.

Benvenuto, Violeta. December 5 and 8, 2005.

Bertea, María Rosa. October 13, 2005.

Boso, Donata. November 11 and 25, 2005.

Caña, Nélida. October 5, 2005.

Di Marco, Rodolfo. October 13 and 18, 2005.

Difilipo, Hortensia. December 8, 2005.

Fernández, Lilia. December 1, 2005.

Foresto, Amelia. October 18, 20, and 23, 2005.

Ghioldi, Rubén. December 2, 2005.

Gómez, Filomena. October 11, 2005.

Legas, Juan Carlos. December 21 and 28, 2005.

Lucero, Ema. November 3, 2005.

Martínez, Adelma. December 27, 2005.

Miranda, Ernesto. October 14, 2005.

Mordini, Norma. October 4, 2005.

Murray Lagos, Elena. October 12, 14, and 16, 2005.

Perera, Laura. December 14, 2005.

Pozzi, Eloísa. October 13, 2005.

Romero, Luis Ricardo. December 21, 2005.

Rubani, Margarita. October 4 and 5, 2005.

Salvatierra, Irma. October 11 and 20, 2005.

Sobrino Aranda, Luis. December 27, 2005.

Sosa, Eduardo. December 7, 2005.

Tomasini, Norberto. December 9, 2005.

Secondary Sources

Aboy, Rosa. *Viviendas para el pueblo: Espacio urbano y sociabilidad en el barrio Los Perales, 1946–1955.* Buenos Aires: Fondo de Cultura Económica, 2005.

Adamovsky, Ezequiel. *Historia de la clase media en Argentina: Apogeo y decadencia de una ilusión, 1919–2003.* Buenos Aires: Planeta, 2010.

Agnew, Jean-Christophe. "Coming Up for Air: Consumer Culture in Historical Perspective." In *Consumer Society in American History: A Reader*, edited by Lawrence B. Glickman, 373–97. Ithaca, NY: Cornell University Press, 1999.

Appadurai, Arjun, ed. *The Social Life of Things: Commodities in Cultural Perspective.* New York: Cambridge University Press, 1986.

Armus, Diego. "El viaje al centro: Tísicas, costureritas y milonguitas en Buenos Aires, 1910–1940." *Boletín del Instituto de Historia Argentina y Americana Dr. Emilio Ravignani*, no. 22 (2000): 101–24.

Auyero, Javier. *Poor People's Politics: Peronist Survival and the Legacy of Evita.* Durham, NC: Duke University Press, 2001.

Ballent, Anahí. *Las huellas de la política: Vivienda, ciudad, peronismo en Buenos Aires, 1943–1955.* Buenos Aires: Universidad Nacional de Quilmes/Prometeo, 2005.

Barbero, María Inés, and Fernando Rocchi. "Industry." In *A New Economic History of Argentina*, edited by Gerardo Della Paolera and Alan Taylor, 261–94. Cambridge: Cambridge University Press, 2003.

Baudrillard, Jean. *For a Critique of the Political Economy of the Sign.* St. Louis, MO: Telos Press, 1981.

Bauer, Arnold J. *Goods, Power, History: Latin America's Material Culture.* New York: Cambridge University Press, 2001.

Bauer, Arnold J., and Benjamin Orlove. "Giving Importance to Imports." In *The Allure of the Foreign: Imported Goods in Postcolonial Latin America*, edited by Benjamin Orlove, 1–31. Ann Harbor: University of Michigan Press, 1997.

Belini, Claudio. *La industria peronista*. Buenos Aires: Edhasa, 2009.

Berger Gluck, Sherna, and Daphne Patai, eds. *Women's Words: The Feminist Practice of Oral History*. New York: Routledge, 1991.

Bergero, Adriana J. *Intersecting Tango: Cultural Geographies of Buenos Aires, 1900–1930*. Translated by Richard Young, Pittsburgh: University of Pittsburgh Press, 2008.

Berrotarán, Patricia, Aníbal Jaúregui, and Marcelo Rougier, eds. *Sueños de bienestar en la Nueva Argentina: Estado y políticas públicas durante el peronismo, 1946–1955*. Buenos Aires: Imago Mundi, 2004.

Bianchi, Susana. *Catolicismo y Peronismo: Religión y política en la Argentina, 1943–1955*. Tandil, Argentina: Instituto de Estudios Históricos Sociales, 2001.

———. "Las mujeres en el Peronismo (Argentina, 1945–1955)." In *Historia de las mujeres en Occidente, Siglo XX*, edited by George Duby and Michelle Perrot, 313–23. Madrid: Taurus, 2000.

Bianchi, Susana, and Norma Sanchis. *El Partido Peronista Femenino, 1949–1955*. Buenos Aires: CEAL, 1988.

Bioy Casares, Adolfo. *Borges*. Barcelona: Destino, 2006.

Borrini, Alberto. *El siglo de la publicidad, 1898–1998: Historia de la publicidad gráfica argentina*. Buenos Aires: Atlántida, 1998.

Bourdieu, Pierre. *Distinction: A Social Critique of the Judgement of Taste*. Translated by Richard Nice. Cambridge, MA: Harvard University Press, 1984.

Brennan, James P. *The Labor Wars in Córdoba, 1955–1976: Ideology, Work, and Labor Politics in an Argentine Industrial City*. Cambridge, MA: Harvard University Press, 1994.

Brennan, James P., and Marcelo Rougier. *The Politics of National Capitalism: Peronism and the Argentine Bourgeoisie, 1946–1976*. University Park: Pennsylvania State University Press, 2002.

Buchrucker, Cristián. *Peronismo y nacionalismo: La Argentina en la crisis ideológica mundial (1927–1955)*. Buenos Aires: Sudamericana, 1987.

Buck-Morss, Susan. *The Dialectics of Seeing: Walter Benjamin and the Arcades Project*. Cambridge, MA: MIT Press, 1991.

Burke, Timothy. *Lifebuoy Men, Lux Women: Commodification, Consumption, and Cleanliness in Modern Zimbabwe*. Durham, NC: Duke University Press, 1996.

Buszek, María Elena. *Pin-Up Grrls: Feminism, Sexuality, Popular Culture*. Durham, NC: Duke University Press, 2006.

Camarero, Hernán. *A la conquista de la clase obrera: Los comunistas y el mundo del trabajo en la Argentina, 1920–1935*. Buenos Aires: Siglo Veintiuno, 2007.

Cascioli, Andrés. *La Argentina que ríe: El humor gráfico en las décadas de 1940 y 1950*. Buenos Aires: Fondo Nacional de las Artes, 2008.

Chamberlain, Mary, and Paul Thompson, eds. *Narrative and Genre*. London: Routledge, 1998.

Chamosa, Oscar. *The Argentine Folklore Movement: Sugar Elites, Criollo Workers, and the Politics of Cultural Nationalism, 1900–1955*. Tucson: University of Arizona Press, 2010.

Chanfrault-Duchet, Marie Francoise. "Narrative Structures, Social Models, and Symbolic Representation in the Life Story." In *Women's Words: The Feminist Practice of Oral History*, edited by Sherna Berger Gluck and Daphne Patai, 77–92. New York: Routledge, 1991.

Clunas, Craig. "Modernity Global and Local: Consumption and the Rise of the West." *American Historical Review* 104, no. 5 (December 1999): 1497–511.

Cochran, Thomas, and Ruben Reina. *Entrepreneurship in Argentine Culture: Torcuato Di Tella and S.I.A.M.* Philadelphia: University of Pennsylvania Press, 1962.

Cohen, Lizabeth. *A Consumers' Republic: The Politics of Mass Consumption in Postwar America*. New York: Vintage, 2004.

———. *Making a New Deal: Industrial Workers in Chicago, 1919–1939*. New York: Cambridge University Press, 1990.

Confino, Alon. "Collective Memory and Cultural History: Problems of Method." *American Historical Review* 102, no. 5 (December 1997): 1386–403.

Cook, Daniel Thomas. *The Commodification of Childhood: The Children's Clothing Industry and the Rise of the Child Consumer*. Durham, NC: Duke University Press, 2004.

Cosse, Isabella. "Relaciones de pareja a mediados de siglo en las representaciones de la radio porteña: Entre sueños románticos y visos de realidad." *Estudios Sociológicos* 25, no. 73 (2007): 131–53.

Cross, Gary S. *Time and Money: The Making of Consumer Culture*. New York: Routledge, 1993.

Cross, Gary S., and John K. Walton. *The Playful Crowd: Pleasure Places in the Twentieth Century*. New York: Columbia University Press, 2005.

De Grazia, Victoria. "Changing Consumption Regimes in Europe, 1930–1970: Comparative Perspectives on the Distribution Problem." In *Getting and Spending: European and American Consumer Societies in the Twentieth Century*, edited by Susan Strasser, Charles McGovern, and Matthias Judt, 59–83. Cambridge: Cambridge University Press, 1998.

De Grazia, Victoria, and Ellen Furlough, eds. *The Sex of Things: Gender and Consumption in Historical Perspective*. Berkeley: University of California Press, 1996.

Delaney, Jeane. "Making Sense of Modernity: Changing Attitudes Toward the Immigrant and the Gaucho in Turn-of-the-Century Argentina." *Comparative Studies in Society and History* 38, no. 3 (July 1986): 434–59.

Di Liscia, María Herminia. "'Ser madre es un deber': Maternidad en los gobiernos peronistas, 1946–1955." In *Historia y género: Seis estudios sobre la condición femenina*, edited by Daniel Villar, María Herminia Di Liscia, and María Jorgelina Caviglia, 33–49. Buenos Aires: Biblos, 1999.

De Santis, Pablo. *Rico Tipo y las chicas de Divito*. Buenos Aires: Espasa Humor Gráfico, 1994.

Dorfman, Adolfo. *Cincuenta años de industrialización en la Argentina, 1930–1980: Desarrollo y perspectivas*. Buenos Aires: Solar, 1983.

Douglas, Mary, and Baron Isherwood. *The World of Goods: Towards an Anthropology of Consumption*. 2nd ed. New York: Routledge, 1996.

Dunn, Robert G. *Identifying Consumption: Subjects and Objects in Consumer Society*. Philadelphia: Temple University Press, 2008.

Elena, Eduardo. *Dignifying Argentina: Peronism, Citizenship, and Mass Consumption*. Pittsburg: University of Pittsburgh Press, 2011.

———. "Peronism in 'Good Taste': Culture and Consumption in the Magazine *Argentina*." In *The New Cultural History of Peronism: Power and Identity in Mid-Twentieth-Century Argentina*, edited by Matthew B. Karush and Oscar Chamosa, 209–37. Durham, NC: Duke University Press, 2010.

———. "Peronist Consumer Politics and the Problem of Domesticating Markets in Argentina, 1943–1955." *Hispanic American Historical Review* 87, no. 1 (2007): 111–49.

Ferioli, Néstor. *La Fundación Eva Perón*. Vol. 1. Buenos Aires: CEAL, 1990.

Finkelstein, Joanne. *The Fashioned Self*. Philadelphia: Temple University Press, 1991.

Fitzpatrick, Sheila. *Everyday Stalinism: Ordinary Life in Extraordinary Times; Soviet Russia in the 1930s*. New York: Oxford University Press, 1999.

Francois, Marie Eileen. *A Culture of Everyday Credit: Housekeeping, Pawnbroking, and Governance in Mexico City, 1750–1920*. Lincoln: University of Nebraska Press, 2006.

French, John D., and Daniel James, eds. *The Gendered Worlds of Latin American Women Workers: From Household and Factory to the Union Hall and Ballot Box*. Durham, NC: Duke University Press, 1997.

Gambini, Hugo. *Historia del Peronismo: El poder total (1943–1951)*. Buenos Aires: Planeta, 1999.

García Canclini, Néstor. *Consumers and Citizens: Globalization and Multicultural Conflicts*. Minneapolis: University of Minnesota Press, 2001.

Garguin, Enrique. "'Los Argentinos Descendemos de los Barcos': The Racial Articulation of Middle-Class Identity in Argentina (1920–1960)." *Latin American and Caribbean Ethnic Studies* 2, no. 2 (September 2007): 161–84.

Gené, Marcela. *Un mundo feliz: Imágenes de los trabajadores en el primer peronismo, 1946–1955*. Buenos Aires: Fondo de Cultura Económica, 2005.

Gerchunoff, Pablo, and Lucas Llach. *El ciclo de la ilusión y el desencanto: Un siglo de políticas económicas argentinas*. Buenos Aires: Ariel, 1998.

Gerth, Karl. *China Made: Consumer Culture and the Creation of the Nation*. Cambridge, MA: Harvard University Press, 2003.

Ginsberg, Elaine, ed. *Passing and the Fictions of Identity*. Durham, NC: Duke University Press, 1996.

Girbal-Blacha, Noemí. "El hogar o la fábrica: De costureras y tejedoras en la Argentina Peronista (1946–1955)." *Revista de Ciencias Sociales*, no. 6 (September 1997): 217–30.

———. *Mitos, paradojas y realidades en la Argentina Peronista (1946–1955): Una interpretación histórica de sus decisiones político-económicas*. Bernal, Argentina: Universidad Nacional de Quilmes, 2003.

Glickman, Lawrence B. *A Living Wage: American Workers and the Making of Consumer Society*. Ithaca, NY: Cornell University Press, 1997.

Goldar, Ernesto. *Buenos Aires: Vida cotidiana en la década del 50*. Buenos Aires: Plus Ultra, 1980.

Goldthorpe, John et al. *The Affluent Worker in the Class Structure*. New York: Cambridge University Press, 1969.

González Bollo, Hernán. "La cuestión obrera en números: La estadística socio-laboral en la Argentina y su impacto en la política y la sociedad, 1895–1943." In *El mosaico argentino*, edited by Hernán Otero, 331–77. Buenos Aires: Siglo Veintiuno, 2004.

Guy, Donna. *Sex and Gender in Buenos Aires: Prostitution, Family, and Nation in Argentina*. Lincoln: University of Nebraska Press, 1990.

———. *Women Build the Welfare State: Performing Charity and Creating Rights in Argentina, 1880–1955*. Durham, NC: Duke University Press, 2009.

Halberstam, Judith. *Female Masculinity*. Durham, NC: Duke University Press, 1998.

Hall, Stuart. "Notes on Deconstructing 'the Popular.'" In *People's History and Socialist Theory*, edited by Raphael Samuel, 227–40. London: Routledge and Kegan Paul, 1981.

Healey, Mark A. *The Ruins of the New Argentina: Peronism and the Remaking of San Juan After the 1944 Earthquake*. Durham, NC: Duke University Press, 2011.

Hessler, Julie. *A Social History of Soviet Trade: Trade Policy, Retail Practices, and Consumption, 1917–1953*. Princeton, NJ: Princeton University Press, 2004.

Hill, Daniel Delis. *Advertising to the American Woman, 1900–1999*. Columbus: Ohio State University Press, 2002.

Iscaro, Rubens. *Historia del movimiento sindical*. Vol. 2. Buenos Aires: Fundamentos, 1973.

Jacobs, Meg. *Pocketbook Politics: Economic Citizenship in Twentieth-Century America.* Princeton, NJ: Princeton University Press, 2005.

James, Daniel. *Doña María's Story: Life History, Memory, and Political Identity.* Durham, NC: Duke University Press, 2000.

———. "October 17th and 18th, 1945: Mass Protest, Peronism, and the Argentine Working Class." *Journal of Social History* 21, no. 3 (Spring 1988): 441–61.

———. *Resistance and Integration: Peronism and the Argentine Working Class, 1946–1976.* New York: Cambridge University Press, 1988.

Jáuregui, Aníbal. "Prometeo encadenado: Los industriales y el régimen peronista." In *Sueños de bienestar en la Nueva Argentina: Estado y políticas públicas durante el peronismo, 1946–1955,* edited by Patricia Berrotarán, Aníbal Jáuregui, and Marcelo Rougier, 47–71. Buenos Aires: Imago Mundi, 2004.

Karush, Matthew B. "The Melodramatic Nation: Integration and Polarization in the Argentine Cinema of the 1930s." *Hispanic American Historical Review* 87, no. 2 (May 2007): 293–326.

Kriger, Clara. *Cine y Peronismo: El estado en escena.* Buenos Aires: Siglo Veintiuno, 2009.

Laclau, Ernesto. *Politics and Ideology in Marxist Theory: Capitalism, Fascism, Populism.* London: NLB, 1977.

Lattes, Alfredo. "Esplendor y ocaso en las migraciones internas." In *Población y Bienestar en la Argentina del Primer al Segundo Centenario,* edited by Susana Torrado, 2:11–46. Buenos Aires: Edhasa, 2007.

Lavrin, Asunción. *Women, Feminism and Social Change in Argentina, Chile and Uruguay, 1890–1940.* Lincoln: University of Nebraska Press, 1995.

Lears, Jackson. *Fables of Abundance: A Cultural History of Advertising in America.* New York: Basic Books, 1994.

Llach, Juan José. "El Plan Pinedo de 1940, su significado histórico y los orígenes de la economía política del Peronismo." *Desarrollo Económico* 23, no. 92 (1984): 515–57.

Lobato, Mirta Zaida. *Historia de las trabajadoras en la Argentina (1869–1960).* Buenos Aires: Edhasa, 2007.

———. *La vida en las fábricas: Trabajo, protesta y política en una comunidad obrera, Berisso (1904–1970).* Buenos Aires: Prometeo, 2001.

Lobato, Mirta Zaida, María Damilakou, and Lizel Tornay, "Las reinas del trabajo bajo el peronismo." In *Cuando las mujeres reinaban: Belleza, virtud y poder en la Argentina del siglo XX,* edited by Mirta Zaida Lobato, 77–120. Buenos Aires: Biblos, 2005.

Löfgren, Orvar. "My Life as Consumer: Narratives from the World of Goods." In *Narrative and Genre,* edited by Mary Chamberlain and Paul Thompson, 114–25. London: Routledge, 1998.

Lucchini, Cristina. *Apoyo empresarial en los orígenes del peronismo.* Buenos Aires: CEAL, 1990.

Luna, Félix. *Perón y su tiempo*. Buenos Aires: Sudamericana, 1992.

Marchand, Roland. *Advertising the American Dream: Making Way for Modernity, 1920–1940*. Berkeley: University of California Press, 1985.

Matallana, Andrea. *"Locos por la radio": Una historia social de la radiofonía en la Argentina, 1923–1947*. Buenos Aires: Prometeo, 2006.

Mauss, Marcel. *The Gift: The Form and Reason for Exchange in Archaic Society*. London: Routledge, 2000.

Maynes, Mary Jo. *Taking the Hard Road: Life Course in French and German Workers' Autobiographies in the Era of Industrialization*. Chapel Hill: University of North Carolina Press, 1995.

McCracken, Grant. *Culture and Consumption: New Approaches to the Symbolic Character of Consumer Goods and Activities*. Bloomington: Indiana University Press, 1990.

McCrossen, Alexis, ed. *Land of Necessity: Consumer Culture in the United States–Mexico Borderlands*. Durham, NC: Duke University Press, 2009.

McGee Deutsch, Sandra. *Crossing Borders, Claiming a Nation: A History of Argentine Jewish Women, 1880–1955*. Durham, NC: Duke University Press, 2010.

McGovern, Charles F. *Sold American: Consumption and Citizenship, 1890–1945*. Chapel Hill: University of North Carolina Press, 2006.

McKendrick, Neil, John Brewer, and J. H. Plumb, eds. *The Birth of a Consumer Society: The Commercialization of Eighteenth-Century England*. Bloomington: Indiana University Press, 1982.

Merron, Jeff. "Putting Foreign Consumers on the Map: J. Walter Thompson's Struggle with General Motors' International Advertising Account in the 1920s." *Business History Review* 73, no. 3 (Autumn 1999): 465–502.

Milanesio, Natalia. "Food Politics and Consumption in Peronist Argentina." *Hispanic American Historical Review* 90, no.1 (February 2010): 75–108.

———. "The Guardian Angels of the Domestic Economy: Housewives' Responsible Consumption in Peronist Argentina." *Journal of Women's History* 18, no. 3 (Fall 2006): 91–117.

———. "Peronists and *Cabecitas*: Stereotypes and Anxieties at the Peak of Social Change." In *The New Cultural History of Peronism: Power and Identity in Mid-Twentieth-Century Argentina*, edited by Matthew B. Karush and Oscar Chamosa, 53–84. Durham, NC: Duke University Press, 2010.

Miller, Daniel. *Material Culture and Mass Consumption*. Oxford: Basil Blackwell, 1987.

Moreno, Julio. *Yankee Don't Go Home! Mexican Nationalism, American Business Culture, and the Shaping of Modern Mexico, 1920–1950*. Chapel Hill: University of North Carolina Press, 2003.

Morris, Rosalind, ed. *Can the Subaltern Speak? Reflections on the History of an Idea*. New York: Columbia University Press, 2010.

Moya, José. *Cousins and Strangers: Spanish Immigrants in Buenos Aires, 1850–1930*. Los Angeles: University of California Press, 1998.

Myerhoff, Barbara. "Life History Among the Elderly: Performance, Visibility, and Re-Membering." In *Remembered Lives: The Work of Ritual, Storytelling, and Growing Older*, edited by Marc Kaminsky, 231–47. Ann Arbor: University of Michigan Press, 1992.

———. *Number Our Days*. New York: E. P. Dutton, 1978.

Nari, Marcela. *Políticas de maternidad y maternalismo político: Buenos Aires, 1890–1940*. Buenos Aires: Biblos, 2004.

Navarro, Marysa and Nicholas Fraser. *Evita: The Real Life of Eva Perón*. New York: W.W. Norton, 1996.

Nora, Pierre. "Between Memory and History." In *Realms of Memory: The Construction of the French Past*, edited by Pierre Nora, 1–20. New York: Columbia University Press, 1996.

Novick, Susana. "Argentina (1946–1986): Las políticas de población y los planes nacionales de desarrollo." In *Política, población y políticas de población: Argentina, 1946–1986*, Susana Torrado, Susana Novick, and Silvia Olego de Campos, 25–52. Buenos Aires: CEUR, 1986.

———. *IAPI: Auge y decadencia*. Buenos Aires: CEAL, 1986.

Orlove, Benjamin, ed. *The Allure of the Foreign: Imported Goods in Postcolonial Latin America*. Ann Harbor: University of Michigan Press, 1997.

Otero, Hernán. "El concepto de población en el sistema estadístico nacional." In *Población y bienestar en la Argentina del primero al segundo Centenario*, edited by Susana Torrado, 1:161–86. Buenos Aires, Edhasa, 2007.

Owensby, Brian. *Intimate Ironies: Modernity and the Making of Middle-Class Lives in Brazil*. Stanford, CA: Stanford University Press, 1999.

Parr, Joy. *Domestic Goods: The Material, the Moral, and the Economic in the Postwar Years*. Toronto: University of Toronto Press, 1999.

Passerini, Luisa. *Fascism in Popular Memory: The Cultural Experience of the Turin Working Class*. New York: Cambridge University Press, 1987.

Pastoriza, Elisa, and Juan Carlos Torre. "Mar del Plata: Un sueño argentino." In *Historia de la vida privada*, edited by Fernando Devoto and Marta Madero, 3:49–77. Buenos Aires: Taurus, 1999.

Pineda, Yovanna. *Industrial Development in a Frontier Economy: The Industrialization of Argentina, 1870–1930*. Stanford, CA: Stanford University Press, 2009.

Pite, Rebekah. "Creating a Common Table: Doña Petrona, Cooking, and Consumption in Argentina, 1928–1983." PhD diss., University of Michigan, 2007.

Plotkin, Mariano Ben. *Freud in the Pampas: The Emergence and Development of a Psychoanalytic Culture in Argentina*. Stanford, CA: Stanford University Press, 2001.

———. *Mañana es San Perón: A Cultural History of Perón's Argentina*. Translated by Keith Zahniser. Wilmington, DE: SR Books, 2003.

———. "Tell Me Your Dreams: Psychoanalysis and Popular Culture in Buenos Aires, 1930–1950." *The Americas* 55, no. 4 (April 1999): 601–29.

Podalsky, Laura. *Specular City: Transforming Culture, Consumption, and Space in Buenos Aires, 1955–1973*. Philadelphia: Temple University Press, 2004.

Portelli, Alessandro. *The Death of Luigi Trastulli and Other Stories: Form and Meaning in Oral History*. Albany: State University of New York Press, 1991.

Porter Benson, Susan. *Household Accounts: Working-Class Family Economies in the Interwar United States*. Ithaca, NY: Cornell University Press, 2007.

Ramacciotti, Karina Inés, and Adriana María Valobra, eds. *Generando el Peronismo: Estudios de cultura, política y género (1946–1955)*. Buenos Aires: Proyecto Editorial, 2004.

Ranis, Peter. "Factories Without Bosses: Argentina's Experience with Worker-Run Enterprises." *Labor: Studies in Working-Class History of the Americas* 3, no.1 (Spring 2006): 11–23.

Rappaport, Erika Diane. *Shopping for Pleasure: Women in the Making of London's West End*. Princeton, NJ: Princeton University Press, 2000.

Rechini de Lattes, Zulma. *La participación económica femenina en la Argentina desde la segunda posguerra hasta 1970*. Buenos Aires: CENEP, 1980.

Roberts, Mary Louise. "Gender, Consumption, and Commodity Culture." *American Historical Review* 103, no. 3 (June 1998): 817–44.

Rocchi, Fernando. *Chimneys in the Desert: Industrialization in Argentina During the Export Boom Years, 1870–1930*. Stanford, CA: Stanford University Press, 2006.

———. "La americanización del consumo: Las batallas del mercado argentino, 1920–1945." In *Americanización: Estados Unidos y América Latina en el Siglo XX; Transferencias económicas, tecnológicas y culturales*, edited by María I. Barbero and Andrés M. Regalsky, 131–89. Buenos Aires: EDUNTREF, 2003.

Rodriguez, Julia. *Civilizing Argentina: Science, Medicine, and the Modern State*. Chapel Hill: University of North Carolina Press, 2006.

Romero, Luis Alberto. *A History of Argentina in the Twentieth Century*. University Park: Pennsylvania State University Press, 2002.

Ross, Peter. "Justicia social: Una evaluación de los logros del Peronismo clásico." *Anuario del IEHS*, no. 8 (1993): 105–24.

Sainz, Alfredo. *Negocios exitosos argentinos*. Buenos Aires: Planeta, 2009.

Salvatore, Ricardo. "Yankee Advertising in Buenos Aires: Reflections on Americanization." *Interventions* 7, no. 2 (2005): 216–35.

Sarlo, Beatriz. *El imperio de los sentimientos: Narraciones de circulación periódica en la Argentina (1917–1927)*. Buenos Aires: Catálogos, 1985.

Saulquín, Susana. *Historia de la moda argentina: Del miriñaque al diseño de autor.* Buenos Aires: Emecé, 2006.

Scanlon, Jennifer. "Mediators in the International Marketplace: U.S. Advertising in Latin America in the Early Twentieth Century." *Business History Review* 77, no. 3 (Autumn 2003): 387–415.

Scarzanella, Eugenia. "El ocio peronista: Vacaciones y 'turismo popular' en Argentina (1943–1955)." *Entrepasados* 14 (1998): 65–84.

Schudson, Michael. *Advertising, the Uneasy Persuasion: Its Dubious Impact on American Society.* New York: Routledge, 1993.

Seveso, César. "Political Emotions and the Origins of the Peronist Resistance." In *The New Cultural History of Peronism: Power and Identity in Mid-Twentieth-Century Argentina*, edited by Matthew B. Karush and Oscar Chamosa, 239–69. Durham, NC: Duke University Press, 2010.

Shannon, Brent. *The Cut of His Coat: Men, Dress, and Consumer Culture in Britain, 1860–1914.* Athens: Ohio University Press, 2006.

Soluri, John. *Banana Cultures: Agriculture, Consumption, and Environmental Change in Honduras and the United States.* Austin: University of Texas Press, 2005.

Stawski, Martín. "El populismo paralelo: Política social de la Fundación Eva Perón (1948–1955)." In *Sueños de bienestar en la Nueva Argentina: Estado y políticas públicas durante el peronismo, 1946–1955*, edited by Patricia Berrotarán, Aníbal Jaúregui, and Marcelo Rougier, 193–227. Buenos Aires: Imago Mundi, 2004.

Stearns, Peter. "Stages of Consumerism: Recent Work on the Issues of Periodization." *Journal of Modern History* 69, no. 1 (March 1997): 102–17.

Steigerwald, David. "All Hail the Republic of Choice: Consumer History as Contemporary Thought." *Journal of American History* 93, no. 2 (September 2006): 385–403.

Stern, Grete. *Sueños: Fotomontajes de Grete Stern.* Buenos Aires: CEPPA, 2003.

Stern, Steve. *Remembering Pinochet's Chile: On the Eve of London, 1998.* Durham, NC: Duke University Press, 2004.

Stiglitz, Joseph. *Globalization and Its Discontents.* New York: W. W. Norton, 2003.

Storrs, Landon R.Y. *Civilizing Capitalism: The National Consumers' League, Women's Activism, and Labor Standards in the New Deal Era.* Chapel Hill: University of North Carolina Press, 2000.

Sutton, Denise H. *Globalizing Ideal Beauty: How Female Copywriters of the J. Walter Thompson Advertising Agency Redefined Beauty for the Twentieth Century.* New York: Palgrave Macmillan, 2005.

Svampa, Maristella. *La sociedad excluyente: La Argentina bajo el signo del neoliberalismo*. Buenos Aires: Taurus, 2005.

The Take. Directed by Avi Lewis. Canada: First Run Features / Icarus Films, 2004. DVD.

Tamarin, David. *The Argentine Labor Movement, 1930–1945: A Study in the Origins of Peronism*. Albuquerque: University of New Mexico Press, 1985.

Taylor, Julie. *Eva Perón: The Myths of a Woman*. Chicago: University of Chicago Press, 1979.

Torrado, Susana. *Estructura social de la Argentina, 1945–1983*. Buenos Aires: Ediciones de la Flor, 1992.

———. *Historia de la familia en la Argentina Moderna (1870–2000)*. Buenos Aires: Ediciones de la Flor, 2003.

Torre, Juan Carlos. *La vieja guardia sindical y Perón: Sobre los orígenes del peronismo*. Buenos Aires: Sudamericana, 1990.

Torre, Juan Carlos, and Eliza Pastoriza. "La democratización del bienestar." In *Nueva Historia Argentina*. Vol. 8, *Los años peronistas (1943–1955)*, edited by Juan Carlos Torre, 257–312. Buenos Aires: Sudamericana, 2002.

Walker Laird, Pamela. *Advertising Progress: American Business and the Rise of Consumer Marketing*. Baltimore: John Hopkins University Press, 1998.

Wallendorf, Melanie, and Eric Arnould. "'My Favorite Things': A Cross-Cultural Inquiry into Object Attachment, Possessiveness, and Social Linkage." *Journal of Consumer Research* 14, no. 4 (March 1988): 531–47.

Woodard, James. "Marketing Modernity: The J. Walter Thompson Company and North American Advertising in Brazil, 1929–1939." *Hispanic American Historical Review* 82, no. 2 (May 2002): 257–90.

Zerubabel, Eviatar. *Time Maps: Collective Memory and the Social Shape of the Past*. Chicago: University of Chicago Press, 2003.

Zuppa, Graciela. "Prácticas de sociabilidad en la construcción de la villa balneario: Mar del Plata y el acceso al siglo XX." In *Prácticas de sociabilidad en un escenario argentino: Mar del Plata 1870–1970*, edited by Graciela Zuppa, 54–79. Mar del Plata, Argentina: Universidad Nacional de Mar del Plata, 2004.

INDEX

fascism: accusations of, 35, 50, 140; allusions to Blackshirts, 142; Nazism association, 200

Fernández de Kirchner, Cristina, 230

Figuerola, José, 31

fish canneries, 39, 117, 242n72

Five-Year Plan (1946), 22

Florida Street, 139–40, 148–50, 209

Flower, Henry, 56, 60

food adulteration, 40–43

Food Department, National, 41, 49

Food Police, 42

food products: advertising, 44–45, 107; changes in consumption, 39–40; female names for, 107, *108*; government oversight, 41–42, 49, 223–24; National Food Code, 43, 224, 242n74; new type, 229–30; packaging, 46–48; *pan negro*, 194–95; quality-price ratio, 40, 43; sanitary regulation, 40–43, 47, 242n73; shortages in 1950s, 194–95; weights and measures, 46, 48

food sector: advertising, 89; expansion, 39; National Food Control, 43; self-service grocery stores, 47, *47*; significance of, 39; state assistance, 26; studies of, 11

foreign capital, 27, 221

foreign debt, 224

foreign exchange, 26, 221

Fourth National Census (1947), 58, 64

fringe benefits, 34, 125

galeritas (top hats), 142

gambling, 128–29, 149

garment industries, 148

gas stoves: durability, 95–96; features of, 90–91; humor in ads, 112; marital bliss and, 175, *175*; marketing strategies,

89–91; savings touted, 95; subsidized gas, 93

gaucho, as icon, 86

gender: in advertising, 14; humor in ads, 111–13; impact of consumer culture, 15; Peronist view of roles, 184–85; reversal of roles, 182–83

gender relations: changes summarized, 158–59; consumption, 159; expectations, 182; marriage, 176–88; mass consumer culture related, 188; sources for studying, 159

gender stereotypes. *See* specific stereotypes

geography of shopping, 207–10, 217

Germani, Gino, 59, 151, 166

Ginzo, José Antonio (aka Tristán), 200

Global Barter Network, 227

Gómez Morales, Alfredo, 26

González Alberdi, Paulino, 29

Greenup, Ruth and Leonard, 56, 146–47, 152

Grupo de Oficiales Unidos (GOU), 20, 48

home furnishings, 169–72

Honest Commerce Campaign, 72–73, *74*

household appliances: access to, 213–14; advertising, 88–96; democratization of, 171; installment plans, 35; modernity related, 90; outdoor advertising, 117; postwar growth, 23; significance of, 211–12. *See also* specific appliances

housework: responsibility for, 182; views of, 180–81

housing, 132, 266n39

husbands: "absent," 181; collaboration of, 171; "domestic," 181–82, 186; emasculated, 183; ensuring devotion

of, 178; as exploited, 176; gender
humor, 111–13; stereotypes and
representations, 160, 161, 181–82;
stingy and controlling, 186–88
hyperinflation of 1980s, 194, 223

IAPI (Instituto Argentino para la
Promoción del Intercambio), 22, 26
iceboxes, 214, 215. *See also* refrigerators
imports: commercial fraud, 43–44; as
markers of modernity and distinction,
11, 43–44
import substitution industrialization (ISI),
19; Argentina compared, 28; early
rates, 19–20; Five-Year Plan, 22; gains,
23; GOU view, 21
income redistribution, 4, 10, 31, 34;
recent, 221
industrialization, 18–28; different
paths to, 18; import substitution
industrialization (ISI), 19; internal
market expansion and, 57; as motor
of development, 21; relocation of
factories, 57; Second World War, 4, 20;
state role, 25–26; weaknesses, 26–27;
workers in ads, 97
industry: birth of, 18; low wages, 30;
market competition, 55; postwar
conditions for, 25–26; profit margins,
34; regional breakdown, 64–65;
second-rate substitutes, 72–73;
under military rule, 222; women
workers, 162
Industry and Commerce Ministry, 48
"Infamous Decade," 4
inflation, 27, 37; controls, 39;
hyperinflation, 223; impact on middle
class, 150–51; under Menem, 223;
under military rule, 222

installment plans, 35; for clothing, 210;
refrigerators, 57
internal market: early Perón period, 22;
Peronist economic plan, 4; Perón on,
29; redefined by advertising, 59; size
of, 17
internal migration. *See* migration, internal
International Advertising Association
(IAA), 58
irons, 197

June (1943) Revolution, 21
justicialismo, 35, 37, 213
J. Walter Thompson Company, 54;
attitudes, 56; focus on elites, 59–60;
market study for Frigidaire, 92; men's
shoes, 98; Pond's campaign, 102; on
print ads, 115; on radio advertising,
115; staff backgrounds, 50; using
Mérito shoes, 61; on worker living
conditions, 57

Kelvinator company, 25
Kirchner, Néstor, 230

Labor, National Department of, 30
Labor, Secretariat of, 31–32
labor historians, 8–9, 11–12
labor laws, 36
labor unions, 31; absenteeism issue,
125, 256n6; dressing for meetings,
216; grocery stores, 38; growth,
32; misleading advertising, 45;
publications, 58; in provinces, 129;
state role, 31–32; support for Perón,
36; under military rule, 222; working-
class living conditions, 56
La Campagnola, 107, *108*, 173
Lagomarsino, Raúl, 22

productivity, labor, 27–28, 256n6; early period, 19

prosumers, 228, 275n22

protective tariffs, 19, 26

provinces: admen's view of markets in, 81; advertising in, 55, 64; advertising in small towns, 69, 70; Bunge's regional breakdown, 63; domestic industry, 23; economic disparity, 63–64; food ad regulation, 45–46; food quality control, 42, 43; local newspapers, 58; manufacturer advertising, 69; national territories, 242n69; newspapers, 247n45; opportunities for advertisers, 66, 70; price controls, 38; vis-à-vis Buenos Aires, 63

psychoanalysis, 153, 166

public health, 40–43

public spaces: gender trends, 179; redefining womanhood, 181; women "invading," 179

public transportation, 133

purchasing power: accounts of newly acquired, 191; before Peronist era, 16–17; changes in advertising, 80; as driving force, 28–29; during Peronist era, 17, 39–48; expansion process, 13; leisure activities, 124; in Peronist project, 18, 49; protecting, 39–48; recent, 230–31

Radical Party, 3, 222–23

radio shows, 110, 115

rational saving, culture of, 198

refrigerators, 23–25; A and B groups, 92; advertising costs, 80; Borges on, 214; demand for, 213; durability, 95–96; earlier advertising, 92; frugality to attain, 197–99; installment plans,

57; manufacturers, 25; meanings of, 214; memories of, 213; modernity associated, 91; nationalistic appeals, 93–96; number of owners, 57; as prestige goods, 92, 93; as priority, 214; savings touted, 95; as symbol, 213; technology and health features, 91–92

rent controls, 31, 34–35

restaurants, 127, 131

restaurant workers, 32, 34; complaints about, 134

Revolución Libertadora, 28

Rosario: candy and cookie factory workers, *163*; changes under Peronism, 195; department stores, 191; described, 65; downtown shopping, 209; food advertising, 45–46; food riots, 223; market potential, 65; newspaper advertising, 68–69; Peronist sympathizer's views, 196; shopping venues, 139; street advertisements, 116; urban attractions, 210–12; working-class women with jewelry, 149

rural to urban migration. *See* migration, internal

Sales Managers Association, 59

salespersons, dishonesty of, 73

Sammartino, Ernesto, 149

sanitary food products, 40–43, 47

Second Five-Year Plan, 27, 201–2

Second World War: imports restricted from the United States, 25; import substitution industrialization, 20; neutrality, 21

seductress stereotype, 167–68

self-indulgence, consumer, 162, 165, 176, 200, 215–16

family size, 184; identity reaffirmed, 142–43; images in advertising, 96–103; marketing survey, 71; neat appearance, 216; poorest social groups vis-à-vis, 202; stereotypes, 143; unmaking of, 228. *See also* standard of living, worker

working-class consumers: agency, 193; assumptions about, 10–11; bad taste and vulgarity, 156; content changes in advertising, 92–93; early market research on, 58; as focus of state policy, 18; Germani on, 59; as historical actors, 5; improving conditions for, 56–67; interviewees, 191–92; lack of decorum, 156; in less advantageous conditions, 201–2; magazine ads, 80; peer recommendations, 98–99; recent era, 220; role summarized, 3; significance of consumer goods, 212; as social subject, 5; social visibility, 156; stereotype summarized, 157

working-class masculinity, 207

working-class women: beauty queens, 102; as consumers, 70–80; criticized, 162–63; "double burden," 182; dress ridiculed, 155; early twentieth-century portrayals of, 145–46; educating, 71–72, 73, 75; as fashion icons, 145; glamorization of, 105; historical invisibility, 218–19; impact on labor force, 264n14; on marriage, 162; materialism alleged, 166–68, 185; occupations, 162; Peronist view of, 180; rational spending, 71; redefining womanhood, 181; Rosario candy and cookie factory, *163*; significance of, 14; single, 161–68; single life-style, 163–68; spendthrift characterization, 165–66, 176, 185–86; stereotypes, 165; as trend setters, 154; wage increases, 264–65n15; young, stereotypes of, 159

yerba maté, 89, 250n17

www.ingramcontent.com/pod-product-compliance
Lightning Source LLC
Chambersburg PA
CBHW020656270326
41928CB00005B/147